Governance and Regulation in the Third Sector

Routledge Series in the Management of Voluntary and Non-Profit Organizations

SERIES EDITOR: STEPHEN P. OSBORNE, *University of Edinburgh, UK*

Governance and Regulation in the Third Sector

International Perspectives

Edited by Susan D. Phillips and Steven Rathgeb Smith

Routledge
Taylor & Francis Group
New York   London

First published 2011
by Routledge
270 Madison Avenue, New York, NY 10016

Simultaneously published in the UK
by Routledge
2 Park Square, Milton Park, Abingdon, Oxon OX14 4RN

Routledge is an imprint of the Taylor & Francis Group, an informa business

Typeset in Sabon by IBT Global.
Printed and bound in the United States of America on acid-free paper by IBT Global.

Library of Congress Cataloging-in-Publication Data
    Governance and regulation in the third sector : international perspectives / edited by Susan D. Phillips and Steven Rathgeb Smith.
      p. cm.—(Routledge studies in the management of voluntary and non-profit organizations ; 13)
    Includes bibliographical references and index.
    1. Nonprofit organizations. 2. Non-governmental organizations. 3. Public-private sector cooperation. I. Phillips, Susan D. (Susan Darling), 1954- II. Smith, Steven Rathgeb, 1951-
    HD2769.15.G66 2011
    338.7—dc22
                                    2010024826

ISBN13: 978-0-415-77477-2 (hbk)
ISBN13: 978-0-203-83507-4 (ebk)

This book is dedicated to the memory of Mark Lyons, a pioneering scholar of the third sector who is the author of the chapter on regulation of the Australian third sector in this volume. Mark died after a brief illness before the publication of this book. He was a central figure in building the field of third sector studies in Australia and the rest of the world. Moreover, his enduring commitment to intellectual rigor, the development of younger scholars, teaching excellence, and building a community of scholars continues to serve as an inspiration to countless scholars and researchers throughout the world including both editors of this book. He truly represented the best ideals and aspirations of the academy.

Contents

1 Between Governance and Regulation

Evolving Government– Third Sector Relationships

*Susan D. Phillips and
Steven Rathgeb Smith*

INTRODUCTION: EVOLVING RELATIONSHIPS

In recent years, across many countries, governments have been reviewing and restructuring their relationships with the third sector. The language of partnership and investment in 'community' is pervasive, and the international breadth of experimentation with renewed relationships is far reaching. In the United States, a call to service and bolstering the nonprofit sector including faith-based and neighborhood organizations are central planks of President Obama's change agenda. In the UK, community partnership is a major component of the coalition's "Big Society" program,[1] just as it was a decade earlier of New Labour's Third Way, although the specifics on how to affect such partnership naturally differ. Similarly, the European Union has put engagement with civil society at the heart of its pursuit of democratic legitimacy, integration, and enlargement (European Commission 2001; Dunn, Chapter 7, this volume). So, too, have many transition countries where legal, policy, and regulatory reforms are linked to modernization and democratization processes, and where civil society organizations are establishing a stronger role as more stable democracies develop. Even countries that have long ignored or openly repressed civil society, such as China, are taking steps toward new nonprofit and charity legislation (Kirby 2006). Political rhetoric abounds, but it has also been accompanied by substantial reform in many countries.

The result has been a wide range of experiments, some bold and some tentative, designed to reshape relationships between the state and the third sector—the diverse constellation of nonprofits, voluntary associations, charities, community-based organizations, social movements, social enterprises, and related organizations that fill the organized space of civil society.[2] These experiments include new policy instruments such as compacts, new legislation governing charities, creation of new regulatory agencies and reengineering existing ones to be more responsive regulators, new funding support, expansion of the definition of "public benefit" that underpins the concept of charity, provision of new legal forms for the incorporation of third sector organizations, more liberal use of the tax system to support charities and other public benefit organizations, and more extensive self-regulation.

One explanation for this international spate of reform is instrumental and very practical: both policy problems and service delivery issues are more complex, and governments have recognized that they cannot solve them on their own. Mixed welfare economies have long been the reality in many countries, although the "associational revolution" that occurred in the 1970s and 1980s substantially increased the number of nongovernmental organizations and the reach of their activities (Salamon 1994). Governments need more effective means of working with and enabling voluntary and nonprofit organizations to achieve results. Consequently, they are devising better ways to work together at both a macro level (through reform of broad policy and regulatory frameworks) and a micro one (through fine tuning existing policy instruments and working with specific organizations).

A second explanation is policy transfer: governments and civil society organizations watched the experience of the early adapters and simply followed the same approach and even borrowed the same instruments. For example, many jurisdictions have developed compacts or accords—broad framework agreements between the whole of government and the whole of the voluntary sector—reflecting in part the emulation of England's lead with the development of its compact in 1997 (Casey, Dalton, & Onxy 2008). Even some of the specific wording of the English Compact has been borrowed and implanted in subsequent ones (Phillips 2003; Scottish Government 2003).

For many scholars of public management, especially those steeped in the British policy literature and varieties of European network theory, something more fundamental than creative problem solving or policy transfer is occurring. At root is nothing short of a transformation in the underlying model of public management. The international trend of reshaping government–third sector relationships is argued to be a manifestation of a broad shift in the governing model from New Public Management (NPM) that focused on markets, principal-agent contracting, and performance controls, to more horizontal, relational 'governance' that emphasizes interorganizational networks, collaboration, and a broad range of policy tools (Hood 1991; Osborne 2010, 2006; Rhodes 1996; Salamon 2002).

Although it was never a unitary or single paradigm and was implemented to differing degrees in various jurisdictions during the 1980s and early 1990s, NPM brought a set of management practices and institutional arrangements that created competitive or quasi markets (Hood 1991; Osborne, Mclaughlin, & Ferlie 2002). It thereby carved out a greater role for non-state actors and led to increased use of contracting as a mechanism of accountability and means of managing relationships. Relatedly, it separated responsibility for policy from service delivery and made policy implementation *"organizationally distanced* from the policy makers" (Osborne 2006: 379). It also decentralized management relationships both within government, through the creation of executive agencies and devolution of responsibility to front line managers, and externally, through management by contract. It put an emphasis on efficiency, cost management, and customer satisfaction, and it shifted from input controls to accountability by results through performance measurement and output controls (Vincent-Jones 2006: 43). And, an aspect that is often overlooked, NPM brought with it expanded regulation in a variety of forms. To be sure, NPM created markets in a variety of public services, but these were often accompanied by social controls and regulations that had significant implications for the third sector organizations which provided these services.

NPM was gradually stymied by the impact of its own success and by its inherent limitations in the face of a changing environment. Its focus on intra-governmental organization, managerialism, and efficiency made it less suitable for a highly pluralized world where the challenge is engaging this plurality and innovating through the injection of "policy venture capital" (Knott & McCarthy 2007; see also Mulgan 2006). The success of NPM in creating competitive markets resulted in enormous fragmentation in services and among service providers (Dunleavy, Margetts, Bastow, & Tinkler 2005a). The supply of providers in many markets was insufficient to generate effective competition, and performance contracting in practice did not lead to substantial changes in the mix of providers. The emerging challenge became one of accountability and finding greater policy coherence as the 'supply chain' between policy and delivery was both long and opaque, and non-state actors held considerable power. Over time, then, experience with market competition generated greater interest in collaboration and partnership with these actors from the private and nonprofit sectors. In addition, for many governments, a preoccupation with efficiency was displaced by a concern with democracy. Both in transition countries, where the dominant project was reinforcing the institutions and practices of fledgling democracy, and in established democracies, where declining trust and confidence in government sparked interest in expanded opportunities for citizen engagement, NPM did not offer the appropriate policy tools or solutions. So, evolution is underway to an alternative model of public management that is more collaborative and relational in nature. At least, that is how the theory goes.

The purpose of this volume is to explore how and why relationships between national governments and third sectors are changing in selected countries that intentionally represent a broad spectrum of experience. These range from change leaders, England and Scotland, that have recently implemented comprehensive packages of legal, policy, regulatory, and funding reforms designed to produce more enabling environments for the work of their third sectors to jurisdictions, Canada and Australia, in which change has been incremental at best. In between, we see the introduction and evolution of a diversity of innovations and the emergence of a variety of new policy instruments and hybrids. The authors, all leading experts in public policy related to the third sector, examine whether these changes reflect an underlying transition in the model of public management—from NPM to a more collaborative form of relational governance—and explore the kinds of tensions and conflicts that are encountered in the process. Is there any evidence that the foundational architecture for a more collaborative relationship between the state and the third sector has been laid? How do we reconcile an interest in collaboration and greater trust-based relationships with the hard edge of rule-based regulations that are a legacy of NPM? What are the outstanding challenges for policy and regulatory reform as well as for collaboration?

Our goal in this introduction is to both lay the groundwork by explaining the argument and potential implications for the shift in public management that is so widely theorized and to identify the common trends and issues that arise from the chapters so that the reader is prepared to spot both convergences and differences. The volume is intended to inform current debates in public management and in the study of the third sector, but it is also meant to be inherently practical, providing fresh perspectives and offering recommendations that are directly useful to public managers and third sector leaders who have responsibilities and interest in developing approaches to public management that are up to the challenges of governing in a complex world and that permit the third sector to be as effective as possible in these contexts.

FROM NPM TO RELATIONAL GOVERNANCE: IMPLICATIONS FOR THE THIRD SECTOR

New [Public] Governance, often called horizontal, collaborative, relational, or just plain "governance," starts with a recognition of interdependence inherent in the "pluralization of policy making" (Rhodes 2000: 54; see also Osborne 2010) and underscores the value of networks over markets or hierarchies in this context (see Koppenjan & Klijn 2004). The model rests on interdependence, not power relationships, and centers on negotiation and persuasion, not control (see Hill et al. 2005; Peters 2001; Stoker 1998). Relationships are not taken as given but need to be negotiated in the context of problem solving (Mintzberg 1996), and the skills required shift from those of management to those of enablement (Salamon 2002: 11). Greater collaboration is evident not only between government and its non-governmental partners, but among various government departments as they have come to work in a more coordinated manner, a process often referred to as horizontal management.

If we are witnessing a fundamental shift in governing models, there should be considerable consistency in the types of changes occurring so as to create legal, policy, regulatory, contracting, and financing frameworks—that is, a common meta-governance (Jessop 1998; Meuleman 2008; Peters 2010)—for the terms of engagement between the state and the third sector. This meta-governance should include policies that enable the work of the third sector, develop its capacity, and engage nonprofit organizations in policy development as well as service delivery.

This shift should bring with it new institutions and practices that encourage deeper understanding, trust, and co-management—even co-governance across the sectors (Bode 2006; Osborne 2006). Although contracts may continue to be important policy tools, they would be more than a means of control over the purchase of services (Unwin 2004). The focus on strengthening relationships should be evidenced by more relational contracting which puts an emphasis on working toward common goals, promoting communication and flexibility, and developing trust, rather than on narrowly meeting the terms of pre-specified "deliverables" (Unwin 2004; Vincent-Jones 2006: 19). The focus of accountability and the means for achieving it should be directed toward facilitating learning and investments in infrastructure support, rather than on control and public assurance that rules are being followed (Aucoin & Heintzman 2000). Accountability regimes would be constructed to address both vertical responsibilities, from agent to principal, *and* horizontal ones, among multiple partners involved in the collaborative effort of governing, often through negotiation between the state and intermediary associations representing third sector organizations. Similarly, the objectives of regulation would expand beyond command and control, rule-based compliance to encourage more responsive regulation that is attuned to the institutional environment and overall performance of the regulatory regime (Baldwin & Black 2008; Braithwaite 2008). Funding horizons would give greater stability and promote more strategic planning by nonprofits. Performance measurement would be designed to encourage organizational learning and better programming. In short, the spotlight would be on building more constructive trust-based, longer-term relationships (Gandhori 2006; Poppo & Zenger 2002; Unwin 2004), and this end would be reflected in the use of a variety of policy instruments and cooperation among public and private funders in support of specific partnerships and services. In this sense, then, the move to relational governance would be a departure from the short-term, market-oriented approach embodied in countries that embraced the tenets of NPM.

The challenge of transition in models of public management is that governing ideas get institutionalized in a variety of ways that may not be readily changed. If the legacy of NPM was just the creation of competitive markets, it could quite readily be supplanted as a model of public management because markets, as an institutional form, are relatively easily altered.

However, NPM not only created markets but brought extensive regulation through various means, all of which are comparatively durable policy instruments. Decentralization, including through markets, did not diminish the focus on accountability, but produced rules, performance contracts, institutionalized auditing, and monitoring machinery, and encouraged a shift from self to state regulation (Jordana & Lefi-Faur 2004). During the height of NPM, the number of regulatory agencies grew, as did the niches that they occupied (Levi-Faur 2008a). So, too, did other means of social control. Because NPM encouraged the fragmentation of policy implementation—represented in part by the proliferation of third sector organizations—governments became very creative in imposing new forms of control and oversight (Dunleavy, Margetts, Bastow, & Tinkler 2005b).

In effect, the NPM state was also the "regulatory state" (Majone 1997; Scott 2004) which shifted "the emphasis of control, to a greater or lesser degree, from traditional bureaucratic mechanisms towards instruments of regulation" (Scott 2004: 148; see also Jordana & Levi-Faur 2004). The interest in regulation did not pass with NPM, although regulation has become a more diverse policy instrument than a set of rules backed by sanctions. Over the past decade, "regulation" has morphed into a mixed array of incentive systems, conventions, standards, targets, best practices, benchmarking, certification, and voluntary codes among other forms of negotiated soft law (Doern 2007; Levi-Faur 2008b; Webb 2005). This has been reinforced by the global economic crisis that began in 2008 which was created in part by ineffective regulation of financial institutions and has sparked a renewed interest in regulation in a wide range of sectors across many jurisdictions (Summers 2008).

The third sector, particularly the charitable subsector, was impacted by increased regulation under NPM and in some respects was particularly affected, in part, because of its governance and the niche it occupied in service delivery. Nonprofits are generally exempt from paying taxes, and, in many jurisdictions, designated nonprofits with 'public benefit' or 'charitable' purposes can issue tax receipts for donations, thereby receiving an indirect (and sometimes direct) public subsidy and generating tax expenditures. This means that governments have an incentive to monitor and regulate this sector; as a result, governments have established systems for registration and reporting for 'charities' (referred to as 501(c)(3) organizations in the US), restrictions on political and commercial activities, and compensation of directors, among others rules. Given the connection with taxation and the objective of protecting philanthropic gifts, these regulatory systems have had a preoccupation with financial matters, particularly with improving control of charity finances (O'Halloran, McGregor-Lowndes, & Simon 2008: 16). Further, the volunteer boards of directors were also supposed to play a key oversight role, supplementing government regulations.

Governments also shape performance and relationships through contracting regimes, performance standards, fee payments, and other financing mechanisms (Heinrich 2002; Krauskopf 2008; Smith & Lipsky 1993). Much of this remains traditional command-and-control regulation in which governments unilaterally set the rules and standards, monitor performance, and impose penalties for non-compliance. In recent years, the third sector has also experienced increased demands for self-regulation (Bothwell 2000) and new forms of regulation through relational contracting. For example, government may contract with a nonprofit organization on a performance basis, but it may not change providers and only collect the information for reimbursement purposes. The two parties are engaged in a long term relationship where concerns about quality and performance are resolved through discussion and negotiation—in effect a relational contract (Smith & Smyth 1996).

An understanding of regulation of the third sector and the hypothesis about the impact of a transition from NPM to relational governance needs to be set against a distinctive characteristic of this sector—its enormous dependence on the maintenance of public trust that makes citizens willing to donate both money and time and entrust themselves and their loved ones to the care of social service agencies or children's soccer coaches (see Hansmann 1980). Evidence suggests that public trust in the sector remains strong, so lack of trust is not an adequate explanation for increased regulation. In a 2006 survey of Canadians, for example, three-quarters said that charities are better than government at understanding and meeting the needs of citizens, and leaders of charities are trusted more than most other professions: only nurses and physicians were trusted more (Muttart Foundation 2006). The adage about "one bad apple spoiling the barrel" is felt acutely in this sector, however, as the collective damages caused by scandals over questionable fundraising practices or compensation of executives attest. Consequently, attention to accountability and transparency are preoccupations of the third sector, its partners, and its regulators (see Brown 2008). Increasingly, regulation has a pre-emptive function of promoting better organizational governance as a means of preventing questionable behavior and forestalling the need to impose the 'cure' of penalties after rules have been broken by a few, and media attention produced collateral damage on many. The challenge is how to adapt regulation and accountability to an evolving model of public management.

GOVERNANCE AND REGULATION:
THE RATIONALE FOR THIS VOLUME

The central question that animates this volume is: what happens for the third sector when relational governance, which implies the negotiation and agreement upon shared, relational norms, performance standards, and co-management, meets the embedded rule-based regulatory systems that were part of NPM? We begin by testing the assumption that a transition is, in fact, occurring from NPM to more relational governance. The conviction that NPM is giving way to relational forms of governance emanates mainly from theory, but it has been repeated often enough in the policy literature that it has been accepted as reality. There are few good empirical tests of such a transition, however, and the evidence is mixed (Considine & Lewis 2003; Hill & Lynn 2005). The chapters in this volume are by no means a systematic test of the development of a relational governance model across the jurisdictions examined, but the authors do provide a window onto shifting patterns of governing. Across ten jurisdictions—England, Scotland, Ireland, Hungary, Germany, France, the European Union, the US, Canada, and Australia—the chapters assess the nature and impacts of the policy, regulatory, and related reforms in state–third sector relationships that have been undertaken in recent years. Are these changes reflective of relational governance?

While one theme of this volume focuses on governance, the second concentrates on regulation. In particular, the authors examine the trends in regulation for the third sector and discuss whether regulatory systems are adapting to accommodate a more significant role for the third sector and more constructive relationship building. To what extent is regulatory reform in the third sector reflective of broader movements in use of regulation as a policy instrument? In many other sectors of the economy and society, regulatory philosophies and systems are undergoing considerable change. In both the academic literature on regulation and various government sponsored reports aimed at regulatory reform, especially in the economic sectors, three themes of reform are evident.

The first is more responsive regulation (Ayres & Braithwaite 1992) which addresses the issue of "when to punish, when to persuade?" (Baldwin & Black 2008; Braithwaite 2002). The notion of responsive regulation is often illustrated by the concept of an enforcement pyramid. The broad base of this pyramid is built on education, persuasion, consultation, self-regulation, and capacity building, and it moves up to selected use of deterrents and penalties as needed. Responsive regulation presumes proportionality of response, availability of a wide range of regulatory tools and credible sanctions, and deep knowledge by the regulator of the regulated sector and the environment in which it operates (Baldwin & Black 2008). "Responsibilization," that is, promoting the capacity of nonprofits to better govern and regulate themselves and of the sector to enhance voluntary regulation, is an important approach in this varied toolkit (May 2007; Vincent-Jones 2006). Although the immediate response to the financial crisis shifted attention back to rule-based, sanction-backed regulation, the reality in such a large and diverse sector, in which the vast majority of organizations are very small, is that governments will never be able to devise enough rules and enforce them without incurring and imposing a huge regulatory burden (Irvin 2005). The essence of much of what is being regulated in this sector is in effect good organizational governance—for example, governance of fundraising activities, training and empowering boards to do due diligence, disbursement of funds on charitable purposes, and promotion of transparency—which necessitates a mix of organizational responsibility, ongoing technical assistance, and external regulation.

A second, related trend in regulation is to make rule setting and monitoring more risk based: priorities are developed and enforcement is targeted in relation to the degree of risk involved (Baldwin, Hutter, & Rothstein 2000). A key element in risk-based regulation is sound evidence on which to assess the risks. As a result, pressures for performance assessment and reporting by regulated organizations, expectations of transparency, and demands for regulators to develop more sophisticated risk assessment systems have increased significantly in recent years (Benjamin 2008).

Third, the changing philosophies of regulation are grappling with the realities of multi-level governance, fragmented governments, and polycentric regimes which mean that there are often overlapping and sometimes conflicting rules and inordinate 'red tape' that limit innovation and reduce flexibility (Black 2008; Doern 2006). The pursuit of "smart" or "better" regulation (External Advisory Committee on Smart Regulation 2004; Gunningham and Grabosky 1998; OECD 2003; UK Better Regulation Task Force 2005), supported by new innovations in "digital-era governance" (Dunleavy, Margetts, Bastow, & Tinkler 2005a, 2005b), is aimed at creating more evidence-based, streamlined, and better coordinated regulation, both within and across jurisdictions, as well as more timely processes and more creative use of different regulatory instruments. Smarter regulation also promotes better assessment of the performance of regulatory *regimes* that take into account the cumulative impact of regulations and may include greater centralization in governance. In many sectors in a variety of jurisdictions, these contemporary ideas about regulation are significantly changing regulatory instruments and institutions in a direction that is compatible with a model of relational governance (see Bernstein & Cashore 2007). One question addressed in this volume is: To what extent is a similar move to responsive, risk-based, and smart regulation being felt in the third sector?

Although there is no compelling reason to think that the third sector would be exempt from the diffusion of these and other regulatory reform ideas, regulation of this sector, particularly charities, is distinct in two important respects. In a globalized world, the charitable sector is one of the few still bounded by geography. The perception, and to a large extent the reality, is that the operations of charities and other nonprofits, with some notable exceptions such as those working in international development, humanitarian relief, human rights, and climate change, have been local in nature. Regulatory systems for charities were built on a reasonable assumption that they do not compete internationally, that philanthropy flows domestically not globally, and that there is little need for legal forms that accommodate trans-boundary or multi-national work. Although the vast bulk of charities still work at a local or national level, the changing reality is that philanthropy, services, and advocacy have become transnational and a nation's international competitive advantage is increasingly linked to the suitability of its regulatory regimes for civil society. Unlike regulatory regimes in other sectors where international competitiveness has become a mantra, the regulation of the third sector has been insulated and slow to change in many countries (see Breen, Ford, & Morgan 2009).

The other important factor is a sense that the primary goals of government regulation of charities are to safeguard a public trust—the charitable gift—and to protect the public purse through control of tax expenditures for these gifts. This leaves little scope for other objectives in regulation, such as relationship-building. Even if new forms of relational governance are beginning to take hold, the regulatory systems in this sector may be slow to adapt to new trends or developments because they have been isolated geographically and set on a narrow mission. Consequently, a lack of regulatory reform cannot necessarily be taken as evidence that the model of public management is static.

This takes us to the intersection of governance and regulation. In places where government–third sector relationships are becoming more collaborative, they will inevitably meet regulatory systems that have not yet fully adapted to accommodate evolving relationships. The third theme that runs through this volume is an examination of a dual set of pressures: a desire for closer collaboration, on the one hand, and a perdurable interest in accountability that is expressed through regulation, on the other hand. What kinds of tensions and conflicts are being experienced at this crossroads of collaboration and regulation? Are innovative accommodations being developed? In different ways and with different lenses, the authors in this volume consider the challenges and implications for both the third sector and governments as they work at this changing nexus of relationships and regulation. Some of the differences in these international trends are reflected in differences in naming this sector, and it is thus useful to briefly outline what we mean by the "third sector."

DEFINING THE THIRD SECTOR

In comparative analysis in this field, finding suitable terminology can be a challenge because both the idea of a sector and what to call it are contested. At a generic level, we have settled on the terminology of "third sector" which refers to the diverse mix of associations that occupy the organized part of civil society. The core attributes of these third sector organizations are that they are products of free association, serve a public benefit, are self-governing, and do not distribute profits to owners or stakeholders (see Frumkin 2002; Salamon, Sokolowski, & List 2003). Although the dependence on volunteers for operations varies enormously, and many professionalized third sector organizations depend almost exclusively on paid staff, their governance is normally the responsibility of volunteers acting in the capacity of directors or trustees.

To varying degrees, third sector organizations serve three important functions. First, they contribute to citizenship and democracy by mobilizing citizens in collective action (Boris 1999; Frumkin 2002; Grønbjerg & Smith 2006; Ingram & Smith 1993; Phillips 2009). Through the process of collective action and the need to govern and manage private organizations, citizens may learn and practice the skills of citizenship—public debate, compromise, and responsibility-taking, thereby building social capital and greater societal trust (Putnam 2000; Warren 2001). As Walzer (1991: 294) notes, "the civility that makes democratic politics possible can only be learned in the associational networks" of civil society. A second role pertains to public policy and governing. By representing a plethora of different interests in policy debates and contributing both expert and experiential knowledge, third sector organizations can promote better evidence-based, more legitimate policy. In some cases, their involvement in policy development is deeply embedded and occurs through formalized co-governance arrangements, as described in some of the following chapters, while in other cases, it is sporadic and even adversarial as third sector organizations advocate for their interests and causes without being invited to do so (see Young 1999). Third, but perhaps the first thing that comes to mind when most people think about this sector, is service delivery. Such service provision may be fully integrated into public services as part of a mixed economy of welfare (Evers 2005) or take place independent from any involvement by the state. Our argument is not that third sector organizations are always constructive forces in promoting active citizenship, better public policy, or effective service delivery; indeed, they may at times be exclusionary, obstructionist, parochial, and highly paternalistic (see Brooks 2000; Fiorina 1999). Rather, our point is to establish a frame for understanding government–third sector relationships which recognizes that the relationship is multi-faceted, extending beyond service delivery, and that such relationships will vary across jurisdictions and over time, depending on the mix of roles at play.

Collectively, the third sector is a major economic as well as social force, contributing on average 5 percent of Gross Domestic Product (GDP) in developed countries, which is roughly on par with the construction and financial services industries (Salamon et al. 2007: 4, 6). The distribution of capacity within the third sector tends to be bifurcated, however, with a small percentage of very large organizations (notably universities, hospitals, and multi-service social welfare agencies, among others) and a very large proportion of organizations, generally more than half, that operate with only one or no staff at all (Salamon, Sokolowski, & List 2003; Statistics Canada 2004). How organizations are supported financially also varies considerably with distinctive regional patterns evident. In developed countries, governments generally provide a significant portion of the funding to this sector (on average 27 percent), often through purchase-of-service arrangements; in no country does the third sector receive the bulk of its financial support from private philanthropy (Salamon et al. 2007: 10).[3] Earned income through the sale of goods and services is the fastest growing part of the funding mix, and, indeed, many third sector organizations have become highly entrepreneurial and use a wide range of innovative social finance tools which, as we will see in the following chapters, creates an interesting array of new hybrid types of organizations and blend of social and economic purposes (Anheier & Mertens 2003; Brandsen, van de Donk, & Putters 2005; Evers 2005; Skelcher 2004; see Smith, Chapter 8, this volume). In short, the notions of "nonprofit" and "public benefit" are rapidly evolving as organizations take on new entrepreneurial pursuits; consequently, the boundaries among the nonprofit, for-profit, and public sectors are increasingly blurred as hybrid forms of financing and organizational form are invented.

Given this internal diversity, it comes as no surprise that the third sector often does not see itself as a coherent *sector* at all (see Carmel & Harlock 2008; Donnelly-Cox & McGee, Chapter 4, this volume; Lyons & Dalton, Chapter 10, this volume). Internal understanding of shared issues and external awareness among the public and governments are often essential components of the broader relationship building, as authors of this volume observe. In conceptual terms, the value of referring to a "sector" is that it serves as a reminder that, in spite of internal differences, the collective has a structure that involves both horizontal connections among groups from different policy and service fields and vertical integration through infrastructure organizations, umbrella groups, and federations that connect the local to the national level. Both of these vertical structures and horizontal networks are central to the overall capacity of the third sector to function with any collective interests at all, and, as discussed in several of the following chapters, the capacity of these infrastructure organizations is a key factor in the ability to forge stronger relationships with governments and initiate reform that leads to more enabling policy and regulatory environments.

Putting aside the debate over whether this is a sector, the matter of how to name it differs by context and place and, in many, this too is debated (see Frumkin 2002). The lexicon includes: nonprofit, charity, civil society, NGO (nongovernmental), voluntary; community, and (in the US) 503(c)(3). Although by way of introduction and overall naming, we have reverted to the generic and encompassing term of "third sector," many of the authors have used the labels that are the more common nomenclature in their own countries. As editors, we have not changed these, and thus a variety of terms are used interchangeably throughout the volume.

The exception to this is the reference to "charities" which are the focus of several chapters. In this case, the authors are using the concept in a more precise manner to refer to those nonprofit organizations that meet the common law interpretation of charitable purposes, have been registered or acknowledged as such by the state, and are able to issue tax receipts for donations. The common law interpretation of charity dates back to the 1601 Statute of Charitable Uses and subsequent classification in Britain's Pemsel case of the 1890s that identified four heads of charity: relief of poverty, advancement of education, advancement of religion, and other purposes beneficial to community (in a manner that the common law regards as charitable) (Bourgeois 2002; Fremont-Smith 2004; O'Halloran, McGregor-Lowndes, & Simon 2008). The common law approach not only restricts organizations that do have charitable objects based on this classification (and subsequent case law) from being recognized as charities, but it requires that substantially all of the activities of qualified organizations be charitable, thereby limiting political and business activities. Some countries, notably the United States and, since 2006, England, have supplemented the common law with legislation that codifies the types of purposes and organizations that are eligible to provide tax receipts (see Moore 2005). The limitations imposed by the common law classification of charitable purposes are widely seen to constrain the work of this sector, the restrictions on policy advocacy are actively contested (Berry & Arons 2003; Casey and Dalton 2006; Dunn 2008), and whether regulation should be so closely linked to a taxation frame of reference is being questioned in many jurisdictions (O'Halloran, McGregor-Lowndes, & Simon 2008; Smerdon 2009). These issues of how charity is determined and the independence of the regulatory body are taken up in several chapters in this volume.

INTERNATIONAL DEVELOPMENTS:
AN OVERVIEW OF THE CHAPTERS

The chapters have been deliberately selected to represent a broad spectrum of approaches to governance and regulatory change in the third sector. We have not attempted to impose a template for each chapter. Rather we asked the authors to address the most important changes in recent years in models of public management and third sector regulation in their countries and to address the implications of their intersection. Our international comparison begins with England, which has perhaps gone the furthest in the most systematic way to reform both relationships and regulations, and it ends with an overview of more autocratic countries, many of which have not only resisted reform but actually become more repressive in their regulation and oversight of the third sector.

England

Over the past decade, England has undertaken a program of unprecedented reform and has arguably set the 'standard' that a number of other jurisdictions have attempted to emulate in whole or in part. **Debra Morris** (Chapter 2) demonstrates how these reforms, a combination of hard and soft law, have been positive in enabling the work of the voluntary and community sector, but have also established new forms of regulatory controls.

One longstanding regulatory issue in England, as in other commonwealth countries, stems from a concern that the common law interpretation of charitable purposes has not kept pace with the kinds of causes pursued and work performed by charities in contemporary societies. Following a call for reform from the sector, in 2001 then Prime Minister Blair commissioned a review of the legal and regulatory regimes governing charities. This review eventually led to the passage of the *Charities Act* in late 2006. The significance of the *Charities Act 2006* is that it sets out, for the first time, a statutory definition of charity that updates the scope of charitable aims for a modern society and establishes a public benefit test for charitable purposes. Although the interpretation will continue to rely on existing case law, the test removes the automatic presumption of charity for organizations dedicated to relief of poverty and advancement of education and religion. Morris is optimistic about the benefits of the new Act, arguing that once fully implemented, it "will modernize and reform the legal framework within which charities operate, and will go far towards ensuring that charities are independently regulated in a manner that is open, consistent and proportionate."

Legal reform has been supplemented with new 'soft law' provisions, notably the Compact of 1997 and more recent moves to self-regulation. The manner in which the Compact and the five policy codes that accompany it have been implemented has produced a relational contract with considerable teeth by establishing a mediation scheme for disagreements, annual meetings with ministers, detailed reporting, and an independent Compact Commissioner. The government has also indicated its support for the self-regulation mechanisms covering good governance and fundraising that have recently been developed by umbrella associations, but it is not leaving the results to chance. If voluntary adherence is not successful, government has reserved the powers to introduce a compulsory system of regulation for the governance of charities and their fundraising. Morris sees great value in such a mix of binding legal rules and voluntary initiatives; the challenge is finding the right mix and identifying the tipping point at which voluntary schemes need to be reinforced with harder law.

Scotland

Following devolution, the government of Scotland embraced a nationalist and economic development project of facilitating an innovative, inclusive, and enterprising third sector and of establishing effective means for state–sector partnerships without creating excessive bureaucracy. The result was a new regulatory system for charities, compatible with this relational governance approach. In analyzing the implications of the charities legislation and regulatory machinery introduced in 2005, **Patrick Ford** (Chapter 3) argues that it represents a missed opportunity to build on Scottish foundations in a way that would lead to a more inclusive definition of charity and establish a regulator that is more attuned to the needs and concerns of the third sector.

Ford notes that Scotland has a longstanding concept of "public benefit" and a legal form of a "public trust" which are more expansive than the corresponding English notions of charity and "charitable trust," although under an integrated fiscal system, the English concept of charity has crept into Scots law over the past several decades. When the new Scottish Parliament came to legislate for reform of charities, it could have emancipated itself from English influence and made use of Scotland's own common law of public trusts. The Scottish legislators seem to have been caught between two instincts, however: to have a charity test that is fully compatible with the English version and thus acceptable for the purposes of the UK level tax relief provisions, and to have one sufficiently different to appear distinctively Scottish. The result, Ford argues, is a "kilted cuckoo." In general, Scotland's new charity test is much the same as the English definition, but the kilting nevertheless left some important differences that have the potential to lead Scottish charitable status in a very different direction from its English counterpart. In addition, the system of charities supervision that was created is oddly out of alignment with the government's relational governance vision that emphasizes facilitation, partnership, and social enterprise.

Ford makes a strong case for replacing the new charity test with Scotland's older public benefit concept which is both simpler and more inclusive. He also advocates reducing the functions of the new Scottish charity regulator and transferring the primary responsibility for maintaining public confidence in public benefit organizations to the third sector itself through more effective self-regulation, particularly of fundraising, led by the national umbrella organizations. In sum, Ford presents a vision for squaring regulation with relational governance.

Ireland

In 2009, Ireland also implemented major reform of the supervisory machinery for charities that includes establishment of a register of charities, a new regulatory body and appeals tribunal, a definition of charitable purposes, and an update of fundraising legislation that promotes self-regulation first, state regulation if necessary. This new regulatory regime was intended to sit alongside the established social partnership that guides the government's relationships with both the business and community sectors—a partnership that has displayed elements of corporatism but has long been interlaced with aspects of neo-liberalism, and that is now in substantial disarray as a result of the financial crisis. **Gemma Donnelly-Cox** and **Siobhan McGee** (Chapter 4) assess the implications and potential of Ireland's new regulatory regime in the context of social partnership. As they observe, the push for regulatory reform was a preemptive move led mainly by actors outside the third sector, and it reflects an acknowledgment that changing times require more advanced, formalized approaches to accountability, rather than the facilitating but informal approaches that have long characterized state–third sector relationships in Ireland. While these reforms have been supported by the sector, its fragmentation and lack of infrastructure meant it was incapable of taking a lead or actively participating in their development.

Donnelly-Cox and McGee argue that the key challenges for Ireland's third sector in being serious players in policy development or effective self-regulation are the absence of a core representative body and the limited recognition of the idea of being a "sector." Without such representative structures, Donnelly-Cox and McGee argue that it seems "inevitable that a suboptimal regulatory framework will replace the unsatisfactory informal relationship that the sector has had with the state." The goals of Ireland's new charitable and fundraising regulation seem clear: to enhance public trust and confidence. However, a common understanding—within the sector, from the regulator, and among the funding public—on the criteria for 'success' still seems elusive.

Germany and France

Ingo Bode (Chapter 5) presents a very insightful analysis of the changes underway in two countries with similar traditions of government–third sector interaction, despite quite different welfare state regimes. Germany has a longstanding corporatist tradition that has included a cooperative relationship between German governments, at the national and state levels, and the third sector. Many third sector organizations are very large and receive most of their funding from the government. While France shares corporatist traditions, greater variability in the government–third sector relationship tends to exist at the local level. More recently though, the ripple effects of the tenets of NPM have been felt in both countries, with a pronounced shift toward more market-oriented mechanisms including formal contracting, competitive bidding, and greater regulation.

Bode's chapter raises three important cautions toward our understanding of the intersection of governance and regulation. First, the notion of the fading of NPM and rise of 'new' relational governance is limited in its application and is not the story of most of continental Europe. Indeed, most of what is supposedly new about relational governance—collaboration and dense networks—appears as 'old hat' in much of Europe, whereas the new reality is one of growing marketization of welfare services and hybridization of the corporatist legacy. Second, it is problematic to discuss regulation of charities and nonprofits as a whole without looking more closely at the nature of the welfare state because so much of the regulation that really matters occurs in the specific context of the welfare markets in which nonprofits work. Third, his comparative analysis reminds us of the need to pay attention to scale and examine sub-traditions, given growing differentiation, by geography and by specific welfare services, *within* each country.

Hungary

Éva Kuti (Chapter 6) describes how the dramatic changes in Hungary since the fall of state socialism have produced a rapidly evolving relationship between the government and third sector that exemplifies many of the trends evident elsewhere: a big increase in interest in third sector organizations and a noticeable shift toward more market-oriented reforms including formal contracts. However, Hungary has also adopted many aspects of collaborative governance between government and the third sector, reflecting the primacy placed on democratization and political and economic modernization since 1989. In effect, Hungary has seen parallel efforts to strengthen *both* NPM and relational governance in the post-socialist period, reminding us that the models are not mutually exclusive. In addition, both models of public management have been adapted in Hungary to meet local contexts and needs, and thus differ from theory or practice elsewhere.

Kuti analyzes in detail some of Hungary's innovations in capacity and relationship building with civil society, including the 1 percent tax (whereby citizens can elect to transfer 1 percent of their personal income tax to nonprofit organizations), the public benefit test implemented in 1997, creation of forums for policy dialogue, and the attempt to establish an independent oversight body to ensure professional and ethic standards are met. As Kuti notes, the proponents of relational governance often take it for granted that civil society actors are able and willing to share responsibilities and collaborate with government. This has not been the case in Hungary, where the government has demonstrated a willingness to build institutions of relational governance, but suspicions by civil society organizations of a return to state control have forced some of its proposals to be withdrawn. As a result, the institutionalization of relational governance has not proceeded as quickly as it might, the mechanisms for public scrutiny and support of the third sector remain extremely complicated and bureaucratic, and a climate of distrust pervades the state–third sector relationship.

European Union

Both collaboration and regulation of the third sector are made more complex by multi-level governance and the growing significance of transnational nonprofits. **Alison Dunn** (Chapter 7) addresses governance *by* and *for* civil society organizations at the level of the European Union (EU).

In terms of engagement of civil society organizations, Dunn observes that the current situation is one of flux. The extensive lobbying industry which has grown up around Brussels is becoming ever more strategic and professional, and the growing importance of transnational organizations across all parts of the third sector means that the EU has become a focal point for their engagement in policy. This benefits the EU by facilitating its dialogue with citizens and providing the Union with a greater degree of credibility and transparency in governance. Dunn analyzes recent developments that promote such engagement in EU governance including: the Aarhus Convention which provides greater opportunities to challenge EU decisions, at least for environmental organizations; the Lisbon Treaty which is premised on participatory democracy; the new Register of Interest Representatives; and the potential for codes of conduct and an EU level Compact-like "concordant." The EU is an extremely complex political system with a confusing labyrinth of institutions, however. In spite of formal mechanisms for civil society organizations to have input into its policy processes, the practical reality is that it is easier, and often more effective, for them to continue to act at the Member State level.

Although the EU has recently made a foray into greater regulation of civil society organizations, notably through the creation of a new common legal structure and common good governance standards, here too the Member States remain the gatekeepers. Dunn does not advocate a more interventionist EU but suggests that a balance needs to be struck between maintaining the pivotal role of the Members States as implementers and regulators of standard governance norms *and* promoting cohesive equality across states as well as enhancing the democratic practices of the EU institutions. Ultimately, the changing relationship of the EU with the third sector highlights the centrality of national governments and means that regulatory and policy changes within Member States are of vital importance in shaping and promoting the third sector's position at the EU level.

US

In the US, the situation for nonprofits is also changing significantly due to both the negative consequences of the current economic situation and the investment in the third sector by the Obama administration. **Steven Rathgeb Smith** (Chapter 8) focuses on contracting for public services as a form of regulation and demonstrates how the impact of NPM and "reinventing government" over the past fifteen years has exerted dual pressures on the nonprofit sector. It has led to greater interest in accountability and control of nonprofits by government, while at the same time it has increased incentives for collaboration between government and nonprofits as well as among nonprofit organizations. Performance contracting, widely used by national, state, and local governments in a wide variety of fields, including child welfare, workforce training, and mental health, brought a push for more outcome evaluation, and it ramped up competition among nonprofits and heightened their vulnerability, all of which reinforced the vertical, hierarchical relationships between governments (at all levels) and nonprofits. At the same time, governments and the third sector are engaged in a variety of partnerships and collaborations to address regulatory issues in contracting as well as more substantive issues related to important policy issues such as homelessness, education, and substance abuse prevention.

This contracting regime is, to a large extent, relational in nature, as it embodies longer term relationships even when competitive bidding is required and is supported by the movement of professionals back and forth between government and nonprofit agencies. These partnerships have been abetted to an extent by the diversification of policy tools, such as vouchers, tax credits, and bond financing, employed by government to support the third sector. The changing funding and political landscapes have facilitated the development of hybrid nonprofits which incorporate features of the public and/or for-profit sectors. As the economic crisis deepened, the US government has been faced with the problem of addressing some of the consequences of the devolutionary aspects of NPM. The result is a push for greater consolidation and centralization of social services and, within the third sector, greater interest in mergers by funders and service providers, thereby creating a new set of financial and political tensions and interesting structural innovations.

All of this is part of a broader trend in American public policy of greater regulation of nonprofits. Major new regulation of nonprofits at the federal level has been discussed extensively in recent years, but it has failed to gain substantial political support. Instead, Congress has enacted a series of relatively minor changes in existing law to increase transparency in reporting. The real change over the next few years is not likely to come from increased regulation, however. Rather it will emanate from the new initiatives of the Obama administration, including support for thousands of new stipended volunteers, for social innovation and entrepreneurship, and for networking among local nonprofits and public agencies. Because major coalitions and associations representing nonprofit organizations are major supporters of the Obama administration, it appears highly unlikely that the administration will seek to tighten regulation of political activity or lobbying by nonprofits. There is also good news in bad for the sector as the 2009 stimulus package to help generate jobs and recharge the economy contained money for a multiplicity of programs and services provided by nonprofit organizations. The stimulus money tended to flow first through agencies with longstanding good relationships with state and local government, thus reinforcing the value of collaboration and partnership between public and nonprofit agencies.

Canada

Canada sits in a paradoxical situation in regulation and relationship building. While Canada has a large third sector—second in the world in size relative to paid employment (Hall et al. 2005)—the sector is almost invisible in national political and policy debates. The Canadian story told by **Susan D. Phillips** (Chapter 9) is one of both resistance and reform. At the political level, there has been little interest, indeed resistance, in changing the fundamentals of the regulatory regime despite calls by the third sector over the past fifteen years for a modernized pubic benefit test, an independent regulator, liberalization of restrictions on advocacy, and more sustainable financing and contracting mechanisms. Some regulatory reform has occurred, however, as the regulator (the national tax agency) has been reinventing itself from within by layering new guidelines and administrative practices into existing rules and procedures. Although these incremental changes are having positive effects, Phillips argues that incremental change alone is insufficient: the fundamentals still need to be addressed.

Although Canada took up components of NPM, it did so with less zeal than many other countries and has begun to move off NPM in recent years. But the replacement model is not so clear, other than progressively greater centralization of power in the Prime Minister's office. In 2000, the Canadian government put its toe in the water of relational governance but quickly found the waters too chilly and withdrew. Building on the momentum in the UK, the federal government began a unique five-year collaborative exercise that was intended to establish more constructive ways of working with the voluntary and nonprofit sector, build capacity, and undertake regulatory reform. The initiative produced an Accord, modeled closely on England's compact, funded some excellent research, and generated a deeper understanding of the sector among individual public servants. More constructive government–sector relationships were never institutionalized, however, and particularly since a change in government in 2006, the Accord has become a limp instrument, and many of the nonprofits funded by the initiative are actually worse off in terms of capacity and access to the policy process. Reactions to scandals in contracting (mainly with private sector firms) in 2000 and again in 2005 produced even more stringent accountability requirements on public funds which have placed an enormous burden on both funding recipients and government departments. A current challenge is how to fix this "web of rules" over contracting (Blue Ribbon Panel 2006). The other unfolding challenge is to devise more effective means of self-regulation over governance and fundraising practices within the sector, a challenge that was accelerated in 2009 when the federal regulator articulated its own expectations for good governance systems and that is complicated by under-developed infrastructure organizations. Given the lack of interest in serious regulatory and policy reform at the federal level, Canadian voluntary organizations are refocusing their attention at the provincial and municipal levels or are working in ways that are less reliant on government involvement.

Australia

Of all the countries surveyed, NPM was perhaps most enthusiastically embraced, by a succession of governments of different political stripes, in Australia. **Mark Lyons** and **Bronwen Dalton** (Chapter 10) argue that the case of Australia provides little evidence for a transition to more relational forms of governance because NPM continues to have a strong hold and the national government's stance to the third sector is little changed. Indeed, they refer to Australia as the laggard. Beginning in the 1980s and extended by the long run of the Labor government of John Howard, Australia institutionalized a strong belief in markets, contracting, and government regulation of the third sector. In addition, the Howard government encouraged the growth of for-profit organizations in service categories previously dominated by nonprofits. The result has been a long term decline in the power and political influence of the third sector in policy development and implementation. Lyons and Dalton are careful to note that not all of the changes that have affected the third sector over the past 30 years are related to NPM as population growth and its ageing, rising living standards, changing values and ways of living, and an expansion of services provided by business have been additional factors.

In terms of regulation, Australia's legal and regulatory framework is "extensive, complex and incoherent," and, in contrast with multiple efforts to assist business, governments have made no serious effort to simplify it, undertaking only modest tinkering. In 2001, the Commonwealth government established an inquiry into the definition of charity which produced a report that was generally welcomed by the third sector. The government backed away from its recommendation to establish an independent charities commission and, after heated debate over a proposal on how to clarify restrictions on political advocacy by charities, it walked away from all but a few minor extensions of charity status. In several states, social service nonprofits managed to push governments into developing compacts modelled after those in the UK, but these have proven to be mainly symbolic gestures that have not addressed the sector's main concerns about the inadequacy of government funding and the risk shifting in contracts. In spite of a new found interest in social inclusion, Lyons and Dalton conclude that in Australia little likelihood exists of any weakening of NPM in the foreseeable future and equally little chance of a significant transformation in relations between governments and the third sector.

Developing and Transition Countries

In the final chapter, **Douglas Rutzen** (Chapter 11) provides a cross-cutting synthesis and, by extending the analysis to a wide range of developing and transition countries, offers a sharp reminder that the situation is not entirely rosy or improving for the third sector in many parts of the world.

As Rutzen observes, in recent years over 40 countries have introduced or enacted legislation that limits the civic space and places significant restrictions on civil society organizations. Although many countries—many of the cases presented in this volume are leaders among them—are responding constructively to meet the changing environment and needs of the third sector, the trend among most autocratic countries is toward increased command and control regulation, designed to serve as gatekeeper to limit the democratic functions of civil society organizations. Nevertheless, some surprising pockets of reform are occurring as various jurisdictions struggle to define public benefit, develop appropriate legal forms of incorporation, establish acceptable limits on advocacy, and address the new reality of transnational organizations.

Rutzen concludes by considering the far-reaching effects that the financial crisis is likely to have on the government–third sector relationship. As we have already witnessed, a short term implication is a call for greater regulation and transparency. Deregulation and contracting based on relational norms are probably politically untenable, at least for the short run. However, the financial crisis has also revealed the incredibly complex interconnections that exist among the public, private, and nonprofit sectors, which were made even more complex by the massive bailouts and investment made by governments in response to the crisis. In an important sense, then, the fundamental principles of relational governance have been validated because it will be increasingly necessary, Rutzen suggests, to engage key actors from various sectors to address emerging challenges of entangled relationships.

WHEN RELATIONAL GOVERNANCE MEETS NPM: INTERNATIONAL TRENDS

The international cases surveyed in this volume reveal a diverse mix of approaches to renewing and restructuring relationships between national governments and third sectors. Although experience is mixed, two overarching themes stand out. First, it is clear that government regulation is not antithetical to collaboration. Rather, well crafted regulation plays a very powerful role in establishing incentives for engagement with nonprofit organizations as well as for sound public management regimes. Conversely, highly restrictive regulatory frameworks can easily constrict the civic space, often intentionally so, and create mistrust on the part of both government and civil society organizations. One has only to look to the multiple examples from autocratic states provided by Rutzen to see the negative consequences or to the new charity legislation in England to understand the positive benefits. Given the complexity of the organizational environment, however, it is all too easy to create an opaque regulatory regime that therefore reduces the incentives for individuals to be engaged in local organizations.

Second, in virtually every country examined, policymakers have pushed in recent years for greater accountability and transparency which typically requires increased regulation, regardless of the overall level of collaboration between government and the third sector. Such accountability was a central part of NPM, and it shows no signs of fading given continued high expectations of transparency in demonstrating that public and philanthropic dollars are being used as intended. Accountability has recently been strengthened in various countries through a variety of means, including: easily searchable registries of charities (and also of lobbyists) that give the public a better window on their activities and finances; new rules requiring greater detail of reporting on fundraising (see Breen 2009); and increased demands for performance-based contracting and outcome evaluation that demonstrate value for money. To some extent, this investment in accountability strategies reinforces a hierarchical relationship with governments, but to an even greater extent it can also increase the space for citizens to become more informed and actively engaged as consumers, members, supporters, and leaders of well-run nonprofit organizations. With more complex forms of collaboration and denser networks, a major challenge for governments and nonprofits alike is to develop approaches that effectively enable horizontal accountability among partners while still maintaining effective vertical accountabilities of contractors to purchasers or regulated organizations to regulators.

The Emergence of Relational Governance

The picture on the purported shift from NPM to relational governance is quite mixed among the jurisdictions included in this volume. In England, Scotland, Ireland, Hungary, the EU, and the US, governments in the past few years have begun to develop much more collaborative relationships with the third sector that include more relational forms of contracting, creation of more responsive regulators, and, in several cases, the establishment of institutionalized means of dialogue and relationship management. Germany and France also have models of public management that might be labelled relational governance, but these are not new; rather they are legacies of an evolving corporatism. As Bode (Chapter 5, this volume) observes, the emerging trend in much of continental Europe is not shared governance but creeping marketization. In contrast, Canada had a short-lived attempt at relationship and capacity building from 2000 to 2002 which has not been carried on in any formal way, and the Commonwealth government of Australia appears to be lagging behind most others because the hold of NPM remains very strong. What explains these significant differences in approaches to more relational forms of governance?

One possibility is that the differences are manifestations of the evolution of different types of welfare states. The countries surveyed include a range of different types of welfare states, to roughly apply Esping-Andersen's

(1990) typology, from the more firmly liberal with their strong emphasis on connection to the labor force as the basis of social security (e.g. US, Canada, Australia, and England) to social democratic welfare states where social policies have been built on principles of universality, quality, and citizenship rights (e.g. Germany and France). One might argue that, given the emphasis on markets, liberal regimes were more open to NPM and, when it ran its course, were the first to turn to more relational forms of governance. The argument does not hold, however, as some of the greatest variation in adoption of relational governance is among liberal welfare states. The US and England, for instance, have moved much farther in this direction than have Canada or Australia. Nor is the explanation simply one of policy transfer, although policy transfer has clearly occurred as witnessed by the spread of the soft law of compacts following England's lead. Canada is a good example of borrowing this policy instrument but failing to institutionalize it into a meaningful tool of relationship building. Whereas the English Compact has gained quasi-statutory status, the Canadian Accord is largely defunct.

The chapters suggest that there is one key factor that differentiates jurisdictions that have intentionally and actively moved to more institutionalized forms of relational governance, and in the process adapted their regulatory regimes, from those that have done little by way of building more constructive state–third sector relationships. That factor is a vision of the role of the third sector that sees it as more than a social safety net or delivery agent of services, but that advances the value of the sector for democracy and citizenship and/or economic development. The vision then needs to be driven by strong political leadership. A connection to democratization or economic development is evident in all the cases in which major reform has occurred: in England where the goal was to promote more active citizenship; in Scotland where there was both a nationalist and economic development project; in Ireland where the social partnership helped transform the country's economic fortunes; in Hungary where both promotion of democracy and modernization of public services were core goals; and in the US where deep economic recession coupled with the Obama administration's commitment to the value of community service are driving new policy directions. However, it is also clear that such a reform project has to be mutual and that neither government nor the third sector can drive it alone. As Kuti (Chapter 6, this volume) discusses, the government's plans for a more collaborative relationship fell short in Hungary because the sector was not willing to engage as a full partner. Conversely, the potential of the third sector's participation in Ireland's social partnership was not fully realized due to the lack of infrastructure organizations within the sector (see Donnelly-Cox and McGee, Chapter 4, this volume).

An understanding of differential shifts in public management models also depends, in part, on our perspectives on NPM and relational governance. So often, both are presented as simplified caricatures: NPM as a focus on markets and governance as centered on collaboration. As the chapters in this volume demonstrate, however, both models are inherently fuzzy sets with significant internal variations and even inherent contradictions. In particular, NPM essentially has two separate tracks: the market competition component and the devolution, community partnership approach. The former creates fragmentation and is often mismatched with the nature of the problem so that, over time, experience with market competition tends to generate greater interest in collaboration and partnership. Market competition models are often at variance with an interest in democracy, as Kuti discusses in the case of Hungary or as Smith shows in the US where greater interest in community partnerships have been pursued as an opportunity for citizen engagement rather than as an antidote to markets. Similarly, the arrival of relational models of governance has occurred through quite different routes: through continuation and adaptation of longstanding corporatist approaches and through the introduction of new forms of collaboration. Thus, relational governance institutionalizes partnership to varying degrees, from formal machinery and entrenched norms, to extended but nevertheless targeted project-specific partnerships, to more episodic collaboration. The transformation to relational governance is akin to Jastrow's famous duck-rabbit ambiguous figure which some may see as a duck and others as a rabbit. What the chapters in this volume indicate is that it is often difficult to tell precisely when the NPM duck becomes the governance rabbit. Hence, we see considerable hybrid forms of public management and the co-existence—sometimes comfortable, perhaps symbiotic, and at other times conflictual in nature—of both marketization and collaboration. As Bode notes in his analysis of Germany and France, the more nuanced story is often one of greater differentiation *within* countries as specific welfare markets or subnational levels evolve in distinctive ways due to the differing degrees and combinations of marketization and partnership. The analyses presented in the following chapters are intentionally high level as they attempt to capture recent developments at a national level, but the full picture clearly demands more detailed analyses that pay serious attention to both scale and subsector.

Tensions at the Intersection of Governance and Regulation

While the intersection of NPM and relational governance can produce a hybridization of models of public management and enabled elements of both to co-exist, tensions can also develop when relational norms meet existing regulatory regimes. First, the desire for accountability, particularly safeguards on public funding, often collides directly with an interest in a more collaborative and decentralized approach. The latter necessarily forces a loosening of government control, which governments are often reluctant to relinquish, and makes accountability inherently more complex. The recent push by the Internal Revenue Service (IRS) for reporting on fundraising (Williams

2007) or the re-centralization of funding for many social and health services at the federal level in the US, described by Smith (Chapter 8, this volume), illustrate this tension. In extreme cases, the strictures and constraints developed in the name of accountability have become so great that they actually undermine real accountability and are a major source of tension in the relationship between government and the third sector. For example, the 2006 report of an independent panel established by the Canadian government to investigate how to reduce the onerous requirements that had been attached to federal government contracting and funding as crisis reactions to scandals expressed shock that the "morass of rules and general red tape" was even worse than imagined, to the extent that they hampered "sensible" reporting and evaluation (Blue Ribbon Panel 2006: vii; see also Elson 2009; Phillips, Chapter 9, this volume). A 2009 comparative study commissioned by the Baring Foundation suggests that the cumulative effect of such accountability demands has been to create a culture in which governments effectively "direct the decisions of individual organisations about how they deliver their mission" (Cairns 2009: 43). A major challenge then for both governments and the third sector as they move forward in restructuring relationships is to square accountability with collaboration.

A second tension relates to the mismatch between regulation and the changing realities of the third sector. Emerging forms of social finance were not anticipated when rules on the "unrelated business" activities of charities were devised, and in some places existing rules would, for example, limit program related investments by foundations and dissuade many forms of social entrepreneurship (Edwards 2008; Young 2003). As Smith notes, the hybridization of organizational forms is stretching the boundaries of both legal and accountability frameworks in the US, and as Dunn observes, the growth of transnational nonprofits challenges the ability of a single jurisdiction to administer appropriate legal forms or regulate effectively, thus prompting interest at the EU level in developing a legal form suitable to multi-jurisdictions. The limitations of the Pemsel classification of charity and the desire to develop a modern public benefit test to replace or supplement it are felt in many common law jurisdictions and have been a source of innovation in some and resistance in others. Related to this is the challenge of modernizing regulatory institutions to be more responsive and less mired in the conflict between serving the regulated sector and protecting the integrity of the tax system. While many look to the independent Charity Commission of England and Wales as the prototype of a more suitable regulatory institution, Ford (Chapter 3, this volume) argues that, when the model was imported into Scotland, it remained too paternalistic: in short, more contemporary institutions compatible with relational governance still need to be invented.

A third, compounding tension is that regulation occurs by many means. While the rules imposed on organizations related to their status as charities and ability to issue tax receipts may be significant in shaping their behavior, greater constraints may actually come through other channels such as contracting and performance measurement. Given the multiple actors this may entail, including different departments and levels of government, foundations, and corporate sponsors, regulation seldom operates as a coherent regime (see Pross & Webb 2005). Nor should we expect to see fully integrated and mutually self reinforcing contracting, performance, and regulatory systems when the trend is toward greater complexity of financing as well as of relationships. Perhaps the best we can count on is that various parts of the system do not consistently undermine each other and do not inhibit constructive reform.

This international survey indicates that the adaptation of regulatory systems is occurring in many countries, but it is nevertheless striking how relatively isolated the regulation of charities remains from most other economic sectors and from the 'big ideas' in the current regulatory literature. Despite the growing adoption of risk based regulatory approaches, it has lagged behind other fields of regulation, and the development of sophisticated risk related systems for charities is generally still at nascent stages (see Evans 2009). Only in a few countries, notably England and the US, does the regulation of charities appear to be significantly influenced by the smart regulation movement that has advocated for better proportionality of regulatory effort to benefit and greater transparency in processes.[4] In part, this isolation may be due to the attachment of the regulatory function to the tax agency in many places, and in part to the relative invisibility of the third sector as a subject of serious public policy (Lyons & Passey 2006; Phillips 2009). Taking up opportunities for learning from other sectors and other jurisdictions will be important given that we appear to be entering an era of renewed attention to regulation, and learning how to be innovators for more effective regulation will increasingly be part of a nation's competitiveness.

Finally, a consistent theme is that lack of capacity, particularly of national infrastructure organizations, undermines the ability of the third sector to embrace and work effectively in genuine partnerships with government. The ability to be effective partners in governing requires mechanisms for representation and engagement *within* the third sector, as well as *to* governments. It also requires a capacity to conduct research so as to have a value in policymaking that is increasingly evidence based and an ability to monitor the state–sector relationship. As the following chapters indicate, the existence of national infrastructure organizations that play such important mediating, representational, research, and supporting roles in the third sector varies greatly. With the exception of the US and to a lesser extent England and Scotland, the under-development of infrastructure organizations is a serious limitation in any transformation to more relational forms of governing. Support for capacity building does not always accompany policy and regulatory reform, however, and increasingly the third sector has had to rely on its own entrepreneurial activities to finance this infrastructure.

CONCLUSION: LOOKING AHEAD

In recent years, the public management literature has worked hard to convince us that a major shift is occurring from a model of NPM to one of shared, collaborative governance. And, it has done a good job as the notion of such a transformation has been widely accepted. Empirical evidence has not kept pace with theory, however. The purpose of this volume is to explore the extent to which such a shift is occurring and to examine the implications for the third sector. The legacy of NPM was not only markets but regulation, and the central question we address is: to what extent are these rule-based regulatory systems and institutions adapting to accommodate more relational forms of governing? The test is by no means systematic or even across the selected countries, and the evidence has to be treated with caution because in many places the third sector is undergoing change faster than models of public management are evolving. Sorting out drivers of change is not simple or straightforward.

The unfolding picture in each of the countries examined is somewhat different, but definite patterns are apparent. In the UK and Ireland, extensive reform is underway, albeit not without a few hiccups, which is designed to enable greater collaboration between the state and the third sector and put in place regulatory systems that facilitate such relationships. Several of the authors would like to see reform go further toward enabling the sector and establishing more responsive regulatory institutions, but in comparison to other countries, England, Scotland, and Ireland would appear to be leaders in creating a *collaborative* model. Several transition countries, notably Hungary, are similarly demonstrating leadership in establishing mechanisms for greater collaboration and support of the third sector, but the sector's lingering suspicions of the state means that it is not yet prepared to be a full partner. A different pattern of *post-corporatist hybridization* is apparent in Germany, France, and other parts of continental Europe that are not included in this volume. Here, too, evidence of institutionalized collaboration between governments and nonprofits exists, but such collaboration is not new; rather it is a legacy of longstanding corporatist arrangements. With increased marketization being introduced into many welfare services, the emergent model is increasingly a hybrid one in which welfare markets are layered into relational governance, with growing differentiation by service field and subnational region. The laggard states are Canada and Australia as here reform has been marginal at best and the model remains one of the *regulatory state*, exercised through both rules on charities and contracting regimes, with little movement toward widespread, institutionalized collaboration. The US is in many respects in a distinctive category of its own with a truly *mixed model*. In the US, several competing forces—performance contracting, calls for greater regulation, political support for the nonprofit sector, and more developed infrastructure within the sector—have produced extensive experimentation in hybrid forms of organization, financing, and relationships. Finally, in many autocratic and developing countries where democracy is still fragile, *state control* remains, and, indeed, political fears of civil society organizations have led in recent years to more restrictive legislation and controls.

The key factor that distinguishes those countries that are moving toward more relational governance and are adapting regulatory and contracting regimes to be more enabling of the third sector is a political vision, supported by sustained political leadership, which sees this sector as more than a provider of services. Only when the value of the third sector as a constructive force for citizenship, democracy, and economic development is appreciated has significant and comprehensive change been led by governments so as to establish a greater role for the sector, enable it to function more effectively, and build more constructive relationships with the state.

At the intersection of relational governance and post-NPM regulation, a number of tensions are evident, and outstanding challenges remain. Accountability mechanisms need to be adapted to function more effectively within emerging forms of collaboration. Governments may seek partnership with nonprofits but are also concerned about public subsidies of advocacy, and thus the regulation of advocacy remains a sore point in relationship building. Regulations often have not caught up with changes in social finance, hybrid legal forms, and modern definitions of public benefit. Regulatory bodies still have to figure out how to balance a compliance and audit function with a responsive and enabling one. Taken as a whole, regulatory regimes often lack coherence because the rules associated with contracting may pile on a regulatory burden and give governments more directive control than partnership arrangements anticipated. In most places, capacity of the third sector to engage in co-management and co-governance remains an issue, and the lack of strong infrastructure organizations may hinder the ability of the third sector to function as a *sector*.

Finally, nettlesome challenges remain that governments and the third sector in most countries are not seriously engaging. In contrast to most other sectors of the economy, the regulation of the third sector is centered on a national (or subnational) frame of reference; consequently, the need to address issues of multi-level governance has been largely ignored. Yet, transnational third sector organizations are becoming much more important, and the contribution of effective regulation and governance of the third sector is increasingly a factor in the ability of states to compete internationally. Even with effective government regulation, a large part of good governance by individual organizations and control of sound fundraising practices will depend on effective self-regulation by the third sector. Finding ways to develop and adapt policy, legal, regulatory, contracting, and financing frameworks for the third sector that enable it to function effectively and that are compatible with changing approaches to public management deserves to be a major focus of public policy in coming years.

NOTES

This project grew out of a panel at the International Research Society for Public Management (IRSPM) conference in Glasgow in 2006. The original set of papers have been added to, revised, and updated, several times in some cases. The graduate student research assistance of Robin Wisener and Katherine Ball of the School of Public Policy and Administration, Carleton University, Mara Brain and Tim Cormier of the Evans School of Public Affairs at the University of Washington, and Lauren Marra of the Georgetown Public Policy Institute is greatly appreciated. We are also indebted to Richard Fries, former Chief Commissioner of the Charity Commission of England and Wales, for providing feedback on the original IRSPM papers.

1. For an early view of David Cameron's "Compassionate Conservatism", see David Cameron, "Victory Speech," *Guardian*, December 6, 2005. Accessed at: http://www.guardian.co.uk/politics/2005/dec/06/toryleadership2005.conservatives3. Cameron stated that, "I want to set free the voluntary sector and social enterprises to deal with the linked problems that blight so many of our communities, of drug abuse, family breakdown, poor public space, chaotic home environments, high crime."
2. Civil society is defined as the space of "uncoerced human association and the set of relational networks—formed for the sake of family, faith, interest and ideology—that fill this space" (Walzer 1992).
3. In a comparison of seven countries that have implemented national satellite accounts for the nonprofit sector, Salamon and colleagues (2007) report that government funding accounts for 27 percent of the revenues of third sector organizations; fees and sales for 28 percent; and philanthropy, including volunteer time, for 35 percent. A broader 34 country comparison (for reference years 1995–2000) conducted as part of the Johns Hopkins Comparative Nonprofit Sector Project indicates a major difference in financing patterns between developed and developing countries. For instance, in developed countries, governments provide, on average, 37.5 percent of the revenues of the sector and in developing countries provide only 16.7 percent of the revenues (see Table 4, accessed at http://www.ccss.jhu.edu/pdfs/CNP/CNP_table401.pdf). In recent years, the only real source of growth in revenues for this sector has come from fees and charges as government funding has been stable or declining and philanthropy took at major hit in 2008–2009 as a consequence of the economic crisis (see Salamon, Geller, and Spence, 2009).
4. In England, the independent Task Force on Better Regulation, appointed by the Minister for the Cabinet Office, extended its analysis of regulation in various sectors to the voluntary and community sector (UK Better Regulation Task Force, 2005), to which it applied the principles of "better regulation": proportionality, accountability, consistency, transparency, and targeting. Although there have been committees and task forces in other countries that have examined regulation within the charitable sector, these have not been connected or informed by such broad cross-sectoral reviews or been part of broader movements of regulatory reform.

REFERENCES

Anheier, H., and Mertens, S. (2003). "International and European perspectives on the non-profit sector: Data, theory and statistics." In *The Non-profit Sector in a Changing Economy* (pp. 269–336). Paris: OECD.

Aucoin, P., and Heintzman, R. (2000). "The dialectics of accountability for performance in public management reform." *International Review of Administrative Sciences*, 66(1): 45–56.

Ayres, I., and Braithwaite, J. (1992). *Responsive Regulation: Transcending the deregulation debate.* Oxford: Oxford University Press.

Baldwin, R., and Black, J. (2008). "Really responsive regulation." *Modern Law Review*, 71(1): 59–94.

Baldwin, R., Hutter, B., and Rothstein, H. (2000). "Risk regulation, management and compliance." Paper prepared for the BRI Inquiry. London: Bristol Inquiry. Available at <http://www.bristol-inquiry.org.uk/Documents/Risk%20regulation%20report.pdf> (accessed 20 April 2008).

Benjamin, L. M. (2008). "Bearing more risk for results: Performance accountability and nonprofit relational work." *Administration & Society*, 39(8): 959–983.

Bernstein, S., and Cashore, B. (2007). "Can non-state global governance be legitimate? An analytical framework." *Regulation & Governance*, 1: 347–371.

Berry, J., and Arons, D. (2003). *A Voice for Nonprofits.* Washington, DC: Brookings Institution Press.

Black, J. (2008). "Constructing and contesting legitimacy and accountability in polycentric regulatory regimes." *Regulation & Governance*, 2: 137–164.

Blue Ribbon Panel. (2006). *From Red Tape to Clear Results: The Report of the Blue Ribbon Panel on Grants and Contribution Programs.* Ottawa: Treasury Board Secretariat.

Bode, I. (2006). "Co-governance within networks and the non-profit-for-profit divide: A cross-cultural perspective on the evolution of domiciliary elderly care. *Public Management Review*, 8(4): 551–566.

Boris, E. T. (1999). "Nonprofit organizations in a democracy: Varied roles and responsibilities." In E. T. Boris and D. E. Steuerle (eds.), *Nonprofits & Government.* Washington, DC: The Urban Institute Press.

Bothwell, R. O. (2000). "Trends in self-regulation and transparency of nonprofits in the U.S." *International Journal of Not-for-Profit Law*, 2(3). Available at < http://www.icnl.org/knowledge/ijnl/vol2iss3/sg_1.htm> (accessed 12 September 2008).

Bourgeois, D. J. (2002). *The Law of Charitable and Not-for-profit Organizations* (3rd ed.). Markham: LexisNexis Butterworths.

Braithwaite, J. (2008). *Regulatory Capitalism: How it works, ideas for making it better.* Cheltenham, UK: Edward Elgar.

Braithwaite, J. (2002). "Rewards and regulation." *Journal of Law and Society*, 29(1): 12–26.

Brandsen, T., van de Donk, W., and Putters, K. (2005). "Griffins or chameleons? Hybridity as a permanent and inevitable characteristic of the third sector." *International Journal of Public Administration*, 28: 749–765.

Breen, O. B. (2009). "Regulating charitable solicitation practices—the search for a hybrid solution." *Financial Accountability & Management*, 25(1): 115–143.

Breen, O. B., Ford, P., and Morgan, G. G. (2009). "Cross-border issues in the regulation of charities experiences from the UK and Ireland." *International Journal of Not-for-Profit Law*, 11(3). Available at < http://www.icnl.org/knowledge/ijnl/vol11iss3/special_1.htm> (accessed 20 June 2009).

Brooks, A. C. (2000). "Is there a dark side to government support of nonprofits?" *Public Administration Review*, 60(3): 211–218.

Brown, L. D. (2008). *Creating Credibility: Legitimacy and accountability for transnational civil society.* Sterling,VA: Kumarian Press.

Cairns, B. (2009). "England—The independence of the voluntary sector from government in England." In M. Smerdon (ed.), *The First Principle of Voluntary Action: Essays on the independence of the voluntary sector from government in Canada,*

England, Germany, Northern Ireland, Scotland, United States of America and Wales. Working Paper No. 3. London: Baring Foundation. Available at < http:// www.baringfoundation.org.uk/FirstPrincipleofVA.pdf> (accessed 3 June 2009).

Carmel, E., and Harlock, J. (2008). "Instituting the 'third sector' as a governable terrain: Partnership, procurement and performance in the UK." *Policy & Politics*, 36(2): 155–171.

Casey, J., and Dalton, B. (2006). "The best of times, the worst of times: Community sector advocacy in the age of 'Compact.' " *Australian Journal of Political Science*, 41(1): 23–38.

Casey, J., Dalton, B., and Onxy, J. (2008). "International perspectives on strengthening government-nonprofit relations: Are compacts applicable to the USA?" Working Paper Series, Centre for Nonprofit Strategy and Management, Baruch College, City University of New York.

Considine, M., and Lewis, J. M. (2003). "Bureaucracy, network, or enterprise? Comparing models of governance in Australia, Britain, the Netherlands, and New Zealand." *Public Administration Review*, 63(2): 131–140.

Doern, G. B. (2007). *Red Tape, Red Flags: Regulation for the innovation age.* Ottawa, Ontario: Conference Board of Canada.

Doern, G. B. (2006). "Multilevel regulatory governance: Concepts, context, and key issues." In G. B. Doern and R. Johnson (eds.), *Rules, Rules, Rules, Rules: Multilevel regulatory governance.* Toronto: University of Toronto Press.

Dunleavy, P., Margetts, H., Bastow, S., and Tinkler, J. (2005a). "New Public Management is Dead—Long Live Digital Era Governance." *Journal of Public Administration Research and Theory*, 16: 467–494.

Dunleavy, P., Margetts, H., Bastow, S., and Tinkler, J. (2005b). *Digital Era Governance: IT corporations, the state and e-government.* Oxford: Oxford University Press.

Dunn, A. (2008). "Charities and restrictions on political activities: Developments by the Charity Commission for England and Wales in determining the regulatory barriers." *The International Journal for Not-for-Profit Law*, 11(1). Available at <http://www.icnl.org/knowledge/ijnl/vol11iss1/special_3.htm> (accessed 20 May 2009).

Edwards, M. (2008). *Just another Emperor? The myths and realities of philanthrocapitalism.* New York: Demos. Available at < http://www.futurepositive.org/edwards_WEB.pdf> (accessed 3 May 2009).

Elson, P. R. (2009). "Canada–Independence in a cold climate: A profile of the nonprofit and voluntary sector in Canada." In M. Smerdon (ed.), *The First Principle of Voluntary Action: Essays on the independence of the voluntary sector from government in Canada, England, Germany, Northern Ireland, Scotland, United States of America and Wales.* Working Paper No. 3. London: Baring Foundation. Available at < http://www.baringfoundation.org.uk/FirstPrincipleofVA.pdf> (accessed 3 June 2009).

Esping-Andersen, G. (1990). *The Three Worlds of Welfare Capitalism.* Princeton, NJ: Princeton University Press.

European Commission. (2001). *European Governance—A White Paper.* Brussels: European Commission.

Evans, S. (2009). "Interpretation and legitimacy in charity regulation." Unpublished doctoral dissertation, Imperial College London.

Evers, A. (2005). "Mixed welfare systems and hybrid organizations: Changes in the governance and provision of social services." *International Journal of Public Administration*, 28: 737–748.

External Advisory Committee on Smart Regulation. (2004). *A Regulatory Strategy for Canada, Report to the Government of Canada.* Ottawa: External Advisory Committee on Smart Regulation.

Fiorina, M. (1999). "Extreme voices: A dark side of civic engagement." In T. Skocpol and M. P. Fiorina (eds.), *Civic Engagement in American Democracy.* Washington, DC, and New York: The Brookings Institution Press and Russell Sage Foundation.

Fremont-Smith, M. R. (2004). *Governing Nonprofit Organizations: Federal and State law and regulation.* Harvard edition. Cambridge, MA: World Belknap Press.

Frumkin, P. (2002). *On Being Nonprofit: A conceptual and policy primer.* Cambridge, MA: Harvard University Press.

Gandhori, A. (2006). "Innovation, uncertainty and relational governance." *Industry and Innovation,* 13(2): 127–133.

Grønbjerg, K., and Smith, S. R. (2006). "Scope and theory of government-nonprofit relations." In W. W. Powell and R. Steinberg (eds.), *The Non-Profit Sector: A research handbook* (2nd ed.). New Haven, CT: Yale University Press.

Gunningham, N., and Grabosky, P. (1998). *Smart Regulation.* Oxford: Clarendon Press.

Hall, Michael H. et al. (2005). *The Canadian Nonprofit and Voluntary Sector in Comparative Perspective.* Toronto: Imagine Canada.

Hansmann, H. B. (1980). "The Role of Nonprofit Enterprise." *Yale Law Journal,* 89: 835–901.

Heinrich, C. J. (2002). "Outcomes-based performance management in the public sector: Implication for government accountability and effectiveness," *Public Administration Review,* 62: 712–725.

Hill, C. J., and Lynn, L. E., Jr. (2005). "Is hierarchical governance in decline? Evidence from empirical research." *Journal of Public Administration Research and Theory,* 15(2): 173–195.

Hill, C. J., Lynn, L. E., Jr., Proeller, I., and Schedler, K. (2005). "Introduction to a Symposium on Public Governance." *Policy Studies Journal,* 33(2): 203–211.

Hood, C. (1991). "A Public management for all seasons?" *Public Administration,* 69: 3–19.

Ingram, H., and Smith, S. R. (eds.). (1993). *Public Policy for Democracy.* Washington, DC: Brookings Institution Press.

Irvin, R. A. (2005). "State regulation of nonprofit organizations: Accountability regardless of outcomes." *Nonprofit and Voluntary Sector Quarterly,* 34(2): 161–178.

Jessop, B. (1998). "The rise of governance and the risks of failure: The case of economic development." *International Social Science Journal,* 50(155): 29–45.

Jordana, J., and Levi-Faur, D. (2004). "The politics of regulation in the age of governance." In J. Jordana and D. Levi-Faur (eds.), *The Politics of Regulation: Institutions and regulatory reforms for the age of governance.* Cheltenham, UK: Edward Elgar.

Kirby, J. (2006, July 25). "Learning to give." *Financial Post,* p. FP3.

Knott, J. H., and McCarthy, D. (2007). "Policy venture capital: Foundations, government partnerships, and child care programs." *Administration & Society,* 39(3): 319–353.

Koppenjan, J., and Klijn, E.-H. (2004). *Managing Uncertainties in Networks: A network approach to problem solving and decision-making.* London: Routledge.

Krauskopf, J. (2008, February). "Performance measurement in human services contracts: Utilization, operational feasibility, and value in New York City." *New York Nonprofit Press.* Available at: <http://www.unhny.org/news/NYNP%20February%202008%20-%20Jack%20Krauskopf%20Article.pdf> (accessed 20 May 2009).

Levi-Faur, D. (2008a). "Foreword." In J. Braithwaite (ed.), *Regulatory Capitalism: How it works, ideas for making it better.* Cheltenham, UK: Edward Elgar.

Levi-Faur, D. (2008b). "Regulatory capitalism and the reassertion of the public interest." *Policy and Society*, 27(3): 181–191.

Lyons, M., and Passey, A. (2006). "Need public policy ignore the third sector? Government policy in Australia and the United Kingdom." *Australian Journal of Public Administration*, 65(3): 90–102.

Majone, G. (1997). "From the positive to the regulatory state: Causes and consequences of changes in the mode of governance." *Journal of Public Policy*, 17(2): 139–167.

May, P. J. (2007). "Regulatory regimes and accountability." *Regulation & Governance*, 1: 8–26.

Meuleman, L. (2008). *Public Management and the Metagovernance of Hierarchies, Networks and Markets: The feasibility of designing and managing governance style combinations*. Heidelberg: Physica-Verlag.

Mintzberg, H. (1996). "Managing government, governing management." *Harvard Business Review*, 74(3): 75–83.

Moore, D. (2005). "Public benefit status: A comparative overview." *International Journal of Not-for-Profit Law*, 7(3). Available at < http://www.icnl.org/knowledge/ijnl/vol7iss3/special_2.htm> (accessed 1 December 2008).

Mulgan, G. (2006, Spring). "The process of social innovation." *Innovations*, pp. 145–162.

Muttart Foundation. (2006). *Talking about Charities*. Edmonton, AB: Muttart Foundation.

OECD. (2003). *From Red Tape to Smart Tape—Administrative Simplification in OECD Countries*. Paris: OECD.

O'Halloran, K., McGregor-Lowndes, M., and Simon, K. W. (2008). *Charity Law & Social Policy: National and international perspectives on the functions of the law relating to charities*. New York: Springer.

Osborne. S. P. (2010). "The (New) Public Governance: A suitable case for treatment?" In S. P. Osborne (ed.), *The New Public Governance? Emerging Perspectives on the Theory and Practice of Public Governance*. London: Routledge.

Osborne. S. P. (2006). "The new public governance?" *Public Management Review*, 8(3): 277–287.

Osborne. S. P., Mclaughlin, K., and Ferlie, E. (eds.). (2002). *New Public Management: Current trends and future prospects*. London: Routledge.

Peters, G. (2010). "Meta-governance and public management." In S. P. Osborne (ed.). *The New Public Governance? Emerging Perspectives on the Theory and Practice of Public Governance*. London: Routledge.

Peters, G. (2001). *The Future of Governing* (2nd ed.). Lawrence, KS: University Press of Kansas.

Phillips, S. D. (2009). "Canada's Conservative government and the voluntary sector: Whither a policy agenda?" In R. Laforest (ed.), *The New Federal Policy Agenda and the Voluntary Sector: On the cutting edge*. Montreal and Kingston: McGill-Queen's University Press.

Phillips, S. D. (2003). "In accordance: Canada's federal government–voluntary sector Accord from idea to implementation." In K. L. Brock (ed.), *Delicate Dances: Public policy and the nonprofit sector*. Montreal and Kingston: McGill-Queen's University Press.

Poppo, L., and Zenger, T. (2002). "Do formal contracts and relational governance function as substitutes or complements?" *Strategic Management Journal*, 23: 707–725.

Pross, A. P., and Webb, K. R. (2003). "Embedded regulation: Advocacy and the federal regulation of public interest groups." In K. L. Brock (ed.), *Delicate Dances: Public policy and the nonprofit sector*. Montreal and Kingston: McGill-Queen's University Press.

Putnam, R. D. (2000). *Bowling Alone: The collapse and revival of American community*. New York: Simon & Schuster.

Rhodes, R. A. W. (2000). "Governance and public administration." In J. Pierre (ed.), *Debating Governance*. Oxford: Oxford University Press.

Rhodes, R. A. W. (1996). "The New Governance: Governing without government." *Political Studies*, XLIV: 652–667.

Salamon, L. M. (2002). "The New Governance and the tools of public action: An introduction." In L. M. Salamon (ed.), *The Tools of Governance: A guide to the New Governance*. Oxford: Oxford University Press.

Salamon, L. M. (1994). "The rise of the nonprofit sector." *Foreign Affairs*, 73(4): 109–122.

Salamon, L. M., Geller, S. L., and Spence, K. L. (2009). "Impact of the 2007–09 economic recession on nonprofit organizations." Communiqué No. 14, Listening Post Project, Center for Civil Society Studies, Johns Hopkins University. Available at <http://www.ccss.jhu.edu/pdfs/LP_Communiques/LP_Communique_14.pdf> (accessed 15 May 2009).

Salamon, L. M., Haddock, M. A., Sokolowski, S. Wojciech, and Tice, H. S. (2007). *Measuring Civil Society and Volunteering: Initial findings from implementation of the UN handbook on Nonprofit Institutions*. Working Paper No. 23. Baltimore: Johns Hopkins Center for Civil Society Studies.

Salamon, L. M., Sokolowski, S. Wojciech, and List, R. (2003). *Global Civil Society: An Overview*. Baltimore: Johns Hopkins Center for Civil Society Studies.

Scott, C. (2004). "Regulation in the age of governance: The rise of the post-regulatory state." In J. Jordana and D. Levi-Faur (eds.), *The Politics of Regulation: Institutions and regulatory reforms for the age of governance*. Cheltenham, UK: Edward Elgar.

Scottish Government. (2003). *Scottish Compact Baseline Review*. Edinburgh: Scottish Government. Available at http://openscotland.gov.uk/Publications/2003/08/17485/22802 (accessed 8 December 2009).

Skelcher, C. (2004). "Public-private partnerships and hybridity." In E. Fairlie, L. E. Lynn, Jr., and C. Pollitt (eds.), *The Oxford Handbook of Public Management*. London: Oxford University Press.

Smerdon, M. (2009). "The first principles of voluntary action." In M. Smerdon (ed.), *The First Principle of Voluntary Action: Essays on the independence of the voluntary sector from government in Canada, England, Germany, Northern Ireland, Scotland, United States of America and Wales*. Working Paper No. 3. London: Baring Foundation. Available at < http://www.baringfoundation.org.uk/FirstPrincipleofVA.pdf> (accessed 3 June 2009).

Smith, S. R., and Smyth, J. (1996, April). "Contracting for services in a decentralized system." *Journal of Public Administration Research and Theory*, 6(2), 277–276.

Smith, S. R., and Lipsky, M. (1993). *Nonprofits for Hire: The welfare state in the age of contracting*. Cambridge, MA: Harvard University Press.

Statistics Canada. (2004). *Cornerstones of Community: Highlights of the National Survey of Nonprofit and Voluntary Organizations*. Ottawa: Minister of Industry.

Stoker, G. (1998). "Governance as theory: Five propositions." *International Social Science Journal*, 50(155): 17–28.

Summers, L. (2008, October 27). "The pendulum swings towards regulation." *Financial Times*, p. 11.

UK Better Regulation Task Force. (2005). *Better Regulation for Civil Society: Making life easier for those who help others*. London: Better Regulation Task Force. Available at < http://archive.cabinetoffice.gov.uk/brc/upload/assets/www.brc.gov.uk/betregforcivil.pdf> (accessed 10 May 2009).

Unwin, J. (2004). *The Grantmaking Tango: Issues for Funders*. London: The Baring Foundation.

Vincent-Jones, P. (2006). *The New Public Contracting: Regulation, responsiveness, relationality*. Oxford: Oxford University Press.

Walzer, M. (1991, Spring). "The civil society argument." *Dissent*, pp. 293–304.

Warren, M. E. (2001). *Democracy and Association*. Princeton, NJ: Princeton University Press.

Webb, K. (2005). "Understanding the voluntary codes phenomenon." In K. Webb (ed.), *Voluntary Codes: Private governance, the public interest and innovation*. Ottawa: Carleton Research Unit on Innovation, Science and Environment. Available at <http://www2.carleton.ca/sppa/ccms/wp-content/ccms-files/ch1.pdf> (accessed 4 January 2009).

Williams, G. (2007, November 1). "Governance issues are a top priority for IRS, official tells regulators." *The Chronicle of Philanthropy*. Available at < http://philanthropy.com/premium/articles/v20/i02/02006701.htm> (accessed 3 March 2009).

Young, D. R. (2003). "New trends in the US non-profit sector: Towards market integration?" In *The Non-Profit Sector in a Changing Economy* (pp. 269–336). Paris: OECD.

Young, D. R. (1999). "Complementary, supplementary or adversarial? A theoretical and historical examination of nonprofit-government relations in the United States." In E. T. Boris and D. E. Steuerle (eds.), Nonprofits & Government. Washington, DC: The Urban Institute.

2 The Case of England and Wales
Striking the Right Balance of 'Hard' Law versus 'Soft' Law

Debra Morris

INTRODUCTION

Recent changes to the regulatory environment for charities in England and Wales mirror the pattern described elsewhere in this volume, whereby the previous contractual relationships that were common between government and service-providing charities in the 1990s are slowly beginning to give way to more partnership-based relationships. These new partnerships, ideally based on mutual trust and confidence, are being developed against a background of growth in a more relational form of governance for charities, and a number of regulatory instruments are being utilized to support this shift.

At the same time, calls to clarify the legal definition of charity and to enhance public trust and confidence in both the concept of charity and charities themselves have been made for some time in England and Wales.[1]

There is recognition that a modern and effective legal framework for charities is vital when they play such a significant role in public life, especially but not exclusively through their delivery of services. There is acceptance of the need for both a more enabling and, in some aspects, a more tightly controlled legal environment for charities. Ideally, a modern and effective regulatory framework should provide a suitable balance so as to support a more relational form of governance but also to meet the demands for enhanced accountability, themes that this chapter will explore. These calls for reform have finally been met, and, consequently, we are witnessing the development of a program of reform of charity law in England and Wales that is unprecedented in its extent. For example, it has, for the first time, answered calls for a statutory definition of 'charity,' hitherto determined only through the common law. The impetus for enhanced legislative and regulatory intervention—largely through demand for greater openness and accountability of charities—seems to derive from a number of somewhat overlapping factors.

First, there is a perception that incentives for improving efficiency, effectiveness, and accountability within the sector are not strong enough. A lack of accessible, appropriate information can make it difficult for donors to assess performance and register their views. Admittedly, this is only an issue if donors care about such matters. There is some evidence to suggest that donors *do* care; for example, a public attitudes survey commissioned by the Charity Commission to investigate the views of the public on the information made available to charities found that the public considers that the principles of transparency and accountability are important (Charity Commission 2004a: Annex A, Table 25). In particular, donors seem to be concerned about the proportion of funds used to support the administrative costs of running charities.[2]

Second, as the sector has grown in scope and size, charities are playing an increasingly important role in the delivery of key public services on behalf of national and local governments (See for example Charity Commission 2007a). Consequently, income from government accounts for 34 per cent of their annual £31 billion income, according to the National Council for Voluntary Organisations (NCVO), with a third of all charities heavily reliant on public sector funding (Reichardt et al. 2008). "Barely a White Paper passes without a ministerial direction that charities should be key providers of public services" (Butler 2006: 2). Their role is likely to be enhanced further under the Coalition government's "Big Society" policy which makes a commitment to even greater involvement of charities and social enterprises in the running of public services (Prime Minister's Office 2010). This, coupled with the fact that many charities receive public subsidies in one form or another, puts them in the spotlight and this increased visibility makes it all the more important that they operate in a transparent manner and are accountable for public money.

Third, there is concern over the declining trend in the levels of individual and corporate charitable giving, which led to a package of tax reforms in the UK in 2000. Well-governed charities are more likely to gain the public's trust, and such confidence is critical for fundraising. Certainly, revelations concerning badly governed charities are detrimental to their fundraising capabilities, and, with charities increasingly in the public eye, their transgressions are more likely to come to the attention of donors. Unfortunately, as in the commercial world, some well-publicized scandals in the charitable sector have affected reputations and damaged trust. For example, in 2003, when a major fundraising scandal hit two breast cancer charities in Scotland and England, leading to intervention by the courts (Scottish Executive 2003: SECO109) and the Charity Commission (2003), the director of communications at another (unconnected) cancer charity observed: "At the end of the day, mud sticks, and it's not just the public that needs to be protected. . . . There need to be far tighter regulations in place to protect the reputation of charities that work hard to be transparent and accountable to supporters" (Third Sector 2003).

After corporate scandals, focus on good governance inevitably filters down to charities. Indeed, against ever-increasing expectations for openness, accountability, and successful service delivery, charities have as much to lose as commercial entities from governance failures, if not more. As Alan Milburn MP[3] said: "The last thing the voluntary sector needs is an Enron-style scandal just at the point when it is becoming such a key part of service delivery in this country" (Milburn 2003). Public trust and confidence are vital for the sector, and yet there is a general decline in public trust and confidence in all social institutions—public, private, and voluntary (Duffy 2003).

In summary, there have been concerns that while the charitable sector was evolving rapidly in response to changing economic and social circumstances, aspects of the legal and regulatory framework had become outdated and may well have been restricting the efficiency and growth of the sector. England's review of the legal and regulatory basis for the charitable sector provided an opportunity to develop a new framework which seeks to encourage the sector to be innovative, dynamic, efficient, and effective, on the one hand, and to protect beneficiaries, donors, staff, and volunteers, on the other.

This chapter begins by reviewing the recent legal changes in England and Wales and then considers other regulatory instruments that could be described as 'soft law' by which a more relational form of governance for charities can also be detected. Two areas in particular are examined: the increased role of self-regulation especially in the areas of charity governance and fundraising, and the development of the 'Compact' between government and the voluntary sector.

A recent survey estimated that there are 865,000 civil society organizations in the UK which, collectively, had total revenues of £109 billion in 2005–2006 and £86.1 billion in assets, and employed 611,000 people (2.2 percent of the paid workforce) (Reichardt et al. 2008). Of these, 180,000 are registered charities (Charity Commission Register 2010). Most are small community based organizations that have little income: small charities represent over 50 percent of registered charities but have less than 1 percent of the income recorded. However, there is also a significant number of large organizations with resources of many millions of pounds that have a strong influence on British society. Just 8 percent of charities receive over 90 percent of the total annual income recorded. Indeed, the largest 706 charities (0.42 percent of those on the register) attract nearly 50 percent of the total income. In 2006, the total income of general charities increased by almost 10 percent in real terms from the previous year to £31 billion, while expenditures increased by almost 15 percent to just over £29 billion. The survey found for the first time that more than half of the income of general charities is 'earned' through the sale of goods and services. In addition, over half of all charities receive no income from statutory sources. In contrast, however, a third of organizations are heavily reliant on statutory funding, the majority of which comes from local governments.

The sector benefits from the existence of a number of major national infrastructure organizations. England's largest umbrella body for the voluntary and community sector, NCVO, which was founded in 1919, has nearly

40   *Debra Morris*

6,000 organizational members that employ over 280,000 staff and utilize over 13 million volunteers. Its sister councils in Scotland, Wales, and Northern Ireland play equivalent roles in both policy development and service to their sectors. In addition, many other infrastructure organizations represent and serve particular sub-sectors or support volunteerism more generally.

CHARITY LAW REFORM

Background to the Reforms

The Charity Commission for England and Wales is established by law as the regulator and registrar of charities in England and Wales (Charities Act 1993, ss.1A–1E). It aims to regulate charities in such a way as to increase their efficiency and effectiveness and also to enhance public confidence and trust in them. The Commission seeks to secure compliance with charity law—whether statutory or developed through the common (case) law—and deals with abuse and poor practice.

Calls for reform to charity law have come from both the voluntary sector, beginning with the Deakin Report in 1996, and also from the government, through the Strategy Unit initiative. While the sector was looking for a stronger legal framework to support its activities, government was also seeking to strengthen the support machinery for the sector so as to enhance accountability and allow the sector to take on a greater role in the delivery of public services. In large part, the concerns and the proposed solutions put forward by both the sector and government coincided.

The legal reforms discussed in this chapter form a relatively coherent package, largely originating from the Strategy Unit report in 2002. The other reforms discussed, referred to as soft law measures such as the Compact and the various voluntary codes, are more fragmented in that they have diverse origins. And, as we will see, they have had varying degrees of success in implementation.

Following on from the report of the Deakin Commission (Commission on the Future of the Voluntary Sector 1996), which called, *inter alia*, for reform of charity law, the Prime Minister commissioned a review of the legal and regulatory framework for charities and other nonprofit organizations in England and Wales in July 2001, with a view to making proposals for reform (Strategy Unit 2001). A consultation document on charity law reform was published by the Prime Minister's Strategy Unit in September 2002 (Strategy Unit 2002) and proposed wide-ranging changes in the law and regulation of the charitable and broader nonprofit sector.[4] Specifically, reforms were proposed in four main areas: (1) modernizing charity law; (2) improving the range of legal forms available to charities and social enterprises; (3) developing greater accountability and transparency to build trust in the sector; and (4) maintaining that trust by independent, open, and proportionate regulation. Following public consultation,[5] the government published its response in July 2003, setting out how it planned to take the reforms forward (Home Office 2003). The government response supported most of the Strategy Unit's main proposals (Morris 2003b: 409).

The Charities Bill was first published in draft in May 2004 for pre-legislative scrutiny by a Joint Committee of both Houses of Parliament. The Joint Committee, having considered evidence during the summer of 2004 (Joint Committee 2003–2004b), published its report in September (Joint Committee 2003–2004a), and the government's response followed in December (Secretary of State for the Home Department 2003–2004), as did the Bill itself. The original Bill was timed-out of parliamentary approval by the May 2005 general election (Charity Commission 2005), but the Queen's Speech in May 2005 confirmed that the government would re-introduce it, and on 18 May 2005, Baroness Scotland (Home Office Minister) moved the First Reading of the Charities Bill. The Bill completed its passage through the House of Lords in November 2005, after more than 60 hours of scrutiny by Peers, and proceeded through the House of Commons in October 2006. Its final debate was in the Lords on 7 November 2006, and, at long last, the Charities Bill received Royal Assent on 8 November 2006.

The Charities Act 2006

The purpose of the *Charities Act 2006*, which is being brought into force in stages until at least 2011 (Office of the Third Sector 2007b, 2010), is to implement the majority of the accepted recommendations of the Strategy Unit.[6] While the reforms in the *Charities Act 2006* (the Act) are wide-ranging and are in line with the four main areas of reform proposed by the Strategy Unit, this chapter focuses on those aspects that are intended to improve the regulatory regime in which charities operate.

Meaning of 'Charity'

The basis for the definition of charity goes back to the preamble to a (now repealed) Act of Elizabeth I (Charitable Uses Act 1601), over 400 years ago (Charities Act 1960: s.38). For the first time, under the 2006 Act, 'charity' has a statutory definition. Charitable status is subjected to a two-stage test. To be considered charitable, an organization must demonstrate that its purposes, as set out in its constitution, fall within one or more of those in the new list of 13 charitable purposes, and also that it is established for the public benefit.

There are two essential elements of the public benefit requirement. First, the pursuit of an organization's purposes must be capable of producing a benefit which can be demonstrated and which is recognized by law as beneficial. Secondly, the benefit must be provided for or available to the public or a sufficient section of the public.

Public benefit has always been an essential element in all charities. It is this factor that distinguishes private trusts from charitable trusts, and it is the public benefit that is said to justify the advantageous taxation treatment afforded to charities. The important difference is that there is no longer a presumption that charities for certain purposes are of public benefit. Previously, there was a presumption that purposes for the relief of poverty, the advancement of education, or the advancement of religion were for the public benefit.[7] No other purposes benefitted from this presumption. The effect of the presumption was that, when the charitable status of an organization established for the relief of poverty, the advancement of education, or the advancement of religion was being considered, the organization's purpose was presumed to be for the public benefit, unless there was evidence that it was not. By contrast, an organization established for any other purpose, which did not have the advantage of this presumption, was required at the time that its status was being considered to provide evidence that its purpose was for the public benefit.

Following the implementation of the Act, *every* organization entered on the Register of Charities needs to show positively that it is set up and operates for the public benefit. So, for example, churches and schools seeking the benefits of charitable status must now demonstrate that they provide a public benefit.

There is no statutory definition of 'public benefit' because the government has decided that the current non-statutory approach will remain, giving flexibility and the capacity to accommodate the diversity of the sector. Decisions about whether a particular charity meets the public benefit requirement will continue to be determined by the Charity Commission as the independent regulator, on the basis of case law, and ultimately by the courts. This should mean that the existing case law definition will remain.

During its passage through parliament, there were calls for amendments to the Charities Bill[8] that would enable the Charity Commission to take account of the impact of fees or charges when considering questions of public benefit.[9] It is interesting to note that the *Charities and Trustee Investment (Scotland) Act 2005*, which began life as a result of a Scottish Review of Charity Law (Scottish Charity Law Review Commission 2001), contains a definition of public benefit (Charities and Trustee Investment (Scotland) Act 2005, s.8), rather than relying on guidance from the Office of the Scottish Charity Regulator (OSCR) and case law to determine whether charitable status should be granted. The level of fees charged by a charity for the provision of its service specifically forms part of the judgment of the OSCR when it decides, under the new law, whether a charity should retain charitable status. Under the legislation, in determining whether a body provides or intends to provide public benefit, the OSCR and the courts must have regard to both any private benefit gained and also to any public 'disbenefit' incurred.[10] In particular, where benefit is, or is likely to be, provided to only a section of the public, the OSCR and the courts must consider whether any condition on obtaining that benefit (including any charge or fee) is unduly restrictive. The words "including any charge or fee" were added to the statutory definition of public benefit under an amendment passed by the Scottish Parliament's Communities Committee and backed by the Scottish Executive. In applying the public benefit test in order to determine charitable status, the OSCR must ask whether there will be any condition on obtaining benefits (such as whether the charity charges or intends to charge for its services) (OSCR 2006: para 8). Where this is the case, the OSCR may need to ask for more information. The specific reference to unduly restrictive fees, together with the approach of the OSCR, will clearly bring the issue into focus in Scotland in a more transparent way than in England and Wales.

Under the English *Charities Act*, the Charity Commission must promote awareness and understanding of the public benefit requirement (Charities Act 2006: s.4) and how it will test this (Charities Act 2006: s.7). It is required to consult with the public and others before issuing or revising any related guidance and, once agreed, must publish this guidance. In early 2008, the Charity Commission published its first set of guidelines, following public consultations, that illustrate what its approach will be to the public benefit requirement (Charity Commission 2008a, 2008b). The guidelines, which must be taken into account by charity trustees when exercising any relevant powers and duties (Charities Act 2006: s.4(6)), effectively reconfirm the Charity Commission's interpretation of the existing (pre-Charities Act 2006) law on public benefit. The removal of the presumption of public benefit mainly serves to emphasize the need for each and every charity to satisfy the public benefit test. This will have a particular impact on fee paying schools and hospitals with charitable status. The tenor of the debate during the Bill's progression (see, for example, HC Deb 2004–2006: 450, part 207, col. 1539–1627), and the subsequent guidance by the Commission, indicate that such organizations should not be complacent because they will need to demonstrate positively their public benefit.[11] The message has been received loud and clear so that, for example, the Chief Executive of the Independent Schools Council has told its fee paying school members—82 percent of which have charitable status (Independent Schools Council (ISC) 2007)—"to think imaginatively of ways in which public benefit might be increased" (Shephard 2006: 2–3).

The categories of charitable purposes laid down specifically in the Act (Charities Act 2006: s.2(2)) include all the previous areas of charity. They also widen the scope of what might be considered charitable. For example, it is now clear that the prevention as well as the relief of poverty is charitable. Like the preamble to the Statute of Elizabeth, the list is illustrative of the types of purposes that are charitable, and it is not definitive. It includes an "any other purposes" clause, enabling an organization to become a charity if its purposes are not named in the list, but can be shown to be "analogous to, or within the spirit of" those that are named or to existing charities.

This will ensure that there is flexibility for the law to evolve in response to changes in society and changing social and economic needs. The range of charities that exists now has clearly evolved considerably since the seventeenth century. By listing these established purposes, the Act updates the scope of charitable aims for a modern society and gives a much clearer idea of what is considered as being 'for charity.'

Other Regulatory Reforms Designed to Enhance Accountability

A number of regulatory provisions in the Act are aimed at greater accountability and transparency. For example, formerly excepted charities[12] with an income of £100,000 or more and some exempt charities[13] (where there is no suitable alternative regulator) are now required to register.[14]

In addition, the Act (Part 2, Chapter 5, sections 19–27) covers the assistance and supervision of charities by the court and the Charity Commission. It gives new powers to the Commission including to: suspend or remove trustees and employees from membership of their charity; direct charity trustees to take certain actions in administering their charity; direct trustees to apply the charity's property in a certain way; give advice and guidance to charity trustees; determine who are the members of a charity; and, in the course of statutory investigations, enter premises and take possession of information and documents. These powers, if used appropriately, should assist in good governance and the prevention of maladministration. The power to determine membership of a charity, for example, should provide specific assistance in the resolution of a number of charity disputes over membership issues that have arisen in recent years.

Enabling Reforms Designed to Increase Flexibility

In order to encourage flexibility, the Act makes a number of de-regulatory changes of benefit to charities, especially smaller ones. For example, the threshold for registering as a charity is raised from £1,000 to £5,000 (Charities Act 2006: s.9), and charities below this threshold will be able to register voluntarily. During Parliamentary debate on the Charities Bill (HL Deb 2005–06: 674, co. 392), the government committed to review all other regulatory and reporting thresholds in the Charities Acts so as to consider whether they are set at an appropriate level.[15]

A significant raft of measures are also included that make merger, evolution, and administration easier for charities.[16] For example, registration of charity mergers is facilitated. Charities that (voluntarily) register their merger with the Charity Commission may take advantage of both a simplified procedure for transferring their assets to the post merger charity and a new procedure for passing gifts from a dissolving charity to the new one. Charities may also spend their permanent endowment (capital) where to do so will provide for a more effective means of fulfilling the purposes of the charity. In addition, various provisions of the Act relax the rules on the advertising of schemes, allow Common Investment Funds and Common Deposit Funds to accept investments from charities in Scotland and Northern Ireland, and extend the circumstances in which the authority of the court or the Charity Commission is not required for the grant of mortgages over charity land.

There is a new legal form, the Charitable Incorporated Organization (CIO), for charities that wish to take a corporate form. This will avoid dual regulation between charity and company law and will provide an alternative to the "company limited by guarantee" model previously used by many charities. The basic framework for the CIO is included in the Act while the detailed structure is dealt with in secondary legislation.

There are a number of helpful provisions relating to trustees.[17] For example, a trustee body is given power to pay an individual trustee in limited circumstances. While the principle of voluntary trusteeship remains at the heart of the role, trustees may pay (in money or in kind) an individual trustee or connected person to provide an additional service to the charity if they think that it is in the charity's interests to do so.

Finally, an independent Charity Tribunal has been introduced to hear appeals against decisions[18] of the Charity Commission.[19] Previously, the only recourse that a charity had if it was unhappy with a decision made by the Charity Commission was to the High Court (Charities Act 1993: s.92). This is expensive, time-consuming, and beyond the reach of most. The creation of a Charity Tribunal will make it much quicker and easier to seek a review.

Other Reforms That Are Both Regulatory and Enabling

Charities have been subject to different degrees of external scrutiny based on income and expenditure levels in the current and preceding two financial years. These complex rules are simplified by the Act.[20] Charities with an income of at least £500,000 or assets valued at £2.8 million or more will be required to have their accounts professionally audited. Charities whose income is more than £10,000 but less than £500,000 must have their accounts independently examined, but they do not have to be audited unless this is required by their governing document. However, organizations whose income is between £250,000 and £500,000 must have their accounts examined by someone who has a relevant professional qualification, as defined in the Act. Auditors and independent examiners of charities will be given statutory protection from the risk of action for breach of confidence or defamation if they report to the Charity Commission abuse or significant breaches of charity law.

The previous legislation on fundraising and public collections was fragmented and inconsistent, and there was a need for a new integrated licensing scheme. In addition to legislative changes to provide a unified licensing scheme for public charitable collections,[21] the Act gives the Minister for the Cabinet Office 'back up' power to introduce statutory regulation of fundraising if the Minister deems self-regulation (Strategy Unit 2002: para 6.29) has failed.[22] It is expected that every effort will be made to allow self-regulation schemes to work, as this is not an area into which government is eager to enter.

Built-in Review

Under provisions in the Act (Charities Act 2006: s.73), within five years of the implementation of the new law, the Minister for the Cabinet Office must instigate a review of the Act and how it has worked.[23] In particular, it will review its effect on: excepted charities, public confidence in charities, the level of public donations, and the willingness of individuals to volunteer. The review should also examine the status of the Charity Commission and its independence from government and anything else that the Minister considers appropriate. Conclusions from the review must be reported to Parliament. This is clearly an enabling provision, giving a very practical emphasis to the implementation of the new framework—the inference being if some provisions have not worked in practice, they will be amended.

The reforms introduced by England's *Charities Act* are wide-reaching, and they have been largely welcomed by charities (see, for example, NCVO 2006a). The Act, once fully implemented, will modernize and reform the legal framework within which charities operate, and it will go far towards ensuring that charities are independently regulated in a manner that is open, consistent, and proportionate. This should increase public trust and confidence in the charity sector as a whole.

SOFT LAW MEASURES

Although a sound legal framework is important, there is more to securing an effective charitable sector than simply ensuring its compliance with the law and financial regulation. In many areas, self-regulation or development of good practice may be more appropriate than compliance-based law. In particular, for purposes of promoting good governance of charities, control of fundraising, and relationship building with governments, measures that go beyond or work outside of legal frameworks are proving to be a better route. Such types of quasi-legal regulatory instruments are sometimes labelled "soft law"—rules or codes of conduct which, in principle, have no legally binding force but which nevertheless may have positive effects (see Snyder 1993: 32; Kirton & Trebilcock 2004). In international law, for example, agreements between states that do not constitute binding treaty obligations would fall within this category. The European Union (EU) increasingly resorts to the use of such alternative instruments—for example, recommendations and guidelines—with the aim of enhancing the effectiveness, legitimacy, and transparency of EU action (Senden 2005).

Soft law measures may be particularly useful when the desired outcome is the enhanced effectiveness of charities or when the diversity of the non-profit sector needs to be accommodated. Even within the subset of organizations that are recognized as charitable in England and Wales, there are over 180,000 registered charities,[24] and they are extremely varied in their spheres of operation, their constituencies, and their size (Reichardt et al. 2008). For example, many of the household names in the charitable world may well be suitable candidates for one form of regulation, but this may not be appropriate for the majority of registered charities as they have annual incomes of £10,000 or less. A regulatory model based partially on soft law measures, including self-regulation, can provide flexible tailor-made responses that can be adjusted as necessary to the specific and changing needs of diverse organizations with different legal forms and differential capacities for compliance. As well as potentially improving the effectiveness of charities, another important by-product of the use of soft law is that both public and government trust in charities is enhanced. The former may lead to an increase in charitable donations, and the latter may well forestall greater statutory regulation.

This may mean that proscriptive law should not have a major role in encouraging and supporting best practice in charity governance. Evidence from empirical research has suggested that there should not be legal requirements for the adoption of particular forms of governance. This view was attributable partly to the diverse nature of the sector and partly due to the need to be able to respond quickly to changes in practice. It was also found that measures compelling greater accountability were considered to be destroying the ethos and richness of the charity sector and that legal rules to enforce accountability should be treated with caution (Warburton 2003: 270).

In addition to the constructive legislative developments outlined above, there is also evidence that more collaborative and trust based relationships between the charitable sector and the state are being built. This arises from two important areas of self-regulation, as well as the creation of a Compact between the government and the voluntary sector. These initiatives indicate that in England and Wales both more effective legal regulation and more relational governance are about to sit side by side.

Self-Regulation through Voluntary Codes

One type of soft law is self-regulation. The term is most often used to describe systems where an industry, profession, or sport regulates its own affairs. Hence, the rules that govern behavior in the market—voluntary codes—are developed, administered, and enforced by the people (or their direct representatives) whose conduct is to be governed (see Gunningham

& Rees 1997). Examples include the code of standards for advertising monitored by the Advertising Standards Authority and the many codes of practice that have become commonplace in the corporate sector.[25] Self-regulatory bodies are often developed by interest groups that may well be threatened with legislation so as to ward off any more binding and perhaps less appropriate form of regulation.

Self-regulation—through the development of tools such as codes of conduct, codes of ethics, standards of accountability, and principles of good practice—is an increasingly prominent mechanism used by charities to achieve greater accountability. An international study (Lloyd & de Las Casas 2005; Sidel 2005) of 35 codes of conduct and certification schemes for self-regulation of non-governmental organizations worldwide revealed that one particular form of accountability tended to dominate. This was defined primarily in terms of setting standards for internal governance, administration, and financial management systems so as to ensure compliance with reporting requirements, laws, and regulations. The authors of the study noted that:

> This bias is primarily a product of the forces driving the accountability debate within the sector. The majority of NGOs are grappling with their accountability in reaction to external threats and bad publicity. Consequently, they are establishing codes of conduct largely out of fear that questions about their accountability will damage their image, scupper their fundraising efforts, reduce levels of public trust and/or lead to more intrusive government regulation. The majority of self-regulation initiatives are therefore centred on setting standards that address the needs of, and clarify and strengthen accountability to, those stakeholders that have the ability to affect them the most—governments, donors and the general public (Lloyd & de Las Casas 2005).

Two areas of such self-regulation that are currently being established in England are of particular relevance. The first—the development of a code of governance, by and for the sector—is a very informal process of self-regulation, without government mandate. The second—a self-regulatory scheme for fundraising—has its origins in statute.

A Code of Governance

In July 2005, following consultation with the voluntary and community sector, including charities, on the need and the contents of a draft code of governance (NCVO 2004), the NCVO launched a Code of Governance for the Voluntary and Community Sector (the Code) (ACEVO et al. 2005). The Code was developed and endorsed by a coalition comprising, in addition to NCVO, the Association of Chief Executives of Voluntary Organisations (ACEVO), Charity Trustee Networks (CTN), and ICSA (the professional body for Chartered Secretaries), with support from the Charity Commission.

A good example of sector-led self improvement, the Code is designed for all those involved in the governance of voluntary and community sector organizations, particularly trustees and chief executives. It will help staff, volunteers, members, and service users to understand what they can expect from a well-governed organization. The Code is intended to be short, user-friendly, universally relevant, and applicable for the voluntary and community sector. The aim is not to specify in detail how trustee boards should be structured, nor how they should operate. Rather, it is to enshrine a number of overarching principles in relation to governance that could be applied across the charitable sector regardless of size of a charity or the sphere in which it operates. The intention is that these agreed set of standards will become part of the sector's best practice tools, not an element of charity law and regulation. The Code has been developed with the aim of being readily understood and widely adopted in parallel with organizations' objects, so that trustees will have in hand the key principles as guidance and a source of reassurance in what may be complex decision-making processes. To ensure that the Code is of use to smaller organizations, an introduction to the principles of good governance for community groups has been developed in a 'sister' leaflet which complements the Code (National Hub of Expertise in Governance 2005).

The Code, produced by the sector for the sector, appears to have been welcomed by trustees.[26] The Code is based on the principles of "comply or explain": organizations using it should be able to either comply with the main principles of the Code or explain why the principles do not apply in particular circumstances. As a voluntary rather than a mandatory code, it reflects the spirit of the charitable sector and should have positive impacts on its effectiveness as well as promoting public trust in the sector (see Dawson & Dunn 2006). Organizations that comply with the Code are invited to state this in their Annual Report and other relevant published material, and to pledge their support for the Code by signing up to an online charter.

The Governance Hub,[27] which was originally responsible for the Code's development, promotion, and evaluation, commissioned research to evaluate its awareness, reach, and influence (NCVO 2007a). The findings include recommendations on how to improve the Code's take up, reach, and ability to reflect the sector's diversity and on what additional support is needed. Although the Governance Hub is now defunct,[28] the recommendations from the program will be taken forward. The Code steering group, comprising the nine partner organizations of the Governance Hub, has confirmed their own organizations' commitment to supporting the further embedding of the Code across the sector (NCVO 2007a).

To confuse matters somewhat, the Charity Commission has also set out its understanding of the principles of sound governance in its publication, *Hallmarks of an Effective Charity* (Charity Commission 2008c), which includes practical examples of the way in which larger charities might demonstrate that they have sound governance. Any confusion seems to be inadvertent, with the Charity Commission appearing keen not to step on others' toes, specifically stating: "the Hallmarks of an Effective Charity is designed to work in a complementary way with—not in place of—other guidance, standards and codes of governance that charities may use. If you are not following another code or standard, Hallmarks is a good place to start" (Charity Commission 2008c: 2). Covering similar ground to the Governance Code, it is stated that compliance with the law is an integral part of good governance and effectiveness. Nevertheless, while the Hallmarks simply set out the standards that the Charity Commission believes an effective charity and its trustees will try to uphold,[29] there is a danger that some will regard its best practice framework as mandatory.[30] This would be regrettable as the governance of charities is an area particularly suitable to soft law mechanisms (Warburton 2003).

Independent of the NCVO initiative, in January 2005, the Independent Commission on Good Governance in Public Services, which was established by the Chartered Institute of Public Finance and Accountancy and the Office for Public Management, launched its Good Governance Standard for Public Services following extensive research and consultation (Independent Commission on Good Governance in Public Services 2004). The Standard is intended to help all organizations in the public sector—including the police, schools, the National Health Service, non-departmental public bodies, and local government—as well as those in the voluntary and community sector who receive public money to provide specific services.

In addition, the National Occupational Standards (NOS) for trustees and management committee members have also recently been approved by the Qualifications and Curriculum Authority after two years of work led by the Voluntary Sector National Training Organisation (which became the Workforce Hub). The Standards consist of four parts setting out the competences, knowledge, and skills that trustees need to acquire in order to carry out their roles effectively (NCVO 2006b). They can be used as a basis for role descriptions or to develop induction or further training for trustees. The Workforce Hub, in partnership with the Governance Hub, also produced a series of 'pocket guides' on the NOS. The NOS are designed specifically for individual trustees and may be used in conjunction with the Code to which their organizations adhere. The idea is that an organization would refer to both on a regular basis.

There is a provision in the Governance Code to the effect that where charities are already covered by existing codes of governance prepared by their representative bodies or regulators, the existing code should take precedence (AVEVO et al. 2005: A7). Bearing in mind the number of competing codes and guidelines currently in existence, some charities may well find themselves confused. The Chief Executive of the NCVO has already noted that trustees are finding the different non-compulsory governance standards confusing and are unsure of the relationship among the Charity Commission's Hallmarks, the Code, and the NOS (Third Sector 2006).

Many of these initiatives are in their early years of development and are yet to take hold to their full effect. For example, in a survey of chief executives of voluntary organizations undertaken in 2006, it was found that only 35 percent of chairs of trustee boards were aware of the Code and were implementing it (ACEVO 2006). It may well be the case that the sector votes with its feet and that the standards which charities choose to pursue will be the ones that are most suited to the practicalities of their work.[31] Alternatively, subsequent refinements (such as the current review of the Governance Code) may integrate other standards within one set. Although refinements are welcome, there is always a concern that, with every new draft of standards and guidelines, the sector has yet more paperwork with which to grapple.

Self-Regulation of Fundraising

A scheme for the self-regulation of fundraising was established as a result of recommendations made in the Strategy Unit (2002) report (para 6.29). With an ultimate goal of increasing public confidence in fundraising and ensuring accountability and transparency in fundraising activities, the aims of the self-regulation of fundraising scheme are to: maintain high standards in fundraising, investigate fundraising complaints from the public, and demonstrate best practice in fundraising.

Following the Strategy Unit recommendation, a scheme was developed by the charitable sector together with key stakeholders. The contribution from sector bodies, consumer groups, and government was crucial in the development of an independent and rigorous scheme in which charitable fundraising organizations, funders, beneficiaries, regulators, and, most importantly, donors can all have confidence. Initially, the Institute of Fundraising (IoF) received the approval of the Home Office to take over the task of investigating the possibility of establishing a self-regulatory governing body (IoF 2003). The IoF is a national, member-based charity which currently represents 250 organizational members and 4,500 individual members. As well as providing continuing professional education, a forum for discussion on issues of common concern, and a source of information, the IoF has developed a Code of Conduct for Fundraisers, which all its members must abide by and support (IoF Online). It has also established codes of practice for different areas of fundraising activity to which members and affiliated charities are committed.

The IoF set up an independent commission to explore different models and recommend a preferred system of self-regulation. Following an 18 month consultation process undertaken by the Buse Commission during 2003–2004,[32] a sector-wide steering committee chaired by the Charities Aid Foundation (CAF) then reviewed the Commission's recommendations and proposed a structure for the voluntary self-regulation of fundraising scheme (Charities Aid Foundation et al. 2004).

The scheme, known as the Fundraising Standards Board (FRSB), was launched to the public in February 2007 and now has over 800 members (FRSB 2008). Members agree to adhere to the highest standards of good practice in fundraising by: signing up to the Fundraising Promise,[33] agreeing to follow the IoF's Codes of Practice, having a robust complaints procedure, and accepting the authority of the FRSB to make the final decision on a fundraising related complaint. Where complaints about fundraising are not resolved directly with the organization concerned, members of the public can complain to the FRSB about organizations that are members of the FRSB. The FRSB will attempt to resolve issues through recommending remedial action and, if necessary, will adjudicate and impose sanctions, which for the most serious cases would include withdrawal of FRSB membership.[34]

The Office of the Third Sector in the Cabinet Office and the Scottish Executive agreed proportionately to fund the first five years of the scheme (which operates throughout the UK), after which it will become self-financing through membership subscriptions. The Strategy Unit contended that, although the government should provide seed funding for the body, the FRSB should be independent of government and self-financing in the long-term.

If the government concludes that this voluntary initiative is failing, the Minister for the Cabinet Office has the power to introduce a compulsory system of regulation. In February 2006, following prior consultation on the criteria that would be used to assess the success of the self-regulation scheme, and determine whether the Minister would need to make use of his powers to bring in statutory regulation (Charities Unit Home Office 2005), Paul Goggins MP set out, in a written ministerial statement, the government's position on assessing the success of self-regulation (HC WS (2005–2006) 442, part 2, col. 38). One of the key measures of success is the level of participation, although it is acknowledged that the scheme will take time to build up high levels of participation. Presumably, as the number of participants grows, the scheme's penetration of the sector will prove important. For example, its ability to attract smaller charities, or charities from a particular sub-sector, will be relevant indicators of its success. The government also expects that the scheme and its participants will provide a clear public promise of what should be expected from fundraisers who are participants in the scheme, and from the scheme itself. The Codes of Practice underpinning the scheme should go beyond requiring compliance with the law and should set a high standard of good practice. Going beyond the letter of the law seeks to raise standards of behavior and promote good practice. One appropriate requirement of the scheme then is that it promotes openness, transparency, and accountability in fundraising practices. Another measure of the scheme's success from the government's point of view relates to compliance issues. Compliance with the scheme must be monitored proportionately. There must be fair and effective sanctions for non-compliance that are proportionate to the nature and extent of any non-compliance, and the initial focus should be on improving performance. The scheme must have a clear and effective complaints handling process which is easily accessible to the public and provides fair redress, and there should not be complete reliance on self-certification. All these measures should enhance the standing of the scheme: the more effective the scheme is, the more charities and other nonprofit organizations will want to join and will want to be bound by its principles. Over time, the self-regulation scheme would be expected to develop performance measures of its own and report its achievements against these in its annual report.

The government will review the development of the scheme on an annual basis and agree on specific targets for the period it funds the scheme. However, the scheme will be given sufficient time to become established and prove its effectiveness before its success is judged. It is therefore envisaged that a formal assessment of the success of self-regula-tion will take place as part of the review of the impact of the *Charities Act 2006*, due to take place within five years of enactment and be formally reported to Parliament (Charities Act 2006: s.73). If self-regulation were to fail, any proposals under the reserve power for statutory regulation of fundraising would require consultation and would be subject to the affir-mative resolution of Parliament.

Although some would question the necessity for such a scheme (see Sargeant 2005), others might argue that it is right to bring in self-regulation at a time when public confidence in charities is relatively high because it will guard against a collapse in confidence and will provide the sector with a platform from which it can robustly defend itself against criticism. The government's view is that "waiting until a crisis which had threatened, or had already damaged, public's confidence in fundraising before tackling the problem could be leaving it too late" (Charities Unit Home Office 2005).

The Compact

Further evidence of a more relational form of governance for charities is provided by the Compact on Relations between Government and the Vol-untary and Community Sector (Home Office 1998).[35] The Compact, which has been described as "completely without precedent" (Kendall 2000: 542), was inspired by the 1996 Deakin Report that recommended a "concordat" between the third sector and the state to lay down basic principles of future relations (Kendall 2000; Lewis 1999). The Compact was drawn up in part-nership following extensive consultation with the voluntary and commu-nity sector and government departments and was published in November 1998. In one respect, the Compact is working well—to the extent that it has helped to ensure that certain third sector issues, such as funding, are in the mainstream of policy debate. Its weakness, however, has been related to compliance and the lack of available sanctions for failure to comply with it and its related Codes.

After statements of "shared vision" and "shared principles," the Compact contains successive lists of "undertakings" (some on behalf of government, some the voluntary and community sector, and some both). The shared vision includes the statement that "voluntary and community activity is fundamental to the development of a democratic, socially inclusive society" (Home Office 1998: para 5) and underlines the effect, positive or negative, that government actions can have on the sector. The shared principles highlight the need for partnership but acknowledge the difference in roles between the two parties, state the values and qualities that should be common to both, and emphasize that "voluntary and community organisations are entitled to campaign within the law in order to advance their aims" (Home Office 1998: para 8.6). The undertakings are expressed at a high level of generality. Indeed, as one observer noted, "To the lawyer approaching them for the first time, the compacts may appear as genuinely baffling documents. They seem to be made up mainly of warm words, platitudes and generalities" (Morrison 2000:113). The Compact is intended to be a general framework and an enabling mechanism to enhance relationships, however, rather than a legally binding document (Home Office 1998: para 1). One of the local Compacts, which were developed subsequent to the national one (Craig, Taylor, Szanto, & Wilkinson 1999), was recently described by a judge in a case against a local authority[36] as "more than a wish list but less than a contract. It is a commitment of intent between the parties concerned."

The Compact has, in turn, formed the basis for the development of five codes of practice in relation to particular areas, each of which lists the rights and responsibilities to which both sectors should adhere in order to make that relationship work.[37] The Codes are, in general, more detailed than the Compact itself so that, in some respects, breaches are more easily identifiable.

The joint foreword to the Compact, by the (then) Home Secretary Jack Straw and Sir Kenneth Stowe (who originally chaired the voluntary and community sector's Working Group on Government Relations), expressed the commitment to carry forward the Compact by encouraging the adoption of its principles and undertakings at a local level where most voluntary and community sector activity takes place. As a result, since the launch of the national Compact, there has been a considerable amount of work undertaken at a local level to develop Compacts between local voluntary and community sectors and local governments and other local public sector partners. It should be noted, however, that early research revealed considerable variation as to the nature and scope of such agreements (Craig, Taylor, Szanto, & Wilkinson 1999). Some merely replicate the national Compact, while others have been constructed specifically in response to local considerations. The latter offer the means of supporting the development of the voluntary sector's capacity so that independent but accountable organizations can do more to meet both their own aims and those of their statutory partners, thereby enhancing their contributions to the community. Although the process of creating Compacts at the local level has been a slower one, compared to the national Compact, it was reported in March 2007 that 99 percent of local authority areas in England were covered by the Compact—94 percent with a published Local Compact and another five percent soon to be (Office of the Third Sector 2007a).

The Compact states that "as far as possible disagreements over the application of the framework should be resolved between the parties . . . mediation may be a useful way to try to reach agreement" (Home Office 1998: para 14). The Compact Mediation Scheme offers a neutral mediator's service to help resolve disputes related either to the letter or the spirit of the Compact. The Home Office appointed CEDR Solve, a recognized leader in the field of dispute resolution, to operate the Scheme which is completely independent and accessible to both government and the voluntary and community sector. In addition, in September 2002, the NCVO launched the Compact Advocacy Programme (CAP). The CAP advocates, campaigns, and provides support and advice to voluntary organizations, helping them to interpret and use the national, local,[38] and regional Compacts in their dealings with government, local authority, and non-departmental public bodies. The aims of CAP include identifying actual (or potential) breaches of the Compact and representing voluntary and community organizations to help resolve Compact disputes. Between November 2006 and 2007, CAP investigated 80 cases (up from 26 cases in the preceding year) where the Compact had been breached, involving more than £3 million worth of funding (NCVO 2007b). An example of a CAP campaign was that aimed at the Department of Health (DofH) in March 2006; CAP was contacted by over 30 organizations that were experiencing problems as a result of delayed decisions on "section 64" funding.[39] The delay was causing the usual difficulties with planning, and some charities were facing closure or redundancies. Partly as a result of campaigning and lobbying by CAP, the DofH finally confirmed funding for ongoing projects and admitted that it had breached the Compact (Butler 2006).[40]

Another element of enforcement and compliance is the annual meeting among the Compact Working Group (now called Compact Voice), government Ministers, and the Local Government Association. The annual meeting reviews progress in development and implementation of both the national and local Compacts. It also agrees on an action plan to take forward the Compacts. Compact Voice carries out a survey each year to inform its submission to the annual meeting. The proceedings of the meeting, the submission from Compact Voice, and the action plan for the year are all contained in an annual report to Parliament (see, for example, Office of the Third Sector 2007a).

The focus for Compact activity, at both the national and local levels, is now switching to quality implementation. In March 2005, the Home Office published proposals for a new Compact Plus scheme (Active Community Unit 2005), which public sector bodies and voluntary organizations will be able to opt into if they wish. It was recognized that the Compact had been criticized for not working as well as it might for a number of reasons (Active Community Unit 2005: 32). For example, the Compact and its five Codes are lengthy, comprising approximately 140 pages. While there are high level principles, it can be difficult for a public sector body or a voluntary organization to know whether the specifics of what it is doing are Compact-compliant. Also, it was suggested that once public sector bodies and sector organizations have signed up to the Compact, there is no mechanism to recognize good practice or highlight behavior that is not compliant with the Compact. Because there are no penalties for those who do not comply with the Compact, over time the initial benefit from having negotiated a Compact might diminish significantly.

Following from the response to this consultation, an independent Commission for the Compact was set up to promote best practices in partnership, oversee the operation of the Compact, and strengthen collaboration between public sector bodies and the voluntary and community sector, leading to better implementation of the Compact (Home Office 2006). The Commission officially launched its policy work program and business plan in April 2007 (Stoker 2007).

There has clearly been much activity related to the Compact. However, many charities have criticized the implementation of the Compact, saying that funders are either unaware of it or do not put its principles into practice (see National Audit Office 2005, 2007; House of Commons Committee of Public Accounts 2005–2006; Financial Secretary 2006). In early 2005, only 15 percent of respondents to a survey (Third Sector 2005) thought that the Compact had made any significant difference. Funding practices have underlain many of the difficulties in the relationship between government and the sector. The Treasury's Cross Cutting Review (HM Treasury 2002) in 2002 identified how some practices in procurement and contracting (such as short-term contracts, spot-funding, and payment in arrears) transfer financial and other risks onto charities, resulting in unsatisfactory outcomes and poor value for charities, funders, service users, and the public. Further research in 2005 (National Audit Office 2005: 3) revealed that most charities had not seen any general improvement in funding practices since 2002, and, in some cases, these practices were perceived to have worsened. The Code of Practice on Funding, originally published in 2000, was updated to include procurement and reissued in March 2005 (Home Office 2005). Although this Code supports the principle of full cost recovery by charities when delivering services for public authorities (Home Office 2005: para 2.10 and Appendix D), in practice, many charities still struggle to obtain full cost recovery. For example, a Charity Commission survey undertaken in 2006 (Charity

Commission 2007b) found that, of the charities responding to the survey, only 12 percent of those delivering public services reported that they obtain full cost recovery in all cases. While 37 percent said that they obtain full cost recovery in some or most cases, most worryingly, 43 percent indicated that they do not obtain full cost recovery for any of the services that they deliver.

Full cost recovery means that charities should receive payment not only for the direct costs that they incur by providing a service—for example, staff salaries in the case of residential care services—but also for legitimate overhead costs, such as the costs of office space, utilities, and information technology services, as well as various other costs such as depreciation and interest on loans (ACEVO 2004). Failure to recover full costs can mean that charities have to divert funding intended for service provision into paying overheads or must subsidize the provision of public services from other sources such as donor income. Ultimately, failure to cover overheads may lead to organizations shrinking or collapsing.

The Compact Code on Funding requires government funders to give adequate notice on funding decisions (Home Office 2005: para 3.11 and 7.6). Where contracts are subject to regular renewal, timely notification of the renewal is important to allow charities to maintain the continuity of the service. However, research published in 2005 found that one of the most frequent problems that charities encounter in relation to funding arrangements with government is their inability, without a confirmed contract renewal, to offer secure employment to project staff (see National Audit Office 2005, 2007; House of Commons Committee of Public Accounts 2006; Financial Secretary 2006). By the time the contract is renewed, key staff may well have left to take up employment elsewhere. Charities consulted reported that it was common for their government funders to confirm funding agreements late, even some time after the agreed start of a time-critical project: in fact, only 18 percent of funding renewals were on time. Without a framework of legal accountability, this sort of behavior will continue.

In May 2006, the government launched its revised Guidance to Funders which promotes the relationship between the third sector and government in public service delivery and furthers the principles embedded in the Compact (HM Treasury 2006). The document addresses a number of specific issues including the need to provide full cost recovery and stability in funding relationships and to move from one year funding to longer-term funding arrangements where appropriate. The Guidance also recognizes that payment in arrears often results in the third sector bearing the upfront costs of borrowing and the risks that this entails. The National Audit Office has also released a web-based tool to guide funders and purchasers through a structured series of decisions about the design of funding programs, ensuring that programs achieve their objectives while also complying with the Compact Funding and Procurement Code.[41]

Separately, and at the same time, in recognition of the increasingly important role that the third sector plays in both society and the economy, Prime

Minister Blair created the Office of the Third Sector (OTS) in the Cabinet Office to drive forward the government's role in supporting a thriving third sector and to join up sector-related work across government.[42] In May 2006, the government launched a review of the future role of the sector in social and economic regeneration (the "Third Sector Review") as part of the 2007 Comprehensive Spending Review process that examined future priorities and allocations for all government spending. The final report of the Third Sector Review (HM Treasury and Cabinet Office 2007), published in July 2007 following the government's largest ever consultation with the sector,[43] set out a strategy to work with sector organizations over the next ten years to promote social and economic regeneration and the partnership between the government and the third sector. The plan was to invest more than £515 million in third sector programs to support thousands of community organizations across the country, help give them a greater voice, strengthen communities, transform public services, encourage social enterprise, and support the conditions for the sector to thrive. Under this last aim, the Report requires all government departments and their agencies to continue to drive improvements in funding practices based on HM Treasury guidance (HM Treasury 2006) and the Compact. All government departments have a responsibility, for example, to reach agreement with voluntary organizations regarding how and when they are going to make payments to them, on the monitoring requirements placed upon the sector, and in acknowledging the legitimacy of the organizations being able to recover all or a proportionate amount of their legitimate overhead costs (HM Treasury and Cabinet Office 2007: para 6.17). Under the Coalition government the OTS has been rebranded as the Office for Civil Society and been given a lead role in implementing the Big Society policy, the impact of which is too early to assess.

Although the Third Sector Review failed to give any formal powers to the Compact Commission, as some had advocated, perhaps all these developments are signs that the high level commitments in the Compact and accompanying Codes are finally being translated into practical results. In any event, many would recognize that the *processes* of producing the Compact and the associated Codes have been valuable in themselves in developing good working relationships. As one American observer has noted:

> What seems clear is that the British Compact ultimately appears more aimed at fomenting dialogue and laying a foundation for communication than at actually carving out a set of binding principles for cross-sector interaction. Absent a fully inclusive group of representative signatories on either side and absent a clear system for resolving conflicts and breaches, the British Compact takes more the form of a set of hypotheses and ideals for effective contracting than a truly actionable cross-sector agreement. This may not be such a bad result, however (Frumkin 2003: 437).

The Compact Commission now clearly has a role to play in further developing good working relationships between government and the third sector. Ultimately, it may provide the enforcement mechanisms that have been lacking. At the launch of the Commission's first work program in April 2007, the Compact Commissioner acknowledged that "there was still a gap to be closed between commitment to Compact principles of good partnership, and their full delivery" (Stoker 2007). In July 2008, the Minister for the Third Sector asked the Compact Commissioner to lead a debate on whether the Compact should be supported by statutory powers. The views of the sector reflected a majority preference for creating an independent statutory commission and also for rewriting the Compact so as to consolidate it and the five associated codes into a single document. Following further consultations, a "refreshed," leaner, and more focused Compact was launched in December 2009 which retains the key principles and commitments of the original but includes some topics (such as the commissioning of public services and subcontracting) on which the original was largely silent (see Commissioner for the Compact 2009). The matter of statutory powers for the Compact Commissioner is still to be resolved.

CONCLUSION

Recent years have witnessed a large number of codes of conduct and other voluntary commitments within the third sector in England and Wales, some of which have been discussed in this chapter. The development of the Compact, in particular, provides evidence that the foundational architecture for a more collaborative relationship between the state and the third sector has been laid. In addition, it has been argued that by simplifying and clarifying the law, the *Charities Act 2006* will make it easier for charities to negotiate their way through it and easier for the public to understand, creating confidence in charities as organizations that benefit the public. This in turn will encourage private philanthropy and other opportunities for people to get involved in causes that they care about and which benefit society as a whole. An independent and diverse charitable sector contributes to a vibrant and active civil society, and a modern and effective legal framework will ensure that the sector continues to make a positive contribution in the 21st century and continues to have public support.

It is fitting that the charitable sector, so diverse in itself, should be subject to a variety of approaches to regulation. The legal obligations should complement the diverse range of soft law approaches to regulation of charities such as the codes of practice described in this chapter. While the *Charities Act 2006* is to be welcomed overall, it is accepted that legal rules (especially new ones) can be difficult to apply. They will not change behavior overnight. Voluntary approaches may well work more easily and may adapt to the circumstances of individual charities. However, the effectiveness of voluntarism relies on the actors themselves. Legal regimes provide a better basis for consistent and fair judgments. Conversely, the legal status of soft law is not as clear as that of legislation, often allowing breaches to be readily tolerated. The weaknesses of voluntary codes are clear: most are not supervised by an independent body and cannot meet the demand of the public for transparent and legal accountability. They often give little remedy or relief to those whose rights are infringed. While the law may assist in the prevention of bad practices, voluntary regulation may well encourage best practice.

It is hoped that the regulation of fundraising scheme will come to have considerable force as soft law. At some point, the soft law duties may well be recognized as, or consciously transformed into, unambiguous and binding obligations. It is difficult to assess at this early stage the extent to which this new scheme will have an impact on fundraising practice. Nevertheless, with the threat of unilateral regulatory action ever present in the background, there is every chance that the scheme will work.[44] Government's (partial) involvement also means that, at least at the start, the scheme was reasonably well resourced. A word of warning though from a comparative point of view (Sidel 2005: 835): "we must be cautious that self-regulation supported and incentivized by government does not become, in effect, a form of government 'nationalization' of nonprofit governance and management through an ostensible 'self-regulatory' process."

While the Governance Code is also in the early stages of implementation, lack of enforcement mechanisms may mean that compliance is simply left to those who are most committed—who probably do not need the Code anyway. It remains to be seen whether this purely voluntary form of compliance can provide effective regulation of the charitable sector. If the prospects of enhanced reputation and greater credibility prove not to provide sufficient incentives of themselves, the provision of some teeth to bite those who do not comply and rewards for those who do (perhaps through an accreditation[45] or a certification program) might be the next stage in development.

The limits of voluntarism mean that it is appropriate to pursue a complementary route towards legal responsibility offered by the new legal framework set up in the *Charities Act 2006*. A mix of voluntary initiatives and binding legal rules are needed to guide the behavior of charities and to ensure effective accountability. The outstanding challenge for regulatory reform, as well as for collaboration, is getting the right mix.

NOTES

1. This chapter is limited to the case of England and Wales. For constitutional purposes, charity law is a devolved matter in the United Kingdom. The supervision and regulation of charities have been devolved to the Scottish Executive (Scottish Charities Office) and to the Northern Ireland Assembly

(the Charities Branch in the Department for Social Development) for purposes other than tax. Reform in Scotland and Northern Ireland is the subject of separate local initiatives. In the past, provisions for regulating charities have differed significantly in each jurisdiction, but Scotland now has a similar regulatory regime to that in England and Wales, as a result of the implementation of the *Charities and Trustee Investment (Scotland) Act 2005*, and it is expected that reforms will result in a similar regime being introduced in Northern Ireland in the future.

2. See also MORI/Charity Commission, *A Survey of Public Attitudes to the Charity Commission—(MORI Poll)*, February 1999. Compare, however, recent research in Australia, suggesting that donors do not care about the ultimate usage of funds (see Berman & Davidson 2003).

3. Labour MP for Darlington, Chair of the Joint Committee on the Draft Charities Bill. See Joint Committee on the Draft Charities Bill (2003–2004a).

4. The Strategy Unit was set up in 2002, bringing together the Performance and Innovation Unit, the Prime Minister's Forward Strategy Unit, and parts of the Centre for Management and Policy Studies. Its aim is to improve government's capacity to address strategic, cross-cutting issues and to promote innovation in the development of policy and the delivery of the government's objectives. The Strategy Unit reports to the Prime Minister through the Cabinet Secretary. For a discussion of the recommendations, see Morris (2002, 2003a).

5. In general, the proposals received resounding support; of the respondents to the public consultation on the Strategy Unit's proposals, 30 were in favor for every one against (Mactaggart 2004).

6. The remainder are being implemented either through other legislation (e.g., *Companies (Audit, Investigations and Community Enterprise) Act 2004*, which contains provisions in Part 2 (s 26–63) for the community interest company) or by administrative action.

7. In *Income Tax Special Purposes Commissioners v Pemsel* [1891] AC 531, Lord Macnaghten classified 'charity' into four principal divisions often referred to as 'heads'. These are trusts for: the relief of poverty, advancement of education, advancement of religion, and other purposes beneficial to the community.

8. See, for example, Lord Phillips' unsuccessful attempt during the Charity Bill's report stage in the House of Lords to introduce an amendment that would have required the Charity Commission to "consider the effect on public benefit of the charging policy of any charity" when consulting in advance of issuing guidance to charities on public benefit. Hansard HL vol 674 col 312 (12 October 2005).

9. The legal principles are derived from the case of *Re Resch* [1969] 1 AC 514. This held that charities which charge high fees for their services are merely obliged to show that people on a low income "are not entirely excluded from benefit." If the fees could be paid for through a private insurance scheme, for example, this would be sufficient to enable the charity to demonstrate public benefit.

10. This can broadly be explained as an instance in which a particular activity not only provides a measure of benefit to the public, but also causes harm to the public (often, but not necessarily, to a different section of the public than the section which may have benefited). See Office of the Scottish Charity Regulator (2006).

11. See, for example, the Charity Commission's (2007c) decision in the Odstock Private Care Limited case. The application (determined by reference to the pre-*Charities Act 2006* law) was rejected largely on the grounds that the effect of

the body's service charges would be to exclude the less well off from benefit, and therefore it could not be held to have satisfied the public benefit test.

12. For example, some religious charities, scouts and guides, and armed forces groups. Excepted charities were those that were not previously obliged to register with the Charity Commission, though they were regulated by it.

13. For example, housing associations, universities, and colleges. Exempt charities were charities that were not previously registered with nor regulated by the Commission.

14. Part 2, Chapter 3 (ss.9–14) and Schedule 5 of Act cover the registration of charities, including new arrangements for the registration of larger excepted charities and for the regulation of exempt charities.

15. See Office of Third Sector and Charity Commission (2007).

16. Part 2, Chapter 4 (ss.15–18) of the Act covers changes to the rules governing the application, by scheme, of charity property "cy-près." Charity property is said to be applied cy-près when it is used for purposes different from, but close to, the purposes for which it was originally given. Part 2, Chapter 10 (ss.40–42) of the Act covers changes to the rules under which small unincorporated charities may transfer their property to other charities, replace their current charitable purposes with new ones, or modify their constitutional powers or procedures. Part 2, Chapter 11 (ss.43–44) of the Act covers the spending of capital endowment funds by charities and the registration of mergers between charities.

17. Part 2, Chapter 9 (ss.35–39) of the Act covers changes to the rules on the disqualification of persons from acting as trustees, the remuneration of charity trustees, the relief of trustees from personal liability for breach of trust or duty, and the purchase by trustees of trustee indemnity insurance.

18. This does not include complaints about the Commission's conduct and service, which will continue to be reviewed by the Independent Complaints Reviewer.

19. Part 2, Chapter 2 (s.8) and Schedules 3 and 4 of the Act cover the creation of a tribunal to hear appeals against some types of decision made by the Charity Commission.

20. Part 2, Chapter 6 (ss.28–30) and Schedule 6 of the Act cover the audit and examination of the accounts of unincorporated charities, the duties of auditors and examiners of those charities, and makes provision for the preparation and audit of group accounts. Part 2, Chapter 7 (ss.31–33) of the Act affects charitable companies only, covering changes to the rules restricting amendments to their constitutions and the audit and examination of their accounts.

21. Previously, collections in public places and door to door fundraising were governed by different statutory regimes.

22. Part 3 of the Act (ss.45–71) deals with fundraising by, and the funding of, charities and other benevolent or philanthropic organizations and is divided into three chapters as follows: Chapter 1 (ss.45–66) establishes the arrangements for the conduct and regulation of public charitable collections; Chapter 2 (ss.67–69) makes changes to the rules requiring statements to be made to donors and consumers by, respectively, paid fundraisers and commercial participators. It also gives the Minister for the Cabinet Office a reserve power to regulate most forms of fundraising by charities and by other benevolent and philanthropic organizations; and Chapter 3 (ss.70–71) contains new powers for the Secretary of State, and for the Welsh Assembly, to give financial assistance to charities and other benevolent and philanthropic organizations.

23. This gives statutory effect to the government's undertaking to carry out an independent review of the operation of the Act, as recommended by the Joint Committee on the Draft Charities Bill (2003–2004a, b).

24. At the end of March 2010, there were 160,690 'main' charities on the Charity Commission Register, plus an addition 21,064 subsidiary or group charities, for a total of 182,034. www.charity-commision.gov.uk
25. See, for example, Financial Reporting Council (2003). This document includes the Code itself and related guidance (the Turnbull guidance on Internal Control, as revised in October 2005, the Smith guidance on Audit Committees, and various pieces of good practice guidance from the Higgs report).
26. The Code has been described as a 'fantastic document' by Seb Elsworth (2007), head of policy at ACEVO. He reported a high level of uptake on the standards outlined in the code.
27. The Governance Hub was a program to improve the quality of governance of voluntary and community organizations in England. It was a partnership of nine infrastructure organizations that provide support to the voluntary and community sector: ACEVO, Black Training and Enterprise Group (BTEG), British Association of Settlements and Social Action Centres (bassac), CTN, East Cornwall Council for Voluntary Services (ECCVS), National Association for Voluntary and Community Action (NACVA), NCVO, Social Enterprise Coalition (SEC), and Volunteering England. The accountable body for the Governance Hub was NCVO. The Hub was a recommendation of the Home Office Active Communities Unit's ChangeUp report, and the Home Office provided funding for the Hub for two years (see Home Office 2004). Funding was then taken over by a new agency, Capacitybuilders (see Capacitybuilders 2006).
28. From April 2008, investment at a national level was refocused from six National Hubs (including the Governance Hub) to nine National Support Service (NSS) workstreams, including Leadership and Governance, to be led by the NCVO (Capacitybuilders 2007).
29. Each of the six Hallmarks describes an overarching principle and not a legal requirement (Charity Commission 2008c: 2).
30. The Charity Commission is aware of the problem and of the need to continue to clarify the difference between what is mandatory and what is advisable by clearly delineating the distinctions. See, for example, Charity Commission (2006).
31. Giles Peel (2006), director of policy and development at the Institute of Chartered Secretaries and Administrators, said that, "judging from the commercial world 'the best code will out in the end.' "
32. See the final report of the Commission (Buse 2004), which calls for the establishment of a Charitable Fundraising Standards Board based on the Office of Fair Trading model.
33. The Fundraising Promise is a commitment made to the public by members of the FRSB scheme. It has been compiled in consultation with fundraisers and the public and is based on six key pledges that center on respect, honesty, accountability, and transparency. The Fundraising Promise represents a commitment to the highest standards of good practice and to ensuring that all fundraising activities are open, legal, and fair.
34. On 25 January 2008, The FRSB published its first adjudication, in which the complaint against a charity was not upheld. Adjudications are published on the FRSB website: http://www.frsb.org.uk/england/adjudications.
35. Parallel Compacts have also been developed in other parts of the United Kingdom. For an examination of the four Compact documents drawn up by government and representatives from the voluntary sectors in England, Scotland, Wales, and Northern Ireland, see Morrison (2000).
36. Mackie J in the case of *R (on the Application of Berry) v Cumbria County Council* [2007] EWHC 3144 (Admin). This seems to be the first case to test whether a breach of the Compact is unlawful.

37. Codes of Practice were developed on: Black and Minority Ethnic Groups, Community Groups, Consultation and Policy Appraisal, Funding and Procurement, and Volunteering.
38. Increased funding from the Big Lottery Fund has allowed the CAP to expand into local Compact work since August 2005. Because government is increasingly seeking to devolve power and decision making to a local level, the CAP has seen local cases overtake national cases, taking on 30 national cases in 2006/2007 compared to 50 local cases.
39. The Secretary of State for Health, through the Section 64 General Scheme of Grants (Health Services and Public Health Act 1968, s.64), has power to make discretionary grants to voluntary organizations in England whose activities support the DofH's policy priorities. Section 64 grants represent the greatest single source of financial support (£17.9 million) that the DofH provides to the voluntary sector.
40. ACEVO also threatened legal action (ACEVO 2007).
41. The toolkit can be found at www.nao.org.uk/better_funding (accessed 12 September 2009).
42. The OTS incorporated the responsibilities of the Active Communities Directorate in the Home Office and the Social Enterprise Unit in (what was) the Department for Trade and Industry.
43. The first phase of the review, which ran from May to October 2006, was the consultation phase, which heard from over 2,000 people representing over 1,000 organizations and also received a substantial number of written responses. This was the largest ever government consultation with the sector and had a much wider remit than previous reviews, which have focused on the role of the sector in service delivery.
44. Harrow (2005) refers to the "fabled 'last chance saloon' which sooner or later gets mention in almost any industry-led self-regulation conversation."
45. In the Netherlands, for example, philanthropic organizations can signal their trustworthiness by conforming to the rules of the branch organization of fundraisers (CBF) which gives them the right to use an accreditation seal (see Bekkers 2003). When it comes to representation in England, a December 2005 survey of subscribers to the Directory of Social Change (DSC) e-newsletter found that 72 percent of respondents did not think a single voice for the voluntary sector was feasible. A key theme that arose from the survey was that the range of organizations involved makes a single voice impossible. http://www.dsc.org.uk/

REFERENCES

Active Community Unit. (2005). *Strengthening Partnerships: Next Steps for Compact. The Relationship between the Government and the Voluntary and Community Sector.* London: Third Sector Office.
Association of Chief Executives of Voluntary Organisations (ACEVO). (2007). *Impact Report 2005/6.* London: ACEVO.
Association of Chief Executives of Voluntary Organisations (ACEVO). (2006). *Raising Our Game.* London: ACEVO.
Association of Chief Executives of Voluntary Organisations (ACEVO). (2004). *Full Cost Recovery: A guide and toolkit on cost allocation.* London: ACEVO.
Association of Chief Executives of Voluntary Organisations (ACEVO), Charity Trustee Networks, ICSA, and NCVO on behalf of the National Hub of Expertise in Governance. (2005). *Good Governance. A Code for the Voluntary and Community Sector.* London: NCVO.

Bekkers, R. (2003). "Trust, accreditation and philanthropy in the Netherlands." *Nonprofit and Voluntary Sector Quarterly*, 32: 596–615.

Berman, G., and Davidson, S. (2003). "Do donors care? Some Australian evidence." *Voluntas*, 14: 421–429.

Buse, R. (2004). *The Future of the Self-Regulation of Charity Fundraising—proposed framework and governance structure.* London: Rodney Buse Associates Ltd.

Butler, P. (2006). "Charities march on Number 10." *The Guardian.* Online. Available at <http://www.guardian.co.uk/society/2006/feb/01/charities.publicservices> (accessed on 12 September 2008).

Capacitybuilders. (2007). *Destination 2014. Our strategy for the delivery of changeup.* Birmingham: Capacitybuilders.

Capacitybuilders. (2006). *Fit for Growth. Building sustainable voluntary and community organisations. Capacitybuilders' strategy 2006.* Birmingham: Capacitybuilders.

Charities Aid Foundation, Institute of Fundraising, Public Fundraising Regulatory Association, NCVO, ACEVO, Scottish Council for Voluntary Organisations, Charity Law Association and the Charity Commission. (2004). *The Self-Regulation of Fundraising.* London: Steering Committee.

Charities Unit Home Office. (2005). *Principles for Assessing the Success of Self-Regulation of Fundraising,* a Consultation Paper. London: Home Office.

Charity Commission. (2008a). *Analysis of the Law Underpinning Charities and Public Benefit.* London: TSO.

Charity Commission. (2008b). *Charities and Public Benefit. The Charity Commission's general guidance on public benefit.* London: TSO.

Charity Commission. (2008c). *Hallmarks of an Effective Charity,* CC10. London: TSO.

Charity Commission. (2007a). *Charities and Public Service Delivery: An introduction and overview,* CC37. London: TSO.

Charity Commission. (2007b). *Stand and Deliver—The future for charities providing public services,* RS15. London: TSO.

Charity Commission. (2007c). *Review Decision Made on the Application for Registration of Odstock Private Care Limited.* London: TSO.

Charity Commission. (2006). *A Report on the Views of Key External Stakeholders on Progress since 2004.* London: TSO.

Charity Commission. (2005). *Charities Bill Fails to be Enacted.* Charity Commission Press Release, GNN ref 114050P. London:TSO.

Charity Commission. (2004a). *Transparency and Accountability,* RS8. London: TSO.

Charity Commission. (2004b). *A Report on the Views of Key External Stakeholders on Progress since 2004.* London: TSO.

Charity Commission. (2003). *Charity Watchdog Steps in to Protect Breast Cancer Charity.* Charity Commission Press Release. London: TSO.

Charity Commission. (1999). *A Survey of Public Attitudes to the Charity Commission (MORI Poll).* London: TSO.

Charity Commission Register. (2010). Online. Available at <www.charity-commision.gov.uk> (accessed March 2008).

Commissioner for the Compact. (2009). Compact Refresh. Available at < http://www.thecompact.org.uk/information/129473/>

Commission on the Future of the Voluntary Sector. (1996). *Meeting the Challenge of Change: Voluntary Action into the 21st Century* (Deakin Report). London: Commission Secretariat/NCVO.

Craig, G., Taylor, M., Szanto, C., and Wilkinson, M. (1999). *Developing Local Compacts. Relationships between local public sector bodies and the voluntary and community sectors.* York: YPS.

Dawson, I., and Dunn, A. (2006). "Governance codes of practice in the not-for-profit sector." *Corporate Governance*, 14, 33–42.

Directory of Social Change (DSC). (2006) E-newsletter. Online. Available at <http://www.dsc.org.uk/>(accessed 20 September 2007)

Duffy, B. (2003). *Who Do We Trust?* London: MORI.

Elsworth, S. (2007, October-November). "A useless redraft?" *Charity Times*.

Financial Reporting Council. (2003). *Combined Code on Corporate Governance.* London: Financial Reporting Council.

Financial Secretary to the Treasury. (2006, June). *Treasury Minutes on the Thirty-second and Thirty-third Reports from the Committee of Public Accounts 2005–2006.* Presented to Parliament by the Financial Secretary to the Treasury by Command of Her Majesty.

Frumkin, P. (2003). "The end of public-nonprofit relations? A comment on Plowden." *Nonprofit and Voluntary Sector Quarterly*, 32: 436–438.

Fundraising Standards Board (FRSB). (2008). *Fundraising Standards Board Annual Review February 2007/2008.* London: FRSB.

Gunningham, N., and Rees, J. (1997). "Industry self-regulation: An institutional perspective." *Law & Policy*, 19: 363–414.

Harrow, J. (2005). "Swift as a shadow, short as any dream . . . institutional and policy perspectives on self-regulation in UK charity fundraising." *Accountable Governance: An International Research Colloquium.* Belfast: Queens University Belfast.

Home Office. (2006). *Report to Parliament of the Sixth Annual Meeting to review the Compact on Relations between Government and the Voluntary and Community Sector.* London: Home Office.

Home Office. (2005). *Funding and Procurement. Compact code of good practice.* London: Home Office.

Home Office. (2004). *ChangeUp. Capacity building and infrastructure framework for the voluntary and community sector.* London: Home Office.

Home Office. (2003). *Charities and Not-for-Profits: A modern legal framework. The government's response to 'Private Action, Public Benefit.'* London: Home Office.

Home Office. (1998). *Getting it Right Together. Compact on relations between government and the voluntary sector in England.* Cm 4100. London: Home Office.

House of Commons Committee of Public Accounts. (2006, March 2). *Working with the voluntary Sector.* HC 717, 32nd Report of Session 2005–2006. London: TSO.

House of Commons Deb (2005–2006) 450, part 207, col. 1539–1627 (25 October 2006).

House of Commons Deb WS (2005–2006) 442, part 2, col. 38 (6 February 2006).

House of Lords Deb. (2005–2006) 674, cols. 312 & 392 (12 October 2005).

HM Treasury. (2006). *Improving Financial Relationships with the Third Sector: Guidance to funders and purchasers.* London: TSO.

HM Treasury. (2002). *The Role of the Voluntary and Community Sector in Service Delivery. A cross cutting review.* London: TSO.

HM Treasury. (1999). *Review of Charity Taxation.* London: TSO.

HM Treasury and Cabinet Office. (2007). *The Future Role of the Third Sector in Social and Economic Regeneration: Final report.* Cm 7189. London: TSO.

House of Commons Committee of Public Accounts. (2005–2006). *Working with the Voluntary Sector* (HC 717). London: TSO.

Independent Commission on Good Governance in Public Services. (2004). *Good Governance Standard for Public Services.* London: OPM/CIFPA.

Independent Schools Council (ISC). (2007). ISC Census 2007. London: ISC.

Institute of Fundraising (IOF). (n.d.), *Code of Conduct for Fundraisers and Codes of Practice*. Online. Available at <http://www.institute-of-fundraising.org.uk/> (accessed on 4 September 2009)

Institute of Fundraising (IOF). (2003, June). *Future of Self-Regulation in Charity Fundraising*. Press Release.

Joint Committee on the Draft Charities Bill. (2003–2004a). *Draft Charities Bill Vol. 1: Report* (HL 167-I, HC 660-I). London: TSO.

Joint Committee on the Draft Charities Bill. (2003–2004b). *Draft Charities Bill Vol. 2: Report* (HL 167-II, HC 660-II). London: TSO.

Kendall, J. (2000). "The mainstreaming of third sector into public policy in England in the late 1990s: whys and wherefores." *Policy & Politics*, 28: 541–562.

Kirton, J. J., and Trebilcock, M. J. (2004). *Hard Choices, Soft Law: Voluntary Standards in Global Trade*. Aldershot: Ashgate.

Lewis, J. (1999). "Reviewing the relationship between the voluntary sector and the state in Britain in the 1990s." *Voluntas*, 10: 255–270.

Lloyd, R., and de Las Casas, L. (2005, December). "NGO Self-Regulation: Enforcing and Balancing Accountability." *Alliance Magazine*. Available at <http://www.alliancemagazine.org/en/content/ngo-self-regulation-enforcing-and-balancing-accountability> (Accessed 15 March 2008).

Mactaggart MP, F. (2004, December). Foreword to *Government Reply to the Report from the Joint Committee on the Draft Charities Bill Session 2003–4, HL 167/HC 660, Cm 6440*. London: TSO.

Milburn, A. (2003, November 12). *Putting the Voluntary Sector Centre Stage*. Speech to the NCVO, London.

Morris, D. (2002). "Strategy unit proposes major shake-up of charity law—Part 1." *Exempt Organisation Tax Review, 38*.

Morris, D. (2003a). "Strategy unit proposes major shake-up of charity law—Part 2." *Exempt Organisation Tax Review, 39*.

Morris, D. (2003b). "Charity law reform: The next step." *Exempt Organisation Tax Review, 41*.

Morrison, J. (2000). "The government-voluntary sector compacts: Governance, governmentality, and civil society." *Journal of Law and Society, 98*.

National Audit Office. (2007). *Office of the Third Sector—Implementation of Full Cost Recovery*. London: TSO.

National Audit Office. (2005). *Working with the Third Sector*. Report by the Comptroller and Auditor General, HC 75 Session 2005–2006. London: TSO.

National Council for Voluntary Organisations (NCVO). (2007a, November 26). *Sector to Have its Say on Ways of Improving Governance*. NCVO Press Release. London: NCVO.

National Council for Voluntary Organisations (NCVO). (2007b, December). *Compact Advocacy Annual Report 2006/07*. London: NCVO.

National Council for Voluntary Organisations (NCVO). (2006a, November 8). *Charities Act Brings Charity Law into the 21st Century*. Press Release. London: NCVO.

National Council for Voluntary Organisations (NCVO). (2006b). *National Occupational Standards for Trustees and Management Committee Members in the Voluntary and Community Sector*. London: NCVO.

National Council for Voluntary Organisations (NCVO). (2004). *A Governance Code for the Voluntary and Community sector? A consultation paper*. London: NCVO.

National Hub of Expertise in Governance. (2005). *Learning to Fly: Piloting your local voluntary or community organisation*. London: Author.

Office of Public Sector Information. (2008). *The Charity Tribunal Rules 2008, SI 2008 No. 221*. United Kingdom.

Office of the Scottish Charity Regulator. (2006). *Meeting the Charity Test. Initial guidance for applicants and for existing charities*. Dundee: OSCR.

68   *Debra Morris*

Office of the Third Sector. (2010). *Charities Act 2006 Updated Implementation Plan March 2010*, Cabinet Office. London: TSO.

Office of the Third Sector. (2006). *Partnership in Public Services: An action plan for third sector involvement*, Cabinet Office. London: TSO.

Office of the Third Sector. (2007a). *Report to Parliament of the Seventh Annual Meeting to Review the Compact on Relations between Government and the Voluntary and Community Sector*, Cabinet Office. London: TSO.

Office of the Third Sector. (2007b). *Charities Act 2006: Implementation Plan*, Cabinet Office. London: TSO.

Office of Third Sector and Charity Commission. (2007). *Financial Thresholds in the Charities Acts. Proposals for Change*. London: TSO.

Peel, G. (2006, February 8). "Charity Commission told to end 'confusing' efforts at guidance." *Third Sector.*

Prime Minister's Office. (2010). "Building the Big Society." London: Prime Minister's Office. Available at <http://www.cabinetoffice.gov.uk/media/407789/building-big-society.pdf> (Accessed 10 August 2010).

Reichardt, O., Kane, D., Pratten, B., and Wilding, K. (2008). *UK Civil Society Almanac 2008.* London: NCVO.

Sargeant, A. (2005, December). "Double Trouble is on the Horizon for the Sector." *Professional Fundraising.*

Scottish Charity Law Review Commission. (2001). *Charity Scotland: The report of the Scottish Charity Law Review Commission.* Edinburgh: Scottish Executive.

Scottish Executive. (2003, June 27). *Breast Cancer Research (Scotland).* Scottish Executive News Release. Edinburgh: Scottish Executive.

Secretary of State for the Home Department. (2003–2004). *The Government Reply to the Report from the Joint Committee on the Draft Charities Bill* (HL Paper 167/HC 660, Cm 6440). London: TSO.

Senden, L. (2005). "Soft law, self-regulation and co-regulation in European law: Where do they meet?" *Electronic Journal of Comparative Law,* 9(1). Online. Available at <http://www.ejcl.org/91/art91-3.html> (accessed on 15 May 2009)

Shephard, J. (2006, December 19). "Charities Act: Next steps." *ISC Bulletin.*

Shifrin, T. (2004). "Pain but no gain." *The Guardian.* Available at <http://www.guardian.co.uk/society/2004/aug/25/primarycare.politics>

Sidel, M. (2005). "The guardians guarding themselves: A comparative perspective on nonprofit self-regulation." *Chicago Kent Law Review,* 80: 803–835.

Snyder, F. (1993). "The effectiveness of European Community law: Institutions, processes, tools and techniques." *Modern Law Review,* 56: 19–54.

Strategy Unit. (2001, July 3). *Prime Minister Announces Voluntary Sector Review.* Strategy Unit Press Release (CAB 128/01). London: TSO.

Strategy Unit. (2002). *Private Action, Public Benefit. A review of charities and the wider not-for-profit sector.* London: TSO.

Stoker, J. (2007, April 11). *Commission for the Compact—taking the compact forward*, Speech to mark the official launch of the Commisioner of the Compact, London.

Third Sector. (2006, February 8). *Charity Commission told to end "confusing" efforts at guidance.*

Third Sector. (2005, January 26) *Working with Government: Second among equals.*

Third Sector. (2003, June 4). *Breast Cancer Groups Demand Stricter Laws.*

Warburton, J. (2003). "Charities and governance: The role of the law." In D. Morris and J. Warburton (eds.), *Charities, Governance and the Law: The way forward.* London: Key Haven Publications.

3 Third Sector Regulation in Post-devolution Scotland

Kilting the Charity Cuckoo

Patrick Ford

INTRODUCTION

Scotland has its own legal system, a hybrid of civil law concepts and a home-grown common law (Sellar 1991). Its separate existence is guaranteed by the Treaty of Union of 1707 between Scotland and England,[1] but the influence of English law on the Scottish system has been pervasive. The London-based legislature for the United Kingdom set up by the Treaty, which after 1707 made law for Scotland in place of the old Parliament of Scotland in Edinburgh, has often foisted on the smaller partner to the Union English terms and concepts which Scots lawyers have been expected to adapt or "kilt" for use in their own system (Sellar 1991: 54–56). This has happened with the English concept of charity, now a long-established cuckoo in the Scottish legal nest.[2] It was originally introduced into Scots law as the criterion for "charitable" tax relief under UK fiscal legislation (*Special Commissioners for the Purposes of Income Tax v. Pemsel*, [1891] AC 531), then much later was made the basis for an elementary—and recently reformed—system for the regulation of "Scottish charities" (Law Reform Miscellaneous Provisions (Scotland) Act 1990: Part I).

In 1999, after almost three centuries without a parliament of its own, Scotland acquired a devolved legislature, the Scottish Parliament, which like its sovereign predecessor sits in Edinburgh. The new parliament is subsidiary to the UK Parliament, which retains overall supremacy in law-making throughout the United Kingdom. The "devolution settlement," given effect by the UK Parliament in the Scotland Act 1998, complements the new devolved legislature with a devolved administration, headed by a "Scottish Executive" of senior "Scottish Ministers" appointed from the membership of the new legislature (Scotland Act 1998: s 44). The devolved institutions may make policy and enact laws for Scotland in all areas other than those expressly reserved to the government and legislature of the United Kingdom. Such "reserved matters" include foreign affairs and defense and, most notably in the present context, fiscal, economic, and monetary policy (Scotland Act 1998: Schedule 5, Part II, Head A). The devolved Scottish Parliament has express authority, however, to legislate for "the creation, operation, regulation and dissolution of charities"—a formula that allows the Parliament to enact its own definition of "charity" (Scotland Act 1998: Schedule 5, Part II, Head C1).

When the new Parliament came to legislate for reform of the Scottish charities system, as it did in the *Charities and Trustee Investment (Scotland) Act 2005*,[3] one might have expected it to emancipate itself from English influence and to make use of the resources of Scotland's own common law. The Parliament might, in particular, have reverted to the Scots common law of public trusts—the indigenous Scottish equivalent of the English law of charities—and based its reform on the concept of "public benefit" developed by the Scottish courts independently of the parallel English concept of charity (see *Wink's Executors v Tallent* 1947 SC 470, 476). But that was not done, and instead the English charity cuckoo was merely adapted, or 're-kilted,' in the guise of a new Scottish "charity test" for use as the basis of the new system of charities supervision provided for by the 2005 Act (s 7).

It is argued here that this approach was mistaken (see also Ford 1999, 2006). The policies announced for the third sector in Scotland, first by the Labour-Liberal Democrat coalition which formed the Scottish Executive during the first eight years after devolution, and more recently by the minority "Scottish Government" of the Scottish Nationalist Party (the term " Scottish Government" is used hereafter to distinguish the Scottish Nationalist administration from its Labour-Liberal Democrat predecessors), would have been better served by legislation taking the Scots common law of public trusts as its starting point. It will be suggested that the common law concept of public benefit, which is both simpler and more inclusive than the new charity test, would have provided a much more satisfactory criterion for identifying those third sector organizations in Scotland that provide sufficient benefit to the public to merit being both facilitated and regulated as "charities." It will also be suggested that the Scottish Parliament's attempt in the 2005 Act to create a paternalistic system of charities regulation on the English model, overseen by a Scottish equivalent of the Charity Commission for England and Wales—the Office of the Scottish Charity Regulator (OSCR)—is inconsistent with third sector policies whose principal aim is to develop the sector's contribution to Scottish society through state–sector partnership and the facilitation of social entrepreneurship. All is not lost, however. A review of the 2005 Act seems inevitable,[4] and it is to be hoped that a future Scottish Parliament will take the opportunity of amending legislation to substitute Scotland's own common law concept of public benefit for the overly complex and unnecessarily restrictive charity test, and to adjust the functions of OSCR to reflect the emphasis of the common law on the facilitation—rather than paternalistic regulation—of voluntary organizations constituted for public benefit.

POLICY-MAKING FOR THE THIRD SECTOR
IN POST-DEVOLUTION SCOTLAND

Scotland is a small country, with a population of just over five million (Scottish Population Statistics 2006). In population terms, as opposed to surface area, that makes it about a tenth of the size of England and Wales (Office for National Statistics 2002). The Scottish third sector, too, is much smaller than its southern counterpart. There are some 45,000 voluntary sector organizations in Scotland, with an annual income between them of approximately £3.87 billion, assets under management of approximately £8.6 billion, a paid workforce of around 129,000, and unpaid support from some 1.2 million volunteers (Scottish Council for Voluntary Organisations 2007a, 2007b). Of Scotland's voluntary organizations, some 23,800 are registered as charities with OSCR (2008a: 3). There are no directly comparable figures for England and Wales (see Reichardt et al. 2008), but the following statistics for charities registered with the Charity Commission will give some idea of the difference in scale between third sector operations north and south of the Border: There are over 190,000 charities registered with the Charity Commission, which between them have incoming resources of nearly £45 billion and a paid workforce of over 600,000 (Charity Commission 2008).

These figures should be sufficient to make the general point that the size of the charities sector, and correspondingly of the third sector as a whole, is so much smaller in Scotland than in England and Wales that policies and legislative arrangements which have been developed for the larger jurisdiction may not necessarily be suitable for the smaller one. For instance, concentrating regulatory and facilitative resources on only one part of the third sector, the charities sector, may be justified in England and Wales on pragmatic grounds alone because it keeps the task of the Charity Commission as regulator within manageable bounds. On the other hand, the small size of the third sector overall in Scotland opens up the possibility of extending OSCR's supervisory jurisdiction beyond a restrictively defined subsector of "charities," to enable its facilitative powers, in particular, to be deployed to assist a broader rather than narrower range of third sector organizations toward maximizing their contribution to Scottish society.

Powers of the Devolved Institutions

Under the devolution settlement, the new Scottish institutions enjoy generous scope for developing third sector policies for Scotland different from those adopted in England and Wales. On the funding side, the Scottish Ministers may, with the approval of the Scottish Parliament, allocate at their discretion the block grant they receive from the UK Parliament, including by making central government grants to third sector organizations (Scotland Act 1998: Part III). They may also control spending on third sector organizations by local authorities.[5] The devolved Parliament has full competence to legislate for local taxes to fund local authority expenditure (Scotland Act 1998: Schedule 5, Part II, Head A1) and may, therefore, control the fiscal concessions to charities and other third sector organizations granted at local level (Local Government (Financial Provisions, etc) (Scotland) Act

1962: s4). Fiscal policy generally, on the other hand, remains reserved to the UK institutions, with the result that the Scottish Parliament has no legislative control over the reliefs conceded to charities from the taxes levied at the UK level, such as those on income and capital gains and on gifts and bequests (Scotland Act 1998: Schedule 5, Part II, Head A1).

So far as regulating the third sector in Scotland is concerned, the Scottish Parliament is, on the face of it, restricted to legislating for "the creation, operation, regulation and dissolution of *charities*" (Scotland Act 1998: Schedule 5, Part II, Head C1). However, because it is accepted that this express power to legislate for charities includes power to define "charities" (Scottish Executive 2004a: 3), the Parliament may, in practice, by adopting a wider rather than a narrower definition of charity, extend its legislative competence across as broad a range of third sector organizations as it chooses. Legislating for third sector organizations which are not defined as charities is a matter reserved to the UK Parliament, such organizations being classed as "business associations" under the devolution settlement, whether or not conducted for profit (Scotland Act 1998: Schedule 5, Part II, Head C1). On the specific issue of fundraising, the devolved Parliament has an unrestricted legislative competence and is free to regulate fundraising for third sector organizations generally, whether or not defined as charities. Fundraising is ultimately a matter of public order underpinned by the criminal law and, like the criminal law generally, within the legislative competence of the Scottish Parliament.

Policies of the Scottish Executive

During its time in government, the Labour-Liberal Democrat Scottish Executive took a number of policy initiatives as part of its "vision for the voluntary sector," with a view in particular to developing the potential of the sector to contribute to the provision of public services in Scotland (Scottish Executive 2005: paras 6 and 15–23). The Executive seems to have accepted the conventional view of the special merits of the sector as a contributor to public services—that it has a particular capacity for innovation, that it is "user focused" and has an ability "to connect with sections of the community which government services often cannot reach," and that it brings a "distinct perspective" to the planning of services acquired through its "knowledge and experience of delivery and the particular needs of groups of users" (Scottish Executive 2005a: 16, 18). To these perhaps speculative virtues of the sector as a partner with government in the delivery of services can be added its undoubted ability to mobilize valuable but inexpensive human resources in the form of volunteers and to attract non-government funding in the form of donations from the public (Scottish Council of Voluntary Organisations 2007a).

The Executive's focus on the "voluntary" rather than "third" sector was, no doubt, simply a continuation of the pre-devolution terminology of the UK government. In setting itself to work in partnership with the "voluntary sector," the Executive renewed a compact originally entered into pre-devolution between the UK government on the one hand and the Scottish Council for Voluntary Organisations (SCVO)—as representative of the sector—on the other, the aim of the post-devolution revival of the compact being "to develop robust relationships" between government and voluntary organizations "for the wider public good" (Scottish Executive and SCVO 2003: 2). The Executive's specific initiatives included a review of funding of the sector, which sought "to maximise its contribution to the common good of Scotland" (Scottish Executive 2005b: 2), a volunteering strategy intended "to embed a robust culture of volunteering in Scotland" (Scottish Executive 2004: 1) and, of course, the reform of the supervision of charities given effect by the 2005 Act. The key aim of the charities reform, taken in combination with an accompanying reform of fundraising for the broader sector, was "to increase transparency without placing the voluntary sector under undue burdens," while yet providing "the public with reassurance that the money they donate is used for the purposes they intended" (Scottish Executive 2005a: 7).

It should be emphasized that the Executive's vision was one for the voluntary sector at large, and not only—despite the particular focus of the 2005 Act on charities—for the charitable sub-sector. Accordingly, the Executive defined the organizations it sought to work with much more inclusively than by reference to any restrictive definition of charity:

> Voluntary organisations are independent bodies with self-governing structures and a wholly or predominantly voluntary governing body. They do not distribute profits and are run for the benefit of others or for the community (Scottish Executive 2004b: part 3.1).

It may be helpful to return to this definition in the next section of the chapter, but it should also be emphasized here that the Executive saw its own role in relation to the sector as above all:

> One of facilitation—removing barriers where they exist, making sure that the voluntary sector has a clear voice, spotting new opportunities for partnership working, and working with public sector providers to better understand the distinctive contribution the sector can make (Scottish Executive 2005a: 3).

Policies of the Scottish Government

The Scottish Nationalist-led Scottish Government has in its turn declared its enthusiasm for a thriving "third sector." The new administration's preference for the term "third sector" over "voluntary sector" signals a significant widening of the policy focus beyond the sector's role as a provider of public services—which nonetheless remains important (see Finance Secretary, 2007)—to a broader role in the Scottish economy:

> The third sector has an important part to play in securing sustainable economic growth. We will seek to secure the development of an innovative, sustainable and inclusive third sector, supporting communities to be more cohesive and contributing to high quality public services and increased economic growth (Scottish Government 2007c: Ch. 10).

The new emphasis on the wider third sector's economic role is part of the Scottish Government's overarching strategy for Scotland to improve the country's economic performance (Scottish Government 2007b: V). With this end in view, the third sector is to take part in a three-way collaboration with the public and private sectors (Scottish Government 2007c: Ch. 2). So far as specifics are concerned, the Scottish Government has announced substantially increased funding for the sector, in particular to encourage volunteering and social enterprise (Scottish Government 2008).

The Scottish Government has not defined what it means by the term "third sector." However, it is clear from the accent on the sector's economic role that it is intended to include not only voluntary organizations as defined by the Scottish Executive but also social enterprises such as cooperatives and community interest companies. These for-profit social enterprises are subject, as "business associations," to their own systems of supervision operating at UK level (Scotland Act 1998: Schedule 5, Part II, Head C1), but the Scottish Government's overarching strategy nevertheless includes, so far as is within its competence under the devolution settlement, a general "commitment to eliminating duplication and unnecessary bureaucracy" (Cabinet Secretary for Finance and Sustainable Growth 2007a). This is to involve, among other things, "significantly reducing the number of quangos" (Cabinet Secretary for Finance and Sustainable Growth 2007b), as well as giving much greater autonomy to local councils in the allocation of resources to public services (Cabinet Secretary for Finance and Sustainable Growth 2007b). What seems to be intended is a latter day Scottish version of "rolling back the frontiers of the state" (in the phrase associated with the free market policies of the former UK Prime Minister, Margaret Thatcher): The new Scottish Government voluntarily shrinking itself to allow room for a flowering, at the local level, of economic and social enterprise (Scottish Government and Convention of Scottish Local Authorities 2007).

The thrust of the policies announced for the third sector in Scotland by the post-devolution administrations is toward facilitation of the sector as a whole as a partner with government, both in the provision of public services and more generally in the encouragement of social enterprise and contributions to "the common good of Scotland." Facilitation, partnership, and enterprise are the key themes in policies embracing the full range of third sector organizations, non-profit and for-profit alike. The 2005 Act and the system of charities supervision it introduced look oddly out of alignment with those policies. The 2005 Act concentrates supervisory resources on charities at the expense of the wider third sector and places a new quango, OSCR, at the head of a system geared as much to centralized monitoring and top-down enforcement as to facilitation. Before considering the 2005 Act and the new charities system in greater detail, it may be helpful, in order to show how this inconsistency has come about and how it might be removed by reform in the future, to sketch out the legislative—as opposed to policy—background against which the statute was enacted.

LEGISLATIVE BACKGROUND

If the policy background to the 2005 Act is made up of the policies for the third sector announced since devolution, the legislative background consists of the legal arrangements for the constitution, taxation, and supervision of charities which the 2005 Act set out to build on and reform. The key arrangements are to be found in a combination of the Scots common law of public trusts, the fiscal legislation governing fiscal reliefs for "charitable" organizations at both UK and local levels, the now superseded system for the supervision of "Scottish charities," and the legislation controlling "public charitable collections" in Scotland.

Scots Common Law of Public Trusts

It is possible to point to a golden age of civic engagement in Scotland (Scottish Charity Law Review Commission 2001: 7), and in particular of involvement by voluntary organizations in the provision of what would now be regarded as public services[6]—a golden age which began sometime in the nineteenth century and faded in the wake of the Second World War, at least partly under the influence of a strong welfare state.[7] Contemporary efforts toward re-engagement of voluntary organizations in the delivery of public services, and in public benefit activity generally, hark back to that golden age, not always consciously, and on occasion while even seeming to repudiate it (Scottish Charity Law Review Commission 2001; Scottish Executive, 2004).

What is significant for present purposes is that the common law of Scotland responded to the needs of that age by developing the concept of the public trust (McLaren 1894: Ch. 8). The law of public trusts, which remains in force, is broadly speaking the equivalent of the law of charitable trusts in England and Wales (and in Anglo-American systems generally), though more recent in origin (*Wink's Executors v Tallent* 1947 SC 470, 476) and with a correspondingly less massive—though still rich—associated case law (Ross et al. 1989; Wilson & Duncan 1995; cf Luxton 2001; Warburton, Morris & Riddle 2003). Indeed, although "public trust" is the strictly correct term, the expression "charitable trust" has often been used loosely in the Scottish courts as a "convenient general name" for the public trust (McLaren 1894: 917). The concept of the public trust is, however, much simpler than its

English equivalent (Ford et al. 2000). In Scots common law, a public trust is nothing more or less than a trust in which "the beneficial interest is intended for the benefit of a section of the public" (Ross et al. 1989: para 6). A public trust is enforceable by "any person interested in the carrying out of the truster's directions" (*Aitken's Trustee v Aitken* 1927 SC 374, 382 (Lord Ashmore)), and in particular—by means of what is sometimes called an *actio populairis* (McLaren 1894: 917), or an "action of the people"—by any member of the section of the public the trust is intended to benefit (*Andrews v Ewart's Trustees* 1886 SC 69, 73 (Lord Watson)). The Lord Advocate, Scotland's principal Law Officer, also has title at common law to raise an action to enforce a public trust in the public interest (*Mitchell v Burness* (1878) 5R 954; *Aitken's Trustees v Aitken* 1927 SC 374). It should be added, given the importance of membership organizations as a proportion of the voluntary organizations active for public benefit in Scotland,[8] that while the common law of public trusts has been developed mainly in the context of the trust in the ordinary sense of a fund entrusted to a small body of trustees under a direction to administer it for specified "public" purposes (*Davidson's Trustees v Arnott* 1951 SC 42, 60 (Lord Patrick)), the common law also accommodates the phenomenon of a larger group of people combining together in an association or membership organization to pursue objects analogous to those of a public trust (McLaren 1894: 917). Parallel arrangements exist for the enforcement of the "quasi-trust" created when such an association is constituted for "public" objects, in the sense of objects intended by the members of the association to confer benefit on a section of the public (*D & J Nicol v Dundee Harbour Trustees* 1915 SC (HL) 7, 13 (Lord Dunedin)).

Two aspects of the Scots common law of public trusts are worth highlighting here because they are markedly different from the parallel features of the law of charitable trusts in England and Wales. The first is that there is in principle no restriction in Scots common law on the type of benefit which may be conferred on a section of the public by a public purpose. The only official restraint on the form public benefit may take is a 'fail-safe' power reserved to the Court of Session to declare invalid a purpose which it judges to be "manifestly extravagant, wasteful or irrational . . . to such a degree as to be contrary to public policy" (Ross et al. 1989: para 87). But for this public policy safety net, the question of what is beneficial to the public is to be determined by the public itself. When assessing whether an object confers benefit:

> the Court is not to make itself the judge of what is for the public benefit. It is enough that the object is one, not immoral or contrary to public order, which a certain section of opinion may regard as of public benefit (*Aitken's Trustees v Aitken* 1927 SC 374, 380 (Lord Sands)).

The concept of public benefit enshrined in the Scots common law of public trusts is an inclusive one, therefore, as well as much simpler and less technical than its equivalent in English law. By contrast, the English definition of charity, even after its rationalization in the Charities Act 2006, combines an elaborate case law on the meaning of public benefit—incorporating a requirement of benefit to the public at large or a section of it—with a restrictive classification of the types of benefit permitted which is drawn ultimately from the preamble to the Charitable Uses Act 1601.[9]

Secondly, the approach of the Scottish authorities to public trusts and analogous associations for public objects has traditionally been non-interventionist and non-paternalistic. As mentioned, the Lord Advocate has power to raise an action of enforcement of a public trust in the public interest, but in practice interventions by the Lord Advocate have been rare, and there is no requirement for members of the public seeking to enforce a public trust by *actio popularis* to obtain the consent of the Lord Advocate to the action (*D & J Nicol v Dundee Harbour Trustees* 1915 SC (HL) 7, 17 (Lord Dunedin)). In principle, therefore, the enforcement of a public trust is a matter for the relevant members of the public themselves. So also the Court of Session, while it has always exercised a jurisdiction of facilitation to approve alterations to the purposes of a public trust which have become outdated or unworkable,[10] has traditionally shown itself reluctant to exercise a jurisdiction of control over membership organizations constituted for public objects.[11]

There is a contrast here with the paternalistic approach of the authorities in England and Wales, where the Crown, as *parens patriae* ("parent of the country"), has a "quasi-parental" relation toward charities, which "makes it the protector of charity in general" (Warburton, Morris, & Riddle 2003, para 10–001, para 1–003). That role has been fulfilled in practice by the Attorney-General, through whom individuals wishing to enforce a charitable trust traditionally had to proceed (Warburton, Morris, & Riddle 2003: para 10–019), and in more recent times also by the Charity Commission, whose consent is still required for enforcement proceedings by individuals (Charities Act 1993: s 33). In England and Wales the court—originally the Court of Chancery—has its own distinctive jurisdiction over charities (*Special Commissioners for the Purposes of Income Tax v Pemsel* [1891] AC 531, 580 (Lord Macnaghten)), and the modern role of the Charity Commission as regulator of charities can be seen as combining the ancient duties of the Crown and the court to safeguard charity property and to monitor charities generally (Warburton, Morris, & Riddle 2003).

A picture can be painted, then, of a nineteenth century and early twentieth century Scots common law of public trusts at the service of civic engagement in Scotland which, by contrast with the law of charities in England and Wales, developed a broadly inclusive definition of public benefit and was concerned primarily with facilitation rather than with paternalistic control. As mentioned, the common law of public trusts remains in force,[12] and many thousands of voluntary organizations in Scotland are constituted as either public trusts or analogous associations with public objects (OSCR 2008a). Had the 2005 Act not been enacted and had the Scottish Parliament still to legislate to give effect to the policies for the third sector announced since devolution, the common law of public trusts might have

seemed the obvious starting point. The public trusts and analogous associations of the common law seem to fit very neatly into the Scottish Executive's definition (quoted above) of the voluntary organizations it sought to
work with for "the common good of Scotland" (Scottish Executive 2005).
By their very nature as trusts and quasi-trusts for public benefit, they are:

> independent bodies with self-governing structures and a wholly or pre-
> dominantly voluntary governing body. They do not distribute profits
> and [by virtue of the common law concept of public benefit] are run for
> the benefit of others [in the guise of a section or sections of the public]
> or for the community [i.e., the public as a whole] (Scottish Executive
> 2004b: para 3.1).

Likewise, the common law's emphasis on facilitation and its tradition of
minimal official involvement in enforcement seem to resonate, not only with
the Executive's view of the role of government in relation to the voluntary
sector "as one of removing barriers where they exist" (Scottish Executive
2005a: 3), but also with the Scottish Government's broader objective of eliminating "unnecessary bureaucracy" to make way for social and economic
enterprise (Cabinet Secretary for Finance and Sustainable Growth 2007a).
It is clear, of course, that even a Scottish Parliament which intended to
legislate with the common law as its starting point would have much to
do to render arrangements developed in the nineteenth and early twentieth centuries fit for purpose as a system of enforcement and facilitation
for today. For instance, an obvious enhancement to the arrangements for
enforcement by members of the public would be a public register of organizations holding themselves out as providing benefit to the public. In an
era of prohibitive court expenses, some more accessible and cost-effective
alternative to the Court of Session would surely have to be devised as a
forum for enforcement proceedings. Nevertheless, the common law of public trusts would provide a natural point of departure for a Scottish Parliament anxious to legislate for charities, both in accordance with the general
policies announced for the third sector since devolution and in a way sensitive to Scotland's own legal traditions.

The Charity Cuckoo

It must be admitted, however, that the merits of the Scots common law
system of public trusts have become increasingly obscured over the past
fifty years by the presence of the English definition of charity in the Scottish
legal nest. The 'cuckoo' was introduced as long ago as the late eighteenth
century, on the first imposition of income tax in the United Kingdom, when
relief was afforded from that tax to organizations with charitable purposes
(Warburton, Morris, & Riddle 2003). It was not until the late nineteenth
century, however, that it was established at the highest judicial level that

"charitable" in this context should be read in its technical meaning in English law, in Scotland as elsewhere in the United Kingdom (*Special Commissioners for the Purposes of Income Tax v Pemsel*, [1891] AC 531). Even then, it was only as charitable reliefs granted on this basis were extended to other United Kingdom-level taxes (Warburton, Morris, & Riddle 2003), and in due course to local government taxation (*Local Government (Financial Provisions etc) (Scotland) Act 1962*), that the significance of the cuckoo grew along with the value of the reliefs (see *Inland Revenue v City of Glasgow Police Athletic Association* [1953] AC 380). In modern practice in Scotland, therefore, while the purposes of a public trust or the objects of an analogous membership organization remain "public" in the language of the common law, it has long been normal to couch them in terms which satisfy the narrower English definition of "charitable" to ensure qualification for the fiscal reliefs.

In the 1990s, the cuckoo acquired new importance when, under the impetus of a report concerned primarily with English charities (Woodfield 1987: para 44), the *Law Reform (Miscellaneous Provisions) (Scotland) Act 1990* introduced, for the first time in Scotland, a statutory system for the regulation of "charities." The common law of public trusts was left in place, but the 1990 Act defined Scottish charities for regulatory purposes as bodies recognized by the Inland Revenue (now HM Revenue and Customs) as eligible for United Kingdom-level tax relief by virtue of their "charitable" purposes, that term being read in its technical meaning in English law (1990 Act: s1(7)).

The style of regulation introduced by the 1990 Act might be described as a pale version of English charity paternalism, drawing selectively on the English charities legislation of the time. The Lord Advocate was given powers of investigation and limited intervention, and an obligation was placed on charities to prepare accounts in set form and to produce them on request to members of the public, but no Charity Commission equivalent was created to oversee the system and monitor compliance arrangements for an "index" of Scottish charities that fell far short of providing a definitive public register of charities, and only very limited provision was made for the facilitation of charities (1990 Act: ss 4–7, 9 and 10).

Fundraising: Public Charitable Collections

The 1990 Act took as the basis of its regulatory regime the English definition of charitable, but there was already a different—and much broader—statutory definition in play for the purpose of regulating public charitable collections in Scotland. This broader definition, too, had originally been introduced into Scotland by way of UK-wide legislation (*House to House Collections Act 1939: s11(1)*), but by the time of the 1990 Act, it was incorporated in a public order statute for Scotland, the *Civic Government (Scotland) Act 1982*. Under the 1982 Act—the relevant provisions of which remain in force for the time being—a public charitable collection is one taken for "any chari-table, benevolent or philanthropic purposes whether or not they are chari-table within the meaning of any rule of law" (Civic Government Act 1982: s 119). The scope of the "charitable, benevolent or philanthropic" formula, which is still also used in fundraising legislation in England and Wales, has been the subject of surprisingly little judicial scrutiny, but is certainly wider than the technical definition of "charitable" on its own: Between them, "benevolent" and "philanthropic" may be regarded as including purposes which, though not technically charitable in the English sense, are nonetheless beneficial to the public, while "benevolent" may also be taken to cover pur-poses benefiting a specified individual or group of individuals (Lloyd 2007; Luxton 2001). The "charitable, benevolent or philanthropic" formula can be seen, therefore, as an attempt to escape the restrictions and technicalities of the English definition of charity so as to permit fundraising in support of a broad range of publicly beneficial activities, alongside fundraising for special-case individuals. Leaving aside the benefit to individuals, the range of purposes covered by the formula seems to be little different from the range of "public" purposes covered by the public benefit concept in Scots common law (*Anderson's Trustees v Scott* 1914 SC 942, 955 (Lord Skerrington)).

To summarize then, the 2005 Act was enacted against the background of a Scots common law of public trusts incorporating an inclusive definition of public benefit accompanied by an official tradition of facilitation rather than paternalistic control. The common law has, however, been overshad-owed by UK tax legislation which concedes special fiscal reliefs to volun-tary organizations in Scotland—as in England and Wales—by virtue of their "charitable" purposes in the comparatively restrictive sense of that term in English law. The 2005 Act replaced a system for the supervision of "Scottish charities"—defined, through the medium of the UK taxation system, by reference to the English definition of charity—which had been a much diluted version of its English counterpart. There had also long been in place statutory arrangements permitting, subject to certain controls, fund-raising by public charitable collection for the benefit of an inclusive range of "charitable, benevolent or philanthropic" purposes, a range which, while allowing for benefit to individuals, otherwise broadly equates to the "pub-lic" purposes of the common law.

THE 2005 ACT: POLICY AND KEY PROVISIONS

The now superseded regime of supervision for Scottish charities was sub-ject to criticism from its earliest days (SCVO 1994), and the 2005 Act was a response to many years of pressure for its reform. The criticisms were directed mainly at the English definition of charity, as outdated and insuffi-ciently inclusive, and at the 'paleness' of the Scottish regime by comparison with its more robust English equivalent. There were corresponding calls

for a redefinition of charity in terms of public benefit and for a strengthened regime of compliance more closely mirroring the English system and
incorporating, in particular, a dedicated Scottish regulator, a definitive register of charities, and improved arrangements for facilitation (Charity Law
Research Unit 2000b; Commission on the Future of the Voluntary Sector
in Scotland 1997; Ford 2006; Scottish Charity Law Review Commission
2001). The 2005 Act also responded to criticisms of the fundraising controls in Scotland, most notably that they were confined to the regulation
of public charitable *collections*. There was a corresponding call in this case
that new controls should be introduced to cover other, more sophisticated
forms of fundraising, again in imitation of provisions already enacted in
England and Wales (Charity Law Research Unit 2000a, 2000b).

A further criticism of the pre-2005 Act arrangements drew attention to
the discrepancy between the scope of the regime for Scottish charities under
the 1990 Act—defined by reference to the term "charity" in its technical
English meaning—and the scope of the fundraising controls under the 1982
Act—defined by reference to the broader "charitable, benevolent or philanthropic" formula (Charity Law Research Unit 2000b; Scottish Charity Law
Review Commission 2001). The discrepancy meant that funds raised under
the wider formula for a benevolent or philanthropic (as opposed to charitable) organization, while they were protected by the controls in the 1982
Act governing the processes of collection, received no continuing protection
once handed over to the recipient body, whereas sums collected for a Scottish
charity received the protection of the ongoing supervisory regime of the 1990
Act. If funds raised from the public for charities were worthy of an ongoing
regime, then why not also the sums collected for the non-charitable—but still
publicly beneficial—activities undertaken by voluntary organizations falling
within the terms "benevolent" or "philanthropic"?

Policy of the 2005 Act

This discrepancy—between the narrower definition of charity used as the
basis of the continuing supervisory regime under the 1990 Act and the
broader formula used in the fundraising legislation—can be seen, with
hindsight, to point forward to a more general problem with the policy-
making behind the 2005 Act. There is an incongruity between the 2005
Act's legislative concentration on a restrictively defined subsector of "charities" and the policies of the Scottish Executive intended to maximize the
contributions to the common good of the voluntary sector as a whole.
While the Executive recognized the importance of supporting voluntary
organizations generally, and in particular of maintaining public confidence in the wider sector by providing "the public with reassurance that
the money they donate is used for the purposes they intended" (Scottish
Executive 2005a: para 7), in the result the emphasis of the legislation is on
protecting the charity "brand" (Scottish Parliament 2005: para 3), and on

establishing "a satisfactory regulatory regime that will encourage public confidence in *charities*" (Scottish Parliament 2005: para 24). The discrepancy which existed under the pre-2005 Act arrangements has been carried forward: The 2005 Act permits fundraising for a wide range of voluntary organizations—with improved controls, certainly, on the processes of fundraising—but makes provision for a strengthened ongoing system of supervision, incorporating improved arrangements for facilitation only in respect of a more narrowly defined range of "charities."

What seems to have happened is that the Executive, followed in its turn by the Scottish Parliament, looked no further than the English definition of charity. The opportunity was missed to follow the logic of the policies declared for the wider voluntary sector by defining charities inclusively, so as to bring into continuing supervision the broader range of organizations—beyond "charities" in the restrictive English sense—entitled to fundraise in support of their contributions to the public good. Instead, charities are defined in the 2005 Act by reference to a charity test intended to be "very similar [to] and compatible with" the English definition, if not exactly the same (Scottish Parliament 2005: para 53).

The Charity Test

Part 1 of the 2005 Act sets up the new supervisory regime for charities in Scotland. Access to the new regime is by entry in the new Scottish Charity Register to be maintained by OSCR, with the principal criterion for entry in the register being satisfaction of the charity test (2005 Act: s 5). No organization is obliged to apply for entry, but a body which does not appear in the register will not be a charity (2005 Act: s106)—whether or not it would satisfy the charity test if it applied—and will neither be subject to the regulatory dimension of the regime nor entitled to its facilitative benefits. As mentioned, the test is modelled on the English definition of charity, and consists of two main elements: first, a requirement that all the purposes of an applicant body must be individually charitable in terms of a restrictive list of permitted "charitable purposes" derived ultimately, like the equivalent list in the revised English definition, from the preamble to Charitable Uses Act 1601,[13] and, second, a statutory sub-test of "public benefit" which seeks to capture the essence of the English case law on public benefit, including the requirement of benefit to the public as a whole or a section of it. Subsidiary elements of the test, each with its origins in English charity law, are intended to assure the non-profit distributing and non-party political character of charities and their independence from central government (2005 Act: ss 7, 8). As also mentioned, however, the test is not exactly the same as the English definition, and there is significant potential for divergence between the two. The Scottish legislators seem to have been caught between two instincts: to have a charity test which was essentially the same as the English definition, and so acceptable for the purposes of the United Kingdom-level tax relief provisions, and to have one sufficiently different to appear distinctively Scottish (Scottish Parliament 2005a: para 53).

The result is the kilted cuckoo: At first sight, the charity test is much the same as the English definition, but the kilting involves two differences, in particular, which have the potential to lead Scottish charitable status in a very different direction from its English equivalent (Ford 2008). First, OSCR, in applying the test, is under no obligation to follow the English case law on charity. Second, the Scottish public benefit sub-test is an "activities" test, whereas public benefit in the English definition is inherent in the notion of a charitable purpose, and requires OSCR to assess the public benefit arising (or likely to arise) from an applicant body's actual (or proposed) activities as well as examining the purposes declared in its constitution. Between them, these two aspects of the charity test confer discretion on OSCR in admitting bodies to charitable status which far exceeds the room for maneuver accorded to the Charity Commission under the English definition. In the result, the charity test and the revised English definition have proved much less compatible than intended, and it cannot be taken for granted that a body which satisfies the charity test also qualifies for charitable tax relief at UK level.

Charities Supervision

Once having met the charity test and been entered in the register, a charity is subject to supervision in broadly the same way as a charity registered with the Charity Commission in England and Wales. There is the same paternalistic emphasis on regulation, as opposed to facilitation. OSCR, the new regulator, is constituted along lines similar to the Charity Commission and in the same *parens patriae* tradition, with a remit to "encourage, facilitate and monitor compliance by charities" with the supervisory regime (2005 Act: s 5C). As explained, OSCR administers the charity test and maintains the definitive public register which is central to the system. Subject to limited exceptions, only bodies that are entered in the register may refer to themselves as charities, and OSCR has power to police improper use of the charity label. A charity may apply to be removed from the register, but on removal an "asset lock" will apply, by which the body will be under a continuing obligation, monitored by OSCR, to administer its pre-removal assets for its purposes as they stood immediately before removal (2005 Act: ss 13, 14, 18, 19, 28).

The Act spells out the duties of charity trustees, and in order to forestall or remedy the effects of misconduct by charity trustees, OSCR is given robust powers of investigation and short-term intervention, and it may apply to the Court of Session where longer-term intervention is required. By contrast with the common law, while a member of the public may 'whistle-blow' by drawing suspected misconduct to the attention of OSCR, members of the public have no powers of intervention of their own under the statute. Financial transparency is provided for through a system of accounting which involves the annual submission of accounts in standard form to OSCR and routine monitoring by the regulator.

While the emphasis of the supervisory regime is *regulatory*, it also has a significant *facilitative* dimension. First, bodies entered in the register have exclusive access to the charity brand because (in principle) only they may refer to themselves as "charities." Secondly, bodies entered in the register have exclusive access to informal procedures for reorganization administered by OSCR, which obviates the need, where the body is constituted as a public trust, for approval by the Court of Session. Thirdly, bodies entered in the register will (in due course) be entitled to adopt a new "dedicated" legal form for charities, the Scottish Charitable Incorporated Organisation (SCIO), which is to offer the benefits of legal personality and limitation of liability by a less cumbersome mechanism than incorporation as a company or industrial and provident society. These facilitative aspects of the regime may be regarded—along with the relief from local government taxation discussed below—as the advantages of charitable status, that is, the benefits conferred by the system in return for a body's submission, on registration, to its regulatory dimension.

Provision is also made for a Scottish Charity Appeals Panel, to which decisions of OSCR on application of the charity test and similar matters may be appealed initially, with a right of secondary appeal to the Court of Session. The aim is to provide a simple and accessible avenue of appeal from OSCR's decisions without the expense and delay inherent in conventional court proceedings.

Fundraising

Part 2 of the 2005 Act deals with controls on the processes of fundraising. Provision is made for modernization of the system of public collections, and new controls, based on provisions long in force in England and Wales, are introduced to regulate fundraising by professional fundraisers and commercial participators. These enhanced and additional controls are to apply to fundraising by and for the benefit of "benevolent bodies," that is, bodies established for "charitable, benevolent or philanthropic" purposes. Retention of the established "charitable, benevolent or philanthropic" formula ensures that the same broad range of voluntary organizations may raise funds from the public as under the pre-2005 Act legislation (2005 Act: ss 79–92). The effect of the new controls is to strengthen the framework within which fundraising for "benevolent bodies" may be carried out, taking account of modern fundraising techniques, but as under the previous legislation, there is no provision for ongoing supervision of the funds raised once in the hands of the recipient organization, other than by virtue of the separate supervisory system for charities under Part 1 of the Act.

Nonetheless, one innovative feature of the fundraising provision is its encouragement of a degree of self-regulation by the fundraising community. The Scottish Ministers are empowered to make regulations setting up, in effect, a compulsory code of practice for fundraisers prohibiting such conduct as unreasonable intrusion on the privacy of potential donors and the making of false or misleading representations (2005 Act: s 83). The intention is, however, that no regulations will be made on these matters unless a new scheme of self-regulation, set up by the fundraising community itself, turns out to be ineffective (Scottish Parliament 2005: para 82).

Consequential Amendments—Local Government Taxation

As explained, Part 1 of the 2005 Act includes a facilitative dimension represented by certain advantages available to a body on registration as a charity. Notably, because of the differences between the charity test and the English definition of charity, charitable relief from taxation at the UK level cannot be regarded as an automatic advantage of charitable status under the *Charities and Trustees Investment Act of 2005*. Part 4 of the Act, however, ensures that the advantage of relief from local taxation is directly related to registration with OSCR. It provides for a "consequential amendment" to the *Local Government (Financial Provisions etc) (Scotland) Act 1962*, to the effect that local authorities must grant automatic relief—currently to the extent of 80 percent—from the non-domestic rates leviable on premises occupied by a "charity," in the sense of a body registered with OSCR. Under the pre-2005 Act arrangements, charity in this context had the same meaning as under UK-level tax legislation.

The effect of the amendment is to break the link between charitable tax relief at the UK and local government levels. There is, however, a secondary relieving provision under the 1962 Act which remains unaffected. Local authorities have power, at discretion, to grant relief from non-domestic rates, in whole or in part, to any nonprofit organization "whose main objects are charitable or otherwise philanthropic or religious or concerned with education, social welfare, science, literature or the fine arts" (1962 Act: s 4(5)(b)). The discretion may be used to 'top up' to 100 percent automatic relief for charities, in the sense of the 2005 Act, or to grant relief, at whatever rate the relevant authority considers appropriate, to a broad range of voluntary organizations which are not charities, but are engaged nonetheless in activities with an identifiable public benefit dimension.

CRITIQUE OF THE 2005 ACT

It was suggested earlier in the chapter that the system of charities supervision introduced by the 2005 Act is out of alignment with the policies for the voluntary sector in Scotland announced, first, by the Scottish Executive and then adopted and developed by the Scottish Government as part of its broader strategy for "an innovative, sustainable and inclusive third sector," embracing nonprofit and for-profit organizations alike and contributing to both "high quality public services and increased economic growth" (Scottish Government 2007a: Ch. 10). The watchwords of these policies are facilitation, partnership, and enterprise. The Scottish Government in particular has committed itself to a minimization of unnecessary bureaucracy and a reduction in the number of quangos, in favor of social and economic enterprise at the local and community level (Cabinet Secretary for Finance and Sustainable Growth 2007a; 2007b). The 2005 Act, however, following a paternalistic model of charities supervision borrowed from England and Wales, has concentrated supervisory attention on the charities subsector and set up a system of supervision dominated by a new quango, OSCR.

The remainder of the chapter will examine those aspects of the new Scottish system most conspicuously out of alignment with the policies of the devolved administrations, and it will suggest how amendments to the 2005 Act drawing on the Scots common law of public trusts might yet give effect to those policies in a way true to Scotland's own legal traditions. The critique of the 2005 Act focuses on three main issues: the defects of the charity test, the paternalistic style of supervision, and the treatment of relief from local taxation.

The Charity Test—Legislative Concentration on "Charities"

The Scottish Executive's policy, adopted by the Scottish Government, of encouraging the contribution of the voluntary sector at large to the "common good of Scotland" (Scottish Executive 2005b: 2) argues for a system facilitating voluntary organizations generally in doing public good. Legislating for such a system could be brought within the competence of the devolved Scottish legislature by its defining charity sufficiently broadly to cover "voluntary organizations" in the sense identified by the Executive as non-profit-distributing bodies "run for the benefit of others or for the community" (Scottish Executive 2004b: para 3.1). This would be to provide for a system of supervision of "common good-doing" voluntary organizations which would take its place as part of the legislative provision for the broader third sector in Scotland alongside the systems operating at the UK level for the supervision of profit-distributing social enterprises such as cooperatives and community interest companies.

Seen from this perspective, the charity test selects too restricted a range of voluntary organizations for inclusion in the charities system. Had the English definition of charity been retained as the principal criterion for entry into the new Scottish system, as it was under the superseded system for "Scottish charities," the conveniences of harmonization with the UK tax system would also have been retained. As it is, the charity test has fallen between two stools: It has all the disadvantages of difference from the English definition, yet misses the opportunity to extend the scope of the supervisory regime across the broad range of common good-doing organizations.

That failure brings with it two specific disadvantages. First, common good-doing organizations that are not eligible to become charities yet are free to raise funds from the public under Part 2 of the 2005 Act as benevolent or philanthropic organizations will not be subject to the ongoing regime of supervision under Part 1 of the Act. From the point of view of donors, this is a significant regulatory deficit in the Act. They cannot contribute to the common good-doing voluntary organizations of their choice which do not qualify for registration under the charity test with the same confidence as to organizations which have passed the test and been entered in the register. It is suggested, however, that the regulatory deficit could be all but removed by substituting the inclusive public benefit concept of the common law for the charity test. The common law concept would offer a ready-made alternative to the charity test that would capture the broad range of voluntary organizations identified by the Executive as contributing to the public good and permitted, under the "charitable, benevolent or philanthropic" formula of Part 2 of the Act, to raise funds from the public.

The second disadvantage is that the facilitative benefits of charitable status are denied to those same common good-doing voluntary organizations that do not qualify for registration as charities. From the point of view of the organizations involved, this is a significant facilitative deficit in the Act. Here again, the deficit could be readily removed by replacing the charity test with the common law concept of public benefit as the gateway criterion for entry in the charities' register. In other words, the common law concept would be a better criterion than the charity test for selecting those voluntary organizations that do sufficient public good to merit the facilitative advantages of charitable status under the Act—with the exception, to be discussed below, of relief from local government taxation.

The Charity Test—Access to the Charity Brand

As we have seen, the advantages of charitable status under Part 1 of the Act are access to the charity brand, the availability of informal procedures for reorganization, and the possibility of adopting the new dedicated legal form for charities, the SCIO. It does not seem controversial to suggest that the informal reorganization procedures and access to the SCIO should be extended to the wider range of voluntary organizations covered by the common law concept of public benefit. The question of access to the charity brand is more difficult.

The assumption behind the concentration on charities in the 2005 Act is that the label "charity" causes a particularly favorable response from the public to an appeal for donations. This is the main policy reason, though not the only one, for subjecting charities, but not benevolent or philanthropic organizations, to a regime of ongoing supervision. The rationale is that a person who is attracted to donate by the special magic of the word "charity" should have his or her contribution protected on an ongoing basis (Deputy Minister of Communities 2005a). One of the difficulties in seeking to protect the charity brand, however, is that it is not easy to distinguish cause and effect in this situation. If a person who contributes to a charity knows that the recipient body is subject to continuing supervision, this may be one motive for preferring to contribute to the charity rather than to a benevolent or philanthropic organization doing broadly similar work.

In any event, one of the principal functions of the charity test in the 2005 Act is to select the range of causes to which the public may contribute in the knowledge that their donations will be protected on an ongoing basis. The legislative intention behind the provisions of the test was that they should enable OSCR to reflect "public expectations of what a charity is" and "the public perception [in Scotland] of what a charity should be" (Minister for Communities 2005). In other words, the intention was that only those bodies that the public think ought to be charities should be entitled to use the charity brand. It is, however, a further difficulty in legislating to protect the charity label that there can be considerable disagreement about what ought and what ought not to be charitable. While a link can be identified between the public's willingness to contribute to charities and the fact that charities provide public benefit, it may well be impossible to devise a test or definition of charity that can be applied with universal approval in every case because there must always be an element of subjectivity in any person's assessment of what amounts to public benefit (Barrie 2005).

Against this background, the 2005 Act follows the English lead of imposing a restrictive official view of what should be regarded as charitable. The effect of the charity test is that OSCR, by its application of the test at registration, decides on behalf of the public which causes are to receive the special protection of ongoing supervision. This is to steer members of the public toward a particular range of causes officially entitled to the label "charity," rather than to allow them to decide for themselves which public benefit causes to contribute to, in the knowledge that their contributions will all be subject to ongoing protection. It is to remove the initiative from members of the public themselves as to which types of public benefit activity they wish to support, and it is inconsistent with the Scottish Government's aim of stimulating social enterprise at local and community level, with a reduced involvement on the part of the state.

Here again, substitution of the common law concept of public benefit for the charity test would offer an alternative approach that is more consistent with both the Scottish Government's policies and the original legislative intention behind the test. Access to the charity brand would be extended (on registration) to all bodies falling within the inclusive scope of the common law concept: all would be subject to the ongoing regime for charities, and the charity label would serve simply as a 'kite mark' indicating that a body entitled to use it was subject to ongoing supervision. The effect would be that members of the public could contribute to whatever public benefit causes they choose from the full range available, knowing that their contributions would receive ongoing protection.

The common law concept would be inclusive but would ensure, nonetheless, through its public policy 'fail-safe,' that only organizations conferring real benefit on the public or a section of the public could take advantage of the charity label. The inclusivity of the concept—its accommodation of differing strands of opinion—would mean inevitably that some causes would not be universally approved of but would recognize that the public's perception of what a charity should be is not a monolith. Members of the public would be under no obligation to contribute to a cause that they did not approve, but they would know that whatever public benefit cause they did contribute to would be subject, as a "charity," to ongoing supervision. For instance, no one would be under an obligation to contribute to a fee-charging school because it was labelled a charity, but anyone who did so, perhaps an alumnus, would have the protection of the ongoing regime.

The Charity Test—Resource-Intensive Administration

The charity test is based on the English definition but is different from it. Two of its distinctive features in particular, as already highlighted, make it difficult and expensive to administer. It has abandoned the resource of the accumulated case law of the English definition, and it incorporates an "activities" sub-test. In the few years since the new system became operational, OSCR has issued initial guidance on the test and then revised guidance, conducting a full public consultation on each occasion in advance of publication. It has proceeded with painstaking care in its 'rolling review' of the register, which requires that each of the bodies transferred to the register from the old "Scottish charities" system, as well as those entered in the register since the start of the new regime, is examined periodically for its conformity with the charity test (OSCR 2008b, 2007). Even so, the guidance remains very general. This is inevitable in the absence of the comparative certainty offered by an established case law. It will take years for OSCR's decisions on the test to build up into an equivalent, and there is in any case a limit to the value of OSCR's past decisions as precedents because, in applying the "activities" element of the test, OSCR is obliged to operate on a case by case basis, examining each set of activities on its own merits The result so far has been resource intensive application of the test by OSCR and uncertainty on the part of both applicants for registration and candidates for review as to how they are likely to fare under the test.

This seems to run counter to the Scottish Government's hopes for the minimization of bureaucracy. Once again, the Scottish public benefit concept would provide an eminently workable alternative to the charity test. It is simple in concept, comes with an existing case law, and avoids the uncertainties inherent in an activities test.

Paternalistic Supervision

A future reform of the 2005 Act regime might look to the common law for no more than its concept of public benefit as a substitute for the charity test. There is, however, another aspect of the regime which might be usefully reviewed in the light of both the policies of the Scottish Government and the traditions of the common law. The importance of the public's financial contribution to public benefit activity is beyond question, and there is no doubt that it justifies the provision by the state of a system of supervision geared to reassuring members of the public that "the money they donate is used for the purposes they intended" (Scottish Executive 2005a: 7). The message of the common law's treatment of public trusts, however, is that there is a workable alternative to the paternalistic, regulator-dominated supervision of the English charities system. It may be impossible to do away with OSCR altogether, but the Scottish Government's aspiration of minimizing bureaucracy and reducing the prominence of quangos in Scottish public life argues in favor of at least reducing its role. As it is, under Part 1 of the 2005 Act, OSCR's functions as a regulator extend to those of registrar, facilitator, investigator, and intervener. Members of the public have little or no standing under the Act to pursue their own interests, whether as contributors, potential beneficiaries, users of public services, or in any other capacity.

An alternative approach suggested by the common law would be to reduce OSCR's role as investigator and intervener to one of default and to revive the *actio popularis* in modern form. It could be declared expressly in amending legislation that the common law right of action by "any person interested" in the performance of public purposes or objects should be available, not only to beneficiaries and users, but also to donors and to umbrella organizations such as SCVO. The involvement of umbrella bodies would introduce an element of self-regulation into the system, along the lines of the stimulus to self-regulation in the field of fundraising contained in Part 2 of the Act. It would be in the interests of the member organizations of SCVO, and of any other bodies representing voluntary organizations engaged in public benefit activity, that their fellow members were administered correctly, and the representative bodies could become, in effect, the guardians of public confidence in the "public benefit" community as a whole. The Scottish Charity Appeals Panel could be recast as a Scottish

Charity Tribunal and have added to its existing appeal responsibilities the functions of an informal first-instance forum of enforcement. In this capacity, it would consider complaints against charity trustees—"actions of the people" raised by members of the public, whether as beneficiaries, users of services or donors, and by umbrella bodies.

While retaining a default power to raise proceedings before the tribunal, similar to the Lord Advocate's power at common law to raise an action of enforcement in the public interest, OSCR's role would become principally one of registrar and facilitator. As registrar its functions would include the provision of information to the public and the gathering of certified accounts for public inspection (a role similar to that of the Registrar of Companies). The public could then obtain the information they needed to decide which organizations to support with their donations and could then follow through the application of funds, if necessary, by means of a complaint to the tribunal.

An amendment of the system along these lines would at least minimize the regulatory involvement of OSCR in the system and would be consistent with the Scottish Government's general policy of stimulating enterprise at a community level by transferring the principal responsibility for maintaining public confidence in "charities"—defined, of course, in terms of the inclusive public benefit concept—to the voluntary sector itself. A sector responsible for its own good name in this way might be a more equal partner with government in the state–sector compact to work for the "wider public good" (Scottish Executive and SCVO 2003: 2) than one subject to the tutelage of a paternalistic regulator in the *parens patriae* tradition.

Relief from Local Taxation

By virtue of the 2005 Act, automatic relief from local taxation—though not, as we have seen, from UK-level taxation—is one of the facilitative advantages of registration as a charity with OSCR. This means in practice that, because of the wide discretion available to OSCR in the application of the charity test, the incidence of charitable tax relief at local level is decided in large part by OSCR, an unelected quango whose members are appointed by the Scottish Ministers. This arrangement seems to be at odds with the Scottish Government's policy of passing greater autonomy to local councils in the allocation of resources. The logic of the policy requires that local authorities be given full discretion as to what reliefs from local taxation, if any, should be conceded to charities. As it is, local authorities already have full discretion in respect of a wide range of voluntary organizations that are not charities but that have a clear public benefit dimension, and the change proposed would simply extend this full discretion to charities (i.e., it would remove the current automatic 80 percent relief from non-domestic rates for charities, making relief fully discretionary). The change would ensure that the incidence of charitable relief from local taxation would be decided entirely at a local level by the elected representatives of the relevant community. Fee-charging schools, for example, would receive relief according to the elected representatives' assessment of their value to the local community.

CONCLUSION

Scotland has a distinctive legal system whose continued existence was guaranteed by the Treaty of Union with England of 1707. Scotland's pre-treaty legislature was, however, absorbed into the Parliament of the Union, and Scotland has only recently re-acquired a legislature of its own under the devolution settlement of 1998, which created a devolved Scottish Parliament and corresponding devolved administration. In the three centuries between the Union and devolution, Scotland's distinctive legal traditions have frequently come under threat from the anglicizing influence of the Union Parliament, the introduction of the English charity cuckoo into the Scottish legal nest, through the medium of UK tax legislation, offering one long-standing example.

It might have been thought that the new Scottish Parliament would legislate, whenever possible, in a way sensitive to Scotland's own legal traditions, in particular in areas where in practice differing circumstances north and south of the Border justify distinctive policy-making for Scotland. Regulation of the third sector is one such area. Scotland is a small country with a correspondingly small third sector, and policies for the sector suitable for the larger partner to the Union may not necessarily be suitable for the smaller one. In the years since devolution, the devolved administrations have in fact developed policies for the third sector adapted to Scottish conditions, but the principal legislative intervention in the area by the devolved Parliament, the 2005 Act, is out of alignment with those policies.

Instead of giving legislative effect to the policies by drawing on Scotland's own legal traditions, as it might have done, the Parliament has sought in the 2005 Act to adapt the English model of charities supervision for Scotland with unsatisfactory results. In particular, there is a legislative focus on "charities," defined by reference to a restrictive charity test based on the English definition of charity, which leaves out of account those voluntary organizations engaged in public benefit activity—common good-doing voluntary organizations—that do not meet the charity test but that should nonetheless be supervised, and above all facilitated, in their efforts to contribute to the wider public good of Scotland. It is also unsatisfactory, against the background of policies expressed in the language of state-sector partnership and the encouragement of enterprise at the local and community level, that the supervisory regime for charities introduced by the Act is heavily paternalistic in character, again in deference to the English model.

The chapter has sought to establish that, by comparatively simple amendments to the 2005 Act, drawing on the Scots common law of public trusts, the new system for the supervision of charities in Scotland could be brought into closer alignment with the policies developed for the third sector since devolution. First, the charity test would be replaced by the public benefit concept of the common law. Second, the functions of the Scottish charity regulator, OSCR, would be reduced so as to leave it with the roles of registrar and facilitator. The main burden of policing and enforcing the proper administration of public benefit organizations would pass to the general public and to the umbrella organizations of the voluntary sector, with power to them to raise enforcement proceedings, based on the *actio popularis* of the common law, before an informal Scottish Charity Tribunal.

The effect of the first of these amendments would be to extend the existing system of charities supervision to an inclusive range of common good-doing voluntary organizations. The system would become a system of regulation and facilitation for nonprofit organizations concerned with public benefit activity in a broad sense, and it would be complementary, within the context of the wider third sector, to the existing systems for the supervision of for-profit third sector organizations. A wide range of public benefit organizations would be supervised under the title of "charities": the Scottish public could contribute to those of their choice in the knowledge that all of them—and not merely a restricted subsector—would be subject to continuing supervision, and OSCR's facilitative powers could be deployed across the same wide range. This would give fuller effect to the policies of passing the initiative for social enterprise to local and community levels and of assisting the voluntary sector as a whole to maximize its contribution to the common good of Scotland.

The effect of the second set of amendments would be to 'de-paternalize' the system. OSCR's role as registrar would be much simplified by replacement of the charity test with the straightforward and inclusive public benefit concept, freeing it up to enhance its provision of information to the public. Members of the public, and the voluntary sector itself through its representative organizations, would acquire responsibility for monitoring and enforcing the correct administration of charities. It would be for the sector itself to win and retain the public's confidence, and to prove itself a worthy partner with government in the provision of public services. This would be to give fuller effect to the policies of minimizing bureaucracy and reducing, where possible, the involvement of quangos in social and economic enterprise, in favor of direct local and community engagement.

As a complement to these amendments, a change could also be made to the existing arrangements for charitable tax relief at a local government level: Complete discretion as to relief could be given to local authorities in implementation of the policy of passing decision-making on resource allocation to the local level where possible. This would complete a package of amendments by which the Scottish Parliament could rescue its credentials, in the area of third sector regulation at least, as a devolved legislature willing to legislate for the distinctive needs of Scotland in a way consistent with the country's own distinctive legal traditions. The effect of the amendments suggested would be to eject the English charity cuckoo from the Scottish legal nest so far as the competence of the devolved Parliament permits. For better or worse, however, the cuckoo would remain significant in Scotland for the purposes of charitable tax relief at UK level.

NOTES

1. Treaty of Union of the Two Kingdoms of Scotland and England, Arts 18 and 19. It is now normal to refer to "England and Wales," which together form a single legal jurisdiction. For convenience the term "English" is used hereafter to refer to the law and legal terminology of the combined jurisdiction. The United Kingdom also incorporates Northern Ireland, a separate jurisdiction with a legal system based on the system for England and Wales.
2. The cuckoo lays its eggs in the nests of other, smaller birds, leaving the "host" birds to hatch and feed the cuckoo's young at the expense of their own.
3. Hereafter the "2005 Act," or "the Act," as the context requires. Part 1 of the Act deals with the supervision of charities, Part 2 with fundraising, and Part 3 with trustee investment powers. Part 3 applies to all Scottish trusts, public and private, and has no special application to trusts which are charities under Part 1 of the Act.
4. Some minor amendments have already been enacted in the Public Services Reform (Scotland) Act 2010, ss 120–128. See also OSCR, *Annual Report and Accounts 2009–10*.
5. In Scotland, the "local authority," or unit of local government, is the council: Local Government, etc (Scotland) Act 1994. There are 32 local councils in Scotland, ranging from the urban such as City of Edinburgh Council to the mainly rural such as Angus Council.
6. For examples from the case law of the time, see *Glasgow Royal Infirmary v Magistrates of Glasgow* (1888) 15 R 264 (provision of clothing for convalescent fever patients); *Morton's Trustees v Aged Christian Friend Society of Scotland* (1899) 2 F 82 (old age pensions); *Trustees of Falkirk Certified Industrial School v Ferguson Bequest Fund* (1899) 1 F 1175 (school for destitute children); *Robertson's Trustees, Petitioners* 1948 SC 1 (convalescent rest home).
7. See Lord President Cooper's description of poverty as "obsolescent:" *Salvesen's Trustees v Wye* 1954 SC 440 at 447. For the impact of the National Health Service, see *East Kilbride District Nursing Association, Petitioners* 1951 SC 64.
8. The majority of charities in Scotland (56 percent) are constituted as unincorporated associations, and a further 18 percent are formed as companies; 18 percent are constituted as trusts (see OSCR 2008a). In principle, all organizations constituted in Scotland with a view to being registered as charities by OSCR will be either public trusts or analogous associations with public objects at common law because the charity test administered by OSCR incorporates as part of its "public benefit" element a requirement of benefit to the public or a section of the public. The same is true in principle

of organizations constituted with a view to qualifying for charitable tax relief at the UK level because the English definition of charity incorporates a similar requirement.

9. The English definition has been rationalized and adjusted by the Charities Act 2006, ss 1–3 and 5. The pre-rationalization definition required, first, that a purpose, to be charitable, should fall within the "spirit and intendment" of the preamble to the 1601 Act, which listed a variety of charitable "uses;" and, secondly, that it should be of a "public character" in accordance with public benefit criteria—including the requirement of benefit to the public or a section of it—developed in the case law (Warburton, Morris, & Riddle 2003: para 1–008). The "uses" of the preamble, extended by the courts principally by a process of analogizing, were famously rationalized by Lord Macnaghten into four "heads" of charity (*Special Commissioners for the Purposes of Income Tax v Pemsel* [1891] AC 531 at 583). The 2006 Act further rationalizes Lord Macnaghten's classification into thirteen "descriptions of purposes." the thirteenth allowing for the addition over time of new types of purposes provided they are analogous to or "within the spirit" of existing charitable purposes. The new classification is to be read in the light of the old case law. The public benefit element of the definition remains entirely a function of the case law, subject to removal of a (rebuttable) presumption in favor of the public character of purposes falling within the first three of Lord Macnaghten's "heads." The net result is that there are still restrictions—set by the extended scope of the 1601 preamble—on what types of purpose of a public character may be accepted as charitable.

10. On the principle of "cy-près" or "approximation" (*Trustees of Carnegie Park Orphanage, Petitioners* (1890) 19 R 605 at 608 per Lord McLaren). For a description of the court's recent practice, see *Mining Institute of Scotland Benevolent Fund Trustees, Petitioners* 1994 SLT 785 at 786H per Lord President Hope, and for a recent example, see *Trustees of the R S Macdonald Charitable Trust, Petitioners* [2008] CSOH 116.

11. *Edinburgh Young Women's Christian Institute, Petitioners* (1893) 20 R 894: Here the court declined to grant authority for an amalgamation of two voluntary associations with similar public objects on the view that, in the absence of an objector, the court had no jurisdiction and its authority was in any case unnecessary. Lord McLaren (at 895) drew attention to the different position in England and Wales, where the authority of the Chancery Division of the High Court would have been required. See also *Leven Penny Savings Bank, Petitioners* 1948 S0 147.

12. For recent cases, see *Tod's Trustees, Petitioners* 1999 SLT 308; *Mohammed Shariff and Another, Petitioners* 2000 SLT 294; *Inverclyde Council v Dunlop* 2005 SLT 967; and *Trustees of the R S Macdonald Charitable Trust, Petitioners* 2008 CSOH 116.

13. See Charities and Trustees Investment (Scotland) Act (2005: s 7(1) and (2).

REFERENCES

Barrie, S. (2005). Remarks to the Communities Committee. *Official Report*. Edinburgh: Scottish Parliament, Communities Committee, 2 February 2005: Col 1717.

Cabinet Secretary for Finance and Sustainable Growth. (2007a) *Official Report*. Edinburgh: Scottish Parliament, Plenary Session, 26 September 2007: Col 2071.

Cabinet Secretary for Finance and Sustainable Growth. (2007b). *Official Report.* Edinburgh: Scottish Parliament, Plenary Session, 14 November 2007: Col 3326.

Charity Commission. (2008). *Annual Report 2007–08.* London: H. M. Stationery Office.

Charity Law Research Unit, University of Dundee. (2000a). *Public Charitable Collections,* Edinburgh: Scottish Executive.

Charity Law Research Unit, University of Dundee. (2000b). *Scottish Charity Legislation: An evaluation.* Edinburgh: Scottish Executive.

Commission on the Future of the Voluntary Sector in Scotland. (1997). *Head and Heart.* Edinburgh: SCVO.

Cross, S. and Ford, P. (2006) . *Greens Annotated Statutes: The Charities and Trustee Investment (Scotland) Act 2005.* Edinburgh: Thomson/W Green.

Deputy Minister for Communities. (2005a). *Official Report.* Edinburgh: Scottish Parliament, Plenary Session, 9 June 2005: Col 17821.

Deputy Minister for Communities. (2005b). *Official Report.* Edinburgh: Scottish Parliament, Communities Committee, 2 February 2005: Col 1705.

Finance Secretary. (2007). *Local Government Finance Settlement 2008–2011, Official Report.* Edinburgh: Scottish Parliament, 13 December 2007: Col 4465.

Ford, P. (2008). "A statute of unintended consequences? The impact of the Charities and Trustee Investment (Scotland) Act 2005 on non-Scottish charities operating in Scotland." *Northern Ireland Legal Quarterly,* 59: 201–222.

Ford, P. (2006). "Supervising charities: A Scottish-civilian alternative", *Edinburgh Law Review,* 10: 352–85.

Ford, P. (2000). "Public benefit versus charity: A Scottish perspective." In C. Mitchell and S. R. Moody (eds.), *Foundations of Charity.* Oxford: Hart Publishing.

Ford, P. (1999). "Scottish charity law reform: An agenda for coherence." *Charity Law & Practice Review,* 5: 187–206.

House of Commons, Public Administration Select Committee. (2008). *Public Services and the Third Sector : Rhetoric and reality.* London: The Stationery Office.

Lloyd, S. (ed.) .(2007). *Charities—The New Law 2006: A practical guide to the Charities Acts.* Bristol: Jordans.

Luxton, P. (2001). *The Law of Charities.* Oxford: Oxford University Press.

McLaren, J. (1894). *The Law of Wills and Succession* (3rd ed). . Edinburgh: Bell and Bradfute/Sweet & Maxwell.

Minister for Communities. (2005). *Official Report.* Edinburgh: Scottish Parliament, Plenary Session Committee, 9 March 2005: Col 15908.

Office for National Statistics. (2002). *Census 2001,* London: H. M. Stationery Office.

Office of the Scottish Charity Regulator (OSCR). (2008a). *Scottish Charities.* Edinburgh: OSCR.

Office of the Scottish Charity Regulator (OSCR). (2008b). *Meeting the Charity Test: Guidance for applicants and for existing charities.* Edinburgh: OSCR.

Office of the Scottish Charity Regulator (OSCR). (2007). *Rolling Review: Pilot study report.* Edinburgh: OSCR.

Reichardt, O., Kane, D., Pratten, B. and Wilding, K. (2008). *The UK Civil Society Almanac 2008.* London: National Council for Voluntary Organisations.

Ross, Lord and others. (1989). "Trusts, trustees and judicial factors." *The Laws of Scotland: Stair Memorial Encyclopaedia,* vol. 24. Edinburgh: Law Society of Scotland/Butterworths.

Scottish Charity Law Review Commission. (2001). *Charity Scotland.* Edinburgh: Scottish Executive.

Scottish Council for Voluntary Organisations (SCVO). (2007a). *Scottish Voluntary Sector Statistics.* Edinburgh: SCVO.

Scottish Council of Voluntary Organisations (SCVO). (2007b). *Third Sector Summit Research Briefing.* Edinburgh: SCVO.
Scottish Council of Voluntary Organisations (SCVO). (1994). *Faith and Hope in Charity?* Edinburgh: SCVO.
Scottish Executive. (2005a). *A Vision for the Voluntary Sector—The next phase of our relationship.* Edinburgh: Scottish Executive.
Scottish Executive. (2005b). *Funding Review: Joint principles and action plan.* Edinburgh: Scottish Executive.
Scottish Executive. (2004a). *Draft Charities and Trustee Investment (Scotland) Bill: Consultation paper.* Edinburgh: Scottish Executive.
Scottish Executive. (2004b). *Scottish Compact Implementation Strategy 2003–2006.* Edinburgh: Scottish Executive.
Scottish Executive. (2004c). *Volunteering Strategy.* Edinburgh: Scottish Executive.
Scottish Executive and SCVO. (2003). *The Scottish Compact.* Edinburgh: Scottish Executive.
Scottish Government. (2008). "Support Package for Third Sector." Online. Available at <http://www.scotland.gov.uk/News/Releases/2008/03/06115639> (accessed 6 March 2008).
Scottish Government. (2007a). *Scottish Budget Spending Review 2007.* Online. Available at <http://www.scotland.gov.uk/Publications/2007/11/13092240/11> (accessed 6 March 2008).
Scottish Government. (2007b). *The Government Economic Strategy.* Edinburgh: Scottish Government.
Scottish Government and Convention of Scottish Local Authorities. (2007). *Concordat between the Scottish Government and the Convention of Scottish Local Authorities.* Edinburgh: Scottish Government.
Scottish Parliament. (2005). *Policy Memorandum issued with the Charities and Trustee Investment (Scotland) Bill (SP Bill 32).* Edinburgh, Scottish Parliament.
Sellar, W.D.H. (1991). "A historical perspective." In S. Styles (ed.), *The Scottish Legal Tradition.* Edinburgh: The Saltire Society/The Stair Society.
Warburton, J., Morris, D. and Riddle, N. F. (2003). *Tudor on Charities*, London: Sweet & Maxwell.
Wilson, W. A. and Duncan, A. G. M. (1995). *Trusts, Trustees and Executors*, (2nd ed.). Edinburgh: Greens/Sweet & Maxwell.
Woodfield, P. (1987). *Efficiency Scrutiny of the Supervision of Charities.* London: Home Office and H M Treasury.

LIST OF CASES

Aitken's Trustee v Aitken 1927 SC 374.
Anderson's Trustees v Scott 1914 SC 942.
Andrews v Ewart's Trustees 1886 SC 69.
D & J Nicol v Dundee Harbour Trustees 1915 SC (HL) 7.
Davidson's Trustees v Arnott 1951 SC 42.
East Kilbride District Nursing Association, Petitioners 1951 SC 64.
Edinburgh Young Women's Christian Institute, Petitioners (1893) 20 R 894.
Glasgow Royal Infirmary v Magistrates of Glasgow (1888) 15 R 264.
Inland Revenue v City of Glasgow Police Athletic Association [1952] AC 380.
Inverclyde Council v Dunlop 2005 SLT 967.
Leven Penny Savings Bank, Petitioners 1948 SC 147.
Mining Institute of Scotland Benevolent Fund Trustees, Petitioners 1994 SLT 785.

Mitchell v Burness (1878) 5 R 954.
Mohammed Shariff and Another, Petitioners 2000 SLT 294.
Morton's Trustees v Aged Christian Friend Society of Scotland (1899) 2 F 82.
Robertson's Trustees, Petitioners 1948 SC 1.
Salvesen's Trustees v Wye 1954 SC 440.
Special Commissioners for the Purpose of Income Tax v Pemsel [1891] 2 AC 531.
Tod's Trustees, Petitioners 1999 SLT 308.
Trustees of Carnegie Park Orphanage, Petitioners (1890) 19 R 605.
Trustees of Falkirk Certified Industrial School v Ferguson Bequest Fund (1899) 1 F 1175.
Trustees of the R S Macdonald Charitable Trust, Petitioners [(2008] CSOH 116.
Wink's Executors v Tallent 1947 SC 470.

4 Between Relational Governance and Regulation of the Third Sector

The Irish Case

Gemma Donnelly-Cox and Siobhan McGee

INTRODUCTION

The impetus for this chapter is the interesting history of statutory–nonprofit relations in Ireland. Core social, education, and health services have historically and to date been delivered by nonprofit organizations and funded by the state. The nature of the relationships underpinning service delivery has variously been described as informal, fragmented, *ad hoc*, heavily dependent on personal relationships, and flexible. Concern with the management and regulation of the relationship has long been expressed by nonprofits and by the various state agencies and government departments interacting with these organizations. More recently, external factors have combined with public interest in accountability and transparency of nonprofit fundraising, and both state and nonprofit concerns about poor regulation to drive the development of a regulatory framework for Irish charities.

The aim of this chapter is to critically examine evolving statutory–nonprofit relations through a review of the relationships that exist between the state and nonprofit organizations and an examination of the development of a regulatory framework for these organizations. The discussion is illustrated with a case study of the development of a Statement of Guiding Principles for Fundraising (Irish Charities Tax Research Ltd. 2008). The *Charities Act* 2009 (enacted in March 2009) has called for implementation of agreed Codes of Good Practice as a mechanism for regulation of the operational and administrative aspects of fundraising and has noted that the Statement is a significant advance to this end.

The chapter is underpinned by an institutional analysis that explores the various forces that have shaped nonprofit–state relations in Ireland. It concludes with consideration of an emerging argument for the enhancement of representative structures to support partnership relations between state and sector. It is argued that representative structures will support a balance between regulation and relational governance, in the interests of both sector and state. However, there is a significant gap between current practice and the proposed model, especially in light of the impact of the financial crisis in Ireland.

A SHORT HISTORY OF SECTOR–STATE RELATIONS

While nonprofit organizations have played an important role in the development of Ireland's socio-economic infrastructure since the establishment of the state and a significant role in both the economy and society, the history of sector–state relations illustrates a variety of patterns of unclear and informal interrelationships. Previous examinations of sector–state relations in Ireland have concluded that there is a need for more clearly defined sector–state relationships (see O'Ferrall 2000). For example, Donoghue (2002) studied relationships between small voluntary organizations and the former Eastern Health Board. She found that, despite a long history of statutory–voluntary relationships in the health sector, they were characterized by an absence of formal reporting procedures, lack of guiding policy, and lack of basic procedures on standards of accountability and criteria for funding. While the key decision makers were known to voluntary sector actors, little was known about how decisions were made or the criteria for selecting partner organizations. Communications with the Health Board tended to be *ad hoc* and intermittent. Formal reporting procedures were found to consist of submission of audited accounts and annual reports. Apart from audited accounts, there were few procedures in place for monitoring of standards and accountability. Four years later, when the state's Comptroller and Auditor General reviewed the relationship between the Health Service Executive and voluntary organizations in the domain of social care, many of the same concerns were raised (Government of Ireland 2005).

Service delivery, how it is resourced, and the mechanisms for its regulation form a substantial element of ongoing sector–state relations. For example, the National Economic and Social Council (NESC) has argued for more formally defined sector–state relations, concluding that, "to *maximize the contribution* of voluntary and community organizations" (italics added), attention must be paid to the relationship between sector and state (NESC 2005: 230). A productive relationship would be characterized by "effective and accountable service provision, where appropriate, transparent and efficient funding arrangements, clear but not burdensome regulation and a coherent policy framework" (NESC 2005: 230).

While the delivery of social services is a core element of sector activity and of the sector–state relationship, if we are to gain a broader understanding of the scope of sector–state relations and their evolution over time, we need to examine the many dimensions of the relationship. In their examination of wider changes in government, public governance, and civic life, Boyle and Butler (2003) proposed a framework that considers the roles of service delivery, regulation, funding, and policy. To these, we add social partnership in Ireland and the place of the nonprofit sector within it. In the last decade, the community and voluntary sector has become engaged in the broader and more formalized social partnership arrangements in Ireland. Partnership talks have formed the basis for planning the future socio-economic development of the nation, and they have set sector–state relations in the broader societal context of state relations with business, agricultural, and labor interests. We review these various dimensions of the relationship and then look in closer detail at the development of a voluntary code for fundraising practice. In the next section, we look at the policy environment and the gradual evolution of a regulatory framework.

THE POLICY ENVIRONMENT

After more than a decade of promises from the state that its relationship with the voluntary sector would be formally recognized within the policy framework, the White Paper *Supporting Voluntary Activity* was published (Department of Social, Community and Family Affairs 2000). It dealt broadly with aspects of statutory–voluntary relations and addressed several issues pertinent to sector regulation. It recognized:

- the nonprofit sector as a core component of a vibrant civil society;
- the need to consult nonprofit service providers and other groups in receipt of state funding about service design and delivery;
- the diversity and autonomy of the sector;
- the role of the sector in contributing to policy and relevant legislation; and
- the legal obligation that rests with the state for the delivery of services.

The White Paper recommended infrastructural supports for state–nonprofit relations. These included voluntary activity units in government departments, establishment of supports for nonprofits' training needs, and clarification of legal and regulatory issues. Recommendations regarding the criteria for securing state funding, the nature of activities that would receive funding support, and the improved management of funding relationships were also included. The White Paper was supportive of the incorporation and regulation of charities generally and of the regulation of charitable fundraising specifically.

The White Paper was a landmark in that it acknowledged the existence of a voluntary and community sector and committed the government to formally recognizing the role of the sector in participative democracy and civil society. Keenan (2008), in a discussion of sector–state relations and the forms of representative structures that would support this relationship, argues that, in Ireland, the block to a more effective relationship is as much about the nonprofit sector as any other factor. He states that, "a strong case can be made for starting the process at the macro, or national, level in defining the role of the sector in society, agreeing the principles of engagement and setting parameters. This would then become the framework for clarifying relationships at the sectoral and agency levels" (Keenan 2008: 32).

Despite the publication of the White Paper, the formal regulatory environment remained unaddressed. In the next sections, we look at the evolution of the legislative framework and the eventual establishment of formal sector regulation, followed by an overview of trends in funding and an assessment of the social partnership.

Legislation and the Development of a Regulatory Framework

For the past two decades, analysts of the legislative framework governing statutory–nonprofit relationships in Ireland have concluded that it is relatively underdeveloped (Acheson et al. 2004; Charities Regulation Study Group 2004; Costello 1990; Cousins 1994, 1997; Donoghue 2002). Prior to March 2006, there was no statutory definition of charity and charitable status. To date, the Revenue Commissioners have determined whether a body is entitled to charitable tax exemption under the *Taxes Consolidation Act 1997*. They have issued a charity reference number (CHY) to bodies which are granted charitable tax exemption.

O'Halloran (2007: 23, 237), in his international comparative study of charity law, described the legal framework in Ireland as more of a facilitative than a regulatory environment, and legislation as concerned primarily with authorizing procedures rather than identifying and proscribing abuses.

Before the enactment of the *Charities Act 2009*, the main charities legislation comprised the *Charities Acts* 1961 and 1973, with significant amendment made by the *Social Welfare (Miscellaneous Provisions) Act 2002*. Aspects of fundraising by charities were addressed in the *Street and House to House Collections Act 1962* and the *Casual Trading Act 1995*. Both of these Acts assigned responsibilities to An Garda Siochána, the Irish police service, regarding the issuing of permits for collections. Fundraising through the National Lottery was governed by the *National Lotteries Act 1986*. Most other fundraising activity was outside statutory control.

The Revenue Commissioners maintained a list of bodies that successfully applied for tax exemption on charitable grounds. Monitoring and supervision responsibilities rested mainly with the Commissioners for Charitable Donations and Bequests, a body that survived intact since the nineteenth century.

There have been a number of reports recommending charitable and fundraising regulation over the past two decades. The first of these was the *Report of the Committee on Fundraising Activities for Charitable and Other Purposes* (Costello 1990). In 1996 the Minister of State in the

Department of Justice, who then had responsibility for this area, convened an Advisory Group which submitted its report on Charities Fundraising Legislation in late 1996 (Department of Justice 1996). These became known as the Costello and Burton reports, respectively. The Costello Report evaluated the adequacy of existing statutory controls but also highlighted the variety of charities providing services in the Republic of Ireland. Statutory incursion into the charitable fundraising sector would have to respect and accommodate those charities with annual revenues of millions of euros and a sizable administrative staff to those with a limited annual income and mostly voluntary administrators. Similarly, the Burton Report encompassed an investigation of the practical applications of the Costello Report, much of which informs the *Charities Act 2009*. Additional examination and research undertaken includes the Law Society (2002) report, which examined and made recommendations concerning the key legal issues at the core of charity law reform. Of relevance, too, in relation to the question of a new form of incorporation for charities was the substantial reform and simplification of company law recommended in the Company Law Review Group (2001) report.

In June 2002, the then newly elected government made a commitment in the *Agreed Programme for Government* that, "A comprehensive reform of the law relating to charities will be enacted to ensure accountability and to protect against abuse of charitable status and fraud." The Department of Community, Rural and Gaeltacht Affairs was charged with implementing this commitment, and a new Charities Unit was established within the department with that remit. The Social Partnership Agreement *Sustaining Progress*, brokered in February 2003, further stated that, "The agreed objective is to ensure that whenever regulation is justified, it is prepared in a fully transparent way that maximizes public participation in its formulation" (Government of Ireland 2003).

Later in 2003, the Department of Community, Rural and Gaeltacht Affairs was charged with bringing forward a comprehensive scheme for charities legislation. In February 2004, a Consultation Paper on "Establishing a Modern Statutory Framework for Charities" was launched by the Department (Department of Community, Rural and Gaeltacht Affairs 2003) and was then followed by a period of public consultation from mid-February to the end of May 2004. In September 2004, an *External Report on the Public Consultation* was published (Breen 2004) and issued by the Minister. Issues raised included formal recognition of sector–state relationships and structures, such as a sector representative body, to improve their effectiveness, statutory recognition of charitable status, and a register of charities. Submissions from voluntary organizations reflected their own concerns with demonstrating accountability and transparency.

The *General Scheme for Charities Regulation Bill 2006* (Department of Community, Rural and Gaeltacht Affairs 2006) was published in March 2006, and in April 2007, *The Charities Bill 2007* was presented to the

Dáil (the Irish Parliament). However, an election was called before the Bill could progress through any further stages, and, consequently, it lapsed in May 2007. On the return of the new Dáil in autumn 2007, the Bill was expected to progress through the next stages towards final enactment but was delayed further. It was eventually signed by the President on 28 February 2009. Formal enactment of the Bill to the *Charities Act 2009* was announced by the Minister of Community, Rural and Gaeltacht Affairs on 2 March 2009.

The Funding Relationship

Almost two decades ago, Faughnan and Kelleher (1993) noted that funding is the primary way in which the state and voluntary sector organizations interact, and this continues to be the case. In its review of literature addressing sector–state relations, the NESC reported that the relationship remained "both unclear and unsatisfactory" (NESC 2005: 224), with *ad hoc* and insecure funding arrangements common.

Notwithstanding the continuing currency of Faughnan and Kelleher's work, the funding environment of community and voluntary organizations has changed very substantially over the past 10 years, during which time there has been a significant increase in state funding, growth in philanthropic giving, and the professionalization of fundraising (Donoghue et al. 2007). In his review of the state of the Irish nonprofit sector, Keenan notes that the sector is faced with the challenge of "securing and maintaining such state funding in a climate of a Government focus on rationalizing funding programs, demonstrating value for money, the achievement of effective outcomes, as well as financial integrity—within a context of increasingly constrained public finances" (Keenan 2008: 21). This statement is even more relevant in the period following the publication of the *Charities Act 2009*, at which time the Irish state entered a period of serious recession.

Social Partnership in Ireland

An important dimension of sector–state relations is the social consensus system of "Social Partnership," formally instituted in Ireland in 1987 and built on the institutional foundations of the National Wage Agreements, which ran from World War II until 1981, the Labour Court, and the Employer Labour Conference. Social Partnership is an agreed, multiannual program among Government, employers, trade unions, and, since 1996, some members of the community and voluntary sector in the form of the Community and Voluntary Pillar. Typically, partnership agreements are developed every three years and deal with wage growth, industrial relations, taxation policy, and social welfare. For example, a partnership agreement may encompass trade-offs among tax cuts, productivity, pay increases, and investment in social services. The first partnership arrangement in 1987 was the *Programme for National Recovery*. It facilitated difficult political and financial decisions that were targeted at growing the economy. The country was close to bankruptcy at the time, and the first agreement was largely an income agreement, with social and other issues dealt with in an almost cursory fashion.

During the 1980s, there emerged a number of organizations active in combating unemployment, campaigning for social welfare improvements and community development. They gradually moved from being external critics of the partnership process to being regarded as necessary participants in the negotiations (see Department of Health 1994, 1997). This eventually culminated in the establishment of the "Community Pillar" in October 1996, when the then Taoiseach (Prime Minister) invited a number of organizations to form a group for the purposes of joining in talks on a new Social Partnership program that winter. The Community Pillar was later renamed the Community and Voluntary Pillar (CV pillar), and it grew to encompass anti-poverty, community development, representative bodies, and service delivery organizations. Membership is still restricted to those community and voluntary organizations invited to join the Pillar by the Taoiseach.

The system of social partnership and its antecedents would seem to lead to the conclusion that Ireland is an increasingly corporatist state. Yet, an interesting backdrop to the study of sector–state relations is the challenge that characterizing either the state or the sector in Ireland presents. Esping-Andersen's (1990, 1996) analysis of welfare regimes presented a mixed picture of the Irish state, and, similarly, Salaman and Anheier's (1998) social origins theory does not compartmentalize the Irish third sector within a single quadrant. Both the state and the sector exhibit characteristics of corporatist and liberal regimes (Donoghue & Donnelly-Cox, forthcoming). While the social partnership agreement process is indicative of a corporatist approach to the development of public policy, there has also been a thrust towards liberal economic policy, most notably for example in the adoption of elements of New Public Management (or what in Ireland has been called the Strategic Management Initiative). Neo-liberal economic policy has been countered at times by various elements within the social partnership process, but it has been noted that in times of economic downturns, even if such downturns are small, the social voices of the partnership process tend to be marginalized in favor of the larger, more traditional social partners concerned with the economy and business (Powell & Geoghegan 2004). Social service provision, therefore, has to be viewed in the context of growing neo-liberalism, while at the same time recognizing the effects of neo-corporatist structures in broadly shaping socio-economic policy (Donoghue & Donnelly-Cox, forthcoming).

In summary, we have reviewed a number of facets of the relationship between the state and the nonprofit sector in Ireland. We have found that the historical analysis of relations as informal, fragmented, and *ad hoc* remains valid despite the integration of community and voluntary organizations into the national system of social partnership. Why should this be so? We argue that, in the absence of a core representative body of the sector and the limited recognition of the concept of *sector*, such fragmentation is almost inevitable. If we look at social partnership, for example, in the absence of a broadly accepted sector representative body, the state can choose which organizations it will bring into partnership negotiations. Keenan (2008) has noted that the Community and Voluntary Pillar in partnership is an informal alliance brought together at the invitation of the Taoiseach. As a collective entity, it has no legal status, it does not exist as an entity outside of the partnership talks, and it has no mandate to engage with the whole sector. The organizations that make up the Pillar are not compelled to deal with organizations outside their own constituencies (Keenan 2008: 37). Thus, while the Pillar makes significant contributions through partnership to the formation of national social policy, it does not serve as a representative body of the sector as a whole. It is within this context that we examine a specific provision of the *Charities Act 2009*— that fundraising charities should be self-regulated under agreed Codes of Practice for fundraising. The case example of fundraising regulation allows us to examine how the historical relationship between sector and state is evolving and consider the implications of the norms of this relationship in a changing regulatory environment.

FUNDRAISING REGULATION: A CASE EXAMPLE

What are the implications of the historical sector–state relationship for fundraising regulation within an evolving regulatory environment? The *Charities Act* published in March 2009 provides for the establishment of the Charities Regulatory Authority (a statutory body for the regulation of charities), a Register of Charities, a definition of charitable purpose, the creation of a Charity Appeals Tribunal, and an update of fundraising legislation. In updating fundraising regulation, the trend evident across Europe of promoting and allowing for co-regulation of fundraising charities has been adopted in Ireland (see Compact Working Group 2001). Self-regulation under agreed Codes of Practice is subject to the provision of reserve powers for the Minister "if such an approach proves ineffective (Department of Community, Rural and Gaeltacht Affairs 2009: 8).

One of the stated purposes of the Irish Act is to "enhance public trust and confidence in charities and increase transparency in the sector." However, it is noteworthy that the impetus for charity regulatory reform in the Republic of Ireland comes not in the wake of major scandals or a particularly high level of public discontent with charitable fundraising. While undoubtedly international forces may have spurred government to act in this area after years of reviews and non-action,[1] and notwithstanding the recommendations of Costello and Burton reports mentioned earlier, the move towards regulatory reform can be seen as a preemptive move led mainly by actors outside the sector, reflecting the fact that changing times require more advanced approaches to accountability and as an attempt to protect the existing high levels of good will and trust towards the sector. Nevertheless, the proposals have so far been welcomed by the sector, albeit without any widespread input or reflection.

The main charities legislation preceding the 2009 Act addressed public collections of cash, and, in particular, it focused on authorizing procedures through the auspices of An Garda Siochána, as opposed to identifying abuses.[2] The *Charities Act 2009* specifies a three-pronged approach to regulating charitable fundraising, which means that: 1) all types of public fundraising will require permits, 2) a Charity Regulator will be appointed and all charities will have to give full details of fundraising activities to the regulator in annual accounts and returns, and 3) the operational and administrative aspects of fundraising will be regulated by agreed upon Codes of Practice developed with the sector. Our analysis focuses on this third component, as it provides a point of interaction among regulation, cross-sectoral interaction to achieve an outcome, and sector–state relations.

The Practical Impact of Regulation: Creating Codes of Practice

The Act specifies that the operational and administrative aspects of fundraising are to be regulated by the Codes of Practice developed with the sector. Unlike many other jurisdictions that have had systems in place for some time for setting standards and dealing with public complaints,[3] there were no such overarching structures in the Republic until the 2008 publication of the *Statement of Guiding Principles for Fundraising* (ICTR 2008). Pre-existing Codes were limited to one for face-to-face fundraising[4] and one for the use of images and messages by international development charities.[5] On the publication of the *Statement*, the Working Group that developed it emphasized that it provide a *framework* of guidelines and principles for fundraising rather than a detailed operational code.

The proposal that the operational and administrative aspects of fundraising would be regulated by Codes of Practice to be developed collaboratively with the sector posed a significant challenge for a sector that had no development body for fundraisers,[6] no representative structures for charities in place, and no existing systems for setting standards. In order to begin addressing this question, a feasibility study and public consultation were undertaken from 2006 to 2007 to explore how the operational aspects of charitable fundraising could be effectively regulated through Codes of Practice.[7]

As part of that and in order to inform decision making about the scope of regulation, a research report (Donoghue et al. 2007) was commissioned to provide the "best estimate of the prevailing scale and practice of charitable fundraising in Ireland." The research found a large concentration of small organizations and a small number of large ones (small and large defined in terms of their publicly fundraised income). Based on these data, it was estimated that more than 90 percent of charities rely on voluntary fundraisers or part-time staff. Two distinct fundraising experiences emerged, depending on whether the organizations in question were large or small in terms of their public fundraised income and on whether they had a national, international, or a local/regional remit (Donoghue et al. 2007). For organizations with a national or an international remit, fundraising is typically larger in scale, more professionalized, and supported by full-time fundraising personnel. Accountability is generally less personal and is likely to be based on strategies such as formal information streams and public relations. These types of organizations are likely to have the capacity to absorb the requirements that regulation will bring.

For organizations with a local or regional focus, investment in fundraising is low, with fundraising efforts regarded as diverting much-needed resources away from service delivery rather than as being a core part of organizational activities. Such organizations are likely to employ more routine fundraising methods (e.g. church gate collections, local business sponsorship). The fundraising 'ask' is likely to be more personal, and support is achieved on the basis of community ties. Accountability operates primarily on the basis of personal trust and observable local evidence. Arguably, these organizations have little capacity to absorb the new regulatory demands.

Submissions to the public consultation emphasized that the design and implementation of Codes need to strike a balance between enhancing public confidence and not being too onerous for the majority of charities which, as was identified in the research, have limited capacity to manage burdensome regulation. In particular, the view was that account should be taken of the needs of smaller organizations for which fundraising is local and personalized, and receiving support depends on community ties and mostly voluntary effort. For these organizations, formalized accountability structures may not add real value while they are likely to add additional bureaucracy.

In recognizing these issues, the Feasibility Study recommended that the Charities sector, allied with professional assistance and a strong independent input, should take the lead in setting the standards and creating Codes. In addition, it suggested that the Regulator establish a Monitoring Group, composed of a majority of independent members and an independent chair, to deal with complaints and to actively monitor usage of the Codes.

In line with the recommendations of the Feasibility Study, a project was initiated in summer 2007 to test the first proposal—that the sector take the lead in setting standards—by establishing a process to agree upon a draft statement of "Guiding Principles for Fundraising" by mid-December 2007. In July 2007, a working group (led by Siobhan McGee[8]) was convened to draft this Statement. The group reviewed best practice guidelines on regulation, undertook a review of codes from several European and international jurisdictions, and considered the feedback received from the earlier consultative processes. An initial draft statement was published for public consultation in the fall 2007. Using feedback from the consultative process, the Statement was finalized and published in January 2008.

This *Statement on Guiding Principles for Fundraising* preceded the publication of the *Charities Act* by over a year. The Act commits the government to implementing agreed upon codes of good practice in relation to fundraising operations. Reserve powers exist for the Minister who, after consultation with the Charities Regulation Authority, may make statutory regulations on the manner and conduct of fundraising if the voluntary code proves ineffective. The Department of Community, Rural and Gaeltacht Affairs noted in March 2009 that the *Statement* represents a significant advance in the work of implementing Codes of Good Practice, and that the work that has been completed so far has been achieved "in partnership with the charities sector" (Department of Community, Rural and Gaeltacht Affairs 2009: 8).

DISCUSSION

There are a number of significant implications for the charity fundraising sector in the context of the framework to regulate fundraising as provided in the *Charities Act*. First, while the charitable sector has been generally supportive of regulation, it lacks coherence and representative structures. Consequently, there has been no opportunity for its engagement in policy development on regulation, and, therefore, the policy formulation around regulation has been largely state-led. This mirrors patterns in the history of sector–state relations and adds credence to the proposition that, without a strong sector with its own coherent representational structures, meaningful engagement is compromised.

Secondly, the Charities Bill challenged the sector to take the lead in devising standards and agreeing upon codes of practice, and a commitment to implementation of these codes is given in the 2009 *Charities Act*. Based on the public consultation, it was generally accepted by the sector that it should, indeed, lead in setting the standards. However, no infrastructure exists to support the development of operational Codes, nor is there any infrastructure to support the professional development of fundraisers and to communicate to the public about fundraising. The process that was undertaken relied heavily on the *Fundraising Landscape* report to set direction. The working group on codes development, the consultative process, and the finalization of the *Statement* were all supported with one-off funding from the Department of Community, Rural and Gaeltacht Affairs.

We argue that the provisions of the Act require that there is a working relationship between the sector and the regulator to address regulatory policy as well as operational and compliance matters. The stated purpose of charitable and fundraising regulation is "to enhance public trust and confidence," and importantly, the Act gives the relevant Minister reserve power to implement statutory regulation if regulation through Codes of Practice is seen to be ineffective. If this is to be achieved, a common understanding of what constitutes 'success' in this context is needed—within the sector, from the regulator, within the Gardai, and amongst the funding public. Establishing a benchmark of current levels of public trust and confidence is required in the first instance. Such a benchmark should, in turn, lead to agreement for measuring the impact of regulation on levels of public trust and confidence as a result of regulation. This represents quite a challenge for a sector without any fundraising development infrastructure or appropriate representative network. It is unclear at this stage how the sector can or will organize to meet this challenge.

There remains the very real issue of the relevance of the evolving regulatory framework to the majority of very small fundraising organizations. The profile of the charity fundraising sector, as presented in the *Fundraising Landscape* report, shows a sector where, for the most part, accountability is achieved on the basis of personal trust and observable local evidence. In that context, what is the value of formalized accountability systems to those sector organizations? How can we ensure that it does not become a burden rather than an enabler?

In a similar vein, it will be crucial to see the response by the public and the media to the availability, for the first time, of data that allow them to compare and judge charities and their fundraising performance. A consequence of the lack of a professional development association for fundraisers is that there has been no attempt made to educate the funding public on fundraising matters. The public in Ireland remain naïve in terms of their understanding of the complexity of managing and resourcing charities as a whole. Irish charities are commonly expected to achieve 'cost free' fundraising, and charities rarely challenge this expectation. Given this significant gap between perception and reality, there is in fact a real chance that the levels of public confidence could be undermined as a result of the availability of comparable information on fundraising activities which will be required by the regulator in annual accounts and returns. There is pressing work to be done to bridge these gaps in understanding, to advocate on the sector's behalf, and to inform and educate the public about the realities of charitable operations.

In the Irish policy context, it can be suggested that social partnership provides the framework within which the relationships between the overall charity sector and the statutory entity that will be the regulator should now be set. In the relationships between voluntary and community organizations and government, inclusion of the community and voluntary platform in the Irish social partnership system has helped to develop a wider ethos of partnership as a useful and effective approach to joint problem solving and decision making. However, the current approach to participation in the Community and Voluntary pillar is not representative of the charity fundraising sector as such. Rather, it represents particular special interests, and these are selected by the state.

CONCLUSION

Given the changing policy context, it appears imperative that the charities sector address the question of representation so that it can engage in dialogue on key questions, the development of the Code, jointly agreed by sector and the government being only the first of these. Such a move would have the added benefit of addressing the general level of understanding that exists about charity organizing *per se*, and also the questions of professional development that professionals are calling for. The history of state–nonprofit relations in Ireland provides evidence of the negative impact on the sector of the persistent challenges in sectoral organizing. Regulation provides additional and now maybe compelling reasons to address the development and infrastructure of the sector.

The development of a regulatory framework, and the particular case of the development of Codes of Practice, make clear the need for not only better sector–state relations but for a working sector–state *partnership*. The need for partnership reinforces the need to develop the nonprofit sector itself so that it can engage more effectively in partnership. Without this, it would seem inevitable that a suboptimal regulatory framework will replace the unsatisfactory informal relationship that the sector has had with the government.

Notwithstanding the difficulties of partnership, given the particular context and history of the voluntary and community sector and social partnership in Ireland, the Social Partnership framework has provided a place wherein the charity fundraising sector can best find an opportunity to facilitate the development of a sector–state relationship that is appropriate to current and future needs. It should be possible to locate an initiative that would enable the development of a representative structure which can, in turn, seek to achieve objectives that no single organization can achieve alone.

Currently, the future of the Social Partnership in Ireland is in considerable question, however. As is all too well known, the country was hit particularly hard by the global crisis, which the NESC (2009) has described as having five dimensions in the case of Ireland—banking and credit, fiscal, economic, social, and reputational. Importantly, the economic failure is also being seen as a failure of democracy. Voluntary and community organizations were not spared serious impact, as 75 percent reported a decrease in revenues and 35 percent experienced a drop in public donations which for many translated into staff layoffs, reductions in salaries and benefits, and projects delayed (The Wheel, 2009). The recession also caused the Social Partnership to buckle under the strain of retrenchment when talks between the government and public sector unions over the government's plan for €1 billion in public service pay cuts collapsed in December 2009. Although discussions among the social partners about the way forward have recently been renewed, the economic situation has raised questions as to whether the social partnership had already reached its 'sell-by' date, on the one hand, and that the way out of the recession will necessarily be achieved through an integrated solution with active involvement of nongovernmental organizations, on the other hand. As social partnership goes through the process of reinventing itself, the importance of representational structures and infrastructure for the voluntary and community sector becomes more important than ever before.

NOTES

1. For example, the Financial Action Task Force (FATF) is an inter-governmental body which works to promote the development and promotion of national and international policies to combat money laundering and terrorist financing.
2. *The Charities Acts 1961* and *1973, the Street and House to House Collections Act 1962,* and the *Casual Trading Act 1995.*
3. For example, the UK Institute of Fundraising promotes a system of voluntary Codes of Practice for charitable fundraising. This was supplemented with the introduction in 2006 of the Fundraising Standards Board, which provides the public with an independent point of contact for queries and complaints about charitable fundraising.
4. The Irish Forum for Direct Recruitment (IFFDR) is a voluntary body of individuals, charities, and providers of face-to-face fundraising services. The IFFDR established a voluntary Code of Practice for organisations who carry out face-to-face fundraising. See www.iffdr.org.
5. Dóchas, the umbrella organisation of Irish Non-Governmental Organisations (NGOs), has drawn up a Code of Conduct on Images and Messages. See www.dochas.ie.
6. Fundraising Ireland was established in 2007 as a networking organization. It does not at this time serve as a professional development body for its members.
7. Report on Feasibility Study on Codes of Practice, from Irish Charities Tax Research to the Department of Community, Rural and Gaeltacht Affairs (2007). See www.ictr.ie.
8. Siobhan McGee was contracted by Irish Charities Tax Research Limited to lead the process between July and December 2007. Other members of the Working Group, drawn mainly from fundraising charitable organizations from across the country, took part on a voluntary basis.

REFERENCES

Acheson, N., Harvey, B., Kearney, J., and Williamson, A. (2004). *Two Paths, One Purpose: Voluntary Action in Ireland, North and South.* Dublin: IPA.

Boyle, R., and Butler, M. (2003). *Autonomy versus Accountability: Managing Government Funding of Voluntary and Community Organisations*. Dublin: IPA.

Breen, O. B. (2004). *Report on the Public Consultation for the Department of Community, Rural and Gaeltacht Affairs*. Dublin.

Charities Regulation Study Group. (2004). *Submission on Establishing a Modern Statutory Framework for Charities*. Dublin: CRSG.

Compact Working Group. (2001). *Guidance for Public/Voluntary Sector Partnerships: A Proposed Supplement to the Funding Code*. London: National Council for Voluntary Organisations.

Company Law Review Group. (2001). *First Report*. Dublin: Company Law Review Group.

Costello, J. D. (1990). *Report of the Committee on Fundraising Activities for Charitable and Other Purposes*. Dublin: Stationery Office.

Cousins, M. (1994). *A Guide to Legal Structures for Voluntary and Community Organisations*. Dublin: Combat Poverty Agency.

Cousins, M. (1997). "Republic of Ireland." In L. Salamon (ed.), *International Guide to Nonprofit Law*. New York: Wiley and Sons.

Department of Community, Rural and Gaeltacht Affairs. (2003). *Establishing a Modern Statutory Framework for Charities*.

Department of Community, Rural and Gaeltacht Affairs. (2006). *General Scheme for the Charities Regulation Bill 2006*.

Department of Community, Rural and Gaeltacht Affairs. (2009). *Principal Features of the Charities Act 2009*.

Department of Health. (1994). *Shaping a Healthier Future*. Dublin: Stationery Office.

Department of Health. (1997). *Enhancing the Partnership*. Dublin: Stationery Office.

Department of Justice. (1996). *Report of the Advisory Group on Charities/Fundraising Legislation*. Dublin: Stationery Office.

Department of Social, Community and Family Affairs. (2000). *Supporting Voluntary Activity: A White Paper for Supporting Voluntary Activity and for Developing the Relationship between the State and the Community and Voluntary Sector*. Dublin: Stationery Office.

Donoghue, F. (2002). *Reflecting the Relationships. An Exploration of the Relationships between the former Eastern Health Board and Voluntary Organisations in the Eastern Region*. Dublin: Eastern Regional Health Authority.

Donoghue, F., and Donnelly-Cox, G. (forthcoming). *Social Service Organisations in Ireland: One Field through which to examine welfare tegimes theory*. Unpublished manuscript.

Donoghue, F., O'Regan, A., McGee, S., and Donovan, A. M. (2007). *Exploring the Irish Fundraising Landscape: A report on the practice and scale of fundraising in Ireland, A report for Irish Charities Tax Research Ltd*. Dublin: ICTR & Dublin: Centre for Nonprofit Management, School of Business, Trinity College.

Esping-Andersen, G. (1990). *The Three Worlds of Welfare Capitalism*. Cambridge: Polity Press.

Esping-Andersen, G. (1996). *Welfare States in Transition: National Adaptations in Global Economies*. London: Sage Publications.

Faughnan, P., and Kelleher, P. (1993). *The Voluntary Sector and the State: A study of organizations in one region*. Dublin: CMRS.

Government of Ireland. (2003). *Sustaining Progress: Social Partnership Agreement 2003–2005*. Dublin: The Stationery Office.

Government of Ireland. (2005). *Report of the Comptroller and Auditor General: Provision of disability services by nonprofit organisations*. Dublin: Stationery Office.

Irish Charities Tax Research Ltd. (2008). *Statement of Guiding Principles for Fundraising.* Dublin.

Keenan, O. (2008). *Relationships and Representation, Challenges and Opportunities for the Voluntary and Community Sector in Ireland.* Dublin: Centre for Nonprofit Management.

Law Society. (2002). *Charity Law: The case for reform.* Dublin: Law Society.

National Economic and Social Council. (2005). *NESC Strategy 2006: People, Productivity and Purpose.* Report No. 114. Dublin: NESC.

National Economic and Social Council. (2009). *Next Steps in Addressing Ireland's Five-Part Crises: Combining retrenchment with reform.* Report No. 120. Dublin: NESC.

O'Ferrall, F. (2000). *Citizenship and Public Service: Voluntary and statutory relationships in Irish healthcare.* Dublin: The Adelaide Hospital Society.

Salamon, L. M., and Anheier, H. K. (1998). "Social origins of civil society: Explaining the nonprofit sector cross-nationally." *Voluntas*, 9(3), 213–248.

The Wheel. (2009). "Impact of the recession on Ireland's community and voluntary organisations: Pre-budget survey." Dublin: The Wheel. Available at <http://www.wheel.ie/user/information/irish_charities_cut_back_on_projects_staff_and_administrative_costs> (accessed 1 April 2010).

5 Creeping Marketization and Post-corporatist Governance

The Transformation of State–Nonprofit Relations in Continental Europe

Ingo Bode

INTRODUCTION

According to widespread assumptions on the international variety of welfare regimes, Continental Europe exhibits a distinctive history of relations between the state and the nonprofit sector (Katz & Sachße 1996; Lahusen 2006; Salamon & Anheier 1998). This history contains a long tradition of close intersectoral collaboration as well as dense network relations among the regime's major stakeholders, including powerful, service-providing nonprofit organizations. In spite of this long recognized pattern, the international debate that began in the late 1990s on the changing governance of the third sector in advanced Western societies has, somewhat surprisingly, stressed the innovative character and relative newness of boundary-spanning intersectoral linkages (Evers 2005; Kooïman 2003: 3, 113; Lewis 2005). In the terms employed by prominent conceptualizations of state–nonprofit relationships (Najam 2000; Young 2000), mere complementarity in the relation between governments and the nonprofit sector is assumed to have been superseded by formalized co-operation or co-optation, even as more distant, if not adversarial, relations seem to turn into collaborative ones. However, this conjecture sits uncomfortably with the fact that mainland Europe (the Netherlands, Belgium, Austria, France, and Germany, to name but a few) witnessed network-based patterns of governance from very early on. What has been substantiated particularly well in the field of social welfare provision, under closer inspection in this chapter, can also be extended to other domains such as cultural production and the social organization of leisure.

Accounts, emanating mainly from Anglo-Saxon countries, that suggest a cross-national transition from government to governance—or from a hierarchy-driven to a network-based architecture of welfare states (e.g. Blomgren-Bingham et al. 2005; Osborne 2006; Pierre 2000; Rhodes

1996)—obviously neglect the Continental tradition. In particular, the contention of the rise of a (more formalized) collaborative interface between state and (organized) civil society seems to be at odds with a long-standing European experience of devolving managerial responsibilities on nonprofit agencies and of concluding intersectoral agreements on public policies. From another perspective, one could even say that Continental European patterns of state–nonprofit partnerships appear as forerunners of a governance model proliferating internationally. At least, distinctive elements of what has commonly been referred to as *corporatist* governance regimes seem to extend to regimes that in former times were either dominated by statutory authorities or characterized by high economic and political autonomy of the third sector.

Things are more complicated, though, than differences in perspectives linked to locale. A major problem with most mainstream accounts of the development of Western governance regimes is a blind spot when it comes to the analysis of the evolutionary dynamics of these regimes. Few have explored how network-based patterns of governance have been, and continue to be, affected by the enduring process of the (quasi-) *marketization* of the relationship between the third sector and its public stakeholders (notable recent exceptions are Carmel & Harlock 2008 and Chapman, Brown, & Crow 2008 for the case of the UK). On the one hand, we have witnessed the increased interconnection of state–nonprofit networks and, on the other hand, a movement toward the deregulation of public service provision though the establishment of what is now widely referred to as "welfare markets" (Bode 2008). Indeed, wherever state–nonprofit partnerships have taken shape on a larger scale throughout the post-war settlement, these partnerships have now become exposed to the logics of competition and rivalry, entrance and exit, bargaining and instrumental behavior. Partnership models based on highly regulated patterns of resource allocation and common planning have, over the last two decades or so, given way to more fluid and dispersed intersectoral relations. Interestingly, this developmental pattern is also, if more implicitly, salient in countries where formalized state–nonprofit partnerships in social welfare provision have emerged more timidly or at a later stage (when compared with mainland Europe), for example, in Britain (Bode 2006a, 2006b).

The international paradox, then, consists of a twofold movement leading to both an *extension* of partnerships and their *permanent disorganization* or, in other words, toward the proliferation of network-like intersectoral arrangements in an era of creeping marketization. While quasi-markets and their impact on intersectoral partnerships have been awarded some attention in the Anglo-Saxon literature dealing with state–nonprofit relations (see Davies 2005; Feiock & Andrew 2006; Smith 2002), the respective dynamics in countries with a longer tradition of institutionalized partnerships between civil society and the state have hitherto been marginal to the international debate. This is a serious lacuna in the literature because taking these dynamics into account may change the overall picture regarding the future of state–nonprofit relations in the twenty-first century.

This is not least because, at closer inspection, the Continental European settlement exhibits a variety of 'sub-traditions' and institutional legacies. As a result, the routes by which state–nonprofit networks meet movements of marketization differ across Continental welfare states. In what follows, this will be illustrated by a comparison between France and Germany, countries deemed to belong to the same (corporatist) family of welfare states. This chapter examines movements of change in both the regulatory frameworks and the 'material' environmental relations concerning major types of nonprofit organizations, and it elucidates how the two countries, exhibiting similar institutional developments throughout the twentieth century, entered the post-corporatist era through different doors by adopting the new 'welfare market agenda' in dissimilar ways.

Hence, Continental Europe sees disparate patterns of post-corporatist state–nonprofit relations even as these relations become more hybrid overall. Yet is this the end of history regarding the intersectoral settlement under study here? One might assume that marketization as a governance model has been profoundly challenged by the recent crisis of the market economy. Indeed, it might be anticipated that the crisis had provoked a return of the state taking responsibilities over from other sectors against the background of what Lambie (2009) refers to as "nemesis of market fundamentalism." The broader question for Continental Europe is whether the strong non-market traditions in the public management of the nonprofit sector will reemerge at the expense of the idea of (quasi-) market governance as a modernization tool. That is why this chapter, in conclusion, briefly assesses whether the crisis of the world (market) economy has had an impact on the way the nonprofit sector is 'handled' in processes of public management nowadays.

GOVERNANCE AFTER CORPORATISM

As noted, Continental European welfare states differ from other nations in that the interface between nonprofit organizations and their environment has adopted a distinctive institutional character. In the comparative literature dealing with this interface (see Casey 2004; Evers & Laville 2004; Salamon & Anheier 1998), the Continental European configuration is often referred to as being *corporatist*. The notion of corporatism addresses various phenomena which include formal arrangements among collective actors, on the one hand, and movements of political exchange between these actors and the state, on the other (see Crouch & Streeck 2006). In a nutshell, corporatism is understood as a particular way of governing society by formalized intersectoral and intermediary collaboration, including at a meso- or even micro-level. Corporatist societies are deemed to rely on organized groups that seek mutual agreements on regulatory norms and then draw on the state in order to have these agreements rolled out across larger sections of the population. Under these circumstances, social affairs are regulated by settlements among major stakeholders of a given societal sector, with the state mobilizing the resources required for the generalization of the agreed norms. All this translates into an 'organic' mode of societal self-steering (within a capitalistic economic order).

In the social sciences, the concept of corporatism has been employed mostly in studies on industrial relations and those players giving shape to them, that is, employer associations and trade unions. However, the organic mode of governing society also features in the social welfare system in which nonprofit agencies, rooted in various strands of civil society, are involved in the provision of services to wider sections of the population (Zimmer 1999 for the case of Germany). Under corporatist governance, these agencies encounter democratically elected authorities in order to agree on regulations to be applied to their sector. Many of them establish highly professionalized, if not quasi-statutory, undertakings running various services on behalf of public authorities. At the same time, however, they embrace a broad rank and file membership, are led by boards composed of lay members, and include a volunteer workforce supplementing the provision of more professionalized services.

Regarding the core fields of social welfare provision, Continental European countries have witnessed an increasing institutionalization of this governance regime during the twentieth century. As will be illustrated at greater length below, these fields became based on highly formalized partnerships between service-providing charities and public bodies (social insurance and welfare bureaucracies) that are expected to subsidize their activities. Importantly, these archetypes of "partners in public service" (Salamon 1995) also engaged with the very design of welfare programs, which enabled nonprofit organizations to end up as major *political* stakeholders of the overall system.

This model of intersectoral collaboration was (and still is) deeply entrenched in the welfare culture of mainland Europe. It also materializes, if much less consistently, in recent debates on Europe-wide regulations of the social welfare system, more precisely in recent controversies around a (failed) European Union (EU) directive on social and health care services (through which these services were meant to become classified as ordinary businesses). Corporatist welfare states and their stakeholders argued that nonprofit service providers have a greater role in the social welfare system than as mere deliverers of pre-tailored services and should not be equated with private businesses contracted by public procurers (or individual clients). Thus far, it seems that this argument is widely endorsed throughout Europe (Kendall 2008; Lahusen 2006; Lloyd 2004).

Overall, network-based patterns of governing social welfare provision are emblematic of the corporatist tradition of state–nonprofit relations. This is why it appears counter-intuitive to posit, for this part of the

Western world, that 'network' or 'relational' governance has emerged as a new phenomenon, following an era of bureaucratic top-down government and (then) the overhaul of the latter by New Public Management (NPM). It is this conjecture which appears to be the core of the narrative that has until recently pervaded the literature on 'new governance' (Entwistle & Martin 2005; Kooïman 2003; Osborne 2006; Rhodes 2007: 1246–1249). At the risk of oversimplification, this narrative maintains that the management of public or social services is far and wide moving toward more collaborative or partnership-based forms of governance. The argument goes like this: First, there was hierarchy-driven bureaucratic governance; then, during the heyday of NPM, the relationship between government and its nonpublic partners was organized around quasi-market-based steering mechanisms (public tendering, contracting-out, mechanistic output control, etc.); this was followed by a transition toward more trust-based partnerships, leading into a new collaborative architecture that enabled the involved partners, including service-providing nonprofit organizations, to bring their distinctive potential to bear. NPM appears here as an "unfulfilled promise" (Noordhoek & Saner 2005: 42), having passed its golden age or even having ended up as a failure. By the same token, 'network governance' is assumed to be a path-breaking innovation, entailing a mode of steering public or social services based on a mixture between hierarchy, consensual agreement and (possibly) performance-based contracts. True, the new settlement is sometimes also understood as an expression of a "'softer' version of NPM" (Budd 2007: 533), but even then it is believed to counteract the impact of competition-oriented NPM policies that are assumed to have caused fragmentation, problems with service quality, and high transaction costs.

This reading of developments in public (and social welfare) sector management is problematic in several respects which make the 'network narrative' hard to believe. First, as Budd (2007) rightly argues, both NPM and the network narrative tend to downplay the limits of non-hierarchical governance in welfare states as the latter are pressured to deliver basic services at reasonable costs *and* with democratic accountability—which is an aspect this chapter will not take up further. Second, the tradition of Continental European corporatism makes the concept of 'new' governance, in particular when used to describe the encounter between state authorities and associational actors, appear as 'old hat.' As Treib and colleagues (2007: 10) note, "fashionable labels of 'old' and 'new' modes of governance" should be avoided when looking at how this encounter is evolving. Third, and most essentially, the penetration of private business values into the public and nonprofit sector, the proliferation of low-trust relations in the encounter between the state and its partners, and shifts in the service providers' strategic position (from relative autonomy to vicarious gatekeeping)—which are all emblematic of the NPM model—have by no means evaporated under a new governmental partnership approach that is now prominent throughout a number of Anglo-Saxon jurisdictions. Rather, studies in the transformation of the health and social care sector have shown that substantial institutional change has taken place internationally, with the enforcement and consolidation of welfare and health care (quasi-) markets as one key tendency (Bode 2008: 23–82; Considine 2001; Gilbert 2002; Pollitt 2007; Taylor-Gooby 2008).

Granted, the network rhetoric has over the last few years surfaced in Continental Europe as well. Public managers have been keen to take more partners on board and to break up existing 'state–nonprofit cartels.' However, network governance as such is anything but new in this part of the world, and the real sea change has been the introduction of competition and rivalry into this mode of governance involving nonprofit organizations (Bode 2006b). Indeed, what Continental Europe has seen is a creeping marketization of state–nonprofit relations and the nonprofits' linkage to their various environments. Thus, although some commentators seem to imply the opposite, the mantra underlying NPM is far from losing ground. This includes the recent period affected by the crisis of the (financial) market. As we will see, however, institutional change throughout Continental European welfare systems, as triggered by the movement to (quasi-) market governance, materializes in hybrid forms infused with particular elements of the corporatist legacy.

TRADITIONAL LANDSCAPES

What are the classical underpinnings of the interface between statutory and associational action in the Continental European settlement? Taking two leading European nations as an example, this section briefly delineates traditional landscapes of state–nonprofit relations in this settlement with a focus on social welfare provision, generally speaking. As space is limited, the two sketches can but outline the basic rationales underlying the development of state–nonprofit relations during the twentieth century (for more detailed accounts see Bode 2003, 2004, 2006b, 2010a; Bode et al. 2006; and other authors cited throughout).

Germany

Taking data on workforce capacities and economic resources as major criteria, the organizational field inhabited by nonprofit agencies in Germany may be viewed as a branch of the public sector. The lion's share of social and health care services in this country is indeed provided or managed by non-statutory organizations. This is not to say that the German state has left everything to such agencies. Rather, it has always made use of extensive 'in-house' facilities. Public authorities run a dense network of agencies, departments, and inspectors concerned with social welfare and health care provision at several territorial levels, and these bodies have a highly formalized remit to fund or to regulate a large range of services (Bahle 2008). In particular, national law obliges municipalities to provide extensive social support facilities for youth, the elderly, and disadvantaged citizens (Wollmann 2008). Funding is partly based on tax revenue distributed across the social service systems on the basis of a formula by which differences in local caseload burdens are balanced out. Municipalities, and sometimes the Länder (the major territorial divisions), employ social workers, health care staff (in hospitals), and agents responsible for case management and social planning. They can also initiate services beyond what is required by national regulation. Altogether, then, a strong state features in the German welfare regime.

And yet, the welfare regime relies on non-statutory bodies to a comparatively great extent. These bodies include social insurance agencies (sickness funds, long-term care funds, and labor offices) which, though subject to far-reaching public regulation, are formally under the control of representatives of the enrollees and of employers (as contributors). Usually, such agencies are not viewed by the third sector literature as belonging to the nonprofit or third sector at all. Although they appear as quasi-public bodies in a number of respects, they embody a broad intersectoral partnership and operate independently of the state in many ways, enjoying a status of conceded institutional autonomy. This chapter will not elaborate on these agencies at greater length (see Bode 2010b), with the exception of the commissioning role they are fulfilling on the basis of both legal provisions and formal agreements with provider associations.

It is these provider associations that are the focus of our discussion. As already noted, the majority of social (and medical care) services in Germany is delivered by formally independent service providers, with most of them carrying a nonprofit label (Evers & Sachße 2003). The bulk of the German nonprofit sector is located in what has been termed *freie Wohlfahrtspflege* (translated literally as "independent caring for welfare"). From the 1920s onwards, local (or regional) umbrella organizations of these associations (*Wohlfahrtsverbände*) developed into major pillars of the German welfare regime. Rooted in faith-based communities (and in the workers' movement as well), they grew as an expression of both a distinctive pattern of entangling the churches with the state and the doctrine of "subsidiarity" which suggests that social welfare (in a broad sense) should be provided by self-governed and decentralised social bodies. In practical terms, this meant that nonprofit organizations became deeply involved in local and sometimes in national social policies (Zimmer 1999). Holding considerable professional expertise, they developed into major government and party consultants. Furthermore, basic institutions relevant to the infrastructure of the social welfare system (universities of applied sciences, professional expert associations, etc.) originated in this universe. To date, this universe is composed of six national umbrellas, with each embracing a large range of local provider associations (Anheier & Seibel 2001: 161–186; Boeße-necker 2005). Providers which had joined one of these umbrellas were until recently automatically entitled to the reimbursement of expenses laid out for the provision of social support services. Hence, these associations were considered as preferred partners of the (quasi-) public bodies that were commissioning social (and health care) services.

It is easy to see that this traditional settlement of state–nonprofit rela-tions embraced a distinctive philosophy of governing modern society. Based on a strong state and a highly integrated, if multi-tiered and plu-ralistic, network of intermediate (nonprofit) organizations, this settlement was emblematic of the corporatist model that pervaded twentieth century Germany. Importantly, these organizations always understood themselves as "multi-purpose" agencies (in the sense of Hasenfeld & Gidron 2005), running diverse undertakings with productive, political, and community building functions. In contrast to what some recent accounts imply (see Rymsza & Zimmer 2004: 195), their strong embeddedness in the welfare state did not prevent them from defending their particular vision of col-lective action. Although they were permanently urged to find consensual agreements with (quasi-) public authorities, distinctive models and prac-tices emerged and were cultivated independently of the state. Lay action and boards composed of volunteers remained cornerstones of their organi-zational model, including during the 1970s and 1980s when the movement toward institutionalization was accelerating.

It holds true that this corporatist 'world of welfare' was often managed as a 'closed shop' at the local level. Therefore, it was challenged by new-comers keen to change routines and methods in social welfare (and health care) provision. However, while some of these newcomers stayed outside the well-entrenched 'welfare cartel,' most joined one of the umbrella orga-nizations in order to access public funding and exert political influence. Thus, fresh ideas were injected into the German welfare regime, particu-larly during the 1970s and 1980s. As an institutional framework, then, the corporatist regime remained pluralistic and also proved able to take challengers on board.

France

In many respects, the French welfare regime resembles the German one, including when it comes to state–nonprofit relations. True, the literature concerned with the history of the nonprofit sector in France emphasizes the conflict-ridden encounter between civil society and the state, on the one hand, and the difficult relations between the Catholic Church and the secu-larized Republic, on the other (see Archambault 2001; Seibel 1992). It has also been argued that state centralism left little space for more symmetric forms of collaboration between statutory actors and non-public agencies. Such observations, however, tend to ignore that the overall organizational settlement taking shape in twentieth century France was akin to the German one. In particular, the configuration established after the Second World War saw major social, educational, and cultural services being delivered by non-statutory organizations under public regulation, although these organizations remained independent in formal and ideological terms. Moreover, with the strong move toward decentralized public administration from the 1980s onward, the political role of the French nonprofit sector, having been a bit masked and localized in the past, was evolving further and became more apparent. Independent associations became accepted as official "partners in reform" (Ullmann 1998) and as carriers of political, cultural, or social innovation (Archambault 2001). Social law-making still remained incumbent on the central state. However, the *départements* (the most essential territorial divisions in France) developed into key players of the social welfare system where the nonprofit sector maintained a strong position, similar to the one held by its German neighbor (Bahle 2008). The remit of regional welfare bureaucracies included (and still includes) the employment of large numbers of professionals, the allocation of tax money, and the development of the infrastructure for the delivery of social support services, including those provided by non-statutory organizations. Municipalities, if compared to Germany, play a minor role in the French social welfare system. That said, the local social assistance bodies (*Centres communaux d'action sociale*, CCAS) offer a range of services and coordinate the activities of other local service providers. The boards supervising these bodies comprise nongovernmental actors, mostly representatives of local associations. This is already indicative of the pluralistic role-set endemic to the French welfare system. As in its German counterpart, self-governance is highly valued, and this is in stark contrast with stereotypes about France epitomizing a bureaucracy-driven 'top-down society.' Besides the CCAS, the approval of self-governance is prominent in the social insurance sector which is administered by representatives of trade unions and employer organizations. While public regulations applying to social insurance are in many respects more imperative than in Germany, both unemployment insurance and part of the pension scheme are under the complete control of the social partners. In addition, part of the health insurance sector is still held by independent 'mutuals' (friendly societies) subsumed under the label of 'social economy' (*économie sociale*) which is often seen in the literature as being so highly developed in France (Archambault 2001: 213).

As noted above, French nonprofit associations are largely involved in social service provision even though the regulatory framework, unlike its German counterpart, does not include an explicit commitment to the principle of subsidiarity: That is, there is no legal norm conveying a preferred provider status to these organizations and no corresponding partnership rationale in the public management of the third sector (Bahle 2008). That said, large sections of the social welfare sector are populated by nonprofits. Drawing to varying degrees on volunteers for both their boards and lay workforce, they operate as professionalized agencies running services in various fields, particularly for youth, the elderly, disabled citizens, and disadvantaged workers.

Public regulation has always been strong in France, though. Nonprofit providers have to be accredited by statutory authorities or social insurance bodies in order to receive public funding; in some fields, accreditation is based on formalized mutual agreements (Lévy 2002). Through this procedure, they become what are known as *associations gestionnaires* (service-managing associations). Although these organizations acquired a quasi-monopolistic position (Archambault 1997: 117), in most sections of the social welfare system throughout the last century, state–nonprofit collaboration was altogether less institutionalized than in Germany (Seibel 1992). Public bodies had more discretion over devolving responsibility on the nonprofit sector. Moreover, informal relations at the local level, involving notables and municipal politicians, frequently proved (and still prove) crucial when it comes to the delegation of service provision to the nonprofit sector. In France's municipalities, mayors have a huge political and administrative leadership capacity and command political mandates that span territorial divisions because many of them are members of Parliament or sit on the councils of the *départements*, which are key commissioning bodies (Wollmann 2008). Hence the roles that nonprofit associations adopt in the local welfare system differ considerably from one setting to the other (Bellaredj et al. 2006).

In general, nonprofit providers that enjoy the status of an *association gestionnaire* present themselves as secular organizations. This is in some way a socio-political construction because the model of collaboration that took shape in twentieth century France was largely inspired by a "social concordat" between the Catholic Church and the state (Bec 1994), not much different from what happened in other parts of Continental Europe. A symbolic precondition for becoming entrusted with quasi-public service provision was that providers dissolved their links to faith-based communities.

It is noteworthy that, to a greater degree than its German neighbor, the nonprofit sector in France embraces relatively strong charitable organizations which have stayed outside institutionalized partnerships (Bode 2003). Based on lay action and a comparatively high reliance on private donations, these organizations were long confined to running emergency services in the field of poverty relief. This has partly changed over the last two decades or so. Alongside the more traditional charities rooted in the Catholic Church or in the workers' movement, bottom-up associations such as *Communauté Emmaüs* or *ATD Quart Monde* took center stage during the 1980s as they embarked on public programs against social exclusion. These new players have been referred to as a "model of a new modern charity" (Ferrand-Bechmann 1992: 235). By the late 1980s, even this charitable part of the nonprofit sector had been embraced by the collaborative approach of public management which dominated throughout the post-war decades.

Nowadays, most welfare-providing nonprofits are members of a national umbrella (*Union nationale interfédérale des oeuvres et organismes privés sanitaires et sociaux*, UNIOPSS) which operates at a greater distance from its more diversified membership than do the six umbrella organizations in Germany. In addition, numerous smaller federations exist within particular service sectors or regions. There is, then, considerable fragmentation of those nonprofit organizations that are partnering with the (welfare) state. That said, during the second part of the last century, UNIOPSS developed into a strong political voice for the sector and acquired collective expertise that was regularly solicited by governments intending to draft new policies (Argoud 1992). Thus, while the French nonprofit sector seems less firmly integrated into the state, important sections of it had become influential junior partners of welfare bureaucracies. There was corporatism 'under the surface'—leading to the development of more (or more visible) intersectoral partnerships—although, in public discourse, the French state has accepted partners in public governance only hesitantly (Cole 2008). Overall, then, the classical French settlement of state–nonprofit relations appears less consistent and institutionalized and more pluralistic than the German one; yet, it has nonetheless become based on a similar collaborative arrangement and was highly integrated in the social welfare system.

DEVELOPMENTS UNTIL THE 'MARKET CRISIS'

Internationally, state–nonprofit relations have undergone considerable change over the past two decades: France and Germany are cases in point. In this section, developments in these relations from the 1990s until the market crisis of 2008 are reviewed with particular attention to two subsectors, domiciliary care to frail elderly people, which is a more traditional domain of the German and French nonprofit sector, and work integration (or 'welfare-to-work'), which is new territory for this sector, especially for what meanwhile is referred to as social enterprises (Nyssens 2006). These examples illustrate both the role that market regulations played over this period and the hybrid character of 'post-corporatist' governance, which emerged prior to the advent of the recent economic crisis.

Germany: Toward Welfare Markets

NPM clearly left its hallmarks on the social welfare system in Germany (Bönker & Wollmann 2000). The 1990s saw a revamping of the two key legal acts that were integrated into the "social law code" (*Sozialgesetzbuch*). Reforms in 1993 and 1996 brought the abolition of commissioning rules which had guaranteed a service-delivery mandate to 'licensed' nonprofit providers, that is, those belonging to the official umbrella organizations. In principle, these rules were replaced by performance-oriented patterns of collaboration. Public funding was now meant to be based on both contracts with (often restrictive) price-per-unit funding and a range of (accountability-related) requirements regarding the use of allocated subsidies. Because these contracts became also understood to be more sensitive to quality issues, negotiations between the involved parties on prices and service norms proved laborious and controversial in many places. True, those long-established corporatist networks did not collapse altogether—in some areas (such as youth help), they were often maintained formally. Yet the distance between many nonprofits and their public partners was growing, and the terms of trade were changing.

Moreover, private providers were admitted to the social welfare system. In the field of elderly care, for example, long-term care insurance which came into force in 1996 started paying allowances to frail citizens. Beneficiaries were permitted to choose any provider willing to offer care services. The idea of running local care support centers based on public-nonprofit partnerships was abandoned. Capacity planning was widely phased out, and the care sector was opened to competition. An overhaul of the Children and Youth Welfare Act in 1998 extended this approach to other fields of organized social support. The new regulations included options for public tenders for which private businesses and nonprofit agencies were invited to bid. More recent regulations in 2002 and 2007 imposed extensive quality inspection on social service suppliers. Provider organizations belonging to the traditional nonprofit sector kept a small privilege in that they remained tax exempted (an advantage awarded on the assumption of their 'social utility'). Furthermore, a general clause stating that public policies were meant to support these organizations where appropriate persisted in the legal framework. On the whole, however, the dominance of nonprofit suppliers in the social (and health) care sector was broken, and the 'terms of trade' were increasingly driven by the rules of the market and those controlling it.

In most sections of the social welfare system, the implementation of the aforementioned reforms were, to some extent, negotiated with representatives from the sector—hence the corporatist interface has not been erased completely. At the same time, change proceeded in an incremental way. While some sub-sectors of the social welfare system were already strongly exposed to the new (quasi-) market regime (e.g. in elderly care), marketization has remained confined to pilot schemes in other sub-sectors (e.g. in residential child care). The market regime became partially influential where the type of service or organization at stake was more recent, as in the case of initiatives combating social exclusion through work integration or workfare (Bode et al. 2006; see also Birkhölzer & Lorenz 2001; Niemeyer 2004).

Across the third sector, then, change was inconsistent. Size was a further issue. For a whole generation of smaller agencies living with irregular and scattered streams of public subsidies, aggressive fundraising became imperative and has also grown in importance throughout the more traditional quarters of the German nonprofit sector. Sweet charity, mass mailings, and professionalized public relations—this was where innovation was now meant to take place. Major nonprofit organizations were now striving to develop 'unique selling points' and strengthen their 'project marketing' vis-à-vis public funders or other stakeholders (including donors and volunteers they seek to attract). Most of them have embarked on bidding for extra money out of the EU purse.

More powerful, traditional providers invested in joint ventures and production chains that allowed for large economies of scale and some protection against market pressures. Others attempted to shelter their organizational core from external pressures through a reduction in the number of skilled employees, replaced by (lower-paid) personnel trained on the job. In some local settings, well-established nonprofit organizations (often together with local partners such as political parties) managed to maintain secure long-term block funding, though at lower levels. The fact remains, however, that during the 2000s, large parts of the third sector had become accustomed to thinking of their activities in market terms and reorganized themselves as 'social businesses' (Flösser & Vollhase 2006; Möhring-Hesse 2008). These dynamics materialized in both well-established and newly emerging sub-sectors.

Elderly care, an established field, became a forerunner on the road toward welfare markets (see Bode 2008: 40–43, 69–72; Kondratowitz et al. 2002). This was largely due to the introduction of mandatory long-term care insurance. The latter was widely based on the logic of direct payment as it was awarding lump sum subsidies which users were meant to take up to buy services from independent suppliers (unless they chose a cash-for-care allowance). One should note that these subsidies, as well as means-tested social assistance paid on top of them by the municipalities, frequently do not suffice to ensure decent care; this requires private co-payment which endorses the new market logic further.

In the residential sector, the number of care homes rose markedly as capacity planning accomplished by state–nonprofit agreements ran out of fashion. Commercial supply was on the rise. Care homes began to compete for residents, including those interested in serviced apartments (a business allowing for some cross-subsidization). In the domiciliary sector, provider rivalry was gaining momentum, too (Bode 2006b). By 2010, only half of the market was held by voluntary sector agencies, providing nursing care and some additional bits of personal care (often with a temporary remit from local authorities). True, there were some efforts to ensure better networking, including through the proactive coordination of service providers (e.g. at the boundary of personal and health care); yet in most cases, institutional support for this was granted on the basis of pilot schemes run for a limited period of time, with the subsidized agencies being expected to take over the burden subsequently.

The old collaborative approach continued to have an effect, though. To some extent, the conditions under which services were reimbursed remained agreed upon between associations of service providers, on the one hand, and regional bodies of long-term care insurance funds, on the other. While the lump sums that these regional bodies granted beneficiaries were capped, some leeway was left to the negotiating parties concerning the design of the service packages on offer. Furthermore, associations of non-profit providers, exerting political pressure on governments through public campaigns, worked hard to suggest amendments in the overall regulation of their sub-sector, for instance concerning general quality norms. However, such norms proved market-embedding rather than market-constraining.

Welfare markets appeared to be even more developed in the field of initiatives combating social exclusion through *organized work integration* (Birkhölzer & Lorenz 2001; Bode et al. 2006; Niemeyer 2004). Against the background of both high long-term unemployment and a reluctance of major stakeholders of the welfare state to admit a volatile "working-poor labor market" (emblematic of Anglo-Saxon societies), the 1980s saw the rise of a new sub-field within the German social welfare system. In this sub-field, independent voluntary agencies and various initiatives often under the auspices of the big welfare associations, created sheltered workshops or similar undertakings in order to provide basic training, social support, and work experience to those facing problems on the ordinary labor market. The essential idea behind these initiatives was to combine job supply with the production of goods and services where both the (mainstream) public sector and the market appeared to fail (e.g. recycling of used items, second-hand trade, etc.). These work integration activities were co-funded by a variety of public sources, including subsidies from the Federal Labor Office, the social budget of the municipalities, and EU programs. Many of the initiatives conceptualized themselves as independent undertakings pursuing both economic and social aims. From this perspective, they were an early expression of what has become common to be coined "social enterprises" (Kerlin 2006; Nyssens 2006). Throughout the 1980s and early 1990s (during the latter period, particularly in Eastern Germany), municipalities embarked on this social business as well. For the time being, such undertakings were, at least partly, subject to corporatist regulations regarding both funding and the terms under which integration programs were run. However, work integration firms never achieved the institutional status that the more traditional social service agencies had enjoyed throughout the twentieth century. Also, many of them were compelled to raise funds independently of public programs, mostly through the sale of goods and services (e.g. in the recycling business). That said, the public promotion of what was referred to as a "second labor market" helped the new nonprofit actors settle in the social welfare system and confront (quasi-) public authorities (including the Labor Offices) with their particular approach to combat unemployment and social exclusion.

While the idea of a second labor market has more or less persisted, public policies and underlying state–nonprofit relations in this particular field changed markedly from the mid-1990s onward. Arguing that work integration initiatives have largely failed to bring their clientele back into ordinary work, subsequent governments have revamped the support schemes in order to downsize the overall sector (especially those parts of it offering vocational training to adults), reduced the salaries paid, and cut the length of employment with these initiatives (from two years to nine months in most cases). Funding was increasingly confined to (ever less generous) wage subsidies, thus exerting increasing pressure on the initiatives to raise resources through the marketing of goods and services.

The so-called "Hartz-reforms," enacted between 2002 and 2006 and geared toward making German labor market policies conform to the international 'work-first' mainstream, put additional strain on work integration initiatives (Seeleib-Kaiser & Fleckenstein 2007). Largely drawing on the NPM model, welfare bureaucracies responsible for (co-) funding these initiatives started to treat them as 'business partners' under contract with public purchasers. Commissioning was meant to be reorganized and tailored on distinctive packages of 'integration services' (including profiling, placement, short-term re-adaptation to a work environment). Moreover, regional units of the Federal Labor Office, as well as some municipal welfare departments, sought to make nonprofit initiatives compete with private businesses. The key idea was to subjugate subsidized employment to rigid efficiency norms in terms of successful short-term placements of the unemployed in the regular labor market. Jobseekers were now being conceived as 'customers' choosing their 'integration provider,' if possible via a voucher scheme. Meanwhile, a growing part of this sub-sector has adopted a business-oriented approach, stressing economic accountancy and measurable performance at the expense of social empowerment and innovation leading to more enabling work settings.

While in some places, the interactions between the initiatives and public bodies continued to be led by an agreement-oriented approach, with both sides bringing their own concepts and visions to bear, the partnership elsewhere became infused by the managerialistic attitudes inherent to the philosophy of NPM. Nonetheless, organizations rooted in the nonprofit sector remained active in the field of work integration, mostly on behalf of public bodies, sometimes by relying on niche markets. Regional or local governments made ample use of the sector's capacity to provide short-term work opportunities to those with low employability, although the terms of employment were much less generous and sustainable than in the early days of the sub-sector.

By the time of the financial crisis, then, the end of the old partnership model was obvious, although the sector continued to exploit its 'political capital' in order to exert influence on regulations and programs. On the whole, one can say that, in this period, Germany saw an uneasy and inconsistent transition to a post-corporatist governance model.

France: Welfare Markets through the Back Door

Until the end of the 2000s, France maintained many of the particularities inherent to its post-war governance model. This also applies to the regulation of social and health care provided by non-statutory agencies. In contrast to other Western countries, fully-fledged welfare markets barely emerged throughout the Hexagon. One reason for this was the reluctance of French elites to embrace the NPM approach as understood from the Anglo-Saxon world, although some of its ingredients were adopted here and there (Cole & Jones 2005; Minvielle 2006).

Concerning state–nonprofit relations, the rules of the game began changing nonetheless. In 2002, an amendment to the so-called "orientation law" of 1975 (the regulatory framework relevant to the social service sector) brought a modification of the provisions governing partnerships between public bodies and non-public service providers. Public subsidies, awarded on a price-per-person basis in most cases, remained largely fixed by state bureaucracies (although based on calculations provided by service agencies). However, the 'public licence' the providers have to obtain in order to enjoy guarantees as regards institutional protection and public resourcing now became subject to regular revisions on the basis of evaluation reports. By the same token, public funding increasingly adopted the form of a contract-based subsidy linked to an agreement on objectives—even though most contracts were rather long-term and often follow cross-party consensus on these objectives. As to non-public organizations working with the long-term unemployed, public support helped hedge their social businesses. However, these latecomers in the social welfare system, like their German counterparts, never enjoyed the same institutional protection as the more traditional agencies in the social and health care field.

Moreover, progressive decentralization altered the patterns of public funding across the whole nonprofit sector, with growing diversity across the national territory because of a shift in responsibilities to the regional layers of public administration. While various governments strengthened the formal acknowledgment of nonprofit organizations as both participants in the public debate and service providers, there was evidence of reduced public funding throughout large parts of the sector (Archambault & Boumendil 2002; Tchernonog 2007). This may be one reason why the third sector in France, like its German counterpart, increasingly invests in charity businesses, mass mailings, and professionalized public relations.

In addition, public tenders became more widespread, albeit not a general pattern. A certain number of social projects run by voluntary agencies were exposed to 'quasi-competition' insofar as these agencies, when suggesting new activities to local authorities, were facing public partners free to decide on whether, and to what extent, they supported them financially, rather than to look out for other providers. This, for instance, became a widespread pattern in out-reach work with homeless citizens which was run by schemes based on year-to-year contracts (Bode 2003). While the respective partnerships appeared quite robust over a longer period of time, secure guarantees were never on offer here.

That said, umbrella associations of nonprofit providers remained important social policy players. When it came to the reform of the overall jurisdiction relevant to the state–nonprofit interface in the French social welfare system, for instance, major umbrellas representing the sector were reported to have operated as "co-préparateurs" of the (amended) orientation law (Lévy 2002: 423). Moreover, after the great heat wave in 2003 involving the deaths of thousands of frail elderly citizens, the then government and representatives of the care industry agreed on a national plan to improve the conditions under which residents of care homes were hosted, with a huge increase in public subsidies awarded to that industry. Thus, corporatism was not abandoned—however, its scope was decreasing.

Again, the subtleties of the new settlement become discernible with a closer examination of the elder care and work integration fields. As regards *elderly care*, nonprofit agencies have remained major service providers, as they have in Germany (see Bode 2008: 48–50, 75–77; Frossard et al. 2004). During the 2000s, the *départements*, by tradition entrusted with the management of the overall care infrastructure, continued resorting to the expertise of nonprofit providers (and their umbrella organizations). Care suppliers were licensed for a given territory and compensated according to evidenced outlays (for care recipients unable to pay). In principle, the state–nonprofit interface inherited from the post-war settlement did not change significantly. However, commercial care homes had mushroomed over the last decades, and, in theory at least, these were eligible for public subsidies as well—notwithstanding the fact that most commercial homes relied almost exclusively on self-paying residents.

More encompassing change was taking place in domiciliary care where governments sought to develop a mixed service market (CERC 2008: 29–57). From the early 1990s onward, various programs aimed at increasing the number of home helpers directly employed by frail senior citizens were launched, with the main support mechanism being exemptions on taxes and social insurance contributions normally paid by employers. Private home helpers proved strong competition for nonprofit agencies providing domiciliary care services on a professional basis (Bode 2006b). The *Plan Borloo*, enacted in 2005, enhanced the tax credit and made the individual purchase of personal care services easier to manage. Also, a national regulation clarified the conditions under which commercial agencies, until then marginal in the field, had a right to be licensed by the *départements*. Furthermore, a law enacted in 2003 stipulated that the provision of domiciliary care was meant to be publicly subsidized according to evidenced performance, agreed in provider-specific contracts; it abolished the monopoly of the previous funding model based on a fee-per-hour arrangement. This opened the doors to more competitive public commissioning.

Concomitantly, a procedure for issuing quality labels was established by the end of the 1990s. This came after associations of nonprofit home care providers sought to further professionalize the industry, including by more formalized partnerships among themselves and with (quasi-) public bodies. Major aims of these initiatives were to ensure sector-wide quality standards and exert influence on public programs meant to boost this sub-sector, including collective agreements on pay rises to which the state is conferring universal validity.

Overall, while commercial provision remained the exception, there were clear tendencies toward increased supplier rivalry. This was reflected by the national umbrellas of nonprofit home care providers investing in broader marketing activities. For instance, these umbrellas and some of their corporate members sought to establish 'service shops' and call centres intended to channel new clients to their services, with the key objective being to attract additional groups of users. Often, such investments were realized through partnerships with businesses seeking cross-selling opportunities (especially insurance companies).

Another competitor of nonprofit care organizations was publicly subsidized welfare-to-work agencies leasing their staff to private households—here, the elderly care sector overlapped with *work integration initiatives* (Barbier & Théret 2000; Bucolo 2006; Chanial & Laville 2004). Similar to what happened in Germany, this sub-branch of the social welfare system took shape from the late 1970s onward against the background of rising long-term unemployment. Likewise, national regulations provided financial support, with local and regional governments offering additional subsidies on a voluntary basis. These support policies became generalized with the promulgation of anti-poverty laws at the end of the 1980s. The new provisions stipulated that recipients of (means-tested) welfare benefits should be given opportunities to find their way back into an ordinary life course (the French term coined for this is *réinsertion*). Initiatives offering these opportunities had to be officially admitted by a commission under the control of the *département*. By this, social enterprises taking disadvantaged citizens on board in order to offer them training or occupational experience became part of the social welfare system in France as they did in Germany—although France's legal framework was less imperative regarding the activities undertaken by these agencies.

Various types of work integration initiatives emerged, including charitable agencies leasing their workforce to private households (or small companies), fully-fledged businesses producing varied goods and services (named *entreprises d'insertion* or *entreprises solidaires*), and commercial (branches of) temporary work agencies specializing in placing disadvantaged employees on the regular labor market. Most initiatives joined umbrella organizations with a remit to represent this new generation of not-for-profit undertakings in the political arena. These umbrellas (often headed by well-known personalities) apparently helped convince the political elites to further institutionalize the partnership between the state and this sub-sector during the 1990s and 2000s. At the local level, spokespersons of the latter were often sitting in multi-party boards entrusted with the design of social integration policies. In that particular respect, this branch of the French social welfare system became included in the corporatist (governance) settlement.

That said, this sub-branch of the French social welfare system was evolving amid a market-driven environment. Although most stakeholders of the French social welfare system would hesitate to admit the very conception of (quasi-) market governance in public administration, the traces of NPM were undeniable. Agencies providing work integration were enabled to adopt a commercial status but remained nevertheless eligible for public support, provided one third of their workforce consists of socially disadvantaged (mostly long-term unemployed) citizens. By the same token, the funding regime was changing. The regulation established in 1998 stipulated that lump-sum subsidies were paid to them for each employment created. Following a reform enacted in 2008, public subsidies awarded to work integration enterprises became premised on contracts setting targets and a number of procedural norms. Overall, most work integration initiatives always depended on self-funding to a much greater degree than their fellow organizations in the remainder of the social and health care sector in France or their counterparts in Germany. Self-funding was ensured, *inter alia*, through encompassing but often precarious, economic activities or niche markets, such as the ones for waste recycling or small-scale personal care.

By the end of the 2000s, welfare markets, while developing more timidly than in Germany, had entered some services provided by the French non-profit sector, if through the back doors. As in Germany, a post-corporatist framework emerged; however, it contained a smaller dose of (quasi-) market governance, which made France lag behind what happened elsewhere in the Western world. But did this imply a more favorable environment for the return of a non-market-based public management of the nonprofit sector in response to the financial crisis? The next section provides some clues for exploring the initial impact of the financial crisis on both countries.

CRISIS? WHAT CRISIS?

It was not before early 2009 that the crisis of the financial market and related market institutions hit Continental Europe. Accounts on how this affected the public management of the nonprofit sector are at a very preliminary state and confined to a snap-shot analysis based on general observations. In France and Germany, major impacts on the nonprofit sector have been twofold: First, public finances were squeezed as governments had to put substantial amounts of money into the banking system. At the same time, economic growth turned into recession, with a reduction in both tax revenues and contributions levied by social security schemes. The public budget out of which service-providing nonprofits were paid was constrained quite heavily, although pressures have been lower than in most parts of the Anglo-Saxon world. That said, the economic contraction proved quite strong in Germany where the GDP shrank by 5 percent in 2009, whereas France was less affected. While both countries were in a state of slow recovery during 2010, continental welfare states have certainly not been preserved from the international crisis.

Concomitantly, the legitimacy of markets as tools of coordination in the economy has been questioned in the public media and by a growing number of academics in this part of the world. The number of newspaper articles and academic essays dealing with the crisis of capitalism, the aberrations of neoliberalism, and the limits to market governance has been quite impressive in both countries. Governments and politicians have proclaimed the end of an era of laissez-faire regulation. Although the call for reform has focused on the financial sector, there has been some debate on the alleged virtues of privatization in the public sector which seems to imply that past policies around the organization of public services have come under scrutiny. Yet what does this imply in terms of the public management of the nonprofit sector?

Three observations can be made at this early stage. First of all, the international response to the crisis has far and wide consisted of deficit spending policies meant to stabilize the wider economy, including through subsidies paid to employers keeping staff on board despite reduced workloads, but also through greater public outlays in general. This has entailed a business-as-usual approach in the French and German nonprofit sectors that work 'on behalf of' government. Social and health care have been among those sub-sectors where employment rates were not touched by the crisis due to unchanged (quasi-) public funding streams. Because foundations relying on capital (interest) income play only a marginal role as funders of the nonprofit sector in both countries, the crisis of endowments and grantmaking felt in the US and elsewhere did not directly affect the revenues of the French or German nonprofit sectors.

Secondly, in some ways, public policy responses to the economic crisis have actually strengthened the resource base of the nonprofit sector in France and Germany. Both countries saw larger subsidies awarded to agencies giving work (and support) to unemployed citizens following the crisis. New workfare jobs in Germany and public employment schemes targeting youth in France brought additional public support to some sections of the nonprofit sector, although this has strengthened the sector's tendency to have a large share of precarious workers. Seen in this light, the crisis has not entailed an additional burden for the sector. It remains to be seen whether it will suffer from the politics of austerity in the near future.

Yet thirdly, and this is striking, those elements of the hybrid governance model that are rooted in the (quasi-) market governance mantra that has infused the public management of the nonprofit sector since the 1990s have *not* been challenged by major political and societal elites in the two countries. Quite the contrary: Policies of exposing nonprofit agencies to market forces have been consolidated in a number of areas. For instance, efforts of the French government to create a mixed market of personal care services were bolstered in 2009, in that the legal provisions as well as infrastructure logistics (such as collective agreements) were rolled out further. In Germany, there have been additional attempts to make users of care services behave like consumers because competitive quality assessments of service providers are now published in public venues. In other fields, the 'habits' established with the implementation of welfare or quasi-markets have not changed notably. This holds true for those fields in which nonprofit providers had already been exposed to tough competition. But it also affects those sections of the sector featuring a (hybrid) post-corporatist framework where nonprofit organizations participate in the public management of the sector through negotiations and contracts. Even as the sector's political influence seems to continue its decline, providers at the local level are ever less sheltered from market pressures. In a word, the legitimacy of (quasi-) market governance in the nonprofit sector has been anything but undermined by the market crisis in the wider economy.

CONCLUSION

This chapter has provided evidence for structural change in state–nonprofit relations in two leading nations of Continental Europe. In the case of Germany, change has come through far-reaching institutional innovation, and in France it has occurred through more incremental dynamics of transformation. Germany has seen the establishment of fully-fledged welfare markets, whereas in France this movement is thus far confined to some niches of the social welfare system, among which is the newly emerging field of work integration. In both countries, the nonprofit sector has undergone creeping marketization over the past two decades, even though the pre-established corporatist framework has not been abandoned entirely. Rather, this framework adopted new forms from the 1990s onward, with partnerships between nonprofit organizations and the state becoming less binding and more volatile, if sometimes more extensive. The scope of substantial regulations was decreasing overall, even as these regulations became less inclusive because newcomers in the sector were facing fewer institutional guarantees than their forerunners. Both countries, then, moved toward a *post-corporatist configuration* exhibiting a hybrid mix of quasi-market governance and agreement-based regulation. At the local level, this has translated into greater situational variety, as the repertoire of governance tools available to welfare bureaucracies has grown markedly. The evidence thus shows that the (post-)corporatist world exhibits some, and probably growing, variety *within the model itself*—which is an observation confirmed by research done on the wider development of Continental welfare states (see e.g. Barbier & Ludwig-Mayerhofer 2004; Morel 2007). What is clear is that this transformation does not accord with the accounts popular in the public management literature of a shift from government to governance or from quasi-markets to networks.

The continental 'family of welfare' does not evolve homogeneously, though. Comparing France and Germany, 'inter-family' differences are obvious indeed. While formerly dense partnerships are becoming looser in twenty-first century Germany, the French nonprofit sector has witnessed the erosion of old-style corporatism (confined to smaller sections of the sector throughout the post-war settlement) in a much less salient way. Rather, the 'new-partnership' discourse that proliferated in the 1980s and 1990s went alongside developments toward more formalized collaboration. However, this collaboration never achieved the same level of reliability as did state–nonprofit partnerships both in the German model and in those parts of the French nonprofit sector which had been subject to corporatist regulation from very early onward. Moreover, in contrast to Germany, France seems to have embarked on NPM in a very reduced and particular version, yet it remains to be seen whether the competition-oriented rationale underlying this approach of public management will grow stronger throughout its welfare and health care system as well.

While the situation was not the same in the two countries prior to the financial crisis, responses to the latter do not differ very much. On the one hand, the sector has, thus far, not seen a growing budgetary pressure as such, especially for those organizations that are entrusted with the delivery of public services. Rather, political responses to the crisis have brought some additional resources to the sector. On the other hand, the obviously decreasing legitimacy of markets as regulatory devices in the wider economy has not been echoed by more critical attitudes concerning quasi-market approaches in the public management of the nonprofit sector. The creeping marketization which, prior to the crisis, had begun to erode network-based forms of governance has persisted and has not been questioned by major stakeholders of the sector.

This implies, however, that push-factors toward marketization are quite robust possibly because they are deeply entrenched in the culture of contemporary civil society (Crouch 2004), including among the academic middle classes who seem to sympathize with growing individualism and less collectivism in the welfare state. More generally, these forces, together with business elites, have come to largely remold public expectations as to what (public) service-providing nonprofit organizations should deliver: Such expectations embrace both choice and user responsiveness *and* measurable outputs delivered to 'commissioners.' This "market populism" (Clarke &

Newman 2009: 86) is an agenda imposed on the welfare state for some time now, and it has largely passed over on to the nonprofit sector (Kelly 2007 for the case of the UK).

This persistence of market orientations alongside network-based collaboration—that is, of the hybrid governance model taking center stage throughout Continental Europe in the new millennium—is not without an impact on how and what nonprofit organizations can deliver. A key issue is sustainability. The post-corporatist approach makes state–nonprofit relations in this part of the world appear more tension-driven overall. While networks grow in scope here and there, the density of the nonprofit sector's networking with public authorities is decreasing even as these networks now embrace 'strangers' from the commercial sector.

The result is permanent *dis- and reorganization* of the cross-sectoral interface. The nonprofit sector is increasingly exposed to volatile inter-linkages (fixed-term contracts, short-lived joint ventures, etc.) and to a somehow schizophrenic experience of being invited to both participate more strongly in collaborative processes and compete more fiercely (see Bode 2006a). Irrespective of the recent economic crisis, then, the overarching trend is toward more nervous patterns of governance, featuring a growing role of competitive orientations mixed up with both multi-party networking and new forms of hierarchical surveillance due to the necessity to control 'partners in public service.' It is too early to discuss the material results that the new post-corporatist configuration will have in terms of social welfare outputs. Thus far, Continental European nonprofit agencies continue to operate, and are publicly perceived, as mission-driven agencies in the first instance. A closer look, however, reveals that a larger share of the organizational energy of these agencies is devoted to marketing policies and business development. Should such tendencies persist, the distinctive capacity of multi-purpose nonprofit undertakings—their ability to combine needs-led service provision, unbiased political advocacy, and mission-led work in the community—can no longer be taken for granted. In the long run, this may even undermine the legitimacy of the sector as such, whether at the expense of a revived bureaucratic state or ever more unleashed market forces.

REFERENCES

Anheier, H. K., & Seibel, W. (2001). *The Nonprofit Sector in Germany. Between state, economy and society.* Manchester: Manchester University Press.

Archambault, E. (2001). "Historical roots of the nonprofit sector in France." *Nonprofit and Voluntary Sector Quarterly*, 30: 204–220.

Archambault, E. (1997). *The Nonprofit Sector in France.* Manchester: Manchester University Press.

Archambault, E., & Boumendil, J. (2002). "Dilemmas of public/private partnership in France." In U. Ascoli and C. Ranci (eds.), *Dilemmas of the Welfare Mix. The new structure of welfare in an era of privatization.* New York: Kluwer Academic/Plenum Publishers.

Argoud, D. (1992). "L'UNIOPPS: un 'ministère privé' des affaires sociales?" *Revue française des affaires sociales*, 46 : 93–104.

Bahle, T. (2008). "The state and social services in Britain, France in Germany since the 1980s: Reform and growth in a period of welfare state crisis." *European Societies*, 10: 25–47.

Barbier, J.-C., & Ludwig-Mayerhofer, W. (2004). "The many worlds of activation." *European Societies*, 6: 423–436.

Barbier, J.-C., & Théret, B. (2000). "Welfare-to-work or work-to-welfare: The French case." In N. Gilbert and R. Van Voorhis (eds.), *Activating the Unemployed. A Comparative Appraisal of Work-oriented Policies*. New Brunswick and London: Transaction Publishers.

Bec, C. (1994). *Assistance République. La recherche d'un nouveau contrat social sous la III^{ieme} République*. Paris: Éditions de l'Atelier.

Bellaredj, F., Douard, O., Pouchadon, M.-L., et al. (2006). "*L'action sociale des communes de taille moyenne. Une analyse monographique dans quatre communes de 50 000 à moins de 100 000 habitants*", *DREES Études et Résultats No.530. October.* Paris.

Birkhölzer, K., & Lorenz, G. (2001). "Germany: Work integration through employment and training companies in Berlin and its surrounding regions." In R. Spear, J. Defourny, L. Favreau, et al. (eds.), *Tackling Social Exclusion in Europe*. Aldershot: Ashgate.

Blomgren-Bingham, L., Nabatchi, T., & O'Leary, R. (2005). "The New Governance: Practices and processes for stakeholder and citizen participation in the work of government." *Public Administration*, 65: 547–585.

Bode, I. (2010a). "Thinking beyond borderlines: A German gaze on a changing interface between society and the voluntary sector." *Voluntary Sector Review*, 1: 139–61.

Bode, I. (2010b). "Towards Disorganised Governance in Public Service Provision? The Case of German Sickness Funds." *International Journal of Public Administration*, 33: 61–72.

Bode, I. (2008). *The Culture of Welfare Markets. The international recasting of care and pension systems*. New York/London: Routledge.

Bode, I. (2006a). "Disorganized welfare mixes: Voluntary agencies and New Governance regimes in Western Europe." *Journal of European Social Policy*, 19: 346–359.

Bode, I. (2006b). "Co-governance within networks and the nonprofit-forprofit Divide: A cross-cultural perspective on the evolution of domiciliary elderly care." *Public Management Review*, 8: 551–566.

Bode, I. (2004). *Disorganisierter Wohlfahrtskapitalismus. Die Reorganisation des Sozialsektors in Deutschland, Frankreich und Großbritannien*. Wiesbaden: Verlag für Sozialwissenschaften.

Bode, I. (2003). "A new agenda for European charity. Catholic welfare and organizational change in France and Germany." *Voluntas*, 14: 205–225.

Bode, I., Evers, A., & Schulz, A. D. (2006). "Where do we go from here? The unfinished story of relations between social enterprises and public policies in Germany." In M. Nyssens (ed.), *Social Enterprise, At the crossroads of market, public policies and civil society*. London/New York: Taylor & Francis.

Boeßenecker, K.-H. (2005). "*Spitzenverbände der Freien Wohlfahrtspflege. Eine Einführung*" *in Organizationsstruktur und Handlungsfelder der deutschen Wohlfahrtsverbände*. Weinheim/München: Juventa.

Bönker, F., & Wollmann, H. (2000). "The rise and fall of a social service regime: Marketisation of German social services in historical perspective." In H. Wollmann and E. Schroeter (eds.), *Comparing Public Sector Reform in Britain and Germany*. Aldershot: Ashgate.

Bucolo, E. (2006). "French social enterprises: A common ethical framework to balance various objectives." In M. Nyssens (ed.), *Social Enterprise, at the Crossroads of Market, Public Policies and Civil Society*. London/New York: Routledge.

Budd, L. (2007). "Post-bureaucracy and reanimating public governance: A discourse and practice of continuity?" *International Journal of Public Sector Management*, 20: 531–547.

Carmel, E., & Harlock, J. (2008). "Instituting the 'third sector' as a governable terrain: Partnership, procurement and performance in the UK." *Policy & Politics*, 36: 155–171.

Casey, J. (2004). "Third sector participation in the policy process: A framework for comparative analysis." *Policy & Politics*, 32: 241–257.

CERC (Conseil Emploi Revenues Cohésion Sociale). (2008). *Les services à la personne*. Rapport No. 8. Paris: CERC.

Chanial, P., & Laville, J.-L. (2004). "French civil society experiences: Attempts to bridge the gap between political and economic dimensions." In A. Evers and J.-L. Laville (eds.), *The Third Sector in Europe*. Cheltenham: Edward Elgar.

Chapman, T., Brown, J., & Crow, R. (2008). "Entering a brave new world? An assessment of third sector readiness to tender for the delivery of public services in the United Kingdom." *Policy Studies*, 29: 1–17.

Clarke, J., & Newman, J. (2009). *Publics, Politics and Power: Remaking the public in public services*. London: Sage.

Cole, A. (2008). *Governing and Governance in France*. Cambridge: Cambridge University Press.

Cole, A., & Jones, G. (2005). "Reshaping the state: Administrative reform and New Public Management in France." *Governance*, 18: 567–588.

Crouch, C., & Streeck, W. (eds.). (2006). *The Diversity of Democracy. Corporatism, social order, and political conflict*. Cheltenham: Edward Elgar.

Davies, J. S. (2005). "Local governance and the dialectics of hierarchy, market and network." *Policy Studies*, 25: 311–335.

Entwistle, T., & Martin, S. (2005). "From competition to collaboration in public service delivery: A new agenda for research." *Public Administration*, 83: 233–242.

Evers, A. (2005). "Mixed welfare systems and hybrid organisations: Changes in the governance and provision of social services." *International Journal of Public Administration*, 28: 737–748.

Evers, A., & Sachße, C. (2003). "Social care services for children and older people in Germany: Distinct and separate histories." In A. Anttonen, J. Baldock, & J. Sipilä (eds.), *The Young, the Old and the State. Social care systems in five industrial nations*. Cheltenham: Edward Elgar.

Feiock, R. C., & Andrew, S. A. (2006). "Understanding the relationships between nonprofit organizations and local governments." *International Journal of Public Administration*, 29: 759–767.

Ferrand-Bechmann, D. (1992). "The mission, purposes, and functions of nonprofit organizations in France." In K. D. McCarthy, V. A. Hodgkinson, R. D. Summariwalla, et al. (eds.), *The Nonprofit Sector in the Global Community*. San Franzisco: Jossey-Bass.

Flösser, G., & Vollhase, M. (2006). "Freie Wohlfahrtspflege zwischen subsidiärer Leistungserbringung und Wettbewerb." In G. Hensen (ed.), *Markt und Wettbewerb in der Jugendhilfe. Ökonomisierung im Kontext von Zukunftsorientierung und fachlicher Notwendigkeit*. Weinheim: Juventa.

Frossard, M., Genin, N., Guisset, M.-J., et al. (2004). "Providing integrated health and social care for older persons in France: An Old Idea with a Great Future." In K. Leichsenring & A. Alaszewski (eds.), *Providing Integrated Health and Social*

Care for Older Persons. An European overview of issues at stake. Aldershot: Ashgate.

Gilbert, N. (2002). *Transformation of the Welfare State: The silent surrender of public responsibility.* Oxford: Oxford University Press.

Hasenfeld, Y., & Gidron, B. (2005). "Understanding multi-purpose hybrid voluntary organizations: The contributions of theories on civil society, social movements and non-profit organizations." *Journal of Civil Society,* 1: 97–112.

Katz, M. B., & Sachße, C. (eds.). (1996). *The Mixed Economy of Social Welfare: Public/private relations in England, Germany and the United States.* Baden-Baden: Nomos.

Kendall, J. (ed.). (2008). *Handbook on Third Sector Policy in Europe. Multi-level processes and organized civil society.* Cheltenham: Edward Elgar.

Kerlin, J. A. (2006). "Social enterprise in the United States and Europe: Understanding and learning from the differences." *Voluntas,* 17: 247–263.

Kondratowitz, H.-J., Tesch-Römer, C., & Motel-Klingebiel, A. (2002). "Establishing systems of care in Germany: A long and winding road." *Aging—Clinical and Experimental Research,* 14: 239–246.

Kooïman, J. (2003). *Governing as Governance.* London: Sage.

Lahusen, C. (2006). "European integration and civil societies: Between welfare regimes and service markets." In M. Bach & G. Vobruba (eds.), *Europe in Motion. Social dynamics and political institutions in an enlarging Europe.* Berlin: Sigma.

Lambie, G. (2009). "Nemesis of 'Market Fundamentalism'? The ideology, deregulation and crisis of Finance." *Contemporary Politics,* 15: 157–177.

Lévy, M. (2002). " La loi du 2 janvier 2002 rénovant l'action sociale et médico-sociale: changement et/ou continuité." *Revue du droit sanitaire et social,* 38: 423–464.

Lewis, J. (2005). "New Labour's approach to the voluntary sector: Independence and the meaning of partnership." *Social Policy & Society,* 4: 121–131.

Liebig, R. (2005). *Wohlfahrtsverbände im Ökonomisierungsdilemma. Analysen zu Strukturveränderungen am Beispiel des Produktionsfaktors Arbeit im Licht der Korporatismus- und der Dritte Sektor-Theorie.* Freiburg: Lambertus.

Lloyd, P. (2004). "The European Union and its programmes related to the third system." In E. Adalbert & J.-L. Laville (eds.), *The Third sector in Europe.* Cheltenham: Edward Elgar.

Minvielle, E. (2006). "The New Public Management à la française: The case of regional hospital agencies." *Public Administration,* 753–763.

Morel, N. (2007). "From Subsidiarity to 'free choice': Child- and elder-care policy reforms in France, Belgium, Germany and the Netherlands." *Social Policy & Administration,* 41: 618–637.

Najam, A. (2000). "The four-C's model of third sector-government relationships." *Nonprofit Management & Leadership,* 10: 375–396.

Niemeyer, B. (2004). "Marketisation vs education? A case study from the micro level of a German programme for vocational preparation." In R. Husemann & A. Heikkinnnen (eds.), *Governance and Marketisation in Vocational and Continuing Education.* Frankfurt etc.: Lang.

Noordhoek, P., & Saner, R. (2005). "Beyond New Public Management: Answering the claims of both politics and society." *Public Organization Review,* 5: 35–53.

Nyssens, M. (ed.). (2006). *Social Enterprise, At the crossroads of market, public policies and civil society.* London: Routledge.

Osborne, S. P. (2006). "The New Public Governance?" *Public Management Review,* 8: 377–387.

Pierre, J. (ed.). (2000). *Debating Governance: Authority, steering, and governance.* New York: Oxford University Press.

Pollitt, C. (2007). "Convergence or divergence? What has been happening in Europe?" In C. Pollitt, S. Van Thiel, & V. Homburg (eds.), *New Public Management in Europe. Adaptation and alternatives.* Basingstoke: Palgrave Macmillan.

Rhodes, R. A. W. (2007). "Understanding governance: Ten years on." *Organization Studies*, 28: 1243–1264.

Rhodes, R. A. W. (1996). "The New Governance: Governing without government." *Political Studies*, 46: 652–667.

Rymsza, M., & Zimmer, A. (2004). "Embeddedness of nonprofit organizations: Government-nonprofit relationships." In A. Zimmer & E. Priller (eds.), *Future of Civil Society. Making Central European nonprofit-organizations Work.* Wiesbaden: Verlag für Sozialwissenschaften.

Salamon, L. M. (1995). *Partners in Public Service: Government-nonprofit relations in the modern welfare state.* Baltimore, MD: Johns Hopkins University Press.

Salamon, L. M., & Anheier, H. K. (1998). "Social origins of civil society: Explaining the nonprofit sector cross-nationally." *Voluntas*, 9: 213–248.

Seeleib-Kaiser, M., & Fleckenstein, T. (2007). "Discourse, learning and welfare state change: The case of German labor market reforms." *Social Policy & Administration*, 41: 427–448.

Seibel, W. (1992). "Government-nonprofit Relationship: Styles and linkage patterns in France and Germany." In S. Kuehnle & P. Selle (eds.), *Government and Voluntary Associations. A relational perspective.* Aldershot: Avebury.

Smith, S. R. (2002). "Privatization, devolution, and the welfare state: Rethinking the prevailing wisdom." In B. Rothstein & S. Steinmo (eds.), *Restructuring the Welfare State: Political institutions and political change.* New York/Houndmills Basingstoke: Palgrave Macmillan.

Taylor-Gooby, P. (2008). "The new welfare state settlement in Europe." *European Societies*, 10: 3–24.

Tchernonog, V. (2007). *L'état des associations. Le paysage associatif français et ses évolutions.* Paris: Dalloz-Juris Associations.

Treib, O., Bähr, H., & Falkner, G. (2007). "Modes of governance: Towards a conceptual clarification." *European Journal of Public Policy*, 14: 1–20.

Wollmann, H. (2008). "Reforming local leadership and local democracy: The cases of England, Sweden, Germany and France in comparative perspective." *Local Government Studies*, 34: 279–298.

Young, D. R. (2000). "Alternative models of government-nonprofit relations: Theoretical and international perspectives." *Nonprofit and Voluntary Sector Quarterly*, 29: 149–172.

Zimmer, A. (1999). "Corporatism revisited—The legacy of history and the German non-profit-sector." *Voluntas*, 10: 37–49.

6 Government–Nonprofit Sector Relations in Hungary
Aspirations, Efforts, and Impacts

Éva Kuti

INTRODUCTION

Though one of the strongest aspirations of post-socialist Hungary is to become a developed democratic country, the challenges its government faces are somewhat different from those common in most developed parts of the world. The issues of New Public Management (NPM), 'new,' 'horizontal,' 'relational,' or 'community' governance and 'smart' or 'responsive' regulation are combined with the need for structural changes and democratization.

Hungary was a state socialist country when NPM started its 'career' as a new paradigm of public administration in the late 1970s. Neither the aims of NPM (improvements in the efficiency and effectiveness of public services, more focus on the citizen/customer, increasing accountability in the public sector) nor its techniques (entrepreneurial leadership, business-type managerialism, competition in resource allocation, contracting out services, etc.) fitted the ideology and practice of the almighty State. While the NPM-inspired public management reforms swept through the developed countries in the 1980s (Hood 1995), the Hungarian public administration remained practically untouched by these new ideas. This also means that the problems which had given rise to NPM in other countries were not properly addressed in Hungary until the collapse of the state socialist regime in 1989.

Thus the popularity of the idea of relational governance and responsive regulation cannot stem from the failure or weaknesses of NPM. The need for more efficiency and more accountability coexists with the need for greater collaboration between government and civil society, for more intense civil society participation in the regulatory process, and for shared responsibility in decision making. The willingness of civil society organizations to be equal and genuine partners in governing is mainly a reaction against their former subordination; it is an important element of the transition from the autocratic regime to a democratic one. The emergence of the governance paradigm in the developed part of the world can be qualified as a lucky coincidence from the point of view of these democratization efforts. Their strength, legitimacy, and influence are obviously enhanced by the fact that the inclusion of different stakeholders in public management, use of networks, and creation of partnerships among public, private, and civic actors have become generally accepted principles (Phillips 2004) in many countries which are regarded as champions of modernization by Hungarian policy makers.

Under these conditions, the government's policy toward civil society and the nonprofit sector[1] is some mixture of initiatives and measures reflecting the transition problems, on the one hand, and modernization efforts, on the other hand. These latter are highly influenced by Western examples and mainstream approaches, while the implementation of regulatory changes and their actual impacts are dependent on the local environment.

The main goal of this chapter is to analyze the actual outcomes of the regulatory measures aimed at the civil society/nonprofit sector in Hungary. This sector is potentially an important partner in the provision of public services and one of the key actors of relational governance. And, the regulatory framework is likely to have a crucial impact on the ability of nonprofit organizations (NPOs) to play these two roles. However, the legislators and other policy makers are not necessarily aware of the far reaching consequences of regulatory reforms, not to mention the complexity of the possible impacts. This chapter examines recent regulatory developments through the theoretical lenses of NPM and relational governance, and it tries to understand how the (sometimes contradictory) aspirations and efforts translate into (sometimes unexpected and unforeseen) outcomes.

This chapter first describes the intellectual and policy background of government–civil society relationships in Hungary, and then it gives an overview of the major regulatory and institutional changes in recent years. As a next step, it analyzes the tendencies embodied in different legislation as it pertains to NPM and relational governance. Finally, the chapter assesses the impact of the regulatory changes, identifies the challenges and conditions needed for further development of collaborative relationships, and draws some general conclusions concerning the relationships between the NPM and relational governance approaches.

BACKGROUND AND CONTEXT

It goes without saying that civil society theory, which is at least partly a product of the Central-Eastern European opposition movements and their intellectual leaders (Havel 1985; Konrád 1984; Michnik 1985), plays an important role in guiding Hungary's transition process. However, on the basis of Berman's (2001) analysis of mainstream thinking, its impact is not as dominant as one would expect:

> Social scientists . . . have devoted increasing attention to explaining what causes democratization in the first place, as well as what makes

democracies vibrant and successful over the long term. Where a generation ago most scholars tackling these questions stressed economic, political or institutional factors, today societal and cultural variables are in vogue. . . . Neo-Tocquevilleans such as Robert Putnam argue that civil society is crucial to 'making democracy work' while authors like Francis Fukuyama and Benjamin Barber who differ on everything else, agree that civil society plays a key role in driving political, social, and even economic outcomes. (32)

Without questioning the importance of building civil society and strengthening citizens' autonomy, the first post-communist Hungarian governments felt also obliged to carry out sweeping institutional reforms. These reforms were regarded as a necessary condition of any further development, including the creation of political democracy, an open society, market economy, a mixed welfare system, public–private partnerships, and shared governance. Neither the objectives nor the ways and means of achieving them were clearly defined. However, the architects of the reforms tended to rely on (sometimes randomly selected) scientific results and foreign experiences. Local experts promoting half-absorbed ideas of 'Western' (thus formerly less known) social science, and foreign advisors selling their own models are also responsible for the eclectic character of the changes. The regulatory measures did not follow any one particular system of thinking or set of ideas, but used parts of many different ones. Neither the common elements of the different approaches nor the tensions and contradictions created by their alternate or parallel use were analyzed in the preparatory phase of the regulatory changes. The implementation details were rarely thought out; the suggested schemes were almost never tested in advance by the decision makers who were far from alike in their thinking. The society was in the process of changing normative structures and basic value priorities. The previous norms underlying state–society relations under state socialism had lost their validity, and the new ones were not yet established. Not only the conventional wisdom but also the machinery of policy making was questioned. New actors were brought to the forefront of change. Their interpretations of the generally accepted aims of democratization, their preferences, their views of the possible solutions, and their actual political intentions were varied and changeable. So, too, was their capacity to influence the policy process. No wonder, then, that the most striking characteristic of the actual outcome of this process is the lack of consistency.

When we try to understand this complex phenomenon, both 'old' and 'new' institutional theories (DiMaggio & Powell 1983; Selznick 1996) provide us with powerful explanatory tools. The present regulatory framework results from adaptive change. If we want to understand its development, we have to study the legal, political, and cultural traditions; the social environment; the administrative ideologies; the generally accepted values; and the interest groups' competition for power and influence. Nevertheless, trans-national similarity of the newly developing nonprofit regulations suggests that isomorphism is also a growing tendency, especially the "coercive iso-morphism" and "mimetic processes" that can be easily detected in Eastern and Central Europe (DiMaggio & Powell 1983).

Traditionally, very different national nonprofit sectors adopt similar reg-ulatory frameworks. One of the obvious reasons to do so is the intention to meet international grant makers' standards, thereby gaining legitimacy and attracting foreign support. Another, albeit no less important factor is the commitment to modernization. Most actors and theoreticians of the transition process are convinced that there is no meaningful alternative to political democracy, market economy, and a modern welfare system (Zapf 2002). Consequently, the legal and institutional frameworks developed by Western countries serve as a model, even if their adoption is difficult and sometimes results in mixed solutions. At the same time, transitions are equally influenced by the original models and local traditions. The majority of observers and stakeholders seem to agree that the reform of regulations helps to bring the "laws into conformity with international good practice, thereby improving the enabling environment for NGOs and enhancing their ability to sustain themselves financially" (ICNL 2003: 7).

The alternative perspective is that a simple adoption of imported models is not satisfactory, not even if the reforms are prepared on the basis of a deep understanding of new paradigms of public policy and management and on a critical evaluation of foreign experiences. The decades of state socialism did too much harm. Private individuals did not have an oppor-tunity to learn how to behave as citizens, and their organizations were not strong enough to become influential and competent partners of the govern-ment. This weakness of the potential civil society partners is an important impediment to the development of horizontal or community governance. A relatively quick recovery is only possible if building a modern regula-tory and institutional framework goes parallel with helping and facilitat-ing democratization. In fact, the recent history of the legal and economic regulations of the Hungarian nonprofit sector reflects these parallel efforts (Bíró 2005; Kuti 1996).

MAJOR REGULATORY AND INSTITUTIONAL CHANGES

An initial step was already taken in 1987 (two years before the collapse of the state socialist regime) when legal provisions pertaining to founda-tions reappeared in the Civil Code. (Formerly, private individuals or institu-tions had not been allowed to establish foundations.) In the same year, Law XI/1987 on legislative procedures provided that an open debate involving stakeholders' voluntary organizations must be a part of the preparation of bills. Two years later, Law II/1989 on association guaranteed the freedom of association, opinion, and religion. It stated that every citizen and any groups or organizations of citizens had the right to create voluntary associations for any purpose that does not explicitly contradict fundamental human values and does not endanger the democratic political order.

Further deregulation of the registration of foundations and generous tax advantages marked the most important stages in building a favorable regulatory framework for the development of civil society in the early 1990s. The subsidiarity principle also began to gain ground, partly as a consequence of Hungary's intention to join the European Union and partly as a result of massive lobbying by the nonprofit community. The number of welfare services that entitle their nonprofit providers to get normative, per capita government support on a contract basis has grown significantly, although rather slowly, since then. The list of these services is determined annually by the law on the state budget.

A series of restrictions were imposed on the tax privileges of nonprofit organizations between 1991 and 1994. First, in 1991, the tax deductibility of in-kind donations was abolished. 1992 was the year of restrictions for all institutions of the Hungarian nonprofit sector. The tax laws limited both the tax exemption of NPOs' income from unrelated business activities and the tax deductibility of individual and corporate donations to foundations. All unrelated business income became taxable if it exceeded 10 percent of an NPO's total revenue (or €40,000). The formerly unconditional tax deductibility of the donations received by foundations was also limited. Registered foundations had to apply to the Tax Authority for tax deductibility. This status was awarded if their activity served a public benefit (the list of "public benefit" activities was included in the tax law) and if their donors did not get any compensation for their donations. Without actually being written down or openly expressed, this regulation made an effort to create a dividing line between the foundations serving a public benefit and all other NPOs.

Another step in the same direction was the amendment of the Civil Code in 1994 which introduced three new nonprofit forms: 1) the public law foundation, established by and kept financially accountable to the state; 2) the public law association, a self-governing professional association or chamber of commerce created by the Parliament by passing a specific law; and 3) the public benefit company, a service providing nonprofit organization similar to a limited liability company but accepting the non-distribution constraint. This time the intention was not disguised at all: The government wanted to create nonprofit organizations that remained under its control. Correspondingly, another set of restrictions was brought about by the 1994 tax law: The tax deductibility of donations was limited. The limit on tax deductible donations of both private persons and companies was 50 percent of the tax they actually paid in the former year. (On the foundation side, the conditions for receiving tax deductible donations did not change.)

In sharp contrast with these restrictions, some other measures significantly increased the scope for civil society involvement in the legislation process. Law LXIII/1992 defined the "data of public interest" and provided that they must be accessible for citizens and their organizations. In 1994, an institutional framework for lobbying by CSOs was also created, known as the "parliamentary lobby list." Registration on the list is open to any nonprofit, and registered organizations are regularly informed about and receive copies of the bills and other proposals that are under preparation by the Parliament. Since 1994, several hundred nonprofit organizations have entered their name on this list (Első Magyar Lobbi Szövetség 2006).

In the following year, the tax deductibility of donations to private foundations was cut again, while the first privileges for public law foundations were introduced. The tax deductibility of individual donations was replaced by a tax credit system. This credit was limited to 30 percent of tax liability, up to €200, thus tax incentives became practically negligible for individual donors. Corporate donations remained deductible from taxable income (up to 20 percent in the case of private foundations and without any limit in the case of public law foundations).

A dramatically different initiative appeared in 1997 when the tax law authorized taxpayers to transfer 1 percent of their personal income tax to nonprofit organizations (Vajda & Kuti 2000). The organizations to receive the support can be designated by the taxpayers themselves, but if they do not declare their intentions, the amount remains in the state budget. The majority of nonprofit organizations are eligible for this support.[2] Although the introduction of the 1 percent system only slightly increased the total revenues of the nonprofit sector, the decentralization of decision making to individual taxpayers more than doubled the number of voluntary organizations that received support from the central budget.

The year 1998 brought about fundamental changes in the regulation of the nonprofit sector. The CLVI/1997 Law on the public benefit organizations (called simply the "Nonprofit Law" by the nonprofit community) represented a paradigm shift in the sense that the definition of the "public benefit character" of an NPO became completely independent from its institutional form, thus the very basis of the direct and indirect public support to this sector was changed. Since then, the registration of NPOs is done by a public benefit test, and only those having received public benefit status are eligible for tax advantages. NPOs can receive the public benefit status if they:

- are engaged in health, social care, research, education and training, culture, sports, emergency relief, rehabilitating employment, promotion of Euro-Atlantic integration, protection of children and youth, environment, human and civic rights, public safety, or services for public benefit organizations;
- serve the general public and not only their own members;

- pursue business activities only in order to raise funds for their public benefit services, without endangering such services;
- do not distribute profit to their members or owners; and
- do not carry on directly political activities and do not support political parties.

In order to acquire an even higher legal status of "eminently public benefit," nonprofit organizations must meet two additional requirements. They have to deliver services that otherwise should be provided by public institutions, and they are obliged to publish information on their activities and financial accounts in the local or national press.

NPOs qualified as public benefit or eminently public benefit organizations are entitled to more public support and much more favorable tax treatment (including tax exemptions, tax deductibility of corporate donations, tax credit of individual donations, and eligibility for other tax advantages) than the 'ordinary' nonprofit organizations that do not directly serve a public benefit. This new regulation can be interpreted as encouragement for NPOs qualified as public benefit organizations, while it represents tight restrictions for those that fail the public benefit test.

This new classification of voluntary organizations significantly helped government agencies find nonprofit partners. Their intention to start a policy dialogue and develop partnership with civil society organizations had already been indicated by the creation of several forums in the second half of the 1990s—for example, a Civil Forum and a Forum of Equal Chances run by the Secretariat for Equal Chances, a Directorate of Civil Relations in the Ministry of Culture and Education, a Civil Club on Employment Issues in the Ministry of Labor, and a Social Council in the Ministry of Welfare. Finally, government–nonprofit sector relations became literally 'institutionalized' in 1998 when a Department of Civil Relations was established in the Prime Minister's Office.

In 2002, the Parliament also established its Civil Office in order to intensify its relations with civil society organizations and promote open legislation. In the same year, the government developed its "Civil Strategy." The final text of the document was an outcome of a whole series of debates with NPO representatives and experts. All suggestions and concerns were discussed in detail, and participants managed to reach an agreement on most of the issues. As a result of these debates, the Civil Strategy listed all relevant challenges faced by the Hungarian nonprofit sector and all measures planned by the government in order to strengthen civil society. The document was endorsed by the government in 2003 (Hungary, Civil Strategy of the Government 2003).

The national Civil Strategy encouraged the development of civil strategies at a ministerial level as well. As a result, a series of specialized strategies were born in the years 2003–2005. These strategies spelled out the ministries' plans to enlarge and deepen their relationships with civil society organizations and to build "strategic partnerships" with them (Nemoda 2005).

The most important promise of the Civil Strategy was met when Law L/2003 created the National Civil Fund (NCF) as an independent institution specialized in supporting civil society organizations (Kuti 2006). The law provided that the new fund's budget be linked to the size of the 1 percent designations. In a given year, the NCF receives from the state budget the same amount of money as taxpayers designated toward NPO recipients in their tax declarations earlier that year.[3] Thus any growth in the 1 percent designations also increases the state support to the NCF. As spelled out in the law, the most important objectives of the NCF are to strengthen civil society, help its organizations take an active role in societal life, and promote partnership and division of labor between government and civil society. Only civil society organizations, such as voluntary associations and private foundations, are eligible to get support from the Fund. Political parties, trade unions, employers' federations, mutual insurance associations, churches, public benefit companies, and public law foundations established by government authorities or municipalities are explicitly excluded. Organizations must be at least one year old and currently be in active operation to be eligible.

Under the provisions of the law, the NCF has to strengthen civil society organizations mainly through covering some part of their operating costs, thus facilitating their institutionalization and professionalization. At least 60 percent of the Fund must be spent on this purpose, while 10 percent covers the administrative costs of the NCF itself. The rest of the money may be devoted to a variety of projects that are likely to strengthen the sustainability of the nonprofit sector as a whole, of which 80 percent is distributed as either non-refundable or refundable grants through open application schemes.

The NCF has two types of decision-making bodies: the Council and the Boards. As a strategic decision-making body, the major roles of the Council are to set priorities, develop the grant-making policy, and decide on the Board structure and division of sources among the Boards. The Boards are the operative grant-makers which decide on acceptance or rejection of the applications for NCF grants. The overwhelming majority of the Council and Board members are civil society representatives, all of whom are selected through an open electoral system. A sophisticated election system has been established in order to ensure that CSO representatives have a decisive voice in the distribution of NCF funds.

In 2005, the Parliament passed Law LXXXVIII/2005 on public benefit voluntary activities. The law defined the boundaries between paid and voluntary work, the allowances available for volunteers, and the procedures of becoming eligible for preferential tax treatment. This was a result of a difficult four-year lobbying process coordinated by the Volunteer Centre Foundation (VCF). The original version of the bill was prepared by an expert group consisting of mainly nonprofit sector representatives. As a second step, the VCF organized a sector-wide debate, and then government representatives joined the process. The final text of the bill resulted from a long dialogue. Though civil society and government positions were sharply different at some points (especially about tax and registration issues), a compromise equally acceptable for both sides was finally reached.

By contrast, in the same year, the Parliament changed the provisions in the personal income tax law on individual donations without any consultation with civil society representatives. All kinds of tax advantages (including the tax credits related to family size, housing, investments, mutual insurance, donations, etc.) became pooled and limited at a very low level. As a further step, the tax preferences to individual donors were completely abolished in 2010. The tax deductibility of corporate donations was also restricted; only the donations to eminently public benefit organizations have remained deductible.

To summarize, the recent history of the legal and economic regulation of nonprofits in Hungary is a series of more or less contradictory laws and government decrees developed by different legislative and government bodies, sometimes in co-operation with civil society representatives, sometimes without them or even against their will. Neither the government intentions behind nor the actual measures themselves are consistent. A thorough analysis of the legal debate on nonprofit regulation reveals divergent political approaches, conflicting interests, different governmental and civil efforts, and even competing expert groups in the background. However, one can identify some more or less clear tendencies which seem to be important from my point of view.

TRENDS IN REGULATORY AND INSTITUTIONAL CHANGES AND THEIR IMPACT ON FORMS OF GOVERNANCE

Hungary's regulatory and institutional changes could be grouped in several different ways. For the purpose of this chapter, I classify them according to their impact on the forms of governance, as shown in Table 6.1.

Roughly speaking, the majority of these regulatory and institutional changes reflect either modernization or democratization efforts (although some have also had side effects), thus their actual impacts were generally in line with a NPM or a relational governance approach. However, the chronology of subsequent regulatory measures reveals a major difference between Hungary and the developed countries. While developed countries have seen a transition from NPM to relational governance (Osborne 2006) for the last few years, Hungary has experienced parallel efforts to strengthen both forms of public management.

Structural Changes, Modernization, and NPM

Post-communist Hungary had an economic crisis in the early 1990s. This crisis and the obvious need for structural adjustment and modernization made strikingly evident that nonprofit organizations must be encouraged

Table 6.1   Regulations and Governance Compared

Measures	New Public Management	Relational Governance
Tax laws, 1991–2010	Strong tendencies of bureaucratization, limitation of eligibility, and stricter control over tax exempt NPOs	Decreasing incentives for citizens' participation through giving
Budget laws, 1991–2010	Growing scope for contracting out services	
Lobby list, 1994		A first step toward open legislation
New NPO forms, 1994	Institutional guarantee for more state control over NPOs providing public services	
Institutions of dialogue, 1995–2010		Government units responsible for relations with civil society organizations
1% law, 1997		Citizens' involvement in the distribution of state support to NPOs
Nonprofit law, 1998	Public benefit test accountability rules	
National Civil Fund, 2004		Civil society representatives' involvement in the distribution of state support to NPOs
Law on volunteering, 2005	Bureaucratic guarantees of transparency	Incentives for citizens' participation through volunteering

and helped to deliver a range of welfare services, especially at the local level. The gradually increasing knowledge of the wave of NPM reforms (Jenei 2005) and the example of "Third Way" modernization of public services (Clark 2004), together with the emotional factors of the fall of state socialism, made this direction unquestionable. However, finding the actual solutions, designing a new division of labor between the public and private service providers, and developing a fully operative system of contracting out services represented a great challenge. No wonder, then, that a series of regulatory efforts have been made in order to create a consistent set of rules. This process is still not finished.

Although since the early 1990s the annual laws on the state budget have defined (and several times redefined) the list of services that can be provided by nonprofit organizations with guaranteed per capita government support, the actual eligibility for this support has remained mainly dependent on the decisions of municipalities because they are the major actors in contracting out services. Unfortunately, the amount of the guaranteed state support rarely covers all the costs of service provision, and municipalities do not always have enough additional funds to equally support the public service providers and the private nonprofit institutions. Because municipalities are directly responsible for the provision of public services, covering their costs has priority over financing nonprofit service providers. As a consequence, the initiatives of nonprofit entrepreneurs to offer new, additional, or innovative services are frequently rejected.

The perspectives of local governments are illustrated by the following excerpt from the social policy program of the municipality of Budapest (1997):

> In order to improve efficiency, decrease costs and raise more funds, the Local Government of the Capital City intends to prepare a comprehensive feasibility study about the transformation of some public institutions of social care into non-governmental organizations. We have to evaluate the possible advantages and disadvantages which can result from the provision of social services through public benefit companies or public law foundations. A strict condition for any such transformation is that neither the service providing capacity nor the quality or availability of the services can decrease. An increase of the relative costs of social services is not acceptable, either. . . .
>
> Another feasibility study must explore the advantages and disadvantages of contracting out social services to non-governmental organizations. The study has to elaborate on
> * the possible schemes of contracting out,
> * the guarantees of quality and reliability,
> * the possible consequences of a violation of contract by the nonprofit contractees,
> * the financial procedure of contracting out services.
>
> The results of the study must be used to develop a 'code of contracting', i.e. a collection of rules which will guide the practice (including competitive tenders, the system of guarantees and the agreement on professional standards) of contracting out social services (12–13).

This growing awareness of various aspects of contracting out services indicates that the NPM approach is quite strong in Hungary. The service-providing segment of the Hungarian nonprofit sector is not far from:

* being propelled from a role as an agent of modernization, able to exert pressure for change over government institutions, and particularly local government, and toward itself being
* a subject of modernization, with consequent challenges for its own governance arrangements and performance management regimes (McLaughlin 2004: 557).

Table 6.2 Number, Revenues, and Paid Employees of Nonprofit Organizations in Hungary, by Type of Activity, 2005

Activity Type	Number of Organizations	%	Total Income Million €	%	Number of Employees FTE*	%
'Classical' civil activities	49,321	87.0	1,427	41.7	29,697	36.0
Advocacy	4,191	7.4	387	11.3	4,902	5.9
Service provision	3,182	5.6	1,605	47.0	48,001	58.1
Total	56,694	100.0	3,419	100.0	82,600	100.0

* Full time equivalent
Source: Central Statistical Office (2007)

Most government officials and many NPO representatives consider this legitimate and timely, all the more because a growing number of nonprofit organizations are involved in service provision. According to statistical data, as shown in Table 6.2, the service-providing NPOs represent only about 6 percent of the sector, but they realize almost half of its total income and employ more than half of its paid employees.

The relative economic strength of the service-providing nonprofit organizations is explained mainly by the fact that they co-operate closely with government agencies. Sometimes they fully take over government responsibilities. More frequently, they contribute to the solution of social problems in some other way. Their engagement in public service delivery is also reflected in the nature of their income. Compared to civil society and advocacy organizations, the nonprofit service providers are much more dependent on government support, as illustrated in Figure 6.1. Almost two thirds of their revenues come from public sources.

These figures strongly support the argument that taxpayers' money transferred to NPOs should be spent in an efficient way. In order to ensure this

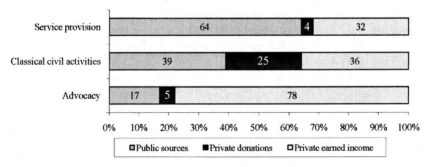

Figure 6.1 Revenue sources of nonprofit organizations by type of activity, 2005.
Source: Central Statistical Office (2007)

efficiency, the eligibility for government support must depend on the professional qualities of the recipients (Hegyesi & Fekete, 2006); in addition, a sophisticated, consistent, and transparent system of public scrutiny must be built (Bíró 2005). Another important point is that the influence of voluntary organizations on public policy and their active role in shared governance should not be undermined by poor performance and deficiencies in their accountability and credibility.

On the other hand, there is also a growing worry about the impact of professionalization on the nonprofit service providers, particularly on their independence and advocacy potential. As noted by a foreign observer of the Hungarian transition process, "the beginnings of a contracting regime with the state raise questions about the future independence of nonprofit organizations and raise danger signals about a new possibility of nonprofit organizations being an extension of state power" (Jenkins 1995: 198).

This worry is even greater among those kinds of voluntary organizations that do not belong to the group of large service providers but still have to meet similar official requirements. As mentioned earlier, regulatory changes created a clear classification of all NPOs according to their public benefit character. By the end of the 1990s, the government has managed to develop a legal framework that allows it to differentiate between nonprofit organizations that directly serve a public benefit (and thus are eligible for public support) and all other NPOs. The public benefit status is a necessary condition for tax advantages and most kinds of government support. Close government control of the public law foundations and associations has also become a part of the system. Any privileges encouraging voluntary work are only available if NPOs develop a fully transparent registrar of their volunteers and make it available for relevant authorities.

On the other hand, it is also true that, in practice, the history of regulation of the nonprofit sector is a series of attempts and failures in this respect. The problems of accountability and public scrutiny were repeatedly identified in the early expert reports and received even greater attention in subsequent debates on the Nonprofit Law. The solutions suggested in several consecutive versions of the bill, however, were quite different.

The original concept of the bill developed by a nonprofit support center suggested the creation of a Nonprofit Chamber (a voluntary umbrella organization of NPOs). This chamber would have overseen whether NPOs operated in accord with the rules, regulations, and professional and ethical standards. According to the bill developed by the experts of the government, this same function would instead have been fulfilled by a government authority (similar to the Charity Commission of England and Wales). The fate of both proposals was exactly the same. Some very visible and noisy groups of the nonprofit community made a strong protest, from purely selfish motives, against such "state control" of the sector. A much larger group of nonprofits seconded for practical reasons, while a silent majority of NPOs did not really ponder the actual issues, but simply and instinctively believed that any attempt at public scrutiny can only be an attack against civil society. During the public debate, minds were poisoned by politicking; reasoned arguments were crowded out by demagoguery. The proposals had to be withdrawn. Even the efforts to reach a compromise failed, and the Nonprofit Law has not solved the problem of public scrutiny. Though accountability and transparency rules are included in the written text of the law, no mechanisms were established for controlling whether these rules are kept or broken. Activity and financial reports are supposed to be prepared, but their existence (not to mention their content) is not checked by any institution.

Under these conditions, government authorities tend to solve the accountability problem 'case by case' when they get in touch with nonprofit organizations. This results in extremely complicated support and service contracts (including ever changing, individually defined standards, accounting rules, and measures of performance and success), long and bureaucratic procedures, and a general climate of distrust, which is equally harmful for all actors. Another outcome has been a cut in indirect state support (tax privileges) where the case by case method is not possible. This is all the more problematic because the over-bureaucratization of the supporting and contract relations counteract the influence of democratization efforts, thus creating an impediment to the development of relational governance.

Relational Governance—A Special Aspect of Democratization

The democratization narrative, which identifies the need for a shift from centralized state bureaucracies to new forms of shared responsibilities and citizen involvement in decision making, is largely consistent with the governance narratives (Bevir & Rhodes 2001). However, there is an important difference between the two approaches. The advocates of relational governance take it for granted that social actors are able and willing to share responsibilities with government. The analysts of the Eastern European developments (Jenei & Kuti 2003; Osborne et al. 2005; Zimmer & Priller 2004) know from experience that this is not always the case.

The long decades of state socialism did not offer much opportunity for individuals to become responsible citizens and form civil society organizations that can be equal partners of the government in developing public policy. Consequently, neither citizens nor their organizations were prepared for a prompt response to the new challenges represented by the unexpected renaissance of a democratic political regime.

As we have already seen, the institutional infrastructure of the policy dialogue between the government and civil society actors has developed relatively quickly. The legal guarantees for access to information and the policy process, the open legislation, the growing number of government units specialized in civil society relations, and the numerous forums of policy dialogue indicate the willingness of government to build the institutions of shared governance (Bódi, Jung, & Lakrovits 2003). Unfortunately, the government efforts to promote partnership have not resulted in similarly rapid changes on the side of the nonprofit sector.

The task of shaping government policy is very demanding and time- and money-consuming. If private citizens and their organizations want to influence government policy, they must follow the political debates; evaluate the different proposals; be knowledgeable about the relationships; keep contacts with politicians, government officials, and other nonprofit organizations; be prepared to analyze the newly emerging issues; and start action at any moment when it is necessary. This advocacy potential cannot be realized by all citizens and all individual organizations, thus co-operation is an incontestable necessity. Unfortunately, for the last 15 years, the general agreement about the necessity of cooperative behavior has been rarely translated into concerted actions in Hungary, although some temporary coalitions of NPOs and some more or less 'improvised' citizens' movements can report on a series of successful concrete actions.

The lack of co-operation skills and the related attitude problems were already recognized in the early 1990s. It took some more time to understand that even carefully designed institutions of shared governance would remain empty without the active participation of civil society actors and to find some methods of accelerating the democratization process. These new methods (the decentralization of redistributive decisions through the 1 percent system and the NCF) are rooted in the belief that, as far as citizens' involvement and democracy-building are concerned, the supporting means can be as important as the actual amount of the state support. Because the actual funding allocation decisions are made by either citizens or NPO representatives, the potential supportees have to approach them, thereby involving them in their work and enlarging the part of society that feels responsible for public affairs. In some sense, this is a 'school of democracy.' Besides intensifying citizen involvement, this method also alleviates the independence/public support problem. Because the government has no voice in the distribution of this special financial support targeted to CSOs, the latter can get some support from the state budget without becoming dependent on government authorities.

The income from the 1 percent designations and NCF grants is not just an additional element of revenues; it also has two other virtues. First, unlike the overwhelming majority of central government support, it is a discretionary grant of money and is not related to concrete projects. This means that it can be used for developing civil society organizations themselves, thus enabling them to become more involved in shared governance. Second, it can be acquired without the need for CSOs to be close to high government officials or other central decision makers, and without being familiar with the rules, procedures and actors of the state redistribution process. This means that grassroots organizations and small local foundations have more chance of receiving this kind of support than any other type of central government grants.

While the 1 percent scheme has delegated decision-making rights to the citizens themselves, their elected representatives have become the key actors of redistribution through the NCF. In their decision-making role, CSO representatives have to go through an important learning process. They have to change their viewpoint; they are obliged to shift from representing their particular organizations to acting in favor of the voluntary sector as a whole. Involved in either developing the policy guidelines or actual grant-making, they have to assume enormous responsibility. Their efforts to live up to these expectations are likely to broaden their horizons, deepen their understanding of sector-wide challenges, and improve their co-operation skills. The same holds true, to some extent, for taxpayers who are supposed to behave as responsible citizens when they decide on the 1 percent designation.

To be sure, none of these government measures can perform a miracle. The first experiences have been rather mixed. About half of the taxpayers are still not ready to make their 1 percent designation. Some of the CSO representatives cannot yet live up to their new responsibilities, and the arguments and debates in the NCF Council and Boards are not always as sophisticated and fruitful as would be ideal. However, the introduction of these new schemes of sharing redistributive power with citizens and civil society leaders can be interpreted as a step toward relational governance— a minor Hungarian contribution to enriching the arsenal of the tools of government in this respect.[4]

On the side of CSOs, the well known necessity "to strengthen their connection to society, by expanding membership and developing effective public relations" (Green 1999: 232) has become strongly reinforced by the new supporting schemes. The emergence of the 1 percent system and the NCF has created some additional motivation for CSOs to build solid relationships, invest in 'goodwill,' and improve their images. The provisions of the Law on volunteering are also likely to facilitate the enlargement of the volunteer base. In the long run, this may result in more visibility and more professionalism—both important conditions of any further development of relational governance.

CHALLENGES FOR REGULATORY REFORM AND COLLABORATIVE RELATIONSHIPS

The directions of this further development of relational governance will incontestably depend on both the intentions of the major actors and their ability to clearly conceptualize the objectives and identify the challenges. One of the main lessons of the experience of the past 15 years is that borrowing foreign concepts "tends to result in institutions that are smoothly adapted to the local conditions, just like borrowed words are adjusted to fit into the broader logic of the language into which they arrive, so that their meaning is subject to change in transfer" (Böröcz 2000: 138). In-depth comparative research would be necessary in order to analyze, interpret, and evaluate all (sometimes contradictory) elements of the Hungarian transition process in the context of NPM and relational governance. For lack of the results of such thorough and sophisticated research, my conclusions will unavoidably remain vulnerable.

On the basis of a sketchy overview of the regulatory and institutional changes and on other sources of information,[5] I venture to conclude that Hungary has made, almost instinctively, important steps toward shared governance without widely using this term or knowing its concept in detail. By contrast, contracting out services has been a frequently mentioned element of the modernization agenda, but its actual practice significantly differs from the foreign models we originally wanted to adopt.

In short, we are in a halfway situation. Under these circumstances both former success and failures, both regulations and practice should be carefully scrutinized. At this point, shared governance should mean, first of all, a jointly managed examination of the achievements behind and the tasks before us, and, second, an agreement on the target areas where efforts should be concentrated. In fact, the government (following the UK example) already tried about five years ago to start consultations on a Compact with civil society. Unfortunately, voluntary sector leaders rejected this idea, partly for fear of a growing government influence, partly because they could not decide which of the umbrella organizations should represent civil society in the course of the consultations.

However, there is at least a silent agreement on some of the regulatory challenges that Hungary has to face in the next couple of years. These are:

- consistency of legal and economic regulation
- financial vulnerability of nonprofit service providers
- accountability, trustworthiness, and legitimacy, and
- deficiencies in cooperation within the voluntary sector

The Consistency of Legal and Economic Regulation

The present regulation of the Hungarian nonprofit sector is a complicated set of particular and more or less contradictory laws and government decrees developed by different legislative and government bodies. In some cases, the recommendations of the Supreme Court and the practice developed by the individual county courts have more influence on the registration and tax treatment of NPOs than the written law itself (Fülöp, 2005; Lominci, 2002). This lack of consistent and comprehensive regulation is a source of conflict with the partners who should share the responsibilities of governance. Clear accounting and tax inspection rules and a correct, carefully thought out, generally known and accepted system of regulations should be developed.

Financial Vulnerability of Nonprofit Service Providers

In order to reform the welfare system and strengthen the nonprofit service providers, the system of funding should also be reformed. The long term strategy of developing a new welfare mix and an appropriate system of financing is still to be developed. The practice tends to be chaotic and contradictory. The tax system has been under 'reconstruction' for several years, and the rules are changing continuously. The disappearing tax incentives for private donations decrease the efficacy of fundraising efforts. The subsidiarity principle is not rooted in the Hungarian political culture. It perfectly fits into the ideology, but it does not guide the behavior and everyday practices of the government. As a consequence, nonprofit organizations find it extremely difficult to diversify their revenues, thereby preserving their independence from the government. A more predictable system of financing would be an important step toward more balanced relationships, thus it would create a more favorable environment for the development of relational governance.

Accountability, Trustworthiness, Legitimacy

As a reaction to the strong government control they suffered under state socialism, the Hungarian nonprofit organizations are extremely reluctant to disclose any financial or management information. Despite the numerous government efforts to build a mechanism of state scrutiny and the attempts of some voluntary umbrella groups to develop self-regulatory schemes and ethical codes, the Hungarian nonprofit sector is still deficient in accountability and transparency. This seriously limits the capacity of NPOs to become influential participants in the new forms of governance. We can only hope that the prediction of Taylor and Warburton (2003: 337) is also valid in Hungary: "All sectors of society (public, private, and voluntary) are being forced, by a reinforcing mixture of legislation and public opinion, to find new forms of accountability that actually strengthen (rather than undermine) trust in institutions."

Deficiencies in Cooperation within the Sector

The lack of coordination and skills of cooperation is one of the most difficult problems in the Hungarian voluntary sector (Sebestény 2005). The different roles they play create some 'natural' divisions among the nonprofit organizations. Advocacy groups frequently resent the pragmatism and opportunism of service providers, while the latter think that their activities are much more important and useful than the ones other NPOs are engaged in. Recreation clubs and membership organizations feel neglected and discriminated against. In addition, there is some tension between the small and big, the rural and urban, the government-funded and foreign-funded organizations, and also between the old fashioned, formerly government-controlled voluntary associations and the new institutions of civil society. Developing sector-wide cooperation is clearly a challenge which needs to be addressed in the very short run because a divided nonprofit community is hardly able to represent civil society and find its place in the new forms of governance.

In short, the institutional infrastructure of the policy dialogue seems to have developed more quickly on the government side than on the side of the Hungarian voluntary and nonprofit sector. Civil society organizations need to significantly increase the professional level of their advocacy activities if they want to be important and influential partners in forming an appropriate regulatory and institutional framework for relational governance.

CONCLUSION

This brief overview of important regulatory changes and analysis of their relationships to NPM and relational governance reveal, on the one hand, the immaturity of the Hungarian civil society and nonprofit sector. It is quite significant that none of the policy actors has been able to clearly define their attitudes toward mainstream and alternative approaches to the problems of government–nonprofit co-operation and co-governance. Many different kinds of ideas, concepts, fragments of models, and foreign examples were floating around, and they were frequently used ad-lib, without paying attention to the compatibility of the proposed measures. In many cases, passionate debates substituted for an in-depth analysis of the problems and an unprejudiced, objective comparison of the possible solutions. Under these conditions, it was quite natural that both the NPM and the relational governance approach have remained influential in Hungary in a period when, in the developed countries, the "NPM paradigm has been challenged by the emergence of 'Third Way' ideas and more specifically, in terms of the organization of public services, an alternative governance paradigm" (Ferlie & Andresani 2006: 391).

On the other hand, one can also draw some more general conclusions from the Hungarian (and broader Eastern European) experience. The parallel presence of the NPM and relational governance approaches in the post-socialist period is probably the consequence of the parallel presence of a series of different problems to be solved and different challenges to be faced. When one of the biggest challenges is that of modernizing public services and developing intersectoral co-operation in their delivery, the policy actors are likely to adopt NPM mechanisms. At the same time, the relational governance mechanisms can also be popular as a result of other challenges—those of democratization, collective problem solving, and civil society participation in policy development.

This suggests that the NPM and relational governance approaches are not mutually exclusive. If they emerged and became dominant consecutively in the public management literature, this is not because of the failure of NPM.

I would even venture to say that the NPM opened the floor for the governance approach because it successfully reached its own genuine limits. When the contractual mechanisms, competition, input and output controls, quality and performance management, and other aspects of NPM had already become ordinary elements of public management, the remaining problems that were unsolved—and unsolvable—by NPM became clearly visible. This is how and why the relational governance approach which argued for cooperative arrangements, could gain ground and, according to Phillips (2004), its rhetoric and assumptions have even outpaced the realities of its practice for the last few years.

From this perspective, the Hungarian experience is not so special. Nor is the main challenge we face. The latecomers, just like the more developed countries, need to develop an optimal configuration of NPM *and* relational governance.

NOTES

This chapter includes some results of a research project which was supported by the Alapítvány a Magyar Felsőoktatásért és Kutatásért (Foundation for the Hungarian Higher Education and Research) and the Általános Vállalkozási Főiskola (Budapest School of Management), whom the author would like to thank for the research grant. She also wishes to thank Steven Rathgeb Smith for helpful comments and suggestions on the first draft of this work.

1. The terms nonprofit sector, civil society, and voluntary sector are used as synonyms in Hungary. Although they share a similar general meaning, their connotations are somewhat different. When voluntary associations and private foundations are mentioned as civil society organizations (CSOs) or voluntary organizations, the emphasis is on the role they play in social participation, advocacy, self-help, and interest articulation. When they are called nonprofit organizations (NPOs), we usually refer to their economic roles related to service provision and income redistribution. The terms third sector and non-governmental organizations (NGOs) are rarely used in Hungary, and they mainly appear in documents prepared for international bodies (European Union, United Nations, World Bank, etc.).
2. NPOs are eligible for the 1 percent support if they are engaged in: preventive medicine; health care; social care; culture; education; research; public security; human rights; environment protection; protection of the cultural heritage; sports and leisure time activities for youth and the disabled; or care for the elderly, children, the poor, the disabled, national and ethnic minorities, or Hungarian minorities in foreign countries. The NPOs must be independent from political parties and cannot support candidates for political office, and they must not be in arrears with tax and duties.
3. However, the law guarantees that this amount cannot be less than 0.5 percent of the personal income tax even if taxpayers' 1 percent designations proved to be extremely low.
4. It is difficult to explain the sharp difference between the Hungarian governments' favorable attitude toward these innovative methods of sharing redistribution of power with citizens and their rigidity, sometimes even animosity, toward the more traditional tax privileges. Maybe the fact that these latter are frequently associated with tax evasion (and almost never with

democratization) is one of the explanatory factors. Another possible explanation is that tax policy is developed under the auspices of the Ministry of Finances where financial considerations are definitely much stronger than concerns about the future of democracy and civil society.
5. Namely, from the nonprofit literature (Bíró 2005; Kinyik and Vitál 2005), statistical data (Central Statistical Office 2007), interviews (Kuti 1996), formal and informal debates with nonprofit leaders and experts, and personal experience.

REFERENCES

Berman, S. (2001). "Civil society and political institutionalization." In B. Edwards, M. W. Foley, and M. Diani (eds.), *Beyond Tocqueville. Civil society and the social capital debate in comparative perspective* (pp. 32–42). Hanover and London: University Press of New England.
Bevir, M., and Rhodes, R. A. W. (2001). "A decentered theory of governance: Rational choice, institutionalism, and interpretation." Working Paper 2001–10. Institute of Governmental Studies, University of California, Berkeley.
Bíró, E. (2005). "A KCR-dimenzió. A közfeladat-ellátásban való civil részvétel jogi akadályai" (The CPPPS dimension. Legal obstacles to the civil participation in the provision of public services). Budapest: EMLA Környezeti Management és Jog Egyesület.
Bódi, G., Jung, A., and Lakrovits, E. (2003). "Civil partnerség" (Civil partnerships). Budapest: KJK Kerszöv Jogi és Üzleti Kiadó Kft.
Böröcz, J. (2000). "Informality and nonprofits in East Central European capitalism." *Voluntas*, 11(2): 123–140.
Budapest. (1997). *Főváros Önkormányzata szociálpolitikai cselekvési programja* (Social policy programme of the Local Government of Budapest). Budapest: Budapest Főváros Önkormányzata.
Central Statistical Office. (2007). *Nonprofit szervezetek Magyarországon, 2005* (Nonprofit organizations in Hungary, 2005). Budapest: Központi Statisztikai Hivatal.
Clark, D. (2004). "Implementing the Third Way. Modernizing governance and public services in Quebec and the UK." *Public Management Review*, 6(4): 493–510.
DiMaggio, P. J., and Powell, W. W. (1983). "The iron cage revisited: Institutional isomorphism and collective rationality in organizational fields." *American Sociological Review*, 48(2): 147–160.
Első Magyar Lobbi Szövetség. (2006). *Kérdőíves felmérés a parlamenti lobbista gyakorlatáról* (A survey of experiences of the parliamentary lobby list). Budapest. Online. Available at <www.parlament.hu/civil/rendezveny/lobbi/lobbi.htm> (accessed 1 June 2009).
Ferlie, E., and Andresani, G. (2006). "Understanding current developments in public sector management—New Public Management, governance or other theoretical perspectives?" *Public Management Review*, 8(3): 389–394.
Fülöp, S. (2005). "Egyesületek bírósági nyilvántartásba vételi gyakorlata" (The practice of registration of voluntary associations at the courts). Budapest: EMLA Egyesület.
Green, A. T. (1999). "Nonprofits and democratic development: Lessons from the Czech Republic." *Voluntas*, 10(3): 217–233.
Havel, V. (1985). *The Power of the Powerless: Citizens against the State in Central-Eastern Europe*. London: Hutchinson.
Hegyesi, G., and Fekete, O. (2006). "Kísérlet a nonprofit szervezetek felmérésére a Társadalmi Igazságosság Index segítségével" (An experiment to gauge nonprofit organizations on the basis of a 'Social Justice Index'). *Civil Szemle*, 1: 5–33.

Hood, C. (1995). "The New Public Management in the 1980s: Variations on a theme." *Accounting, Organizations and Society*, 20(2–3): 93–110.

Hungary. (2003). *Civil Strategy of the Government of Hungary*. Budapest. Online. Available at < www.civil.info.hu> (accessed 15 January 2009).

International Center for Not-for-Profit Law (ICNL). (2003). Survey of tax laws. Affecting non-governmental organizations in Central and Eastern Europe, 2nd ed. Washington, DC: International Center for Not-for-Profit Law. Online. Available at < http://www.icnl.org/knowledge/pubs/TaxSurveyCEE.pdf> (accessed 15 January 2009).

Jenei, G. (2005). *Közigazgatás-menedzsment* (Public Administration Management). Budapest: Századvég Kiadó.

Jenei, G., and Kuti, É. (2003). "Duality in the third sector. The Hungarian case." *The Asian Journal of Public Administration*, 25(1): 133–157.

Jenkins, R. M. (1995). "Politics and the development of the Hungarian nonprofit sector." *Voluntas*, 6(2): 183–201.

Kinyik, M., and Vitál, A. (2005). "Közfeladatok ellátása a nonprofit szektorban" (Public services delivered by the nonprofit sector). *Civil Szemle*, 2(2): 90–105.

Konrád, G. (1984). *Anti-politics*. London: Quartet Books.

Kuti, É. (2006). "Arm's length funding for civil society: Lessons from the first year of the National Civil Fund." *Public Administration Review*, 8(2): 351–365.

Kuti, É. (1996). *The Nonprofit Sector in Hungary*. Manchester and New York: Manchester University Press.

Lominci, Z. (2002). "A közhasznú szervezetekről szóló törvény bírói gyakorlata" (The court practice of implementation of the law on public benefit organizations). Budapest: HVGORAC Lap- és Könyvkiadó Kft.

McLaughlin, K. (2004). "Toward a 'modernized' voluntary and community sector? Emerging lessons from government—Voluntary and community sector relationships in the UK." *Public Management Review*, 6(4): 555–562.

Michnik, A. (1985). *Letters from Prison and Other Essays*. Berkeley, CA: California University Press.

Nemoda, I. (2005). "Stratégiai partnerségben" (In a strategic partnership). *Civil Szemle*, 2(3): 119–130.

Osborne, S. P. (2006). "The New Public Governance?" *Public Management Review*, 8(3): 377–387.

Osborne, S. P., Jenei, G., Fabian, G., and Kuti, É. (2005). "Government/non-profit partnerships, public services delivery, and civil society in the transitional countries of Eastern Europe: Lessons from the Hungarian experience." *International Journal of Public Administration*, 28(7): 767–786.

Phillips, S. D. (2004). "The limits of horizontal governance voluntary sector-government collaboration in Canada." *Society and Economy*, 26(2–3): 383–405.

Sebestény, I. (2005). *Civil Dilemmák—Kihívások és Alternatívák a Civil Szektorban* (Civil dilemmas—Challenges and alternatives in the civil sector). Budapest: Civitalis Egyesület.

Selznick, P. (1996). "Institutionalism 'old' and 'new'." *Administrative Science Quarterly*, 41(2): 270–277.

Taylor, M., and Warburton, D. (2003). "Legitimacy and the role of UK third sector organizations in the policy process." *Voluntas*, 14(3): 321–338.

Vajda, Á., and Kuti, É. (2000). " 'Citizens' votes for nonprofit activities' in 1%. 'Forint votes' for civil society organizations." *Nonprofit Kutatócsoport*, Budapest, 156–220.

Zapf, W. (2002). *Modernizáció, jólét, átmenet* (Modernization, Welfare, Transition). Andorka Rudolf Társadalomtudományi Társaság and Századvég Kiadó, Budapest.

Zimmer, A., and Priller, E. (eds.). (2004). *Future of Civil Society. Making Central European nonprofit organizations work*. Vs Verlag für Socialwissenschaffen, Wiesbaden.

7 Gatekeeper Governance
The European Union and Civil Society Organizations

Alison Dunn

INTRODUCTION

The European Union (EU) has developed apace since its early formation through the Treaty of Rome in 1950. Then it was a body focused upon economic matters set up as a means to ensure peace in Europe. Now it has widened to cover a broad range of social concerns which include the environment, culture, education, justice, security, health, employment, and social rights. Almost sixty years after its inception, the EU has become a significant policy-making and regulatory body which has an influential role in steering the laws and activities of its Member States.[1]

As a political body with widespread interests, the policy- and law-making focus of the EU adds an extra layer of regulation beyond national laws to which civil society organizations, citizens, and Member States are bound. In so doing, the EU does not interfere with Member States' taxation regimes or framework laws concerning the status of nonprofit organizations or the boundaries of the third sector within their jurisdictions. Neither is the EU concerned whether and to what extent sector organizations can undertake lobbying or advocacy activities (except where those activities lead to criminal acts or terrorism). Rather, the EU imposes laws which affect how organizations carry out their activities, for example, employment or trade laws, and laws which concern the fields in which organizations operate and so affect their beneficiaries or users, such as environmental regulations and regulations on social welfare rights and age or gender discrimination.

While the policy and regulatory aspects of the EU have consequences for nonprofit organizations as actors within Member States and the EU, they also present an opportunity and focus for scrutiny and lobbying. An extensive economic and non-economic lobbying industry has grown up around Brussels that is becoming ever more strategic and professional. The European Commission, for example, has drawn up an extensive database of organizations that operate at the EU level and that have members in at least three EU Member States.[2] Although often perceived as weak and uncoordinated actors in the EU field (Geyer 2001:478; Lloyd, 1998), many nonprofit organizations have established bases in Brussels and have joined together as coalitions to strengthen their voice and influence.[3] Indeed, the existence of transnational organizations is a growing phenomenon at the EU level, and it cuts across all traditional fields of third sector concerns including environment, human rights, welfare, and culture. The benefits of nonprofit organizations' engagement with the EU are twofold. For organizations, lobbying the EU represents an opportunity to influence the development of supranational laws and policies and to maintain a check and balance on this process. For the EU institutions, the engagement of nonprofit organizations in developing laws and policies creates 'civil dialogue.' It not only brings the EU closer to its citizens, but it also provides the Union with a degree of credibility and legitimacy by demonstrating transparency in governance. The relationship between the sector and the EU can well be described as a symbiotic one.

The opportunities for lobbying in the EU are legion, mainly due to the multiplicity of institutional bodies. The EU is organized into specific institutions, each with a distinct role in policy and regulation. While the European Parliament is concerned with passing budgetary and legislative provisions, the European Commission, which is divided into specific policy areas, proposes policy and regulation, implementing the same, as well as acting as chief protector of the Treaties. This latter role involves the Commission in bringing proceedings against Member States for infringement. By contrast, the Council of the EU negotiates legislation and represents Member States in the EU process, including policy-making (whereas the Parliament represents citizens through its elected body). The Court of Justice upholds the rule of EU law, and the Court of Auditors ensures proper EU financial management. Although all of the EU's institutions are open to petition and consultation, some are more developed than others in terms of their engagement with nonprofits. As we shall see in this chapter, the opportunities for advocacy, lobbying, and taking on a monitoring role clearly exist, but significant barriers to effective engagement remain.

In addition to the primary EU institutions, there are other bodies that support the development and monitoring of policy and regulation. For the purposes of this chapter, the most significant of these are the Committee of the Regions (COR) and the European Economic and Social Committee (EESC).[4] These bodies were provided with advisory status under the Treaty of Nice. This Treaty made express provision for the COR and the EESC to be consulted by the Council and the Commission, and also for the COR and the EESC to issue non-binding opinions on matters they consider appropriate (Treaty of Nice: Articles 263–265 COR, Articles 257–262 EESC). The memberships of the COR and the EESC are comprised of representative organizations and interest groups nominated by Member States and are concerned with regional policy and economic and social issues, respectively. As advisory bodies, they provide a direct channel into policy and regulatory processes. The EESC has particular significance since Article 257 of the Nice Treaty made it a representative of "various economic and social components of organized civil society."[5] As a check and balance on the exercise of power and as an acknowledged 'bridging' mechanism, the advisory bodies provide nonprofit organizations with the opportunity for involvement with the governance of the EU. Both the COR and the EESC represent a clear institutional effort to incorporate civil society into the EU process, although there is concern over the weight their views are actually afforded (Jeffery 2002).

This chapter is concerned with EU governance *by* and *for* nonprofit organizations which fall within the broader ambit of EU civil society. It begins with an examination of the EU's understanding and recognition of civil society. This can be a complex task given the multiplicity of sector organizations within the 27 EU Member States, the level of maturity and development of the sectors, particularly in the newest Member States, and the different legal traditions arising from the Member States' diverse civil and common law jurisdictions. The chapter then sets out the development of governance within the EU: first, governance *of* the EU institutions and policies undertaken by civil society organizations, and, second, EU governance *for* civil society organizations. In so doing, particular attention is paid to recent developments and key proposals for change.

As we shall see, although there have been some calls at the EU level for more robust internal governance of civil society organizations, the chief focus has been on such organizations scrutinizing the EU institutions and participating in EU policy and decision making. The reason for this governance focus has been to give credibility to the Union and to ensure its legitimacy. Within the process of EU governance by and for civil society organizations, Member States take up a key gatekeeper role. Where civil society organizations contribute to and challenge EU policies and decisions, they may be constrained by the EU institutions, the Treaty provisions, or the policy-making process. Consequently, recourse to Member States may be the only effective mechanism for civil society organizations to ensure governance at the EU level and contribute to policy-making. Similarly, the EU's attempts to provide governance for civil society organizations have placed the Member States in a pivotal role as implementers and regulators of standard governance norms. It will be argued that, as a result, attempts to utilize civil society in providing legitimacy for the EU are undermined, and cohesive equality across the EU is open to question.

A recent major development in the EU–civil society relationship is the ratification in late 2009 of the EU's Constitutional/Reform Treaty, known as the "Lisbon Treaty," and this chapter provides an early analysis of the implications of its implementation. The initial proposed Constitutional Treaty 'hit the buffers' in 2007. Although ratified by some Member States, the Treaty was put into a period of 'reflection' following its rejection by the French and Dutch referendums in 2005. In June 2007, a meeting of the Leaders of the EU Member States agreed that a new Intergovernmental Conference be set up to draft a new "Reform Treaty." The text of this redrafted Treaty was agreed in October and was formally signed in Lisbon on 13 December 2007. Discussion and ratification by each Member State was required before it could be implemented, however, and for a period the fate of this process hung in the balance following initial rejection in a referendum by the Irish people. By the fall 2009, all Member States, including Ireland after a second, more enthusiastic referendum, had ratified the Treaty, and it took effect on 1 December 2009.

EU'S UNDERSTANDING AND
RECOGNITION OF CIVIL SOCIETY

Concern with terminology and the difficulty of defining the boundaries and extent of the sector as well as its constituent elements is as prevalent in the EU as it is in many other jurisdictions. The position for the EU is complicated further by the attempt to bring together diverse understandings and terminology from the Member States which have different civil and common law traditions and legal systems (Kendell 2001: 8; Kendall & Anheier 1999; Lloyd 1988: 191–195). The EU institutions, themselves fragmented, have variously discussed policies relating to the 'voluntary sector,' 'charities and foundations,' 'not-for-profit organizations,' 'non-governmental organizations,' and the 'third sector' with little logic or consistency. The EU institutions, individually or collectively, have not developed a clear or consistent understanding of the sector, either within Brussels or across the Member States. While there is no common phraseology used to identify organizations and the sector as a whole, the term 'civil society' has seen increasing use by the institutions and in the treaties to collectively describe organizations that exist in the space between the market and the state.

The notion of a 'civil society' is itself nebulous. Although there is no formal EU wide definition or understanding of civil society, the EESC has given it a broad description, and this has been employed by the European Parliament and the European Commission.[6] The EESC has classified civil society generically as "all organizational structures whose members have objectives and responsibilities that are of general interest and who also act as mediators between the public authorities and citizens" (EESC 1999: 30, para 7.1).[7] It is clear that this classification includes economic and non-economic actors, and nonprofit groups are just one element of a broader category of organizations. The EU does not specifically distinguish nonprofit organizations but tends to treat them with civil society as a whole. The EESC has determined that civil society comprises:

> labour-market players (i.e. trade unions, employers' federations also known as 'the social partners'); organizations representing social and economic players, which are not social partners in the strict sense of the term; NGOs (non-governmental organizations) which bring people

together in a common cause, such as environmental organizations, human rights organizations, consumer associations, charitable organizations, educational and training organizations etc.; CBOs (community-based organizations), i.e. organizations set up within society at grassroots level which pursue member-oriented objectives, e.g. youth organizations, family associations and all organizations through which citizens participate in local and municipal life; and religious communities (EESC 1999: 30, para 8.1).

The EESC has estimated that there are over 100 million volunteers in Europe (EESC 2006c: para 2.1). Indeed, civil society organizations have been recognized as important actors in EU activities for over a quarter of a century. International civil society organizations, for example, can seek formal participatory status with the Council of the EU.[8] The Fontaine report of 1987 urged greater recognition and a more defined role for civil society.[9] Both Declaration 23 annexed to the Final Act of the Maastricht Treaty and Declaration 38 of the Amsterdam Treaty emphasize cooperation between the EU and the sector. Although prior to the implementation of the Lisbon Treaty civil society organizations have no legal standing in the EU,[10] their value as intermediaries has been recognized in connecting a fragmented and often distant Union to its citizens (Commission of the EU 2001, OJ C 287 of 12.10.2001, paras 3.1–3.2). Indeed, civil society organizations have become indispensable at a time when the Union is expanding and when its democratic (and economic) legitimacy has been open to question. The traditional sector roles of advising policy makers, sharing technical expertise in complex areas, sitting on committees, monitoring institutional activities and implementing policies, as well as raising awareness about EU activities and programs are all carried out by civil society organizations at both the EU level and for the EU in Member States (Commission of the EU 2000: paras 1.3–1.4).

The reason why civil society organizations are vital to the EU's success can be seen from the principles underlying the Union. One of the expressed aims of the EU has been to create social dialogue through civil dialogue. To that end, three key principles underpinning the values and processes of the EU have proved significant in necessitating a role for civil society organizations. The first is the principle of subsidiarity under Article 5 Treaty of the European Community (Treaty of Rome) which devolves policies and their implementation to Member States and grassroots actors in order to ensure that decisions are taken close to EU citizens. Civil society organizations are well placed and connected in this regard at national, regional, and local levels and have an important role in implementation.[11]

Second, there is the principle of integration of the EU. To operate successfully with a diverse range of Member States, which often have different agendas regarding regulation and policy, the EU requires significant levels of cohesion across the European communities. The procedure of integration is concerned with the pooling of national sovereignty toward certain objectives that are deemed to be better achieved if undertaken by the Member States in consort. European integration is both formal—with the creation of institutions and processes through treaties ensuring that there is greater cooperation on policies and decision making—and informal, that is, concerned with creating integration through building citizenship and a common European identity (see Wallace 1990). Given the diverse traditions, customs, and cultures across the Member States, there needs to be a way to bring the different parts together, and this cannot be done without the citizens. Civil society organizations have a significant role in encouraging citizenship, and EU funding (for example through the Structural and Cohesion funds) is made available for organizations to carry out such EU projects. Many civil society organizations participate with the EU in this regard.

Third, and linked to the notion of integration, is the principle of enlargement. This refers to the process by which new Member States join the EU and through which they have to integrate with existing Member States. Civil society organizations are ideally placed to assist countries in preparing for accession, particularly in terms of increasing awareness, bridging cultures, engaging citizens, and supporting fledgling civil societies, a factor readily recognized by the European Commission and in the so-called "Copenhagen Criteria" (Commission of the EU 2005a: para 1.1).[12]

The relationship between civil society and the EU is not without its difficulties, however. There are particular struggles with perceptions and expectations from both sides. Dealing with fragmented institutions, which each have different procedures (for example, for consultation or lobbying[13]), and a lack of institutional knowledge are particular concerns for civil society organizations. There are multiple access points, and different institutions require different strategies (Beyers 2004: 218). While this allows "venue shopping" (Mazey & Richardson 2001), it also creates confusion for the uninitiated and for smaller, poorly resourced organizations. These difficulties are compounded by a perception of institutional inertia, high levels of bureaucracy at the EU level (Kendall & Anheier 1999: 284), and a fear that collaboration may simply be a "public relations exercise" (Civil Society Contact Group 2006: 13). For the institutions' part, civil society can be an unknown and poorly understood entity. A myriad of concerns from bodies from 27 Member States, the sheer multiplicity and cultural diversity in organizations, their dynamic nature and ability to evolve (Commission of the EU 2000: 6), the lack of a single or uniform view, and the political agendas and conflict between organizations (Geyer 2001:478; Lloyd 1988: 189) can be at best challenging and at worst capricious. Equally, civil society's lack of apparent transparency and representativeness are of concern. The EESC in particular has argued that ensuring a proper system of "representativity" of civil society organizations is the only way in which they can properly participate in policy shaping and decision making and avoid accusations of individualism and lack of transparency. To that end, the EESC has proposed that principles of "openness, objectivity, non-discrimination, verifiability and participation" be used to create a procedure to assess the representativeness of organizations (EESC 2006a: paras 2.5, 3.1, 5.4). Thus far, the EU as a whole has avoided creating an accreditation system of favored organizations that satisfy *inter alia* criteria for transparency, representation, and expertise.[14] But the EESC favors encouraging a level of standard organizational norms to ensure legitimacy of those organizations that provide expertise or participate or collaborate with the EU (EESC 2006a: para 3.2.1).

EU GOVERNANCE BY CIVIL SOCIETY ORGANIZATIONS

The European Commission's White Paper and Governance Initiatives

Harnessing civil society more successfully and creating a dialogue with and between the EU institutions and civil society organizations have been at the forefront of discussions on strategic development of the EU in the last decade. Partly this is a response to lobbying from the sector, but it is primarily a recognition of the "democratic deficit" in the EU which, to be credible and to build stronger foundations for the institutions and greater cohesion across the Union, requires more robust transparency and accountability (EESC 1999: para 2.4).[15] In the face of sustained criticism of the EU institutions over a lack of accountability, waste of resources, and corruption, European governance was identified in 2000 as an area for strategic development by the European Commission. Its 2001 White Paper advocated multi-level governance across the EU: that is, "opening up the policy-making process" (Commission of the EU 2001: Executive Summary)[16] and making a commitment to creating a dialogue between the EU's institutions and its citizens and organizations, with clear standards set for consultation and participation (Commission of the EU 2001: 16). In so doing, the Commission argued that this would provide overall policy coherence within the EU (Commission of the EU 2001: 13). The White Paper reaffirmed the connection between civil society organizations and the development of EU policy and the delivery of EU services (Commission of the EU 2001: 14). It also recognized the significance of such organizations in encouraging citizenship and participation (Commission of the EU 2001: 15) and in being an "early warning system for the direction of political debate" (Commission of the EU 2001: 14).

Prior to the White Paper on European Governance, there had been initiatives to strategically involve civil society in the policy-making of the EU but with less urgency and less institutional consensus. The European Commission took the first concrete steps in 1997 by setting out the promotion of the role of this sector in Europe (Commission of the EU 1997). In its communication, the Commission advocated enjoining civil society organizations as a "full partner in the debate on all policy and implementation on matters which concern them" (Commission of the EU 1997: para 10.4). In particular, the Commission focused upon the significance of the sector as a partner in fostering citizenship and democracy in the EU (Dunn 2000). These two key themes remained the underlying focus of both a subsequent discussion paper adopted by the Commission on "building a stronger partnership" with organizations (Commission of the EU 2000) and the Commission's White Paper several years later. Each policy document from the Commission has served to highlight the continuing difficulty that a remote, inadequately understood, and poorly presented political body has in engaging its citizens.[17]While the 1997 Communication prompted interest but very little action, the European Commission's White Paper had wider appeal, even though it was criticized as being vague in its recommendations (De Schutter 2002: 201). The White Paper served as a catalyst for the development of a series of proposals for creating stronger and more transparent policy-making in the EU.[18] Some of these accountability mechanisms were aimed at allowing for wider dissemination of information, such as the introduction of legislation allowing for open access to documents of the Commission, Council and European Parliament.[19] Other initiatives were intended to encourage greater and more transparent participation in policy-making, such as the Commission's minimum standards for consultation.[20] Of these measures, the most recent and significant is the European Transparency Initiative which was launched in 2005 and covers, *inter alia*, proposals for interest lobbying and conducting and participating in consultations.[21]

To combat the difficulty of assessing the credibility, weight, and representativeness of information provided to the EU institutions by civil society and other organizations—a problem earlier highlighted by the EESC—the European Transparency Initiative proposed an "incentive based registration system" for such organizations (Commission of the EU 2006).[22] The *Register of Interest Representatives*, which began operation in June 2008, allows the EU institutions and the public access to information about the mission, funding, and constituency of organizations that take part in consultations and that seek to lobby the EU.[23] The register is not officially an accreditation system, and it is intended to be voluntary. Given that presence on the register ultimately provides sufficient information to the institutions to be an indicator of the weight to be afforded to an organization's views and expertise, it is easy to see how such a system could become *de facto* accreditation and potentially divisive as a result. Notably, an open accessible and transparent register with information on who or what an organization represents and how they are funded could go some way to ameliorate the influence and resource imbalance between economic corporate lobbyists and non-economic civil society organizations. This is a factor recognized by the sector (Commission of the EU 2006: 6, para 2), but it would require the institutions to clearly determine the weight to be afforded different groups. Both the EESC and the COR have argued that a distinction needs to be retained between lobbyists that are profit oriented and those that are not, and credence given accordingly (EESC 2006b: para 4.2.1; COR 2007: para 4.2). Although the levelling of the playing field between different actors is acknowledged by the Transparency Initiative, whether and how emphasis is to be given to one group over another has not been addressed in the initial or the final proposals post consultation. Determining how representative organizations are and what weight to give to their views will be a matter of discretion depending upon the circumstances and focus of individual consultations or calls for expertise. On the institutions' part, this discretion could be difficult to account for, and organizations will need to be clear on how their information is to be used and the inferences that are drawn from it.

Once registered, it is intended that organizations subscribe to a code of conduct (Commission of the EU 2006: 8, para 3.1). Currently, the European Commission relies upon lobbying organizations to individually self-regulate with a series of minimum standards relating to honesty and integrity of actions and veracity of information (Commission of the EU 2006: 9, para 3.2).[24] This system allows organizations to have flexibility and autonomy, with each organization drawing up its own code, and presents a low administrative burden for the Commission. But the current system lacks consistency, certainty, breadth, and teeth as a regulatory tool. The proposal for a common code continues the approach of self-regulation favored by lobbyists but puts forth minimum standards applicable to all and provides for agreed upon enforcement mechanisms. There is the further threat of a compulsory code with compulsory registration if a self-regulatory common code proves inadequate (Commission of the EU 2006: 10, para 3.2).

The Transparency Initiative initially proposed that such a code would be drawn up by lobbyists and that it would have "a common enforcement and sanction system trusted by all" (Commission of the EU 2006: 9, para 3.2). The Commission has now accepted that such a code should be drawn up centrally by the Commission and that it should in principle apply to all the EU institutions (Commission of the EU 2007a: paras 2.1.4–2.1.5). The Transparency Initiative's original scheme for a common code was both ambiguous and naïve. The proposal was light on detail and particularly vague on the genesis of the new code. If not impossible, it would certainly have been impractical and unrealistic for the lobbying community, as broad and diverse as it is with both economic and non-economic actors, to draw up and agree upon a common code with clear provisions and mechanisms for enforcement and sanction. How such enforcement would operate was also unclear, and it would seem to have required umbrella bodies representing the various actors to either work together to police their members or to set up a separate body for this purpose. Agreement on this issue and determining the funding for such a body are overwhelming arguments against such self-regulation. A compulsory code is not an attractive alternative either, given that it reduces independence and creates a less elastic system, but it would at least be a more feasible overall option and would be more likely to ensure parity of treatment.[25] Attaching a code to a voluntary registration system is likewise imperfect if the purpose is to overcome the current lack of coverage of self-regulatory codes, unless of course voluntary registration is *de facto* compulsory.[26]

Although many civil society organizations engage with the EU institutions and contribute extensively to policy-shaping and decision-making, the Transparency Initiative demonstrates the procedural difficulties organizations have in participating and establishing a formal relationship with the EU institutions. It has been suggested that an EU level framework agreement, a "Concordat" similar to the UK compacts, would be more appropriate in regularizing relations between the parties and ensuring that there is adherence to good governance norms. This proposal has been championed by England's National Council for Voluntary Organisations (NCVO) with the support of sector umbrella bodies at EU level such as the European Council for Non Profit Organisations (CEDAG).[27] A sector led, rather than an EU imposed, proposal has much to recommend it, and the experience of the UK compact has been largely positive. The EU, however, has yet to show receptiveness to such proposals, and, in the face of such institutional disinterest, the campaign for this compact will be an uphill struggle. But even if such a compact were adopted, significant practical restrictions would remain. The EU is an extremely complex political system in terms of policy-making, and, for many citizens and organizations, it is a confusing labyrinth of institutions, departments, competencies, and officials. Although there are mechanisms for civil society to have input into the EU policy processes, for the majority of such organizations, the practical reality is that it is easier to act at the Member State level, seeking their desired results from their national governments or pressuring their national governments to take up the policy or governance issues at the EU level on their behalf.[28] The role then for the Member State is an indirect one. It is not forced by the specific actions, policies, or treaty provisions of the EU, but it is born of the practical reality of how organizations, institutions, and policy processes work.

Participatory Democracy

At a broader level, the Commission's 2001 White Paper on promoting multi-level governance (and the initiatives it has spawned) rest upon the principle of encouraging participatory democracy in the Union. As De Schutter (2002) has argued, the EU has steadily become process-focused rather than simply results-based (199). Ensuring input and participation into the Union's activities assists in providing for confidence and legitimacy in the EU's actions; it also helps achieve subsidiarity and integration, and it assists in securing successful accession through enlargement. Participatory democracy is a key aspect of the long debated Lisbon Treaty, which represents a formal acknowledgment of civil society's role. Article 1 paragraph 12 of the Lisbon Treaty amends Article 8 of the Treaty on European Union (Maastricht Treaty), substituting a new Article 8 B (hereafter 'Article 8 B [as amended]') which expressly provides for civil society participation. For the first time, it sets out that the EU institutions "shall maintain an open, transparent and regular dialogue with representative associations and civil society," and that citizens and representative organizations should be given the opportunity to put forward and exchange their views on areas of the EU's acts. In addition, the Article provides that citizens may invite the Commission, which is required to maintain consultations to ensure coherence and transparency in the EU, to make proposals in areas where it is thought necessary to implement the Constitution.[29]

Article 8 B (as amended) will give civil society organizations express legal standing as consultative bodies in the Union for the first time. Formal recognition of their role has long been a goal of the sector (European Citizens Association 2002: 6–7). Whereas the Nice Treaty recognized the EESC as a conduit for civil society representation in the Union, the Lisbon Treaty elevates the sector's status and establishes direct contact. Such recognition of civil society in EU policy and decision-making is significant and more effective given that EESC representation is neither all-embracing nor a strong form of collaboration. However, there is still uncertainty over how this Treaty provision will be interpreted. For a start, there is no definition of civil society in the Treaty, and it is not clear whether the EESC's broad definition (which extends beyond nonprofit organizations) would be adopted or whether a narrower approach would be taken. Article 8 B (as amended) also does not make clear which provisions fall within the "regular dialogue" to be undertaken, be it simply Commission initiatives or more broadly all policy and legislative proposals. In addition, there is uncertainty surrounding the process for regular dialogue. This could simply formalize the Commission's current use of civil society expertise in its specific areas of concern and its general consultation procedures already in operation. This will not effectively change civil society's position beyond allowing it to enforce its right to dialogue under the Article if established procedures are infringed. Alternatively, Article 8 B (as amended) could lead to a revision of the European Commission's dealings with civil society by creating a more formal procedure for exchange of ideas and channels of communication. One concern with this approach will be how the Commission decides to establish contact with civil society, be it through discussions with individual organizations, through representative bodies, or through a system of accreditation, and what credence it will give to the sector's (often diverse) views.

Article 8 B (as amended) will keep the EESC's concern with the representativeness of civil society organizations alive, and in this context the European Transparency Initiative's creation of a Register of Interest Representatives will take on special significance. There are already concerns within the civil society sector with regard to implementation of Article 8 B (as amended) and specifically whether one of its consequences will be state capture of organizations in a sector that prizes its independence. Indeed, some organizations have already chosen not to participate with the EESC as the current representatives of civil society for this very reason (Civil Society Contact Group 2006: 9). There is fear that to do so would give the EESC control over the presentation of sector views and that the institutions' discussions with the EESC could simply become a substitute for proper dialogue with civil society as a whole. Article 8 B (as amended) offers an important opportunity for greater recognition of civil society at the EU level, but it could be in danger of becoming a damp squib if considered attention is not given to the purpose and detail of its operation.

Challenging Decision-Making

Beyond an advisory role and contribution to policy-shaping, many civil society organizations may wish to challenge decision-making in the EU through judicial review, as they would decision-making in their own Member States. Most jurisdictions have provisions for judicial review of public authorities' actions or decision-making procedures, and the new Treaty may similarly assist civil society organizations in bringing actions against the EU institutions, which would go some way toward enhancing their accountability.[30] At the EU level, Article 230 EC makes provision for reviewing acts of the European Parliament, Council, Commission, and European Central Bank, and it allows for them to be annulled by the European Court of Justice (see Cygan 2003). There are three statuses under Article 230 in which a challenge may be brought. Some bodies within the EU, including the Commission, Council, and Member States, have "privileged status" to bring a challenge in any circumstance. Other bodies, including the European Parliament, European Central Bank, and the Court of Auditors, have "semi-privileged status" which allows them to seek review for the purpose of protecting their prerogatives under the Treaties. Finally, there are "non-privileged" applicants provided for under Article 230(4) which permits an action to be brought "if the act which is to be challenged is a decision addressed to the applicant or is a decision addressed to another person which is of *direct and individual concern* to the applicant or is a decision in the form of a regulation which is of *direct and individual concern* to the applicant" (emphasis added). It is under the provisions of Article 230(4) that civil society organizations would seek to challenge Community acts.

The grounds for "direct or individual concern" under Article 230(4) have been restrictively interpreted by the European Court of Justice, and their limited accessibility has been described as one of the least satisfactory aspects of the EU process.[31] Direct concern means establishing a causal link between the Community measure and its impact upon the applicant. Individual concern has also been interpreted into a strict test because the case of *Plaumann* requires the decision to affect the applicants "by reason of certain attributes which are peculiar to them or by reason of circumstances in which they are differentiated from all other persons and by virtue of these factors distinguishes them individually just as in the case of the persons addressed." [32] This means that civil society applicants must show that they are 'singled out' by the decision in a way that distinguishes them from other applicants, as the person to whom the initial decision was addressed was also singled out (Fairhurst 2006: 214). For his part, Plaumann did not satisfy the test. His case concerned a decision addressed to the German government concerning the imposition of a duty on imports of clementines into Germany and regulating taxation control on imports from outside the EU Member States. The Court of Justice found that Plaumann, an importer of clementines who challenged the import decision, undertook a commercial activity that was unlimited in terms of those who could participate. The fact that Plaumann was one of just thirty clementine importers was irrelevant. Under the criteria of Article 230(4) there was nothing to distinguish Plaumann individually. As such, Plaumann was part of a general and open class and could not claim to be individually concerned. Furthermore, it is not acceptable to argue that some issues are of such magnitude that they are "shared and common" and so rise above the *Plaumann* criteria.[33]

This sets the bar very high and makes it difficult to bring public interest challenges of EU decision-making unless an organization can effectively show that it is part of a separate class. This is a complex and restrictive approach to *locus standi* and is certainly less liberal than most Members States would apply to their own judicial review rules.[34] Courts in the UK, for example, have placed emphasis on the expertise of pressure groups and lobbyists as qualities that make them sufficiently interested to be able to bring an action for judicial review.[35] Indeed, the EU rules leave civil society organizations with little alternative than the uphill task of attempting to persuade their own Member States, which have privileged status, to bring an action on their behalf.

As an alternative, it has been argued that protection of specific rights that are high on the EU agenda could be drafted into Article 230 via inclusion in the Charter of Fundamental Rights of the EU. Article 47 of the Charter contains the right to an effective remedy and to a fair trial for all EU citizens. Advocate General Jacobs in *Unión de Pequeños Agricultores v Council* (*UPA*)[36] expressed the view that Article 47 could be used to open up Article 230 by linking an applicant's "individual concern" to "a substantial adverse effect on his interests" due to the applicant's particular circumstances.[37] This would make application for judicial review for non-privileged applicants cause-based, their cases being strengthened by connection to matters within the EU's priorities. This novel approach is less than satisfactory given that the EU's agendas can be transient, and it also removes parity between applicants in different areas of rights protection. If applicants are to be given rights to challenge decision-making, it would be more appropriate to do so in a manner that ensures a level playing field and equality of treatment. That said, such a construction would permit more public interest challenges while still retaining some boundaries to prevent opening of the proverbial floodgates of litigation. But despite Advocate General Jacobs' views, the European Court of Justice in *UPA* made it clear that Member States should have in place clear systems for judicial review for actions to be brought and that any change to Article 230(4) should come by Treaty amendment.

The Lisbon Treaty may provide for a more liberalizing effect for judicial review. Article 2 paragraph 214 of the Lisbon Treaty amends Article 230 of the Treaty establishing the European Community (Treaty of Rome), substituting a new Article 230(4) (hereafter "Article 230(4) [as amended]"). Article 230(4) (as amended) is framed in the following terms:

> any natural or legal person may . . . institute proceedings against an act addressed to that person or which is of direct and individual concern to them, and against a regulatory act which is of direct concern to them and does not entail implementing measures.

Article 230(4) (as amended) retains the requirement of "direct and individual concern" for European Community acts in general but makes a departure for regulatory acts which need only be of direct concern to the applicant. This would leave civil society organizations that wish to challenge such an act to establish a causal link only, rather than the stricter test from *Plaumann*. Of course, the scope of Article 230(4) (as amended) still needs to be judicially determined. Of particular need for interpretation is the term "regulatory acts" which are not defined elsewhere in the Treaty. Indeed, in other provisions, the Treaty refers to legislative and non-legislative provisions such as framework laws, regulations, decisions, recommendations, and opinions, but not regulatory acts. Ward points out that the term can be interpreted either narrowly (to cover only delegated or executive legislation such as regulations and decisions) or broadly (to cover all primary EU legislation) (Ward 2004: 213–214). The narrow approach would accord with other Treaty provisions, such as Article 254 Treaty of Rome as amended by the Lisbon Treaty, Article 2 paragraph 242, which covers non-legislative acts. However, a purposive approach would enable the Treaty to be interpreted broadly and in accordance with the principles of subsidiarity and integration underlying the Union and, as a result, provide greater transparency and legitimacy.

It is not clear which interpretation will predominate, but there is value in lobbying for the widest reading of the provision. Subject to defining terminology, Article 230(4) (as amended) will be a welcome addition as a tool for civil society organizations in ensuring governance at the EU level. Moreover, it accords with the wider principle of participatory democracy upon which the EU is framed. Of course, it would have been a greater cause for celebration if all Community acts were subject to the more liberal requirements under the Article, but this, at least, is a step in the right direction.

Civil society organizations working in the environmental field have more scope for challenging decision-making outside of the original Article 230(4) or the proposed Article 230(4) (as amended). Under Article 1 of the Convention on Access to Information, Public Participation in Decision-making and Access to Justice in Environmental Matters (the "Aarhus Convention"), the public is given access to information, a right to participate, and access to justice. The latter gives the right (Article 9) to challenge acts which breach environmental law to a person who has a sufficient interest or an impairment of a right. Access to justice and determination of sufficient interest and impairment of rights are devolved to national jurisdictions or to the EU level where the EU is the party concerned. Ratified by the EU in 2003, the Aarhus Convention applies to all the EU institutions,[38] albeit the provisions under Article 9 did not come into application until June 2007. In implementing Article 9, the EU expressly gives the right to request an internal review of an administrative act to a non-governmental organization that satisfies four criteria: the organization is independent and nonprofit under national law,[39] its primary object is environmental protection, it has existed and pursued the primary objective of environmental protection for at least two years, and the subject matter of the request for internal review is covered by its objectives and activities.[40] This judicial review procedure is a very novel but extremely significant one within the EU context. It is too early to tell how civil society organizations will use the Convention rights in the environmental field or, indeed, how the EU institutions will respond to requests for internal review.

What is clear is that the Convention highlights the disparity between policy areas. To be sure, environmental rights are an increasing priority for most political systems, but they are not an exclusive concern in the EU field. It will become progressively more difficult to justify the difference in treatment of civil society organizations and other applicants who wish to challenge Community acts in fields other than environmental law. An ultimate consequence of the Aarhus Convention may well be that it compels reform so that parity of judicial review is ensured across all policy areas. Already, the European Commission has suggested that it will examine whether affording more rights to civil society organizations, such as rights similar to those under the Aarhus Convention to launch an internal review procedure, could be a viable incentive to encourage organizations to join the Register of Interest Representatives launched by the European Transparency Initiative (Commission of the EU 2007a: para 2.1.3).

EU governance by civil society organizations is thus in a state of flux. Currently, it represents a curious mix of fundamental principles and rhetorical policy documents, which set great store by the notion of the governance roles that civil society organizations can undertake, and more mundane procedurally focused policy, which can detract from and limit the very principles it is set up to facilitate. Set against this is a promise of future opportunity that may revolutionize the role and possibilities for civil society organizations to contribute to and challenge policy-shaping and decision-making, but that may equally come to nothing given that reform is dependent upon the machinations of the political process. From the EU institutions we see a clear concern with boundary setting, and in this context the Member States unwittingly become significant actors in completing the governance process. This is because, without their own legal standing in the Union, the only effective method for civil society organizations to challenge decision-making is to either persuade their national governments to act on their behalf or seek a remedy at national level.

EU GOVERNANCE FOR CIVIL SOCIETY ORGANIZATIONS

While the engagement of civil society organizations in the governance of the EU is accepted and encouraged, institutions, such as the European Parliament (2001: 11), have made it clear that with better involvement comes greater responsibility, and that civil society organizations need to have sufficient internal mechanisms for their own good governance, accountability, and openness. The Commission has come up with a number of proposals in this regard, but they have yet to come to fruition. What unites the proposals is the focus upon Member States as implementers and regulators to ensure that civil society organizations are properly governed. These are not new powers for Member States, but rather signal an emphasis upon the need for strong governance mechanisms at the Member State level. In these proposals we also see the Commission move away from addressing the broader civil society to a more specific focus upon nonprofit organizations. Within Member States a narrower distinction is often made between different types of nonprofit organizations, often for taxation and regulatory purposes (such as charities in England or foundations in France). These further distinctions among types of organizations and the concerns with taxation are matters for individual Member States in their own regulatory frameworks and are not ones which feature at the EU level.

Statute for a European Association

A longstanding proposal is to establish a Statute for a European Association (EA) that would ensure a common legal structure and common good governance norms across the sector. The proposal for the European

Association Statute was made by the European Commission as long ago as 1991, and it formed part of a broad stream of initiatives from the Commission's then Social Economy Unit.[41] The purpose behind the proposal was to provide one common organizational form with separate legal status available to all nonprofit bodies so that they could easily undertake cross border co-operation and operate in several Member States. The European Parliament approved the Commission's proposal, subject to agreed amendments, in 1993. The EA proposal was then put before the Council of Ministers for approval, and there it languished for many years before eventually being withdrawn (EESC 2006a: paras 6.41–6.42). The EA remains of interest, however, because of the increasing calls for it to be reintroduced. In the current 'good governance' climate, the EA would overcome many of the concerns of the EU institutions about establishing the representativeness of civil society organizations.

The EA would apply to a "permanent grouping of natural and/or legal persons whose members pool their knowledge or activities either for a purpose in the general interest or in order to promote the trade or professional interests of its members in the most diverse areas (Article 1(1))." Although a non-distribution constraint was intrinsic to the proposal (Article 1(3)), it was not clear if this definition would cover all organizations under the Member States nonprofit umbrellas. Some organizations, such as social clubs, might fall outside the trade and professional interests clause and the classification of "a purpose in the general interest," dependent upon how the latter clause was construed. Under the proposals, organizations that wish to become EAs should have a foothold in at least two Member States and would be registered in the Member State where the organization has its central administration (Article 4). Qualifying legal forms include companies limited by guarantee, incorporated by Royal Charter or Act of Parliament, Industrial and Provident Societies, unincorporated associations, and all institutions established for exclusively charitable purposes.[42] Upon registration the EA would acquire legal personality in the Member States, allowing the EA, *inter alia*, to contract, acquire title to property, and be a party to legal proceedings, and limiting its liability to its assets (Article 2).

The EA option would be attractive as a legal form for those nonprofit groups that wish to undertake cross-border activities. As an organizational vehicle, it provides for simplicity and ease of operation without interfering with or attempting to harmonize the regulatory regimes of Member States. The EA allows organizations to operate under just one registration procedure from the Member State in which it is registered. This obviates the need for a transnational nonprofit organization to register in each Member State in which it operates or comply with reporting regulations from different jurisdictions. At present, this can be a bureaucratic process and a particular problem where jurisdictions have different civil and common law traditions. The EA does not, however, give the organizations any extra advocacy or lobbying powers because they would still be regulated in this regard by the Member State in which they are founded.

Many transnational organizations pushed for acceptance of the EA proposal (Kendall & Anheier 1999). Of course, these nonprofit organizations are by no means representative of the whole sector across all the Member States, and most European nonprofits will never have an interest in registering in this new form. Even so, the proposal for the EA remains of interest particularly because it embodies, within the legal form, principles of good governance. For example, the proposal included regulations on an EA's governing committee, rules of the association, and functions of its executive committee.[43] In addition, it would have required an EA to have a model for participation or an information/consultation process, and to normally include in its governing document rules on membership (for the EA and its executive committee) as well as specification of member rights and obligations, executive committee powers, obligations and authorities especially with regard to third parties, and rules on winding up. Absent from the proposals were clear provisions for monitoring and compliance of EAs, which would be devolved to Member States. There was also no consideration of a central register for the EAs.[44] Naturally, the bite of the EA rules would require some teeth to ensure compliance, and, without the creation of a governing body to supervise these provisions, it is hard to see how parity in compliance would be guaranteed across the Member States. Such parity would be difficult to achieve not least because the EA (and the EU more generally) does not seek to harmonize nonprofit framework laws across Member States.

A further consideration is the likely consequences of transnational EAs for other nonprofit organizations. Theoretically, the creation of an EA form should have little or no impact on other nonprofit organizations, whether they operate at a national or EU level because the EA form does not provide an enhanced route to operate at the EU level. In practice, however, EA organizations may well be perceived by the EU institutions as more representative or authoritative than their national counterparts precisely because of their experience and operation in more than one Member State. Given that transnational organizations are already in existence, the EA form would not create this perception, but it could well endorse it at a time when the EESC and the European Commission are moving toward requirements of transparency and representativeness in sector organizations.

The proposals for participatory democracy under Article 8 B Maastricht Treaty (as amended) and the European Transparency Initiative have prompted calls for the EA to be resurrected. The EESC is firmly in favor of the EA as a vehicle for its principles on the representativeness of organizations and also as a way in which freedom of association can be consolidated with an expression of European citizenship (EESC 2006a: paras 6.3, 6.4.2, 6.4.3). As a representative of civil society, the EESC has appealed for the proposals to be put back on the EU agenda. Calls are evident too from the nonprofit sector itself, perhaps buoyed up by the recent acceptance of a similar proposal for a European Cooperative Society and the push for a European Foundation Statute.[45] The EA could be a clear badge of good governance and credibility for those sector organizations working at the EU level which have to comply with different rules for governance from the different EU institutions.[46] Of itself, that would reduce the administrative burden placed on organizations when they wish to engage with multiple EU institutions. While the governance methods in the EA may be viewed as overly prescriptive, the initiative is attractive for its potential in encouraging common procedures and organizational forms, subject of course to consistency of Member State implementation (albeit harmonization of law across Member States is not a goal in this arena). As a uniform vehicle with certain minimum standards and consistency, the EA has much to recommend it. In highlighting the need for clear systems of governance, the proposal carries forward the importance of transparency in the nonprofit sector. Moreover, as noted above, the proposal would obviate the difficulty that currently exists when a nonprofit organization operating in different Member States is required to comply with different levels of accountability and transparency. Given the increasingly strong call for better governance of all civil society organizations, particularly those that operate at the EU level, the current climate is most propitious for the renewal of this proposal.

Anti-Terrorism Code of Conduct

The EA is essentially a sector-oriented initiative drawn from an attempt to make governance of nonprofit organizations transparent and to assist in the creation of an express EU space for organizations. Less obviously sector-propelled is a more recent proposal from the European Commission for a code of conduct for nonprofit organizations. This code is aimed at sector organizations operating at a national level, and it is born out of a concern that organizations are vulnerable and open to exploitation by fundamentalist or terrorist groups. It was proposed at a time when the EU institutions were beginning to show great concern with security and preventing terrorism following an escalation in terror campaigns across the globe (Commission of the EU 2005c). The code is one part of a broader initiative to co-ordinate national agencies across the EU Member States dealing with security and financial intelligence (Commission of the EU 2005c: 1–7). The code is aimed at preventing terrorist financing through or by nonprofit organizations and, in so doing, ensuring that such organizations are transparent in their accounts and activities (Commission of the EU 2005b: para B). Significantly, the Commission eschews the notion of 'one size fits all' and proposes via the code to lay down a set of minimum standards and common principles to be implemented individually by each Member State. Member States, then, have a key role in interpreting these provisions. The proposed code is expressed to be for nonprofit organizations in all Member

States (as opposed to the broader field of civil society) (Dunn 2006)[47] and would be adopted on a voluntary basis, albeit there is strong encouragement for compliance with the code.

The Commission's proposals seek to "maintain trust" and "enhance public confidence" in nonprofit organizations (Commission of the EU 2005b: para B). To that end, the code suggests that procedures should be put in place by organizations to ensure that their work is open and honest by having proper accounts, audit trails, and compliance with financial reporting arrangements and that they utilize the appropriate channels for money flows into and out (Commission of the EU 2005c: para 3). To ensure organizational compliance, the code suggests that Member States could use incentives to nonprofit organizations, such as privileged legal and taxation status or seals of approval (Commission of the EU 2005c: para 2.2). It also proposes oversight systems that Member States should put in place (Commission of the EU 2005c: para 2.2). Such supervisory or regulatory mechanisms are to enable Member States and their institutional representatives, such as public agencies, to monitor organizations, their activities, and funding arrangements. In addition, the information gleaned should allow for "cooperation/information exchange" at the EU level (Commission of the EU 2005c: para 2.4). Under the code, the oversight mechanism that Member States as regulators are encouraged to employ is a publicly accessible national registration scheme for nonprofit organizations, under which the regulator should have investigatory powers (Commission of the EU 2005c: para 2.4).[48] To highlight potential or actual risk and to provide an oversight body with information to enable supervision and monitoring, the code recommends that organizations submit and maintain "basic information forms" to be held by a registering body. These forms would contain general organizational details, such as: the full name and address of the organization and any branches, mission statements, organizational and decision-making structures, internal financial control mechanisms, details of officers and their responsibilities, and financial information such as bank account details and information on the countries from which the organization receives or transfers funds (Commission of the EU 2005c: para 3). Donors, too, have responsibilities under the draft code, which is keen to promote the idea of "responsible giving" (Commission of the EU 2005b: para C.3). The code places an onus on individual donors to verify that their donations are going to legitimate organizations not ones supporting terrorist-related political activity. While this would be impossible to police, it is proposed that this be ensured through Member States informing and educating their citizenry and allowing basic information from the organizations to be publicly accessible (Commission of the EU 2005b: para C.3).[49]

Many Member States already have registration schemes in place for their nonprofit sectors. Some of these schemes, such as the Charity Commission's Register of charities in England and Wales, cover only part of the sector operating within a Member State and would not be sufficient on their own to comply with the European Commission's proposed code. Because the responsibility for operating and monitoring a national registration scheme for nonprofits lies with national governments, each Member State would be required to develop their existing arrangements to ensure compliance, be that through a separate registration system or the development of an existing one. As with the EA, there is no attempt under the code to create or enforce harmonization of nonprofit framework laws in Member States. The Member States would be given free reign to set up or develop existing registration systems appropriate to their jurisdictions. In addition, the code does not attempt to determine the rules on advocacy and lobbying by sector organizations at the national level. Neither are organizations given extra powers to lobby at the EU level beyond Member States' laws. National non-profit organizations undertaking lobbying or advocacy activities at the EU level can only do so under the limits set by the regulations in the Member State jurisdiction within which they are registered.

The Commission's proposal for a code of conduct is rooted on a defensible premise of protecting organizations, their donors, and the general public from extremist or criminal activity through ensuring open, accountable, and transparent governance. The proposal's level of flexibility, leaving the onus on Member States to interpret and implement in accordance with their own legal traditions, is likewise encouraging and necessary given the different concepts of nonprofit organizations across the many European jurisdictions. But practical implementation and ensuring compliance may well prove a complex task, particularly for those Member States that have recently joined the Union and those gearing up for accession. Similarly, the proposals are result-focused: They seek to make certain that there is oversight of the whole EU nonprofit sector. Little thought is given to the process and burden that the registration mechanisms will place upon Member States, which may not have full nonprofit registration in place already, or upon organizations, particularly smaller and poorly resourced ones which may find they are saddled with formal regulation or with multiple regulators calling for similar information.[50]

For its part, the Commission has promised further dialogue with the sector in ensuring that there is an "appropriate balance between statutory and self-regulation" (Commission of the EU 2005c : 10). A formal Contact Group, consisting of representatives from the nonprofit sector and interested authorities, has been established to take this dialogue forward. In voicing its support of the proposals, the Council of the EU nevertheless counselled that, when implementing the Commission's proposals, the Member States would need to take into account that there is a joint responsibility between the Member States and nonprofit organizations for safeguarding the integrity of the sector, that there should be dialogue between all parties, and that Member States should have full and current knowledge of the nonprofit sector within their jurisdiction. Likewise, the Council emphasized that accountability is an essential requirement for credibility and confidence in the nonprofit sector, and for accountability to work there should be effective oversight (Council of the EU 2005: 31–32). A principle missed by the Council, but of vital importance, is that these proposals and their implementation should neither discourage freedom of association nor affect the very flexible evolution of sector organizations that has been permitted in some Member States, such as the UK. The success with which Member States interpret these proposals and how at the EU level the constructive information exchange is achieved remains to be seen.

CONCLUSION

For many years, EU governance by and for nonprofit organizations operated more at the level of conceptual policy than reality. Nonprofit organizations, as one component of the wider construct of civil society, were part of the EU landscape but given very little genuine admittance into policy-making and the decision review process by the EU institutions and under Treaty provisions. Civil society's activities were often considered limited, and concerns were raised over nonprofits' lack of organizational accountability and representativeness as well as their unrealistic expectations of the EU institutions (EESC 2006a, Commission of the EU 1997: para 9.3). Even today, with the greater institutional recognition of the fundamental role that civil society can play in the EU, the relationship between the two remains a limited one. In particular, it highlights the centrality of Member States and national political and legal arenas for engaging with civil society organizations across the wide range of normal sector activities and for harnessing governance by and of the sector. There has been the traditional two-way governance process at work between the EU institutions and civil society organizations, but standing in the middle have been the Member States with a gatekeeper role. The centrality of national governments means that regulatory changes within Member States and the policies and agendas of Member States toward the nonprofit sectors in their jurisdictions remain of vital importance in shaping and promoting the sector at the EU level.

In terms of the input engagement in the EU from the bottom up, for example, through participating in policy-shaping, acting as a check and balance on the EU institutions, and ensuring their transparency as well as accountability in policies and decision-making, civil society's contribution has been relatively constrained by the EU institutions, the complexity of the EU policy process, and by their legal standing. True, civil society organizations are consulted; they provide expertise, implement EU policies, and are used as a badge to demonstrate the democratic credibility and legitimacy of the Union. It is also true that many civil society organizations are successful in this role, particularly those that are transnational. But, in general, they follow an institutional agenda, have a largely reactive role, are limited in bringing legal challenges against EU decision-making, and, as a body, currently have no specific legal standing in the Union. The consequence is a displacement focus by the overall sector upon national governments and national legal processes to gain their desired output at the EU level. Ultimately, a civil society organization's primary chance of success in fostering governance of the EU is to go through its Member State. This is so even though it remains difficult to convince national governments to act, given the nuances of the national and EU political landscapes and their own policy agendas. Limiting access for the civil society sector at the EU level has the effect of filtering issues through Member States but also maintaining the principle of representative democracy upon which the Union is primarily based.[51] But the gatekeeper role of Member States indicates that civil society organizations, despite the EU's many plaudits, do not in reality have direct access to review EU policy and decision-making beyond the EESC conduit.

Looking at governance from the top downward, that is, the EU institutions' regulation of the behavior of nonprofit organizations in terms of ensuring transparency and accountability, we are starting to see the EU seek to put in place some standards. These governance standards are broad brush, with the purpose of setting down generalized norms upon which more specific regulations can be developed. The implementation of these governance mechanisms is to be completed not by the EU's institutions or its regulatory processes, but by Member States and national laws. Much of the detail of the operation of nonprofit and wider civil society organizations has always been determined at the national level under Member State laws. This is clearly appropriate given the diverse common and civil law traditions across the 27 Member States and the different terminology and conceptions that exist of sector organizations. Of course, there are other areas in which the EU regulates at a national level, but these are in significant social rights such as employment and discrimination law. In these areas, the EU regulation is generally applicable to all organizations and is not directed specifically or solely at the civil society sector. But it has generally not been within the purview of the EU to be concerned with each Member State's private law of organizations, and this explains why the EU regulation in this field is undeveloped. Where we see the EU taking a hand with governance of nonprofit organizations is in those situations where there are wider policy issues at stake, such as concerns with security, terrorism, and proper financial management of EU funds, or simply to assist the EU in understanding and putting in context the civil society organizations with which they have contact. In governing the sector, then, the EU very clearly uses the Member States as gatekeepers, and it is through such national governments that implementation and regulation of governance standards will take place.

The gatekeeper role of Members States has much to commend it, and it does accord with the EU's principle of subsidiarity. It also maintains a barrier which can filter out vexatious and undeserving challenges that would inevitably draw the EU institutions' time and resources away from more appropriate concerns (compare De Schutter 2002: 216–217). But the Member States' gatekeeper position is not without its difficulties which raises questions about its appropriateness. The Member States' subsidiarity role only works where the organizations are national as opposed to transnational. In addition, even though the principle of representative democracy is maintained, the lauded role of civil society organizations in addressing the EU's democratic deficit is severely undermined by limiting their effective access to EU policy and decision-making. Filtering through Member States also does little to support civil society's role in assisting the EU to achieve its principles of integration and enlargement. Emasculated organizations are ineffective ambassadors for citizenship. In addition, while some provisions, such as the EA and the anti-terrorism code of conduct, will encourage a degree of commonality in the approach to nonprofit organizations within Member States, leaving national governments to develop governance standards for the sector will lead to inconsistency across the Union. While some Member States, such as France, Germany, and the UK, have advanced regulatory frameworks in place for the civil society sectors within their jurisdictions, other Member States (particularly accession states) are either less well developed or lack sufficient political will to regulate. Such differentiation could undermine the EU's proposals, particularly if transnational organizations seek to register as EAs in the Member States with the least well-developed regulatory and governance procedures or those with the most advantageous advocacy and lobbying laws.

A more interventionist EU at this level is not recommended, but a balance needs to be struck here, with greater support offered to Member States so that appropriate, consistent, and balanced governance is achievable. This is necessary not least because it is only a strong, accountable civil society sector which has the support of citizens that can successfully operate as a check and balance on the EU institutions.

As we have seen in this chapter, there are signs that the traditional governance connections between the EU and civil society organizations are changing. Some of the proposals, if they come to fruition, are significant. The Aarhus Convention in particular could prove to be a catalyst for more open access for civil society in the review of EU processes. To be sure, the Convention only applies to nonprofit organizations working in the field of environmental protection. But affording rights to one section of civil society highlights an untenable differentiation between different parts of the sector. The Aarhus Convention may well become a model for nonprofit organizations beyond the environmental field and may compel reform to ensure parity of judicial review across all policy areas. In addition, the principle of participatory democracy which is embedded in the Lisbon Treaty will provide civil society with its own legal standing in the EU for the first time and, as a consequence, promises greater depth to its relationship with the Union. The changes in approach that both of these developments could bring are not to be underestimated. If followed through, the move from the EESC as the conduit for civil society to direct individual access and specific legal standing for organizations in the Union will mark a new era that will revolutionize EU governance by and for civil society organizations. If the EU process is serious about using civil society to demonstrate the credibility and legitimacy of the Union, it will move to implement these changes without delay.

ACKNOWLEDGEMENT

The author would like to thank the AHRC who funded this work, Anthony Zito for discussion on the issues and Ann Sinclair for her research assistance.

NOTES

1. Following recent enlargement, there are now 27 Member States (Austria, Belgium, Bulgaria, Cyprus, Czech Republic, Denmark, Estonia, Finland, France, Germany, Greece, Hungary, Ireland, Italy, Latvia, Lithuania, Luxembourg, Malta, the Netherlands, Poland, Portugal, Romania, Slovakia, Slovenia, Spain, Sweden and the UK), 2 accession candidate countries (Croatia and Turkey), and an application pending from the former Yugoslav Republic of Macedonia.
2. The Register of Interest Representatives was established in 2008 as a voluntary register and replaces the earlier "Consultation, the European Commission and Civil Society" (CONECCS); see https://webgate.ec.europa.eu/transparency/regrin/welcome.do.
3. For example, the Platform of Social NGOs, the European Confederation for Relief and Development, European Council for Nonprofit Organizations, EU Civil Society Contact Group, and Green 10.
4. Other bodies include the European Central Bank, the European Investment Bank, and the European Ombudsman.
5. To that end, the EESC has regular dialogue with the EU institutions and with the sector. It has a Liaison Group for European Civil Society Organizations and Networks which maintains contact with civil society organizations.
6. See, for example, European Parliament (2001) *Resolution on the Commission White Paper on European Governance* (COM (2001) 428—C5–0454/2001—2001/2181(COS)) 29 November 2001, para 11; Commission of the EU, *Civil Society Dialogue between the EU and Candidate Countries* COM (2005) 290, 29 June 2005, para 1.3.
7. This definition has been used in subsequent EESC opinions; see, for example, EESC, *Opinion on the Communication from the Commission to the Council, the European Parliament, the European Economic and Social Committee and the Committee of the Regions on Civil Society Dialogue between the EU and Candidate Countries*, OJ C 28 of 3.02.2006: 97.
8. Participatory status is a relatively new provision laid down in Council of Europe, Committee of Ministers, Resolution Res(2003)8, adopted by the Committee of Ministers on 19 November 2003.
9. *Resolution on Nonprofit Making Association in the European Communities*, OJ C 099, 13/04/1987 p. 205. For a history of the development of EU policy toward the sector, see Kendall & Anheier (1999).

10. This contrasts with their standing with the United Nations and the Council of Europe.

11. For example, in setting the "Lisbon Strategy" (created at the European Council Meeting in Lisbon in 2000), the importance of the role of civil society in contributing to and achieving these targets was acknowledged. This strategy is an attempt by the Member State governments to agree upon a set of targets in order to enhance their individual country's economic competitiveness, for example, through enhancing knowledge and education, technology, and employment.

12. The Copenhagen Criteria, decided by the Member States at the Copenhagen European Council in 1993, is a set of requirements for countries wishing to join the EU and set out in Articles 6(1) and 49 EC, including the need for stability of institutions guaranteeing democracy, the rule of law, and human rights (of which having a vibrant civil society would play a part).

13. For example, the European Parliament under its Rules of Procedure has extensive rules for lobbying which do not apply to the other institutions.

14. Under its Rules of Procedure, the European Parliament has a process of accreditation which requires organizations to register and adhere to a code of conduct if they seek at least five days access to the Parliament per year (see Article 3, Annex IX of the Rules). This register does not require information on who an organization represents.

15. As the EESC acknowledged in 1999, the EU "faces low confidence among its citizens who accuse it of inefficiency, point to democratic deficits and call for greater responsiveness to grassroots opinion. European integration needs the commitment and support of ordinary people more urgently than ever before and at present does not seem to have enough of either," *Opinion on 'The role and contribution of civil society organizations in the building of Europe.'*

16. The White Paper defines governance as "rules processes and behaviour that affect the way in which powers are exercised at European level, particularly as regards openness, participation, accountability, effectiveness and coherence" (Commission of the EU 2001: Executive Summary).

17. The lack of an "EU wide public space" and media contributes to poor understanding and a perception of elitism within the system (Greenwood 2007).

18. See, for example, the European Commission's launch of a 'Partnership for European Renewal' COM(2005) 12, 26.1.2005.

19. Regulation (EC) No 1049/2001 of 30 May 2001 provides for access and a register of published and unpublished EU documents. The European Commission is currently reviewing the operation of this Regulation and is considering extending it to all EU institutions (Commission of the EU 2007b).

20. The Commission's standards covering participation, accountability, and coherence are articulated in Commission of the EU COM (2002) 704, Chapter V. See also Commission of the EU COM (2002b) 713.

21. See Commission of the EU (2006), *Green Paper: European Transparency Initiative* COM (2006) 194, 3.5.2006. The Transparency Initiative also covers disclosure of data on beneficiaries of EU funds proposing that Member States have an obligation of disclosure, pages 13–14. See generally the European Transparency Initiative website http://ec.europa.eu/transparency/eti/index_en.htm

22. The initial incentive, which proposed to encourage voluntary registration, was not a strong one: It involved simply an automatic alert of consultations within the area of interest specified by the organization. Post consultation, the Commission has agreed to look into also allowing registered organizations advanced recognition to launch an internal review, such as under the Aarhus Convention. It is certainly clear that stronger incentives are needed if the registration system is to be a success.

23. The Register replaced the CONECCS database.
24. See Commission of the EU (2002a), *Toward a reinforced culture of consultation*, covering, *inter alia*, declaration of interests, accuracy of information lack of inducements.
25. The EESC favors a compulsory code similar to the one used by the European Parliament (EESC 2006b: Para 5.2.1).
26. An example of a compulsory code is the Combined Code on Corporate Governance in England and Wales. The COR favors compulsory registration (COR 2007: Para 4.3).
27. The English Compact is discussed in the chapter by Debra Morris in this volume. NCVO's proposal for a Concordant is available at: http://www.ncvo-vol.org.uk/policy/index.asp?id=2810.
28. There is also a process of self-selection at work. The policy process at the EU level creates an abundance of knowledge resources and intellectual capital so that the vast majority of civil society organizations can opt not to pursue the EU process and focus more on the national arena (Jacobs & Zito 2003).
29. This is not an open invitation to individuals but rather requires "not less than one million citizens who are nationals of a significant number of Member States" (Article 8 B [as amended]).
30. The Lisbon Treaty also expressly incorporates the European Convention on Human Rights into the EU process. This will give a broader scope for protection of the fundamental human right freedoms in the Convention and greater recourse for citizens and organizations to enforce their rights beyond their Member States.
31. Advocate General Jacobs, Case C-40/00P, *Unión de Pequeños Agricultores v Council*.
32. Case 25/62, *Plaumann & Co v Commission*.
33. See Case C-321/95, *Stichting Greenpeace Council (Greenpeace International) v Commission* [1998] ECR 1–1651. In this case, the Advocate General was prepared to accept individual concern had Greenpeace been specifically requested by an EU body such as the Commission to become a formal participant, but a representation to an open consultation was not acceptable: see Cygan (2003: 1002–1005).
34. Article 230 can be extended by the courts; for example, it was extended for the European Parliament in *European Parliament v Council (Re Chernobyl)* (1990). But attempts have not been permitted to extend Article 230 for public interest litigation (Cygan 2003: 1001–1002).
35. See Sedley LJ *R (The Refugee Legal Centre) v Secretary of State for the Home Department* [2004] EWCA Civ 1481, para 5. The Supreme Court Act 1981, section 31(3) laid down that an action could be brought where an applicant demonstrated "sufficient interest," see *Inland Revenue Commissioners v National Federation of Self-employed and Small Businesses Ltd* [1981] 2 WLR 722.
36. Advocate General Jacobs, Case C-40/00P, *Unión de Pequeños Agricultores v Council*.
37. Before the court made its decision in *UPA* a similar approach to Article 47 was taken in Case T-177/01 *Jégo-Quéré v Commission* in 2002, but that case was limited by the decision of the Court in *UPA*. For discussion on the use of Article 47, see Cygan (2003: 1008–1010).
38. Decision 2005/370/EC. The access to justice provisions were adopted by the European Parliament and Council on 6 September 2006 with Regulation (EC) No 1367/2006.

39. It is interesting that the regulation uses the term "nonprofit-making" rather than "nonprofit-distributing." If this is meant literally, it will limit the number of sector organizations that can take advantage of the Regulation.

40. Regulation (EC) No 1367/2006, Article 10 and 11. The request for review must be made within six weeks of the act being adopted, published, notified, or omitted.

41. The proposal began some years earlier, see initially European Parliament, *Resolution on nonprofit-making associations in the European Union*, OJ C 99/205, 13 April 1987. On proposals for the EA, see COM(91) 273/I and II, COM(93) 252, COD0386, and COD0387. At the same time, similar proposals were also made for a European Co-operative Society (Com(91) 273/III and IV), a European mutual society (Com(91) 273/V and VI), and a statute for a European company (COM(91) 174/I and II). There is also a proposal for a European Foundation Statute, currently subject to a feasibility study, see the European Foundation Centre which is leading the proposal lobby: www.efc.be

42. Article 3(1) of the proposal provides three methods for becoming an EA: where there are at least seven natural persons who are nationals of at least two EC Member States; where there are two or more legal entities where any two are resident in at least two Member States; and where an already established association, registered in one Member State, has had an establishment in another Member State for at least two years.

43. Articles 11–15 deal with regulations for general meetings. Article 16 provides for an equal right to information for the members of the EA. Voting rights and decision-making are covered in Articles 17–21. Article 22 covers the functions of the executive committee, including the power to represent the EA in dealings with third parties and the power to delegate. The term of office of the executive committee (not to exceed six years, subject to reappointment), conditions of membership, and alternative appointments are laid down in Articles 25–27. Power of representation is covered in Article 29, rights and obligations in Article 31, and civil liability in Article 33, such that "members of the executive committee shall be liable for loss or damage sustained by the EA as a result of breach of the obligations attaching to their functions." The liability of the executive committee is joint and several (Article 33(2)).

44. Article 9 provides that the Member State will give notice of the creation of the EA in the Official Journal.

45. Council Regulation (EC) No 1435/2003, 22 July 2003 on the Statute for a European Cooperative Society (SCE) in force from 18 August 2006 and given effect in UK law via The European Cooperative Society Regulations 2006, Statutory Instrument 2006 No. 2078. The European Company Statute was approved by the European Council at its Summit in Nice on 8 December 2000.

46. The European Council for Nonprofit Organizations (CEDAG) has argued for the statute to be revived in order to simplify the EU institutions' different measures for accountability: CEDAG, *Answer to the EESC Consultation on "Representativeness of the European civil society organizations within the civil dialogue"* (SC/023 14 February 2006), 28 June 2006, p. 15.

47. Nonprofit organizations are defined as those that "engage in the raising and/or disbursing funds for charitable, religious, cultural, educational, social or fraternal purposes, or for the carrying out of other types of good works" (p. 1). For a fuller discussion see Dunn (2006).

48. Investigations should be 'proportionate to the weight of the identified risk.'

49. Confidential bank account details would be excluded.

50. Indeed the consultation on these proposals brought little commendation from the sector.

51. See Article 8 A (1) Treaty of Maastricht as amended by Article 1 paragraph 12 of the Lisbon Treaty.

REFERENCES

Beyers, J. (2004). "Voice and access: Political practices of European interest associations." *European Union Politics*, 5(2): 211–240.

Civil Society Contact Group. (2006). *Making your voice heard in the EU: A guide for NGOs.*

Commission of the European Union. (1997). *Promoting the Role of Voluntary Organizations and Foundations in Europe*, COM (97) 241, 6 June.

Commission of the European Union. (2000). *The Commission and Non-Governmental Organizations: Building a stronger partnership*, COM (2000) 11, 18 January.

Commission of the European Union. (2001). *European Governance—A White Paper*, COM (2001) 428, 25 July.

Commission of the European Union. (2002a). *Toward a Reinforced Culture of Consultation and Dialogue—General principles and minimum standards for consultation of interested parties by the Commission*, COM (2002) 704, 5 June.

Commission of the European Union. (2002b). *Communication on the Collection and use of expertise by the Commission: Principles and guidelines*, COM (2002) 713, 11 December.

Commission of the European Union. (2005a). *Civil Society Dialogue between the EU and Candidate Countries*, COM (2005) 290, 29 June.

Commission of the European Union. (2005b). *Draft Recommendations to Member States Regarding a Code of Conduct for Nonprofit Organizations to Promote Transparency and Accountability Best Practices*, JLS/D2/DB/NSK D (2005) 8208, 22 July.

Commission of the European Union. (2005c). *Communication on The Prevention of and Fight against Terrorist Financing through enhanced national level coordination and greater transparency of the nonprofit sector*, COM(205) 620, 29 November.

Commission of the European Union. (2006). *Green Paper: European Transparency Initiative*, COM (2006) 194, 3 May.

Commission of the European Union. (2007a). *Communication on Follow-up to the Green Paper 'European Transparency Initiative'* COM (2007) 127, SEC 360, 21 March.

Commission of the European Union. (2007b). *Green Paper, Public Access to Documents held by Institutions of the European Community: A review*, COM (2007) 185, 18 April.

Committee of the Regions (COR). (2007). *Opinion on European Transparency Initiative*, CONS T-IV-008, 13–14 February.

Council of the European Union. (2005). *2696th Council Meeting*, Justice and Home Affairs, Brussels, 14390/05 (Presse 296) 1–2 December.

Cygan, A. (2003). "Protecting the interests of civil society in community decision-making—the limits of Article 230 EC." *International and Comparative Law Quarterly* 52: 995–1012.

De Schutter,O. (2002). "Europe in search of its civil society." *European Law Journal*, 8(2): 198–217.

Dunn, A. (2000). "Shoots among the Grassroots: Political activity and the independence of the voluntary sector." In A. Dunn (ed.), *The Voluntary Sector, The State and The Law*. Oxford: Hart Publishing.

Dunn, A. (2006). "To Foster or to temper? Regulating the political activities of the voluntary and community sector." *Legal Studies*, 26(4): 500–523.

European Citizens Association. (2002). *Listening to Civil Society: What relationship between the European Commission and NGOs?* 2 March.

European Economic and Social Committee (EESC). (1999). *Opinion on The Role and contribution of civil society organizations in the building of Europe*, OJ C 329, 17 October.

European Economic and Social Committee (EESC). (2006a). *Opinion on The representativeness of European civil society organizations in civil dialogue*, SC/023—CESE 240, 14 February.

European Economic and Social Committee (EESC). (2006b). *Opinion on The Green Paper—European Transparency Initiative*, SC/028, 26 October.

European Economic and Social Committee (EESC). (2006c). *Opinion on The Voluntary activity: Its role in European society and its impact*, SOC/243—CESE 1575, 13 December.

European Parliament. (2001). *Resolution on the Commission White Paper on European Governance* (COM (2001) 428—C5-0454/2001—2001/2181(COS)) 29 November.

Fairhurst, J. (2006). *Law of the European Union*, 5th ed., London: Pearson.

Geyer, R. (2001). "Can European Union (EU) social NGOs co-operate to promote EU social policy?" *Journal of Social Policy*, 30(3): 477–493.

Gjems-Onstad, O. (1995). "The proposed European Association: A symbol in need of friends?" *Voluntas*, 6(1): 3–21.

Greenwood, J. (2007). "Organized civil society and Democratic legitimacy in the European Union." *British Journal of Political Science*, 37: 333–357.

Jacobs, J., and Zito, A. (2003, September). "A cross-regional comparison of civil society in the environmental policy-making of the MERCOSUR and the European Union." Paper presented at UACES 33rd Annual Conference, Newcastle upon Tyne.

Jeffery, C. (2002). "Social and Regional Interests: ESC and Committee of the Regions." In John Peterson and Michael Shackleton (eds.), *The Institutions of the European Union*. Oxford: Oxford University Press.

Kendall, J. (2001). "The third sector and the development of European public policy: Frameworks for analysis?" *Civil Society Working Paper 19*. London: The Centre for Civil Society.

Kendall, J., and Anheier, H. K. (1999). "The third sector and the European Union policy process: An initial evaluation." *Journal of European Public Policy*, 6(2): 283–307.

Lloyd, P. (1988). "The European Union and its programmes related to the third system." In A. Evers and J. Laville (eds.), *The Third Sector in Europe*. Cheltenham: Edward Elgar.

Mazey, S., and Richardson, J. (2001). "Interest groups and EU policy-making: Organizational logic and venue-shopping." In J. Richardson (ed.), *European Union: Power and Policy Making*, 2nd ed. London: Routledge.

Treaty of Nice Articles 257–262 (concerning the EESC) and Articles 263–265 (concerning the COR).

Wallace, W. (1990). *The Transformation of Western Europe*. London: RIIA/Pinter.

Ward, A. (2004). "The Draft EU Constitution and private party access to judicial review of EU measures." In T. Tridimas and P. Nebbia (eds.), *European Union Law for the Twenty-First Century*. Oxford: Hart Publishing.

8 The Government–Nonprofit Relationship in the US
New Challenges and Possibilities

Steven Rathgeb Smith

INTRODUCTION

Today, nonprofit agencies in the US are facing a financial crisis unlike any time since the Great Depression. State and local governments are slashing spending for countless agencies, even many longstanding ones providing vital services. The assets of foundations have plunged, leading them to cut their grant levels substantially. And individual donors are facing declines in their asset values in a time of major layoffs and economic uncertainty. This dramatic shift in the revenues of nonprofits is exacerbated to an extent by its timing: The number of nonprofit agencies has grown dramatically in the last 15 years, so more agencies than ever are competing for rapidly shrinking public and private funding.

The economic crisis that began in late 2008 has put the relationship between government and the nonprofit sector at a crucial transition stage. Since the 1960s, government funding of nonprofits had been on the rise, especially for social and health organizations. But the reversal and contraction of public and private support due to the economic crisis has been especially severe at the state and local levels, although great variation exists across the country. The federal stimulus package of 2009 moderated some of these cutbacks, but it is not likely to help many smaller nonprofits which are not well-positioned to take advantage of the stimulus money.

The high profile politics of government funding and its implications for many nonprofit organizations has tended to overshadow the ongoing transformation and diversification of the ways government financially supports nonprofits (Salamon 2002; Smith 2006). Initially, government financing of nonprofits tended to be in the form of grants and contracts (often with relatively minimal accountability). Increasingly, tax credits, tax-exempt bonds, tax deductions, vouchers, and fees for services are important as forms of government financing for nonprofits. This diversification of funding or "policy tools" (Salamon 2002) tends to mask the extent of public funding of nonprofits and, simultaneously, the increased centralization of government funding at the federal level in many areas such as health and social services. The variety of policy tools has also had important and far-reaching effects on the actual operations of nonprofit organizations, notably by facilitating the development of hybrid nonprofit organizations with features of the public and/or for-profit sector and by promoting much greater cross-sectoral initiatives involving multiple organizations including nonprofits, for-profit businesses, and different government agencies.

In addition, the current economy highlights and intensifies two contradictory pressures on nonprofits. One the one hand, there is greater competition for funding and increased attention to accountability and outcome evaluation. Further regulation could be forthcoming. On the other hand, the economic recession and the diversification of policy tools also encourages the growth of relational governance at the local level (Phillips, Chapter 9, this volume; Van Slyke 2009), including more cooperation in the provision of services and greater interest in different types of alliances and network relationships. Thus, trends in the US mirror the two fundamental strands of New Public Management (NPM): the desire for improved performance and the goal of shifting away from large public bureaucracies toward more flexibility and decentralization in public service delivery (Behn 2003; Hill & Lynn 2004; Hood 1991; Rhodes 1991; Smith 2006).

This chapter analyzes and discusses the ongoing evolution of the government–nonprofit relationship in the US within the context of broader trends in public and nonprofit management. In the US, the emergence of new policy tools and devolutionary and economic pressures have promoted greater interest in the development of horizontal networks and collaboration even as government has tried to assert more accountability and authority over nonprofit agencies, especially agencies that are providing public services with government funds.

NONPROFITS AND GOVERNMENT: THE GROWTH AND DEVELOPMENT OF THE RELATIONSHIP

Government financial support of nonprofit organizations has a long tradition in the US dating back to the colonial period (Hall 1987; Salamon 1987; Smith & Lipsky 1993). Harvard University, the Massachusetts General Hospital, and other leading educational and health institutions received public funding in their formative years. Throughout the 19th and early 20th centuries, government funding of nonprofit service agencies continued, although it tended to be most extensive in the urban areas of the Northeast and Midwest. Overall, government oversight tended to be quite minimal. The relatively few agencies receiving public funds were subject to little ongoing scrutiny; indeed government relied upon these agencies themselves (and their boards) to conduct program monitoring.

Beginning in the 1960s, government funding of nonprofit organizations increased sharply, fueled by extensive new federal spending on many new social and health programs and organizations including Medicare and Medicaid, community action agencies, community mental health centers, neighborhood health centers, drug, and alcohol treatment, and child protection agencies. Other innovative community agencies receiving federal funds were battered women shelters, rape crisis programs, and emergency shelters for runaway youth. In the 1980s, the federal government also funded an array of new programs for persons with AIDS, homelessness, community care, and hunger relief, among others—most under contract with nonprofit service agencies (Smith 2006; Smith & Lipsky 1993). The funds for these programs were typically distributed directly to local nonprofit organizations through contracts or given to state and local governments who then subcontracted the funds to local nonprofits. Initially, the accountability expectations on these programs tended to be very modest, especially as they pertained to program outcomes.

Government policy toward nonprofit agencies took a different turn in the 1980s with the election of President Ronald Reagan, who won passage in 1981 of the OmniBus Reconciliation Act which initially reduced federal spending and regulations on many federal social and health programs and devolved responsibility for the administration of these programs, at least in part, to the states (Gutowski & Koshel 1984). Some nonprofit agencies, especially community based agencies, experienced sharp reductions in government funding, at least initially. Overall, the goal of the changes was to shift funding and oversight of federal programs, including many social and health programs delivered by nonprofit agencies, to state and local governments and to the private philanthropic sector.

Yet, even before the end of the second Reagan term in 1988, government funding and oversight of many different types of nonprofit services agencies recovered and in many cases increased substantially. Many states and localities substituted their own funds for lost federal money, refinanced their contracts with nonprofit agencies, or reconfigured programs to maximize federal assistance in order to take advantage of federal programs with increasing budgets (GAO 1984; Milroy 1999). This shift was particularly apparent in policy areas such as mental health, developmental disabilities, child welfare, home health, and counseling where state government increasingly tapped Medicaid to fund services previously funded through federal, state, and local categorical grant programs (GAO 1995; Smith 2006).

In addition, federal funding to address urgent public problems such as low income housing, immigrant assistance, child care and child welfare, drug and alcohol treatment, and community development rose, often substantially, during the late 1980s and 1990s (Smith 2006). For instance, nonprofit low income housing agencies proliferated throughout the country, spurred in part by the federal Low Income Housing Tax Credit (LIHTC) program of 1986.

More recently, the devolution of federal policy entered a new stage with the implementation of welfare reform, signed into law in 1996 by President Clinton. This legislation replaced the Aid for Dependent Children (AFDC) program enacted in 1935 as a shared federal/state program with wide variations in payment levels to individuals and eligibility standards nationwide. In place of AFDC, the Temporary Assistance for Needy Families (TANF) was established, initially with higher levels of funding than under AFDC but with a reduced number of recipients. TANF includes new state block grant programs and greater discretion for states to design income assistance programs, although new strict federal regulations governing the expenditure of federal TANF money by the states exist, including specific performance targets for states on the number of people on the welfare rolls, rates of teenage pregnancy, and work participation by welfare recipients. The welfare reform legislation also included a so-called Charitable Choice amendment to encourage states to fund faith-based agencies providing social services.

The impact of TANF on nonprofit organizations was complex. Almost immediately, many of the clients of nonprofit social welfare agencies lost their income maintenance support. However, these same clients, to greatly varying degrees across the country, were eligible for additional services (funded in part with new federal grants) to help them seek permanent employment. Overall, the size and character of welfare rolls and the expenditure of funds on welfare related programs changed dramatically, with a sharp drop in the number of individuals receiving cash assistance through TANF and an increase in funding of welfare-related social services (House Ways and Means 2004: 7–3, 7–4; Scarcella, Bess, Zielowski, & Geen 2006; Winston & Castenada 2007).

The federal share of total public funding to support nonprofit health and social welfare organizations also rose, until the financial crisis began in 2008, due to the increased reliance of state and local government and many nonprofit service agencies on Medicaid, the shared federal-state health care program. Medicaid, for instance, is critical to funding services to the developmentally disabled, especially community based programs (Braddock et al. 2005). And, Medicaid funds a broad group of programs provided by nonprofit agencies including hospitals, child welfare, home care, hospices, counseling, residential foster care, drug and alcohol treatment, and services for the mentally ill (although the extent of coverage varies depending upon the state). Several other federal programs experienced significant expansion until 2008 as well, including programs to support: community re-entry for criminals and parolees, child care, foster care and adoption, health promotion and prevention, home health care, emergency shelter, and the prevention of homelessness. Other types of nonprofit agencies such as arts and cultural agencies or charter schools did not experience the rise in federal support; instead their growth has been fueled by state and local government support and private donations.

Arguably, the growth of fiscal centralization through Medicaid and other federal programs in service categories such as mental health and child welfare has been facilitated and enabled by nonprofit organizations, especially community agencies which are perceived as legitimate, neutral organizations with local roots. This community connection has been especially valuable in providing support for different types of community services. Indeed, even many nationally recognized nonprofits with roots in voluntarism and civic engagement, such as Teach for America, City Year, and YouthBuild, rely upon partnerships with government for funding and referrals. They also depend substantially upon stipended volunteers through AmeriCorps.

In short, the relationship between nonprofits and government in terms of funding has been profoundly changed in the last 40 years. Prior to the 1960s, nonprofit agencies (except for hospitals and universities) were small and largely reliant on private contributions (especially the United Way) supplemented with client fees; their services were relatively narrow and restricted. Many agencies depended upon volunteers and lacked high levels of professionalism and accountability. The growth of government funding fueled the sharp rise in the number of nonprofit agencies with many agencies, especially in the area of health and social care, now primarily reliant upon government funds. Indeed, data from the National Center for Charitable Statistics (NCCS) suggest that nonprofits in some categories such as development disabilities and foster care depend upon government for most of their revenue. Some services such as child care do receive significant amounts of private fee income, while other services such as food banks and emergency shelters receive a mix of government funds supplemented by private contributions (NCCS 2009). Overall, the number of 501(c)(3) charitable nonprofits has almost doubled since 1996 to just under 1 million (NCCS 2009). Today, nonprofits are crucial to the implementation of public policy and the ability of government to achieve pressing policy goals and priorities, despite a deep economic recession.

The Diversification of Policy Tools

Importantly, government support for nonprofits also diversified substantially in the last 15 years, resulting in important shifts in the revenue streams of nonprofit agencies. One key change has been the shift away from the traditional contracts that were the hallmark of the initial period of widespread government funding of nonprofit social and health agencies in the 1960s and 1970s. Most contracts in this period were on a cost-reimbursement basis that paid agencies for their costs based upon the contract terms and budget. As a result, government funding primarily flowed to nonprofits through block contracts for certain levels of service or program units. However, many current forms of government support are tied to the client or consumer rather than the agency (and hence are reflected as program service revenue or fee income in the annual reporting of the non-profit to the Internal Revenue Service). A vivid example is Medicaid which functions like a "quasi-voucher" because eligibility is tied to the client. Agencies are reimbursed for providing qualifying services to eligible clients; their reimbursement rate is a vendor rate whereupon government will pay a certain amount for a specific service regardless of the costs incurred by specific agencies. In general, Medicaid vendor rates encourage competition for clients because it may only be possible to generate surpluses at high levels of service volume because each new Medicaid eligible client is more revenue for the agency at only marginally more cost. This financing arrangement is dramatically different than the traditional cost-reimbursement contract. Under the latter, agencies actually faced disincentives for service expansion because additional services added to an agency's cost without any certainty that these costs would be reimbursed. Many other contracts for services such as welfare to work, job training, mental health, and drug treatment are now structured as per client reimbursements based upon a specific rate schedule.

Other types of voucher programs are also more important to nonprofit funding. For example, many nonprofit housing programs for the disadvantaged rely upon the Section 8 housing voucher program. Child care vouchers for low-income people to promote permanent employment were an important component of the TANF legislation and grew substantially until the economic crisis hit in 2008. The appeal of vouchers is rooted in the attraction of greater client choice for services. Other similar funding initiatives are certain tax credits including the child care tax credit which can be claimed by individuals and couples on their tax returns. This credit partially offsets the cost of child care and dependent care (such as home health services), making nonprofit (and for-profit) services more affordable. The Work Opportunity Tax Credit offers financial incentives for for-profit firms to hire disadvantaged clients of nonprofit agencies. Also, the Welfare-to-Work tax credit, implemented in 1998, provides firms potentially larger subsidies for hiring long-term welfare recipients (Hamersma 2005). Both tax credit programs boost the demand for nonprofit programs.

In addition, the LIHTC allows private investors to reduce their tax liability by purchasing tax credits to build low-income housing with the hope that the tax savings will be passed on to low-income renters in the form of lower rent payments. This tax credit program is vital to the ability of nonprofit community development and housing organizations to build low-income and affordable housing (Jackson 2007; Keyes et al. 1996; Mayer & Temkin 2007). In addition, some nonprofit organizations can also tap historic preservation tax credits to help preserve historic structures or facades, sometimes in combination with the LIHTC (Jackson 2007; National Park Service 2009).

The other policy tool with much greater utilization by government and nonprofit organizations is tax-exempt bonds. Large nonprofit institutions such as hospitals and universities (as well as for-profits) have taken advantage of tax-exempt bonds for decades. These bonds help nonprofit organizations finance the cost of capital improvements such as new construction or renovation. What is new in the last 15 years is the growing use of tax-exempt bonds by smaller nonprofit organizations such as housing development organizations, child welfare agencies, and mental health centers. This increase in tax-exempt bond financing reflects in part the steady rise in the number of nonprofit organizations, especially smaller community-based organizations. Most of these community organizations are undercapitalized so, as they develop and evolve, they face substantial challenges in adequately funding their capital costs. This situation is exacerbated by the lack of financing for capital costs within government contracts. As a result, nonprofit organizations have turned to policy makers at the federal, state, and local levels to help them address these important capital costs. For example, state housing finance agencies have supported low income housing development by issuing bonds. Some states such as Massachusetts, Washington, and New Jersey established state agencies for economic development or housing development that offer tax-exempt bond financing programs for qualifying 501(c)(3) organizations. Tax-exempt bonds are an attractive financing option for nonprofits because they can obtain sizable financing for their capital needs; few foundation sources of extensive capital financing exist by comparison, although some big national foundations have begun to offer programs specifically targeted to capital needs (Ryan 2001). Targeted fundraising through capital campaigns can be a very labor intensive and expensive process that is especially difficult for smaller agencies to undertake.

Importantly, the economic crisis created havoc in the market for tax-exempt bonds and certain types of tax credits such as the LIHTC and historic preservation tax credits. To the extent that the economy recovers, these tools should continue to grow in utilization. However, the shift away from the older traditional cost-reimbursement contracts to greater reliance on fee revenue tied to the client is likely to continue even in the economic downturn.

GOVERNING THE RELATIONSHIP: CONTRADICTIONS AND COMPLEXITY

The diversification of policy tools and the growth of nonprofits providing valued public services have changed the political and market environments for nonprofits and created contradictory tendencies: greater interest in control of nonprofits by government, while at the same time increased incentives for collaboration between government and nonprofits as well as among nonprofit organizations. These different tendencies embody the inherent contradictions within NPM which encourages greater competition and control as well as greater decentralization, community participation, and collaboration (Rhodes 1996). These contradictions exist because, in practice, the increasingly intertwined relationship between government and nonprofits occurs within a political context that profoundly shapes its evolution and development. These conflicting tendencies are especially apparent in new regulatory and accountability standards by government for nonprofit organizations.

Regulation and Accountability

Even before the financial crisis hit in late 2008, the growth of nonprofits and the increased dependence of government on nonprofits for service delivery, especially in social services and health care, was forcing important shifts in the government–nonprofit relationship. First, contracts have become more performance-based. In the initial build-up of government contracting with nonprofit agencies in the 1960s and 1970s, government administrators tended to emphasize 'process' accountability which focused on the outputs and activities of the contract agencies. The advent of the government reform movement of the 1990s (Hood 1991; Osborne & Gaebler 1992; Rhodes 1996) encouraged government administrators to restructure their contracts with nonprofit agencies to be more performance or outcome based. To varying degrees, many key contracts including welfare to work, mental health, workforce development, and foster care are now performance based contracts whereupon agencies are reimbursed for services only if they meet specific performance targets (Behn & Kant 1999; Forsythe 2001). Many private funders, United Ways, and national foundations such as the Edna McConnell Clark Foundation are also tying their grants to an expectation of meeting certain agreed-upon performance measures. Overall, nonprofits face increased pressure to improve their performance from both the public and private sectors (Light 2004).

This heightened interest in performance has a number of implications for public policy and nonprofit organizations. First, this shift to outcome evaluation often involves a revolution in management thinking. Agencies need new investments in information systems in order to track outcomes and compile relevant programmatic and financial data. A key ripple effect is the 'professionalization' of the administrative and programmatic infrastructure of nonprofits, especially for smaller community organizations which may have roots in local voluntarism. Greater investment in administration and programs can be a severe challenge for these community organizations given their relative undercapitalization. Also, the resources necessary to comply with performance contracts can raise questions about mission and programmatic focus because the performance contracts may contain expectations at odds with the longstanding client and program emphasis of the program. To be sure, many nonprofit social service agencies continue to rely upon volunteers even with the growing emphasis on performance contracts. However, volunteers tend to be involved in support activities such as board service and fundraising or less intensive direct service roles such as soup kitchens, crisis hot-lines, tutoring for youth, and building homes.

This shift to professionalization and performance contracting can be especially consequential for nonprofits such as local community organizations that emerge out of a desire of a group of like-minded 'community' of people to address a problem or social need such as homelessness. These individuals create a service agency that regards its mission as logically being responsive to their community of interest (Smith & Lipsky 1993). Government, by contrast, tends to approach services and clients from the norm of equity, consistent with the need of government officials to treat groups and individuals fairly. Equity can be interpreted in a variety of ways, but in social and health services, it usually means defining need in order to allocate resources by criteria deemed to be fair—for example, by income, geographic location, and severity of illness or need. Because of their emphasis on responsiveness, nonprofit agencies may clash with government, particularly on policy matters relating to services, clients, and staff. This clash can be especially pronounced under a performance contracting regime that can leave nonprofit service agencies little discretion on the performance targets to be met and may require the agency to shift its programmatic focus toward short-term goals and client groups that are at variance with their original community of interest (Smith & Lipsky 1993).

Thus, performance contracting and, more broadly, the movement toward greater outcome evaluation can represent an intensified form of control over the operations of nonprofit organizations. In this sense, it can be conceptualized as another form of hierarchical governance whereupon government administrators try to control the activities and performance of their agents (Hill & Lynn 2004; Kettl 2002). The economic recession has intensified pressure for hierarchy because government cutbacks and the drop in private giving places nonprofits in a particularly vulnerable position vis-à-vis government and limits their ability and/or willingness to challenge government decisions. Further, the economic situation has significantly increased the interest of many legislators and administrators in targeting services and ensuring accountability for public money; thus, performance contracting might expand and become more restrictive, creating a more rigid vertical relationship between government and nonprofits, with even less discretion for nonprofits to influence government policy and performance regulations.

The logic of performance contracting also tends to promote market competition among providers: Government is supposed to hold agencies accountable for specific outcomes, and if they do not meet these outcomes, government will turn to a different provider. Thus the very existence of performance contracting promotes greater uncertainty and more competition from nonprofit and for-provider providers. To the extent that nonprofit agencies are subject to contract termination (for non-performance), then agencies will be understandably more concerned about potential competitors and may adjust their programs and management styles accordingly. Agencies which may not have considered bidding upon particular contracts may do so in a performance contract arrangement as an 'insurance policy' in case other contracts are lost. By creating greater vulnerability among nonprofit agencies, market competition can reinforce the vertical, hierarchical relationships between government and nonprofits.

However, some qualifications to the general observation are necessary. First, the fiscal crisis has already reduced public and private revenues for nonprofits, creating less money for nonprofits to use to track outcomes and undertake evaluation. Second, the logic of performance contracting is that government (and private funders and the United Way) will switch providers if performance targets are not achieved. However, the economic crisis could, in both the short and longer term, shrink the number of providers in local communities, leaving government with fewer providers, spurring a reassessment of performance contracting, and providing an incentive for government to work collaboratively with nonprofits.

Third, the advent of performance contracting and the increased attention to program evaluation and outcomes encourages government and nonprofit agencies, to varying degrees depending upon the jurisdiction, to explore ways to achieve accountability through accreditation and self-regulation. For example, the Maryland Association of Nonprofits has developed a "Standards of Excellence" to promote high standards of ethical behavior and good governance in nonprofits. And nonprofit agencies in specific service categories, such as addiction services, are using accreditation to help support their efforts to enhance their impact and effectiveness. And, greater interest exists among nonprofits in particular service categories such as child welfare or drug treatment for cooperation to agree upon standards of good care and practice. To the extent that self-regulation develops, it could mitigate some of the pressure for additional regulation on performance and promote more collaborative, or horizontal, relationships between government and the nonprofit sector.

Fourth, government and nonprofits agencies providing public services are often engaged in a long-term relationship (Smith & Smyth 1996), despite the pressures of performance contracting and market competition, so both parties have an incentive to work together on performance measures and overall accountability. Indeed, nonprofits often work through their associations and coalitions to influence government contracting policy on rates and key regulatory issues. This intertwined and complex government–nonprofit relationship also encourages movement of staff between the two sectors. Many nonprofit agencies now have executive directors who previously held important government positions. Hiring staff with government experience is a very public acknowledgment that government contracting can be a long-term relationship. Today, nonprofit organizations provide an incredibly diverse array of services, often under very difficult circumstances.

204 *Steven Rathgeb Smith*

Many government contracts are for ongoing services such as child welfare, prisoner re-entry, community programs for the developmentally disabled and mentally ill, home care for the elderly, and workforce development. To be sure, the certainty of funding is often very unclear and unpredictable. Many agencies, especially larger agencies, may experience declines in some contracts and increases in other contracts in any particular year (Allard 2009; Sosin et al. 2010). However, agencies tend to have long-term relationships with government and are expected to be able to weather the cyclical nature of government funding. As a result, nonprofit organizations need to invest in their staff with the goal of building productive long-term relationships with government in order to be effective and sustainable; staff with government experience can be of great assistance.

Thinking about the relationship with government as a long-term relationship is reflected in other organizational adaptations to contracting. Government contract administrators place great priority on several key management components: sound financial management, including regular audits; attention to performance management, including the use of current program evaluation models; up-to-date tracking of clients and services; and a good reputation in the local community. In order to meet government expectations on these important priorities, nonprofit agencies with contracts (or interested in obtaining contracts) need to invest in expertise in financial management, program evaluation, and information technology. Over time, then, government contracting tends to profoundly change the internal agency dynamics and management style.

The movement of professionals back and forth between government and nonprofit agencies encourages a consensus on programmatic standards in particular service categories. This consensus can become a characteristic of the "contracting regime" whereupon government and nonprofit agencies develop a common set of assumption to guide their relationships. The regime concept—which was originally applied in the field of international relations—suggests that two parties are mutually dependent upon each other so that each party cannot easily exit the relationship. However, an equally important aspect of regimes is that one party is typically much more powerful than the other. In the case of contracting regimes, government tends to be the more powerful partner and is in a position to dictate programmatic and financial expectations even in the face of opposition from their contract agencies (Smith & Lipsky 1993; see also Considine 2003; Considine & Lewis 2003). For example, a public child welfare department and a set of nonprofit child welfare agencies may develop specific norms about acceptable practice, referral policies, and reimbursement rates. These norms then guide the behavior and strategic management of the government department and the providers. In this relationship, government is able to drive the evolution of these norms given its resources and political influence and the relative absence of alternative funding sources for their programs.

Contracting regimes tend to operate based upon a certain level of trust among the two parties, despite this power imbalance. Contracts are often relational and long term even in instances where competitive bidding is required (Smith & Smyth 1996). This "relational contracting" does not preclude differences of opinion or outright conflict, but it does underscore the stability of many contracting arrangements and the importance of cooperation among the two parties (Deakin & Michie 1997; Ring & Van de Ven 1992; Van Slyke 2007). But this cooperation occurs within a framework established by the more powerful partner. For example, nonprofit organizations may cooperate with government on a contract for community care for the chronic mentally ill, but the standards of care, financial regulations, and outcome measures are still set largely by government. Put another way, a nonprofit agency, by its decision to contract, indicates a willingness to cooperate with government on the implementation of a government program. Consequently, relational contracting (or horizontal governance) does not capture the nature of typical contracting relationships because it implies equity in decision-making among the two parties when, in fact, government is the much more powerful partner.

It should also be noted that performance contracting is part of a broader trend in American public policy of greater regulation of nonprofits. The federal Internal Revenue Service (IRS) has for example revised its longstanding reporting forms for nonprofit organizations in an effort to promote greater transparency and greater accountability, especially as it pertains to governance and financial management. Congress has debated many different proposals for new regulations governing nonprofits and foundations, including a requirement that nonprofits formally evaluate their activities on a regular basis. However, Congress passed legislation in 2006 that made only minor changes to existing law, mostly focused on foundations and charitable giving. Overall, then, the relationship between government and the nonprofit sector in terms of federal law governing their reporting and financial management did not change substantially, despite concerted attention from some members of Congress.

New Organizational Relationships and Forms

The contradictions within NPM are evident in the proliferation of new organizational forms and new relationships among nonprofit, for-profit, and public organizations. This development reflects in part the effects of the diversification of policy tools and the greater incentive for collaboration produced by the ongoing evolution of public policy toward nonprofits.

One important effect of tool diversification is "hybridization" of organizational forms, both formal and informal (Skelcher 2004). Many of these new forms represent a more collaborative and horizontal relationship among many different organizations. A good illustration is low income housing organizations. The LIHTC allows private investors to receive tax credits for investments in eligible housing projects. Low income housing agencies and community development organizations interested in accessing the LIHTC need to develop ongoing partnerships with for-profit organizations including investment houses, banks, and for-profit businesses. Nonprofit housing agencies also need to forge ongoing partnerships with local and state governments and often with local nonprofits that provide social services because new low income housing projects often need to integrate a variety of needed social services for eligible low income or disabled renters.

Moreover, nonprofit housing developers need to create for-profit, limited partnerships for their tax credit projects (so the private investors can receive their tax credits). Sometimes, the limited partnership is effectively owned by the nonprofit; in other cases, the nonprofit may be a minority partner. Significantly, the complexity of tax-credit deals and their multiple revenue streams tend to mask the extent to which the projects of low income housing organizations depend upon indirect government support and partnerships that are not tied directly to the tax credits including: 1) donations of land by local government to the housing organization at no cost or substantially below market; and 2) the use of Section 8 housing vouchers to support the rent payments of the tenants. In an important sense, then, low income housing organizations are a good example of an emergent form of nonprofit organization reliant on a mix of public and private revenue and embedded within a web of partnerships and collaborations that support its programs.

This movement away from direct contracts to much greater reliance on a mix of revenue is increasingly common among nonprofits providing social and health services. A good example is an agency in Seattle (Washington), founded in the early 1970s to create and improve affordable housing and physical facilities for low income populations by providing architectural design and technical support to nonprofit agencies. Initially, the agency functioned as a 'technical assistance' arm of the Seattle Department of Housing and Human Services, but in the last 15 years, the mission and activities of the agency broadened substantially. Twenty years ago, the agency relied almost completely on funding from the federal Community Development Block Grant (CDBG). This money was given to the state which then gave it to the city of Seattle which then contracted with the agency for technical assistance and design work with local nonprofits. In the mid-1990s, the agency experienced a funding crisis when the city notified the agency that it would terminate its funding entirely. Pushed by this funding crisis to diversify, the agency bought a for-profit architectural firm which became a for-profit subsidiary of the agency. Ultimately, the city decided to continue to fund the agency, but the level of CDBG funds has declined steadily. However, the agency has been able to increase its revenue substantially by generating fee income from other nonprofit agencies (which they typically receive from government sources). For example, a low income housing organization might receive funding from the LIHTC program to build affordable housing: The budget for the housing project includes funding for design services that the housing agency directly pays to the architectural design agency.

The shift in revenue streams is very consequential in terms of accountability, performance expectations, and competition among agencies for funding. The fee income for the design agency is based largely on its relationships, market position, and performance. No formal contracts exist, and the money tends to be project by project. Nonetheless, the relationships tend to encourage repeat business, either directly or indirectly (because much of the public money is channeled through other organizations). Indeed, this agency is representative of a new wave of nonprofits—from community development organizations to emergent job training programs to innovative programs for the homeless—that mixes direct and indirect public funding complemented by occasional project specific grants from foundations and corporations and by individual donations.

Moreover, many nonprofit agencies are now tapping this mix of public and private money and an array of different network relationships to build large projects. For instance, the Seattle Art Museum (SAM) recently completed a major new project: the Olympic Sculpture Park (OSP) on the city's waterfront. OSP evolved from the joint efforts of SAM, private donors, a large oil company, Unocal, and the nonprofit Trust for Public Land (TPL). Unocal had owned a project site for several decades. SAM staff viewed this site as the perfect location for a new sculpture park and thus sought funds to buy the property from Unocal, which assisted by selling the land at a below market price and taking the eligible tax deduction for the difference between the selling and appraised price. TPL, working with SAM, raised the $16 million for the purchase price from private donors. TPL then transferred title of the land to the Museum Development Authority, a public development authority (PDA) which owns the land on which the current SAM building resides. (A PDA is a quasi-public institution in Washington State that can issue bonds and possesses more financing flexibility than a traditional nonprofit.) The total cost of the project was over $80 million, with this money being a mix of many different government funding sources, foundation grants, and individual donations. The overall success of this project relied extensively on different network relationships and partnerships among an array of public and private agencies.

The OSP project illustrates a number of important trends in public and nonprofit management. First, OSP underscores the emergence of land trusts and the national Trust for Public Lands (TPL), in particular, as central players in various types of nonprofit—for-profit partnerships (and public–for-profit partnerships). The ability of corporations and individuals to take a tax deduction for a gift of land at its appraised market value is a significant financial incentive (over and above the existing incentives for cash contributions) to give appreciated land for public purposes. Also, corporations may save substantial sums in environmental remediation and associated transaction costs. TPL and other similar organizations have the expertise and the professional capacity to manage these land deals and facilitate the raising of money for the purchase price.

Second, these projects are complicated, not unlike tax credit deals. They rely heavily on professional and social networks to connect donors, the TPL, government agencies, and nonprofit institutions. Further, the complexity of the project and the many players tends to mask the sometimes substantial public funding role, either directly or indirectly. It also illustrates that government funding remains important for nonprofit initiatives even though it is not structured as a performance contract. For example, the OSP project received many *grants* (similar to a foundation grant) from government agencies to help with different parts of the project. The city also provided in-kind assistance.

Third, the OSP deal underscores the importance of hybrid organizations to help attract the necessary financing for nonprofit organizations. OSP is technically owned by the Museum PDA. SAM also has created an affiliated Seattle Art Museum Foundation to help attract private donations. In this sense, OSP and SAM fit with the broader trend evident in housing and many other types of nonprofit organizations to create new organizational structures in order to gain greater financing and programmatic flexibility. The affiliated foundation, for instance, is an increasingly common organizational vehicle used by nonprofit organizations to raise revenue for the parent organization. (The board is typically controlled by the parent organization, although great variation exists in the specific by-laws and rules governing the boards of the affiliated foundation.)

Initially, these affiliated foundations were limited to very large institutions such as hospitals and universities. The impetus for these foundations was the argument that private donors would be more likely to give money to a foundation than the parent organization because donors would have greater control over the money and more certainty on the disposition of their donations. Over time, affiliated foundations have proliferated, with many relatively modest sized nonprofit agencies creating foundations. A contributing factor was the perception of scarcity and the uncertain environment faced by many nonprofits worried about their financial sustainability. These foundations also can forge partnerships between nonprofits and for-profit companies.

In addition, a veritable continuum of new inter- and intra-organizational relationships among nonprofits has been created by the changing funding and political landscape for nonprofits. One example is a more integrated relationship between two nonprofits. As noted, the number of nonprofit organizations has, until recently, risen sharply. Many of these organizations are small and undercapitalized, creating severe financial sustainability problems, especially given the current economy. One option for small organizations in trouble is to merge with a more stable organization. However, mergers are often difficult: Boards of directors want to protect the integrity and mission of their organizations, and a larger, more stable organization may be understandably reluctant to assume the liabilities of a financially weaker one.

The difficulties of merger present a serious problem for public (and private) funders. Funders are increasingly concerned about the many relatively small agencies with overlapping missions, thus creating service fragmentation, obstacles to service access, and quality assurance problems. And, each of these agencies has an administrative infrastructure to support which is inefficient from a government's perspective. Given that governments may be relying upon small, financially unstable agencies to provide vital public services using public funds, government contract administrators may feel that their clients are vulnerable to service disruptions unless the clients can be moved to a more stable organization.

In short, government is faced with the problem of addressing some of the consequences of the devolutionary aspects of NPM. Because consolidation and the accompanying greater centralization of services is problematic politically and financially, new structural innovations are emerging. One recent example illustrates the point. In Seattle, a relatively small social service agency, supported almost entirely by government contracts, was experiencing serious financial and programmatic distress. The agency serves a very disadvantaged homeless population, and thus the clients would almost certainly encounter major problems if service were precipitously cut. At the same time, a larger, established agency serving a similar population was scanning their environment for new programmatic and funding opportunities. The city encouraged the larger agency to approach the smaller agency about a merger or takeover. The board of the acquiring agency, however, was concerned about its financial exposure, especially given the uncertainty surrounding the future of the smaller agency. After a series of discussions, it was decided that the acquiring agency would take over the smaller agency, but that it would remain a legally separate entity. The bylaws of the latter were changed so that the board of directors of the acquiring agency could appoint the board of the smaller agency, giving it effective control even though the agency remained legally separate.

This complex arrangement has advantages for all three parties to the transaction. The acquiring agency gains control of the substantial assets and programs of the failing agency, while limiting its risk by keeping the agency distinctively separate. The smaller agency is relieved of the daunting legal and financial obligations without having to go through an expensive and complex merger process. It also preserves the identity of the agency and its programs, at least in the short term, so the appearance of continuity is maintained. And the city, the principal funder of both organizations, gains a more stable agency partner without the disruption of transferring contracts and clients to a new organization.

Other examples of new inter-organizational linkages include collaboration among different agencies to co-produce a specific service. For example, a nonprofit agency serving the chronic mentally ill might collaborate with a housing agency to offer support services in a low income housing residence. This collaboration may also be required by the stipulations of the government contract. The economic crisis has also encouraged many nonprofits to discuss ways in which they can share expenses such as office and support staff. Indeed, many innovative cost-sharing arrangements have been created across the country, often with the participation of a wide range of nonprofits.

The other notable example of new inter-organizational relationships is the increase in collaboration among nonprofit service agencies to lobby government administrators and legislators for more funding and higher rates on service contracts. This collaboration can be informal, so the executive directors of service agencies such as child welfare organizations might cooperate to pursue higher rates. Or, collaboration might evolve into a formal, membership-based coalition or association, with the mission of representing their member agencies in the political realm. In many states and larger localities, each major service category—e.g. home care, developmental disabilities, mental health, child welfare—has their own statewide association to pursue their public policy priorities. These associations also can provide greater networking among nonprofit agencies and an organizational vehicle to lower costs through bulk purchasing and other revenue saving strategies. These 'infrastructure' associations representing nonprofits have also tended to provide collaborative relations with government, including mutual problem solving on key issues such as contract rates and regulations.

THE AMERICAN STATE AND THE GOVERNMENT–NONPROFIT RELATIONSHIP

In many ways, the complexity of the government–nonprofit relationship reflects the particular features of the American state in the context of general trends in public management such as NPM. That is, the American welfare state has expanded in recent years through direct and indirect funding support for nonprofits. The federal government's funding role has become more important through contract funding as well as other funding programs including Medicaid, tax credits, and vouchers. Yet, the states remain very important in regulating and funding nonprofits as well, reflecting the federal system in the US that gives states and localities a strong role in public policy, especially in social and health policy. Indeed, many key funding programs such as Medicaid and TANF are shared federal/state programs. This federal system leaves nonprofits receiving funding highly vulnerable to the changes in local economic conditions which in turn affects state and local budgets. Indeed, this vulnerability has been heightened in recent years because of changes in federal programs that have granted greater discretion to state and local governments in the administration and funding of important social and health programs which affect hundreds of thousands of nonprofit organizations and their users.

The pressure for performance management is particularly keen at the state and local levels given their economic pressures, the rising demand for services, and the sharp rise in the number of nonprofit and for-profit service providers. In this sense, the US at the state and local levels has adopted many of the practices of other countries including Australia (Lyons & Dalton, Chapter 10, this volume) and Canada (Phillips, Chapter 9, this volume). However, the particular federal structure of the US has also promoted the development of new inter-organizational relationships among nonprofits, as well as long-term relationships between government and many nonprofit service providers, to a much greater extent than in other federal systems. This reflects the relative absence of many service providers in some areas as well as the political character of the government–nonprofit relationship which makes it very difficult for government administrators to switch contracts.

Major new regulation of nonprofits at the federal level has certainly been discussed extensively in recent years, but it has failed to gain substantial political support. The result has been a series of relatively minor changes in existing law to increase transparency in reporting. State governments continue to devote relatively scant resources to regulating the non-programmatic aspects of nonprofits, leaving this role to the federal government.

Further, several recent developments and trends appear certain to increase the incentives for nonprofits to engage in inter-organizational collaborations and adopt different types of hybrid governance structures. First, in 2009, Congress passed the *Serve America Act* which provides funding for thousands of new stipended volunteers through AmeriCorps and VISTA (Volunteers in Service to America) and which will promote support for local nonprofits and increased networking among local nonprofits and public agencies. Second, major coalitions and associations representing nonprofit organizations are major supporters of the Obama administration, thus it appears highly unlikely that the administration will seek to tighten regulation of political activity or lobbying by nonprofits. Third, the recently passed stimulus package to help generate jobs and recharge the economy contains money for a multiplicity of programs and services provided by nonprofit organizations. This money was to be distributed as quickly as feasible to a wide variety of providers, and the most likely recipients are agencies with longstanding good relationships with state and local governments (because a substantial portion of the stimulus money is given to state and local governments to spend).

The economic crisis may also hasten the shift away from the "disaggregation" tendencies characteristic of the governmental reform movement of the last 15 years (see Dunleavy et al. 2006). The increase in contracting and the proliferation of service agencies tended to promote service fragmentation and decentralization which complicates the governance of key public services such as child welfare or mental health. Even before the economic crisis, government and nonprofit leaders were experimenting with strategies to achieve greater service integration and collaboration. Fiscal pressures have increased the interest in collaboration, and even consolidation, in the interests of improved efficiency and program effectiveness. Yet, the concentration of power that has occurred in other countries such as Australia and Canada seems unlikely in the US context given the characteristics of America's federal structure which offers many access points for individuals and groups to influence public policy, as well as a decentralized administrative structure coupled with greater centralization in public financing. Further, the push for performance management and greater competition in service among nonprofits providing public services will continue but will also be attenuated by the fiscal crisis and the relative dearth of qualified nonprofit providers in many communities.

Yet, the fiscal situation will likely put the spotlight on one centrally important aspect of nonprofit service delivery: the relationship between nonprofit agencies and their clients. The expansion and diversification of government financing of nonprofit service agencies that took place until 2008 puts nonprofits on the front lines of public services. Thus, social citizenship for millions of individuals hinges on the capacity and effectiveness of nonprofits. The current cutbacks in funding are severely curtailing social citizenship rights as access to vital services is reduced. Reversing this situation will require sustained public investment and an invigorated policy role for nonprofits that recognizes the importance of government policy and funding to the effectiveness and quality of nonprofit services. Nonprofits will also need to invest on an ongoing basis in developing effective governance and to broaden and deepen their own community and political support.

ACKNOWLEDGMENTS

The graduate student assistance of Mara Brain, Tim Cormier, and Lauren Marra is greatly appreciated. I would also like to acknowledge the support of the Nancy Bell Evans Center on Nonprofits and Philanthropy at the Evans School of Public Affairs at the University of Washington and the Public Policy Institute at Georgetown University. Finally, I would like to thank Putnam Barber, Julita Eleveld, and Cory Sbarbaro for their feedback on earlier versions of this chapter.

REFERENCES

Allard, S. W. (2009). *Out of Reach: Place, poverty, and the New American Welfare State*. New Haven, CT: Yale University Press.
Behn, R. D. (2003). *Rethinking Democratic Accountability*. Washington, DC: Brookings.

Behn, R. D., and Kant, P. A. (1999, June). "Strategies for avoiding the pitfalls of performance contracting." *Public Productivity and Management Review*, 22(4): 470–489.

Braddock, D., Hemp, R., Rizzolo, M. C., Rizzolo, Coulter, D., Haffer, L., and Thompson, M. (2005). *The State of the State in Developmental Disabilities: 2005*. Preliminary Report. Washington, DC: American Association of Mental Retardation.

Considine, M. (2003). "Governance and competition: The role of non-profit organisations in the delivery of public services." *Australian Journal of Political Science*, 38(1): 63–77.

Considine, M., and Lewis, J. M. (2003, March/April). "Bureaucracy, network, or enterprise? Comparing models of governance in Australia, Britain, the Netherlands, and New Zealand." *Public Administration Review*, 63(2): 131–140.

Deakin, S., and Michie, J. (1997). "Contracts and competition: An Introduction." *Cambridge Journal of Economics*, 21: 121–125.

Dunleavy, P., Margetts, H., Bastow, S., and Tinkler, J. (2006). "New Public Management Is dead—Long live Digital-Era Governance." *Journal of Public Administration Research and Theory*, 16: 467–494.

Forsythe, D. W. (ed.). (2001). *Quicker, Better, Cheaper? Managing performance in American Government*. Albany, NY: The Rockefeller Institute Press.

General Accounting Office (GAO). (1995). *Medicaid: Spending pressures drive states toward program reinvention*. Washington, DC: GAO. GAO/HEHS-95-122.

General Accounting Office (GAO). (1984). *States Use Several Strategies To Cope With Funding Reductions Under Social Services Block Grant (SSBG)*. Washington, DC: GAO. GAO/HRD-84-68.

Gutowski, M. F., and Koshel, J. J. (1984). "Social Services." In J. L. Palmer and I. V. Sawhill (eds.), *The Reagan Experiment*. Washington, DC: Urban Institute.

Hall, P. D. (1987). "A historical overview of the private nonprofit sector." In W. W. Powell (ed.), *The Nonprofit Sector: A research handbook*. New Haven, CT: Yale University Press.

Hamersma, S. (2005). *The Work Opportunity and Welfare-to-Work Tax Credits*. Urban-Brookings Tax Policy Center. No. 15. Online. Available at <http://www.urban.org/url.cfm?ID=311233> (accessed 15 April 2009).

Hill, C. J., and Lynn, L. E., Jr. (2004). "Is hierarchical governance in decline? Evidence from empirical research." *Journal of Public Administration Research and Theory*, 15(2): 173–195.

Hood, C. (1991). "A Public management for all seasons." *Public Administration*, 69: 3–19.

House Ways and Means Committee. (2004). *The Green Book*. Online. Available at <www.gpoaccess.gov/wmprints/green/index.html> (accessed 15 April 2009).

Jackson, P. J. (2007). *The Low-Income Housing Tax Credit: A framework of evaluation*. Washington, DC: Congressional Research Service.

Kettl, D. F. (2002). *The Transformation of Governance: Public Administration for the Twenty-First Century America*. Baltimore: Johns Hopkins University Press.

Keyes, L. C., Shwartz, A., Vidal, A. C., and Bratt, R. G. (1996). "Networks and nonprofits: Opportunities and challenges in an era of federal devolution." *Housing Policy Debate*, 7(2): 201–229.

Light, P. C. (2004). *Sustaining Nonprofit Performance: The case of capacity building and the evidence to support it*. Washington, DC: Brookings.

Mayer, N., and Temkin K. (2007). *Housing Partnerships: The Work of Large-Scale Regional Nonprofits in Affordable Housing*. Washington, DC: Urban Institute. Online. Available at < http://www.urban.org/UploadedPDF/411454_Housing_Partnerships.pdf> (accessed 10 April 2009).

214   *Steven Rathgeb Smith*

Milroy, J. B. (1999). *"The impact of federal budget cuts on the community-based nonprofit service sector: A case study."* Unpublished doctoral dissertation, Department of Political Science, State University of New York at Buffalo.

National Center for Charitable Statistics (NCCS). (2009). *Quick Facts about Nonprofits. Available at* <http://nccs.urban.org/statistics/quickfacts.cfm> *(accessed 15 April 2009).*

National Park Service. (2009). *Federal Tax Incentives for Rehabilitating Historic Buildings. Annual Report for FY 2008.* Online. Available at <http://www.novoco.com/related_program/resource_files/nps_annualreport_08.pdf> (accessed 5 April 2009).

Osborne, D., and Gaebler, T. (1992). *Reinventing Government.* Reading, MA: Addison-Wesley.

Ring, P. S., and Van De Ven A. H. (1992, October). "Structuring cooperative relationships between organizations." *Strategic Management Journal,* 13(7): 483–498.

Ryan, W. P. (2001). *Nonprofit Capital: A review of problems and strategies.* Report prepared for The Rockefeller Foundation and Fannie Mae Foundation.

Salamon, L. M. (ed.). (2002). *The Tools of Government.* New York: Oxford University Press.

Salamon, L. M. (1987). "Partners in public service: The scope and theory of government-nonprofit relations." In W. W. Powell (ed.), *The Nonprofit Sector: A research handbook.* New Haven, CT: Yale University Press.

Scarcella, C., Bess R., Zielewski, E., and Geen, R. (2006). *The Cost of Protecting Vulnerable Children V: Understanding state variation in child welfare financing.* Washington, DC: The Urban Institute, Available at < http://www.urban.org/UploadedPDF/311314_vulnerable_children.pdf? (accessed 20 April 2009).

Skelcher, C. (2004). "Public-private partnerships and hybridity." In E. Fairlie, L. E. Lynn, Jr., and C. Pollitt (eds.), *The Oxford Handbook of Public Management.* London: Oxford University Press.

Smith, S. Rathgeb. (2006). "Government financing of nonprofit services." In E. T. Boris and C. E. Steuerle (eds.), *Nonprofits and Government.* Washington, DC: Urban Institute Press.

Smith, S. Rathgeb, and Lipsky, M. (1993). *Nonprofits for Hire: The welfare state in the age of contracting.* Cambridge, MA: Harvard University Press.

Smith, S. Rathgeb, and J. Smyth. (1996, April). "Contracting for services in a decentralized system." *Journal of Public Administration Research and Theory,* 6(2): 277–276.

Sosin, M., Smith, S. R., Hilton, T., and Jordan, L. P. (2010). "Temporary crises and policy change: The case of state substance abuse systems." *Journal of Public Administration Research and Theory.* 20(3): 539–575.

Van Slyke, D. M. (2009). "Collaboration and relational contracting." In Rosemary O'Leary and Lisa Blomgren Bingham (eds.), *The Collaborative Public Manager: New Ideas for the twenty-first century.* Washington, DC: Georgetown University Press.

Van Slyke, D. M. (2007). "Agents or stewards: Using theory to understand the government-nonprofit social service contracting relationship." *Journal of Public Administration Research and Theory,* 17(2): 157–187.

Winston, P., and Castaneda, R. M. (2007). *Assessing Federalism: ANF and the recent evolution of American social policy federalism.* Washington, DC: The Urban Institute.

9 Incrementalism at its Best, and Worst

Regulatory Reform and Relational Governance in Canada

Susan D. Phillips

INTRODUCTION

Canada is a strange paradox in its approach to regulation and government collaboration with the third sector: Over the past decade, so much and so little has changed simultaneously. On the one hand, successive increases in the level of the charitable tax credit, introduced by both Liberal and Conservative governments, have given Canadian taxpayers comparatively generous incentives for giving. A novel and much vaunted two year experiment in collaboration beginning in 2000 attempted to build more constructive relationships between the whole-of-government and the third sector, although these relationships were never institutionalized. Ongoing incremental change within the primary regulator of charities, the federal tax agency, has promoted greater transparency and communication. On the other hand, Canada has fallen far behind other countries in modernizing its policy, institutional, and regulatory architecture governing this sector.

Unlike most of the other jurisdictions discussed in this volume, Canada has not introduced new legislation specifically for charities or undertaken a high level review of the criteria that guide which kinds of organizations qualify for charitable status (in spite of an invitation from the Supreme Court to do so). It has not built ongoing forums for cross-sector policy discussions, revamped regulatory frameworks and institutions, and it has exerted only minimal effort at expanding the range of financing tools available to charities, nonprofits, and social enterprises. Unlike the US or the UK, the Canadian government's strategy for financial stimulus to address the economic crisis of 2008–2009 had no serious role for nonprofit organizations. There was no social innovation fund or promotion of volunteerism, as in the US, and very little funding directed to nonprofits to help individuals and communities through the crisis, as occurred in the UK and elsewhere. Indeed, for a country with a comparatively large third sector—reportedly second largest in the world relative to the economically active population (Hall et al. 2005: 9)—Canadian governments have virtually ignored this sector as a focus of public policy.

This chapter analyzes the Canadian experience with government–third sector relationship building and regulatory reform over the past decade. As a policy tool, regulation traditionally involves rules, sanctions for non-compliance, and an independent body to enforce these rules and administer sanctions as required (Doern 2007; May 2002). In recent years—the reaction to the financial crisis notwithstanding—thinking and practice related to regulation has begun to change in many sectors in two ways. First, there has been a movement toward more "responsive" regulation which involves promoting compliance primarily through deeper understanding and more constructive relationships with the regulated sector and only secondarily using command style regulation (Ayres & Braithwaite 1997; Baldwin & Black 2007; Scott 2004). Second, a focus on "smart" regulation (or "better" regulation as it is known in the UK) has advocated a more coordinated, results-based approach, ensuring that regulation "is never more complicated or costly than it has to be" (Smart Regulation External Advisory Committee 2004; see Better Regulation Task Force 2005; Doern 2007; Harrow 2006). The push toward responsive, smart regulation is in large part a consequence of relational and multi-level governance, and it presents a new set of challenges for regulatory bodies: how to develop more effective relationships with the regulated sector, and how to balance the role of enforcer of rules with that of enabler. While these ideas have permeated regulation in many sectors, they have not had a serious impact on regulation of Canada's third sector. Why has Canada been so reluctant to modernize its regulatory approaches for this sector? And more broadly, why is the third sector so consistently ignored in Canadian philosophies of public management and on policy agendas?

The case is made that the inattention to the third sector is not primarily a reflection of the ideology of any specific political party as it has endured through many changes in government (Phillips 2009). Rather, this lack of interest reflects the specific ways in which public management has evolved at the federal level in Canada, the increased concentration of power in the Prime Minister's office, and the overwhelming preoccupation with rule-based accountability. Although Canada took up various aspects of New Public Management (NPM) in the 1980s and early 1990s, creating quasi-markets in many public services, focusing attention on "customer" service, promoting managerialism, and decentralizing operations, it did so with much less zeal than many other countries (Aucoin 1995). Like other jurisdictions, it has begun to move away from NPM in recent years. In Canada, this has not come as an explicit repudiation of NPM, but as a drift in any guiding philosophy of public management given that successive governments, particularly the minority governments which have been in power since 2004, have been preoccupied with accountability and maintaining power. Although the replacement model of public management for NPM is not yet evident, it is clearly not one of relational governance which puts a premium on collaboration and networks. Rather, external relationships are increasingly controlled from the political center, and the legacy of regulation left by NPM has been reinforced in recent years with a "morass" of rules on public spending that were born out of reaction to crisis and that have been slow to be rectified (Blue Ribbon Panel 2006).

The Canadian case reveals a clear tension between regulation and more collaborative relationships as outdated regulation hamstrings organizations and creates a 'firewall' between government and nonprofits, leading to a lack of government understanding of (and interest in) the sector (Eakin, Graham, Blickstead, & Shapcott 2009). The focus of this chapter is specifically on charities, although one of the central issues is how to determine which organizations qualify as charities in the first place and what constitutes charitable activity. The analysis is centered on the federal government which admittedly does not represent the complete picture of government–third sector relationships in Canada because social, health, and education services are the responsibility of provincial governments, albeit supported by relatively unconditional federal block funding and often delivered by charities and other nonprofits. Because the federal tax agency is the *de facto* regulator of charities and the federal government still provides significant funding to nonprofits, however, its stance toward regulation and relationships with the third sector remains important.

AN OVERVIEW OF THE THIRD SECTOR IN CANADA

Canada's third sector is estimated to comprise approximately 165,000 organizations of which almost 85,000 are registered by the Canada Revenue Agency (CRA) as charities and are thus able to issue receipts for donations that can be claimed as tax credits. In terms of economic impact, the sector contributes 7 percent of Gross Domestic Product (GDP), making it eleven times larger than the automobile industry and larger than the value of mining, oil, and gas extraction (McMullen & Schellenberg 2002; Statistics Canada 2007: 9, 11). The organizations that are part of this sector are enormously diverse in both size and purpose: The largest portion is in the sports and recreation field, followed by religion and social services (Statistics Canada et al. 2005: 10). While impressive in the aggregate, there is an enormous bifurcation within the sector between a very small slice of large organizations and a multitude of very small ones. The 1 percent of charitable and nonprofit organizations with over $10 million CDN in annual revenues account for over 60 percent of the entire revenues of the sector, half the staff, and a fifth of volunteers (Statistics Canada et al. 2005: 22). By contrast, two thirds of the organizations have annual revenues of under $100,000 CDN, and half are operated primarily by volunteers (Statistics Canada et al. 2005: 22).

Governments, mainly provincial governments which contract for social and health services, account for 36 percent of the total revenues of the sector. However, the reliance on government funding varies enormously. While social service organization relies heavily on government funding (on average 68 percent of all revenues), sports and recreation, religious, and advocacy organizations depend primarily on donations or fees and memberships. The reality facing all charities and nonprofits is that they have become much more dependent on earned income in recent years which, on average, accounts for 43 percent of revenues (Statistics Canada et al. 2005). Just as in other countries, the impact of the recession has meant increased operating costs and service demands and an erosion of all sources of revenues (Imagine Canada 2010)[1]

This description could be a snapshot of the third sector in most developed countries, with only modifications to the specific numbers (Salamon, Sokolowski, & List 2003). Several features distinguish the Canadian third sector, however. First, it is relatively compartmentalized between 1) charities, themselves divided by mission or service field, 2) nonprofit organizations primarily invested in advocacy (and thus do not qualify as or do not wish to become registered charities), 3) other nonprofits such as professional and industry associations, and 4) social enterprises (which may be incorporated as either nonprofit or for-profit entities). These silos are created, in part, by the limited corporate forms available and, in part, by regulations on 'political' and business activities by charities.[2] Consequently, the creative hybridization of organizational forms that Smith (this volume) describes in the US is much less developed in Canada, as is the intertwining of networks that such hybridization encourages. Another important implication is that this sector very actively questions whether it is a coherent 'sector' at all and hence often fails to actively pursue cross-cutting sectoral policy issues.

A second characteristic is a lack of sector infrastructure, notably the national umbrellas, federations, and research organizations that serve, coordinate, and represent their member interests. Although national federations of provincial and local organizations exist in most subsectors, they are generally poorly funded and lack policy research and advocacy capacity. This partly reflects the strong preference by governments and foundations to fund direct services to individual 'clients' rather than policy research or advocacy, and it is compounded by the fact that Canadian foundations are comparatively small and undercapitalized so they are not significant sources of discretionary funds. The problem of underdeveloped infrastructure also arises from the third sector itself, however, because it does not fully appreciate the value of such infrastructure and does not push hard or collaborate for its improvement.

Third, there are considerable and growing subnational variations in the relationships of provincial governments to the sector. Although constitutionally their jurisdiction, provincial governments have shown little interest in regulating charities; indeed, their stance has been described as one of "benign neglect" (PAGVS 1999). In terms of relational governance at the provincial level, Quebec stands out as distinct as the only jurisdiction to have promoted the development of an active social economy, supported advocacy organizations and social movements, and provided regular vehicles for government dialogue with them (Laforest 2006). In part because third sector organizations elsewhere in the country have become disenchanted with the likelihood of regulatory reform or input into policy at the federal level, many are turning their attention to the creation of regional networks and relationship building with provincial governments. This growing subnational activity is an increasingly important factor in pressures for regulatory and institutional reform, albeit directing attention away from the national stage.

TOWARD REGULATORY REFORM IN CANADA

An anomaly of government regulation of Canada's charitable sector is that, while jurisdiction is provincial under the constitution, the federal government has assumed a *de facto* regulatory role for determining which organizations can be considered charities because of its control over the tax system.[3] The link between taxation and regulation is therefore entrenched institutionally and in approaches to reform, or lack thereof. Within the federal government, regulatory responsibility for charities is divided between the Department of Finance which establishes policy through the *Income Tax Act* (ITA) and the Charities Directorate of the CRA which administers and enforces compliance with regulations under the Act, registers eligible charities, monitors and audits them, and provides guidance through information bulletins. Nowhere in the ITA or in other legislation is the definition of charity articulated. Rather, it is established through common law interpretation using the original list of charitable uses established as part of the 1601 Statute of Elizabeth and consolidated in the Pemsel case of the late 1800s under four main heads: advancement of religion, advancement of education, relief of poverty, and other purposes beneficial to community (in a way the law regards as charitable). Status as a registered charity brings with it annual reporting requirements, limitations on advocacy and business activities, and the need, until recently, to meet an annual disbursement quota by spending 80 percent of revenues on charitable activities (thereby restricting spending on administration and fundraising and creating a substantial administrative and reporting burden). In contrast, nonprofits face very few requirements. Regulation of both nonprofits and charities occurs through other channels as well, notably via rules related to financing and contracting, lobbyist registration, and anti-terrorism legislation. Over the past decade, three key issues have persisted as the targets of reform: determination of charitable status;

regulation of charitable activities, including business and advocacy activities; and financing instruments and accountabilities.

Regulating the 'Definition' of Charity

As in other common law countries, the concept of 'charity' has come under fire in Canada, perhaps to an even greater degree than elsewhere, because its regulatory frameworks and institutions have been so resistant to change. In many respects, Canada's approach to the third sector remains rooted in a Victorian view of "cold charity" in which the main role of the voluntary sector was to help the less fortunate by providing services and support (Deakin 2002; Phillips 2003: 18; Warren 2001). As one Canadian charity lawyer, Blake Bromley, pointedly states in his blog: "The law of charity as applied by Canada Revenue Agency (CRA) is entirely hostile to innovation and creativity when addressing social problems. The societal values which shape the law of charity are the attitudes towards the poor of Victorian England. If you want to understand the policy values which inform the law of charity you should read Charles Dickens, preferably beginning with *Oliver Twist*" (Bromley http://beneficgroup.com/blog).

How we determine which kinds of organizations are eligible to issue tax receipts for donations helps define the kind of civil society we want. How governments approach public policy on the 'definition' of charity establishes whether it views the treatment of charities as a matter of social and economic policy or merely one of fiscal policy (Wyatt 2009). Having charitable status is not only an incentive to giving for individuals and corporations but influences foundations as well because they can transfer funds or assets only to other registered charities. Such status thus becomes an important factor in determining how funding flows inter-organizationally and, given associated restrictions on business activities by charities, on the ability to raise funds through social enterprise. More than a financial benefit, charitable status is a hallmark of legitimacy, indicating a kind of official sanction as having a public benefit and being trustworthy and accountable (see Levasseur 2008). The issue, then, is how to bring the criteria for determining charitable status in line with the kind of civil society that we want to encourage as a matter of public policy.

In the common law tradition, such alignment and the flexibility to realign comes through the process of case review. In one respect, the beauty of the common law is that it is inherently flexible, setting new law based on the last case heard; in another respect, the common law can be quite calcified depending on the last case heard. It places an emphasis on the rights and duties of individuals determined on a case by case basis that relies on precedent, and, because it is fact-based rather than principle-oriented, the common law is typified by a certain rigidity of what can be specified or argued by analogy (for instance, allowing a Freenet association to be considered charitable because the information highway is analogous to an asphalt one and thus falls under the reference in the original Elizabethan Statute to roads and bridges) (see Webb 2000). By embodying a respect for the prevailing social order, the common law has an implicit bias toward maintenance of the status quo in society requiring, as O'Halloran (2002) observes, "an almost feudal respect for king and for country and for the institutions of the land."

The adaptability of the common law depends on regular judicial review which in Canada is not working for charities. If denied application for registration by the CRA, the organization can appeal to the Federal Court of Appeal which requires representation by counsel and is thus both expensive and time consuming and puts the primary onus on the charity to defend its eligibility, not the CRA to defend its rejection. From the Federal Court an appeal can be made to the Supreme Court. In the past 50 years, the Supreme Court has heard only three cases on the concept of charity and the Federal Court only nine cases, none of which has modernized the law (Wyatt 2009).

In perhaps the most contentious case, the Supreme Court denied registration to the Vancouver Society of Immigrant and Visible Minority Women on the grounds that the kind of life skills and job training it provides does not qualify as advancement of education under the common law and that the category of people who benefit from its services (immigrant and visible minority women) was not sufficiently broad to be considered under the fourth head of charity, other purposes beneficial to 'community' (Stevens 2000). In addition, because not all immigrant and visible minority women are disadvantaged, the organization would not qualify under relief of poverty. Although the Supreme Court refused to significantly expand the common law definition, it openly invited Parliament to step in with a legislated definition, an invitation that has not been accepted.

In its 2007 decision on an amateur youth soccer association (AYSA), the Supreme Court determined that sport, as 'mere' sport, does not quality as charitable under Canadian law, although a sports organization would not be precluded if it had other charitable benefits such as promoting health. The Court thus confirmed, and slightly muddied, the existing common law. The importance of the case is that the Court also noted that to allow sports to be considered charitable could have a significant fiscal impact given that 21 percent of nonprofits are in the sports and recreation field (although actual evidence of the impact was not presented). Using this fiscal consequences test, the Court determined that recognition of sport as charitable would not be an incremental change but a major one best left to Parliament. As Parachin (2008) argues, the AYSA case could result in a "frozen definition of charity" because courts may refuse to expand the definition if there are adverse fiscal consequences and, by definition, virtually every proposed expansion of charity could have fiscal consequences. In effect, this case establishes that revenue considerations guide the common law test and, as in the Vancouver Society case, the Supreme Court lobbed major reform back to the legislators.

By international comparisons, then, Canada has been conservative in its determination of charitable status, in part, because the tax agency as regulator is seen to be reluctant to hand out tax expenditures and, even more significantly, because the appeal mechanisms are so expensive that they are seldom used. As a result, groups promoting racial harmony, environmental protection, patriotism, or volunteerism are likely to have qualified as charitable in the UK or the US, whereas they would likely have been denied status in Canada. A legislated approach that 'tops up' the common law with additional categories of public benefit has recently been adopted in several countries including England (Morris this volume) and Scotland (Ford this volume) and has long been embedded in the US tax code for defining a 503(c)(3) organization. While a legislative approach has been dismissed by the Canadian government, incremental change has nevertheless occurred through new CRA "guidance." These guidelines have dealt with the main problematic categories in which there were major inconsistencies in how different organizations are treated and are aimed primarily at clarifying existing law rather than changing it (because CRA does not have authority to change the law). In 2005, for instance, guidance was issued on ethnocultural organizations that was long overdue given that 40 percent of the population of the major urban centers are immigrants and/or visible minorities and multiculturalism is formally recognized in the Canadian Charter of Rights and Freedoms (Canada Revenue Agency 2005; Drache 2005). These guidelines do not create a new category of charity but provide clarity on how ethnocultural organizations can qualify using the existing common law test which means that the underlying rationale is still primarily linked to a sense of disadvantage. A 2006 guidance clarifying the "public benefit" test provides some expansion of previous interpretations by noting that the public may be somewhat restrictive in terms of need or geography (Canada Revenue Agency 2006). The combined effect, presumably, would be to allow an organization such as the Vancouver Society to now be registered, although the courts are not bound by the CRA's guidance, and they have not been put to the test.

These adjustments are at the margins, however, and a high level review and separate charities legislation remain off the table in Canada for several reasons. The federal government is loath for jurisdictional reasons to push its authority by creating separate charities legislation. While it could undertake a review of the charities provisions of the ITA as it does for banking and other sectors, the Department of Finance, which has sole access to making amendments, has no apparent interest. Without a guiding philosophy of public management that recognizes a relationship of interdependence between government and the third sector, the political level sees no political gain and feels no imperative for reform. In the late 1990s, an independent expert panel established by the sector made a strong pitch for a modern public benefit test embodied in new legislation (PAGVS 1999), a case that is still regularly advanced by some charity lawyers. However, in recent years, the charitable sector has not been actively pressing the matter (Wyatt 2009). While the sector remains too distracted with urgent issues such as financing and lacks decent lobbying capacity to mount any strong campaign for reform, the outdated and relatively inflexible approach to the concept of charity leaves Canada unprepared to deal with a rapidly changing environment in which the push for social innovation and more creative social finance are changing how nonprofits and charities operate. Interestingly, the emergent pressure for reform is likely to come from social enterprise for which the Victorian concept of charity is an anathema, but this is likely to take a few years to become a well organized movement and have its impact fully felt.

Regulating Advocacy and Policy Participation

The regulation of advocacy has been one of the sore points in the relationship between government and charities. As in other common law countries, in order to qualify for charitable registration, an organization must have charitable purposes, thereby excluding organizations dedicated primarily to advocacy from being registered. In addition, their activities must be substantially charitable: The regulatory question is how much is "substantial"? This has been interpreted to mean that no more than 10 percent (recently increased on a sliding scale to 20 percent for small organizations) of a charity's resources can be devoted to advocacy and "political activity." In addition, no partisan political activity is permitted, but in practice this is not particularly restrictive because third sector organizations are rarely allied with political parties, nor do they feel any benefit to being partisan or expect the public to support partisan activity with the use of tax expenditures (Pross & Webb 2003). At the other end of the spectrum, consultations invited by governments are unrestricted. There is a large swath of policy related activity between these two extremes, however, that can be done under existing rules.

Charities have long argued that the regulations are too restrictive, creating a chill on advocacy activities because organizations fear losing their charitable status if they overstep the limits. As Pross and Webb (2003) observe in a longitudinal study, they were struck by the number of times the charities said they restricted their participation in public policy advocacy for fear of jeopardizing their status as registered charities. Leaders from the third sector have been vociferous in their criticism of the "10 percent rule": "The law in this field is unclear, badly dated, poorly reasoned, and poorly stated. As a result its application and enforcement by the [CRA] are inconsistent and arbitrary. . . . This leaves charities to distribute band-aids rather than to speak freely on behalf of their clients and members to participate fully in the development of long-term solutions to important problems and issues" (IMPACS 2004, accessed 4 October 2008).[4]

In 2005 the boundaries on advocacy were significantly tested by the debate over same sex marriage. Several religious leaders were vociferous in their opposition, including in national newspaper ads and Sunday sermons, and they argued that they had a right and a responsibility to participate in this public policy debate using whatever resources and means they deemed necessary. This stance propelled the Charities Directorate to issue a warning to one particularly vocal Roman Catholic Bishop to refrain from engaging in partisan rhetoric on this issue (Valpy 2005). Had the issue not been decided relatively quickly with legislation permitting same sex marriage, it would have been intriguing to see how far the regulator would have taken the issue, potentially de-registering churches—undoubtedly to outrage among segments of the public and putting a new light on the appropriate limits to advocacy.

Slightly expanded limits on advocacy established in 2003 enable the charitable sector collectively to spend an *additional* $113.5 million CDN (for an annual total of $5.7 billion CDN), but there is no evidence that even if the advocacy chill thawed that they would be interested in or capable of spending anything close to this amount on advocacy (Elson 2008). As Elson (2008: 119) argues, "the lack of advocacy activity by charities, rather than being limited by an overly restrictive or ambiguous regulatory regime, is more likely due to the absence of concerted and collective representation." Lacking such infrastructure, charities for the most part are not particularly effective advocates in Canada (Wyatt 2009).

The criticism of the regulation is also a lament for the absence of effective, institutionalized mechanisms for constructive dialogue with the federal government. To be sure, there are pockets of good working relationships of government departments with key third sector organizations, as well as annual consultations with a wide array of organizations in preparation for the federal budget and public consultations on many other issues. In general, however, the routes to influence have become increasingly closed to charities in recent years, and many parliamentarians have made it very clear that they see advocacy organizations as competition (Phillips 2009). At various times over the past 20 years, both Liberal and Conservative governments have signaled a strong preference for nonprofits that produce services rather than research or policy advice which at various times has resulted in sudden cuts to government grants and contributions. One of the most blatant round of cuts came in 2006 when the Harper government surgically eliminated funding to certain think tanks, literacy and volunteerism programs and took a run at women's organizations by changing the terms and conditions on funding provided by the federal Department of Status of Women to remove the pursuit of "equality" for women and social justice from its mandate and impose a requirement that any organization it funded must refrain from any advocacy of federal, provincial, or municipal governments (Phillips 2009). Given such a stance to advocacy on the part of government, whether or not the regulations actually restrict spending on advocacy, it is not surprising that a relational approach between the federal government and the third sector has been slow to develop in Canada.

Financing Nonprofits: Regulatory Constraints

The financing of charities and nonprofits has perhaps been the greatest arena of change since the late 1990s, with both positive and negative consequences for organizations and with significant implications for both regulation and relationships. The positive development has been significant increases in the value of the tax credit in 1996 and 1997 and expanded opportunities to donate securities beginning in 2006.[5] While the expanded tax credits have not increased the number of tax filers claiming a credit— as claims have been decreasing since 1990—the amounts donated have increased slightly (Imagine Canada 2009). As a means of increasing incentives for new giving and reversing further declines that occurred during the recession, Imagine Canada, the leading infrastructure organization, has proposed the implementation of a "stretch" tax credit that would provide a top up credit for new giving above the highest amount donated in the past. So far, the idea has not been implemented. Although increases in tax credits may benefit some charities, they do little by way of enhancing government– third sector relationships because they are formulaic in nature, requiring some monitoring and auditing but little policy-related interaction with charities. In addition, the increased tax expenditures were accompanied by massive cuts to direct government funding of charities and nonprofits, leaving many worse off (Eakin 2007; Scott 2003).

Government also has a hand in regulating how charities finance their work by setting limits on business and fundraising activities. This sphere of regulation will change in coming years due to new rules on charitable fundraising, the implementation of which is still unfolding, and is under pressure for more significant reform by those interested in expanding social enterprise. In 2009, the federal government introduced a new policy on charitable fundraising, an area that has been weakly regulated by provincial governments and one that the federal government was hesitant to enter directly as its jurisdiction is open to question. Although the CRA has long regulated amounts spent on fundraising through the disbursement quota, it will now do so more explicitly. The new policy establishes acceptable limits on amounts spent annually on fundraising (with less than 35 percent regarded as generally acceptable) and articulates sound 'conduct' and management and control systems that CRA will expect to see as part of charities' risk mitigation strategies when it audits them (such guidelines may long have been used in auditing but were never transparent) (CRA 2009). Whatever its impact on fundraising practices, the new policy is likely to have two other important effects. First, because the underlying premise is that both individual charities and the third sector as a whole will effectively monitor and comply with good fundraising practices, it is likely to pull the sector into more active self-regulation. Imagine Canada has already relaunched its voluntary Ethical Fundraising and Financial Management Code and is testing plans for a more formal certification system of good governance. Second, the new policy takes the CRA into regulating organizational governance by identifying the management and control systems that it expects to be in place. But, better governance by charities will not be achieved through a rule-based compliance system. Rather, it puts a new onus on the CRA to become a more responsive regulator, working with and educating charities as to better practices. The question remains if the tax agency can make this transformation to being a different kind of regulator.

The other major pressure point for regulatory reform revolves around social enterprise. Canadian regulations have been less favorable to the development of social enterprise than those in the US, the UK, and many other countries (Carter & Man 2009). One constraint is that charities may only carry on business that is directly related to their charitable purposes or is run substantially by volunteers; unrelated business is not permitted (whereas in other countries, it is simply taxed).[6] What the CRA determines to be related business has been inconsistent, so in the interests of greater transparency, it has issued clearer guidance on business (Canada Revenue Agency 2003) and community development activities (Canada Revenue Agency 2009). The current pressure to facilitate investment in social enterprise, however, will take much more than clarifying existing rules. Rather, it is likely to demand a more fundamental review and reform of current regulatory frameworks. Interestingly, it may be the social enterprise wedge that eventually pries open the door to substantial regulatory reform.

The negative development in financing as a means of regulation has been the heightened accountability requirements on government contracts and contributions. Although worldwide NPM brought with it a major increase in reporting rules and audit (Powers 1994), these requirements have been particularly onerous in Canada due to stringent controls imposed as a reaction to scandal. In 2000, newspapers across the country carried headlines of a "billion dollar boondoggle," the story that the lead federal social policy department had supposedly lost track of and could not account for huge amounts of transfers to voluntary and private sector organizations in a job creation program (Good 2003). While the stories were misleading because only a very small amount of funding could not be properly accounted for, the consequences for organizations funded by the federal government were very real as accountability requirements were tightened enormously (Good 2003; Phillips & Levasseur 2004). Reaction to another scandal a few years later, in which federal funds from advertising contracts with private firms found their way to the Liberal Party of Quebec, layered on even more contracting rules and oversight. The resulting "web of rules" has placed an enormous burden on both funding recipients and government departments (Blue Ribbon Panel 2006) and made any form of relational contracting almost impossible. It has also contributed to a lack of trust and hindered the possibility of more relational forms of governance because the main point of contact with third sector organizations, the program officers, have had to take on a policing and auditing function, rather than being advocates for their programs and constituencies. In 2006 an independent expert panel was established to recommend a way to cut through this morass, and its members expressed surprise and concern that the problem was much worse than imagined, noting that the red tape "has served only to undermine accountability and hamper sensible reporting and evaluation" (Blue Ribbon Panel 2006: vii). The panel's recommendations, which included simplifying the rules, providing full cost recovery in funding programs, and encouraging innovation, are being implemented but more slowly than anticipated and with little impact as yet on funding recipients. Given the political capital that was expended on commitments to ensuring accountability, it is difficult for government to make a case that rules should be relaxed or greater flexibility based on relational criteria should be accommodated. Canadian federalism has also enabled a slow response to fixing the web of federal rules because most health, education, and social services are the responsibility of provincial governments. While the rigidity of the federal system of grants and contributions has been a huge burden for recipient organizations, it has not paralyzed the delivery of core services and did not produce a nation-wide outcry directly from citizens.

The debate over accountability associated with government funding masks a much bigger problem—that Canada has a limited array of financing instruments for the third sector, forcing a reliance on contracting and contribution agreements (which require a pre-specified project or service to be delivered with measurable outcomes). The lead department with responsibility for the third sector established a task force to examine how to create a broader range of financing tools for supporting community investment and social innovation. However, the timing was unfortunate as the work of the Task Force on Community Investments was completely overshadowed by the more visible Blue Ribbon Panel, and, given the lack of political interest, its report (2006) was ignored by government. It appears that if a more diversified set of financing instruments is to be developed, it will happen through the regulatory route under pressure from the growing movement for social enterprise.

REFORM, RESISTANCE, AND INCREMENTALISM

Explaining Resistance

With the exception of the increased tax credit, substantial change in the underlying premises, governing legislation, and regulations that define and direct the work of the charitable sector has not occurred in Canada—indeed, reform has generally been resisted by governments. Although the sector itself has been less than an effective advocate on these matters, primarily due to the lack of capacity in the national infrastructure organizations, advocacy strategies alone do not explain the resistance to modernize regulation. Rather, it stems from the Canadian philosophy of public management and lack of political and institutional leadership.

First, it has to be recognized that the institutional impediments to reform are significant. With federal jurisdiction hanging on the thread of control over tax collection and provincial governments having shown little interest in regulating charities, the federal government has been careful not to overstep its authority, at least until its recent policy on charitable fundraising which arguably tiptoes on provincial jurisdiction and which may still be contested as beyond federal authority. If it is contested, the provinces may be compelled to step up their regulatory regimes which could lead to a confused patchwork of new rules. Good policy is more than a matter of defending jurisdiction, however. If Canadian governments are going to produce better policy and regulation, they will need to find ways of better intergovernmental cooperation. In most other major areas of the economy, federal–provincial cooperation works through various institutionalized meetings of officials and ministers: Not so for the third sector (Wyatt 2009). Not only are collaborative mechanisms absent, but information sharing is difficult because the ITA prohibits disclosure of taxpayer information with only limited exceptions for charities (Oosterhoff 2004). The need for greater multi-level coordination and the bias in favor of privacy in the ITA are compelling reasons to consider the enactment of separate charity legislation and, more radically, a joint national regulatory institution. A parallel can be drawn with the regulation of securities which has also been fragmented by jurisdiction, producing 13 separate provincial and territorial regulators and, overall, uncoordinated and inconsistent regulation. After 40 years of debate, agreement was reached in 2009 to establish a single national securities regulator. A similar concept of a coordinated federal-provincial charities regulator has been floated several times (Joint Regulatory Table 2004; PAGVS 1999), but so far it has been a nonstarter.

Within the federal level, institutional fragmentation means there is no strong advocate for change. The Department of Finance, which guards its authority over the ITA, has little contact with charities outside of the annual budget consultations and is not a proponent of reform. The Charities Directorate, a small part of the tax agency, can only instill change through administrative guidance. No central agency has a mandate to coordinate policy for the third sector, and the small unit in a line department with responsibility for the sector has little claim on other departments and has seen its budget cut significantly in recent years. The trend toward the centralization of power in the Prime Minister's office, a phenomenon referred to as "court government" (Savoie 2008), coupled with minority government, means that little of significance happens unless it accords with the direction set by the center. If departments are doing anything creative by way of engaging with or testing policy about the sector, they tend to intentionally fly low under the political radar.

Second, the high level of mobility in the public service, created by opportunities for advancement given retirements and the demographic profile, contributes to a lack of internal leadership. Even if inclined toward a more relational approach, the public service has lost much of its internal capacity for sustaining relationships with the staff of third (and private) sector organizations due to high turnover. Most senior public servants stay in their positions, on average, only two years which makes getting to know the players and establishing trust relationships very difficult. Over the past 14 years, for example, the Charities Directorate has had eight directors (or acting directors), and, while several attempted to make positive change, only so much can be accomplished in such a short tenure. In addition, there is very little exchange of personnel between government and nonprofit organizations, and such exchange has been made more difficult by the 2006 *Federal Accountability Act* which prevents senior public servants from working for organizations that communicate with their former departments for five years after they leave public office.

The third, and arguably most important, impediment is a lack of vision of the role of the third sector in the guiding philosophy of public management. In Canadian approaches to public management, nonprofits have been either relatively invisible, instrumental, or seen as problematic. Under NPM, their role was understood to be part of "alternative service delivery," and in this they were grouped with privatization, contracting, partnerships, and other 'methods' (Treasury Board Secretariat 2002). In trying to address the web of accountability rules on contracts and contributions imposed after recent scandals, they were a problem that had to be fixed. In addition, many politicians have seen them as competitors for public attention which led to arguments that governments should not fund its critics. Without a political vision of a more constructive role for the third sector and its relationship with the state, governments have not had a compelling reason for policy and regulatory change.

Attempts at Relational Governance

Beginning in 2000, the Liberal government experimented with a novel approach to relational governance. This came as a result of the sector's own initiative and leadership, and it was driven in part by a desire for the federal government to more effectively engage with citizens and avoid having such relationships mediated through provincial governments. What better way to engage citizens than through their voluntary organizations. An informal coalition of sector leaders, known as the Voluntary Sector Roundtable, was formed in 1995, and two years later it commissioned an independent panel (modeled to some extent after the Deakin Commission in the UK) to examine issues of accountability and governance. In its 1999 report, the [Broadbent]

Panel on Accountability and Governance (PAGVS 1999) outlined an agenda for reform that included: the development of a compact; replacing the tax agency with an independent commission akin, with modification, to the Charity Commission of England and Wales; introducing a legislated 'definition of charity' and advancing stronger self-regulation by the sector itself. Government recognized that any change regarded as legitimate had to come through a collaborative effort, and in 2000 it established a unique joint process known as the Voluntary Sector Initiative (VSI). For the first two years of its five year mandate, the VSI was to work primarily through seven joint tables (consisting of about 14 members chosen equally from government and the third sector) to build a better relationship with the sector, expand its capacity, and advance regulatory reform (within limits). The dedication of participants was impressive, and the amount of time many devoted to the VSI was significant: For example, the third sector co-chair of one of the tables made the four hour flight to Ottawa 108 times in one year. The VSI produced some important new research on the sector and a variety of other special projects, but it got bogged down in process and operational issues rather than dealing with higher level policy. And, the big policy issues of financing, regulation of advocacy, new charity legislation, and reform of the regulator were never up for joint consideration (Social Development Canada 2004).

An Accord similar to the English compact was signed, but without being backed by strong monitoring machinery or support for implementation, it was never widely used and, when the government changed in 2006, it was largely abandoned. Greater trust and deeper understanding of the 'other' was produced among public servants and sector leaders, but over the span of two years, 50 percent of the public servants had changed jobs and exited participation in the VSI, and new institutionalized means for collaboration were not established (Social Development Canada 2004). The leadership of the third sector also dissipated after the initiative; a new national organization that was intended to provide collective leadership was poorly funded on short term horizons so it quickly folded, and many of the key individuals moved out of active policy leadership roles. In many respects, the leadership capacity of the third sector was weaker after the VSI than it had been going into it, and it remains so today. The one area in which change did occur was in the regulator's relationship with the sector, but this occurred through incremental steps rather than by major reform.

Incrementalism at Work

Although the VSI joint table that dealt with regulation did not have the mandate to address the big framework issues, it made a number of constructive proposals related to the compliance regime, virtually all of which were implemented in 2004.[7] In addition to these changes to rules, in the early 2000s, the Charities Directorate began to improve many of its business, administrative, and communication practices which have moved it to being a more responsive regulator with a somewhat greater focus on service rather than merely on audit and compliance. The primary impetus seems to have come from senior management within the CRA who got to know the sector better through participation in the VSI. The range of administrative changes include: greater transparency and communications (with a much better website, regular newsletters, and information sessions); training regarding compliance (conducted by other nonprofits under contract to CRA); issuance of better policy guidance; and, in response to many years of advocacy by the sector, eliminating the disbursement quota that imposed an unduly complex and costly administrative burden, particularly for smaller charities (Department of Finance 2010). The advantage of small adjustments is that they could be relatively easily facilitated because they do not necessitate more formal legislative change. Early evidence suggests that these reform initiatives are paying off as the credibility and working relationships of the CRA with the third sector have improved in the past few years.

At the same time as engaging in relationship building with the sector, however, the regulator has greatly increased its compliance activity and audit machinery in response to a series of cases involving charities being used as tax shelters (see Donovan 2009). In 2009, the Charities Directorate undertook to audit all tax-sheltered arrangements (where the tax receipts are worth more than the actual donations) which resulted in the status of several charities being revoked. In addition, the anti-terrorism legislation enacted in 2001 has greatly increased the regulator's oversight potential, particularly over organizations with international activities or partners. The Anti-Terrorism law casts a broad net in its definitions of what kinds of actions contribute to and facilitate terrorism, its enforcement mechanisms are draconian without provisions for due process, and it creates open-ended liability for nonprofits because they cannot claim due diligence as a defense (Carter, 2004). The future relationship between regulator and sector will hinge, to an important extent, on the balance achieved between these enhanced audit and compliance activities and the softer side of education, advice, and communication.

Can administrative change alone go far enough toward achieving better, smarter regulation? I argue it cannot because such internal change does not open representational spaces for debate about policy goals and how best to achieve them. Given the fundamental changes that are occurring in the third sector and in public management in Canada, debate about policy goals and policy instruments is exactly what is needed as a first step.

CONCLUSION: REGULATING FOR RELATIONAL GOVERNANCE

The Canadian story told in this chapter is essentially one of policy drift, punctuated by occasional active resistance to change, that has inhibited the development of both relational governance and regulatory reform. While there has been some regulatory change, it has been quietly incremental, layered in as new administrative practices and clarified interpretations of existing law. Although such incremental adjustments have been constructive, they do not represent major shifts in strategic direction, and Canada will not get to transformational change through incrementalism alone. A key challenge is to dislodge the underlying premise of charity—that focuses on encouraging the advantaged to help the disadvantaged—on which the regulatory system has been built and which still endures.

The Canadian model of the welfare state has long been a well developed mixed economy in which services are delivered by governments, nonprofits, and for-profit firms in varying mixes depending on the particular service. NPM reinforced this mixed economy by shifting a greater range of services from governments to nonprofit delivery and by promoting more open competition between nonprofit and for-profit providers. In many other countries, the service fragmentation that resulted from increased market competition eventually led to a greater interest in collaboration and partnership (which in parts of Europe was already present as a legacy of corporatism) and to an increased hybridization of the third sector with new corporate forms, social enterprise, intra- and inter-sectoral partnerships, and diversified financing tools. To be sure, new markets were created in public services and service fragmentation was felt in Canada, but the impact of a modulated version of NPM was more one of degree than of fundamental change in an already mixed economy. In addition, the rules on business activity, incorporation, and advocacy by registered charities restrained hybridization and social enterprise. While government greatly expanded tax credits for charitable giving, it also cut funding for organizations that were not delivering 'client' services, thereby reaffirming the charity model and further privatizing funding decisions from government to private donors.

For a national government that has thought of the third sector primarily as "alternative service delivery," rather than being a force for democracy, citizen engagement, or community and economic development, there has been no imperative to change the regulatory regime. In addition, the Canadian preoccupation with accountability as control has restricted the development of any form of relational contracting and diverted attention away from expanding the array of financing tools available to the third sector. When enthusiasm for NPM as a guiding philosophy of public management faded, no alternative took its place that would provide a compelling ideational basis for change. Pragmatism—of muddling through in service delivery with reasonable cost controls and of the politics of minority government—was more consuming than big new ideas. Because third sector advocacy and infrastructure organizations were under developed to begin with and had been hit hard with funding cuts, they have not been effective proponents of reform for the past decade.

The lack of substantial change in the regulatory regime or in government-sector relationships has left Canada ill prepared to deal with a changing environment that includes increased vulnerability of financing, growing presence of social enterprise, pressures for greater transparency, performance assessment and self-regulation, and the need to be nimble and more effective at social innovation. Is the future necessarily one of continued drift? Without a political vision for the role of the third sector and its relationship with government that moves beyond a narrow view of service delivery and charitable giving, the status quo seems likely. Potential wedges that may create openings for change are emerging from both social enterprise and an interest in social innovation that is finding some resonance in government. Whether these are seen as opportunities or are met with resistance is still an open question.

NOTES

1. Until the recession, donations (11 percent of income for this sector) had been growing year by year, but the donor base has been shrinking slightly; 10 percent of donors are responsible for 62 percent of donations (Imagine Canada et al. 2009). In 2008, charitable donations were down by about 5.3 percent ($450 million CDN), although there is speculation that some of this drop was due to a crackdown on illegal tax sheltered donations (Blumberg 2009). A 2010 survey of over 1,500 charities indicated that most, especially small ones, had difficulty covering their expenses because revenues have declined (on average, 17.5 percent) while demand has increased (on average, by 1.6 percent). To cope, organizations said they were trying to increase revenues, use reserve funds (if they had any), cut staff, and make greater use of volunteers. One quarter of the organizations surveyed indicated that they had cut services, and a quarter noted that the very existence of their organizations was at risk (Imagine Canada, 2010). Interestingly, these organizations, on the whole, were remarkably confident about the future, perhaps more than their current situations warrant. The very large charities (annual revenues over $5 million) had been much less affected by the financial situation, with 62 percent indicating that they were not stressed at all.
2. In 2009, for the first time since last revised in 1919, the federal *Nonprofit Corporations Act* was updated (to come into effect in 2010 or 2011) after dying on the order table in Parliament three times since 2004. Most incorporation is done under provincial legislation, however, and this has also been highly restrictive. For example, until repealed in 2009, legislation in the province of Ontario prohibited charities from owning more than 10 percent of a business or land and investments that they did not occupy or use for three years (Carter & Man 2009).
3. Quebec operates its own tax system and its own registration of charities. Normally, charities seeking to operate in Quebec attain status from both the federal and Quebec governments, and the provincial system is normally congruent with the federal.
4. The limitations on advocacy are also seen to be out of touch with the views of Canadians. A 2004 national survey on the roles of charities found that Canadians have higher levels of trust in charities than they do in governments, and 78 percent felt that charities should be able to speak out on policy

issues, with over 90 percent support in some fields such as social policy and health (Muttart Foundation 2004).
5. The charitable tax credit is calculated at 15 percent for donations under $200 CDN and at 29 percent for larger amounts. See http://www.cra-arc.gc.ca/tx/ chrts/dnrs/svngs/2-eng.html. In the 1990s, the ceiling on annual donations that a taxpayer can claim was increased from 50 to 75 percent of net income, and in 2006 donations of publicly listed securities became fully exempt from capital gains.
6. An additional constraint is that the ITA recognizes only three types of entities: taxpaying corporations, tax-exempt nonprofit organizations, and charities. This limits the creation of hybrid organizations. In addition, charitable foundations cannot incur debt or own a corporation, and the disbursement quota requires all gifts and asset transfer to go to other charities. The effect is to greatly limit the feasibility of program related investments and support for social enterprise by foundations (Carter & Man 2009).
7. Specifically, the changes include intermediate sanctions involving fines and suspension of tax receipting privileges (previously the only sanction was revocation of status), a change in the appeal process related to sanctions (only) that allows for appeals to proceed to the less cumbersome Federal Tax Court, and increased transparency on the kind of information that can be provided by the CRA (Hayhoe 2005).

REFERENCES

Aucoin, P. (1995). *The New Public Management: Canada in comparative perspective*. Montreal: Institute for Research on Public Policy.
Ayres, I., and Braithwaite, J. (1997). *Responsive Regulation: Transcending the deregulation debate*. Oxford: Oxford University Press.
Baldwin, R., and Black, J. (2007). "Really responsive regulation." *LSE Legal Studies Working Paper 15*. London: London School of Economics.
Better Regulation Task Force. (2005). *Better Regulation for Civil Society*. London: Better Regulation Task Force.
Blue Ribbon Panel. (2006). *From Red Tape to Clear Results. Report of the Independent Blue Ribbon Panel on Grant and Contribution Programs*. Ottawa: Treasury Board Secretariat.
Blumberg, M. (2009). "Are charitable donations in Canada down in 2008? Depends how you define donation/legitimate charity." *GlobalPhilanthropy.ca*. Available at www.globalphilanthropy.ca/index.php/blog/comments/are_charitable_donations_in_canada_down_in_2008_depends_how_you_define_dona/\ (accessed 3 January 2010).
Canada Revenue Agency. (2009). *Policy guidance CPS-028: Fundraising by registered charities*. Ottawa: Charities Directorate, CRA. Available at < http://www.cra-arc.gc.ca/tx/chrts/plcy/cps/cps-028-eng.html#h1> (accessed 11 December 2009).
Canada Revenue Agency. (2006). *Guidelines for registering a charity: Meeting the public benefit test*. Ottawa: Charities Directorate, CRA. Available at <http://www.cra-arc.gc.ca/tx/chrts/plcy/cps/cps-024-eng.html> (accessed 2 July 2007).
Canada Revenue Agency. (2005). *Policy statement: Applicants assisting ethnocultural communities*. Ottawa: Charities Directorate, CRA. Available at < http://www.cra-arc.gc.ca/tx/chrts/plcy/cps/cps-023-eng.html> (accessed 19 June 2006).
Canada Revenue Agency. (2003). *Policy statement: What is a related business?* Ottawa: Charities Directorate, CRA. Available at <http://www.cra-arc.gc.ca/tx/chrts/plcy/cps/cps-019-eng.html> (accessed 18 June 2009).

CRA. (1999). *Registered charities: Community economic development programs.* Ottawa: Charities Directorate, CRA. Available at < http://www.cra-arc.gc.ca/E/pub/tg/rc4143/rc4143-e.html> (accessed 13 June 2004).

Carter, T. S. (2004). "Charities and compliance with anti-terrorism legislation in Canada: The shadow of the law." *International Journal of Not-for-Profit Law,* 6(3).

Carter, T. S., and Man, T. L. M. (2009). Business activities and social enterprise: Towards a new paradigm. Discussion paper, Carters Professional Corporation.

Deakin, N. (2001). *In Search of Civil Society.* Basingstoke, UK: Palgrave Press.

Department of Finance. (2010). *Budget 2010: Leading the way on jobs and growth.* Ottawa: Public Works and Government Services Canada.

Doern, G. B. (2007). *Red Tape, Red Flags: Regulation for the innovation age.* Ottawa: Conference Board of Canada.

Donovan, K. (2009, August 12). "Charity stripped of licence in probe: Funds for Canada deemed to be tax shelter."*Toronto Star*, p. A.13.

Drache, A. B. C. (2005, August). "CRA publishes ethnocultural statement." *MillerThomson LLP Charities and Not-for-Profit Newsletter*, pp. 2–3.

Eakin, L. (2007). *We Can't Afford to Do Business This Way: A study of the administrative burden resulting from funder accountability and compliance practices.* Toronto: Wellesley Institute. Available at <http://wellesleyinstitute.com/files/cant_do_business_this_way_report_web.pdf > (accessed 9 June 2008)

Eakin, L., Graham, H., Blickstead, R., and Shapcott, M. (2009). *A Policy Perspective on Canada's Non-profit Maze of Regulatory and Legislative Barriers.* Toronto: Wellesley Institute.

Elson, P. (2008). *A historical institutional analysis of voluntary sector/government relations in Canada.* Unpublished PhD dissertation, University of Toronto, Toronto, Canada.

External Advisory Committee on Smart Regulation, Government of Canada. (2004). *Smart Regulation: A regulatory strategy for Canada.* Ottawa: Privy Council Office.

Good, D. (2003). *The Politics of Public Management: The HRDC audit of grants and contributions.* IPAC Series in Public Management and Governance. Toronto: University of Toronto Press.

Hall, M., Barr, C. W., Easwaramoorthy, M., Wojciech Sokolowski, S., and Salamon, L. M. (2005). *The Canadian Nonprofit and Voluntary Sector in Comparative Perspective.* Toronto: Imagine Canada.

Harrow, J. (2006). "Chasing shadows? Perspectives on self-regulation in UK charity fundraising." *Public Policy and Administration*, 21(3): 86–104.

Hayhoe, R. B. (2004, January). "An introduction to Canadian tax treatment of the third sector." *International Journal of Not-for-Profit Law*, 6(2).

Imagine Canada. (2010, April). *Imagine Canada's Sector Monitor,* 1(1). Available at <http://www.imaginecanada.ca/files/www/en/sectormonitor/sectormonitor_vol1_no1_2010.pdf> (accessed 30 April 2010),.

Imagine Canada. (2009, August 14). Pre-budget brief submitted by Imagine Canada to the House of Commons Standing Committee on Finance. Toronto: Imagine Canada.

Imagine Canada et al. (2009). *Caring Canadians, Involved Canadians: Highlights of the 2007 Canada Survey of Giving, Volunteering and Participating.* Ottawa: Statistics Canada. Available at <http://www.givingandvolunteering.ca/files/giving/en/csgvp_highlights_2007.pdf> (accessed 2 November 2009).

Joint Regulatory Table (JRT) of the Voluntary Sector Initiative. (2003). *Final Report of the Joint Regulatory Table: Strengthening Canada's charitable sector, Regulatory reform.* Ottawa: Voluntary Sector Initiative. Available aT <http://www.vsi-isbc.ca/eng/regulations/reports.cfm> (accessed 10 June 2009).

Laforest, R. (2006). "State and community sector relations: Crisis and challenges in Quebec." *The Philanthropist/ Le Philanthrope*, 20(4): 171–184.

Levasseur, K. (2008). *Charity in Canada: A governance and historical institutional lens on charitable registration.* Unpublished doctoral dissertation, School of Public Policy and Administration, Carleton University, Ottawa, Canada.

May, P. J. (2002). "Social regulation." in L. M. Salamon (ed.), *The Tools of Government: A guide to the New Governance* (pp. 156–185). New York: Oxford University Press.

McMullen, K., and Schellenberg, G. (2002). *Mapping the Non-Profit Sector.* CPRN Research Series on Human Resources in the Non-Profit Sector. Ottawa: Canadian Policy Research Networks.

Muttart Foundation. (2004). *Talking About Charities.* Edmonton: Muttart Foundation.

O'Halloran, K. J. (2002, September). "Charity law review in Ireland and the challenges for the state/third sector partnership." *International Journal of Not-for-Profit Law*, 5(1).

Oosterhoff, A. H. (2004). "Charitable fundraising research paper." Prepared for the Uniform Law Conference of Canada, Civil Law Section, Toronto.

Panel on Accountability and Governance in the Voluntary Sector (PAGVS). (1999). *Building on Strength: Improving governance and accountability in Canada's voluntary sector.* Ottawa: Voluntary Sector Roundtable.

Parachin, A. (2009, March 6). "Unraveling the definition of charity Fiscal objectives shouldn't govern the granting of charitable status." *Lawyers Weekly.* Available at <http://www.lawyersweekly.ca/index.php?section=article&articleid=869> (accessed 15 January 2010).

Phillips, S. D. (2009). Canada's Conservative government and the voluntary sector: Whither a policy agenda?" In R. Laforest (ed.), *The New Federal Policy Agenda and the Voluntary Sector: On the cutting edge* (pp. 1–27). Montreal and Kingston: McGill-Queen's University Press.

Phillips, S. D. (2003). "Voluntary sector-government relationships in transition: Learning from international experience for the Canadian context." In K. L. Brock (ed.), *The Voluntary Sector in Interesting Times* (pp. 17–70). Montreal and Kingston: McGill-Queen's University Press.

Powers, M. (1994). *The Audit Explosion.* London: Demos.

Pross, A. P., and Webb, K. R. (2003). "Embedded regulation: Advocacy and the federal regulation of public interest groups." In K. L. Brock and K. G. Banting (eds.), *Delicate Dances: The nonprofit sector and government in Canada* (pp. 63–122). Kingston: McGill-Queen's University Press.

Salamon, L. M. Sokolowski, S. Wojciech, and List, R. (2003). *Global Civil Society: An Overview.* Baltimore: Johns Hopkins Center for Civil Society Studies.

Savoie, D. (2008). *Court Government and the Collapse of Accountability in Canada and the United Kingdom.* Toronto: Institute of Public Administration of Canada.

Scott, C. (2004). "Regulation in the age of governance: The rise of the post-regulatory state." In J. Jordana and D. Levi-Faur (eds.), *The Politics of Regulation: Institutions and regulatory reforms for the age of governance* (pp. 145–176). Cheltenham, UK: Edward Elgar,

Scott, K. (2003). *Funding Matters: The Impact of Canada's New Funding Regime on Nonprofit and Voluntary Organizations.* Ottawa: CCSD (in collaboration with the Coalition of National Voluntary Organizations).

Social Development Canada. (2004). *The Voluntary Sector Initiative Process Evaluation.* Ottawa: Social Development Canada. Available at < http://www.hrsdc.gc.ca/eng/cs/sp/sdc/evaluation/sp-ah213e/page00.shtml> (accessed 1 September 2007).

Statistics Canada. (2007). *Satellite Account of Nonprofit Institutions and Volunteering 1997–1999*. Ottawa: Minister of Industry.

Statistics Canada et al. (2005). *Cornerstones of Community: Highlights of the National Survey of Nonprofit and Voluntary Organizations*. Ottawa: Minister of Industry.

Stevens, D. (2000). "Vancouver Society of Immigrant and Visible Minority Women v. M.N.R." *The Philanthropist/ Le Philanthrope*, 15(2):, 4–13.

Task Force on Community Investments. (2006). *Achieving Coherence in Government of Canada Funding Practices in Communities*. Ottawa: Human Resources and Social Development Canada.

Treasury Board Secretariat. (2002). *Policy on Alternative Service Delivery*. Ottawa: Treasury Board Secretariat.

Valpy, M. (2005, January 18). "Bishop blasted for calling on the state to target gays." *Globe and Mail*, p. A1.

Warren, M. E. (2001). *Democracy and Association*. Princeton: Princeton University Press.

Webb, K. (2000). *Cinderella's Slippers? The Role of Charitable Tax Status in Financing Canadian interest groups*. Vancouver: SFU-UBC Centre for the Study of Government and Business.

Wyatt, B. (2009). "Overview from Canada: Modernising charity law." *The Philanthropist/Le Philanthrope*, 22(2): 59–74.

10 Australia

A Continuing Love Affair with the New Public Management

Mark Lyons and Bronwen Dalton

INTRODUCTION

The purpose of this book is to explore the implications for nonprofit organizations of the transition from New Public Management (NPM) to more
collaborative forms of relational or distributed governance. The case of
Australia, which is examined in this chapter, does not provide strong evidence for such a transition. It also shows the difficulty of generalizing about
relations between governments and the third sector.

During the 1980s Australian governments—both state and national,
Labor and Liberal—gradually embraced the set of beliefs and practices that
came to be known as NPM. This embrace was not without its critics, but it
had powerful supporters and transformed the role of government and the
practice of governing. It also had direct implications for the third sector.

Australia has a large and varied nonprofit sector. However, it is generally not viewed as a sector, and certainly not by governments. Instead,
different parts of government interact with different groups of nonprofit
organizations, but these interactions are not underpinned by a consistent
philosophy or understanding of the sector. The adoption by governments
of NPM impacted some parts of the nonprofit sector, mostly to their detriment. Parts of the sector have grown while others have declined: Some of
this growth, but also some of the decline, is a direct consequence of NPM.
During this period other government initiatives, independent of NPM,
have also had significant effects on parts of the nonprofit sector. NPM still
dominates Australia, however, ensuring that any movement toward more
relational forms of governance are little more than gestures. Consequently,
examples of government interactions with nonprofits informed by a relational approach to governance are few and unimportant. The chapter concludes that in Australia there is little likelihood of any weakening of NPM
in the foreseeable future and equally little chance of a significant transformation in relations between governments and the nonprofit sector.

NEW PUBIC MANAGEMENT IN AUSTRALIA

The term "New Public Management," soon abbreviated to NPM, came into
use around 1990 to describe a number of changes in the way governments

went about their tasks: changes that one scholar has called a "cultural revolution" (Yeatman 1990). Although there is some disagreement about the drivers of these changes (Flynn 2002; Yeatman 1994), there is broad agreement that they entail privatization of and competition in the provision of public services, parsimony in resource allocation, an entrepreneurial rather than a bureaucratic approach to management, an emphasis on specifying outputs and measuring performance, and a clearer separation of the political responsibility for setting policy and its implementation or administration (Hood 1990; Osborne and McLaughlin 2002).

Although the term NPM only began to be used around 1990, the changes that it sought to encompass can be seen emerging as early as the late 1970s. In order to summarize the impact of NPM in Australia and to understand its dynamics, it is helpful to see it as generated by two interrelated core beliefs.

The Belief in Markets

One belief was that markets are the most efficient and effective mechanisms for the distribution of resources, and that therefore the role of governments is to protect and create markets. A corollary of this was a belief that for-profit enterprises or businesses are, under most circumstances, the most efficient providers of services. Governments gradually came to believe that their main role was to extend the operation of markets and to enable the growth of business, though needing to develop and patrol a regulatory framework to ensure that some firms did not behave in ways that undermined the operation of the market and thus the public good.

These changes flowed from the apparent failure of Keynesian economic management to prevent or successfully address the stagflation of the mid-1970s. They represented a victory for a revived neo-classical economics and its more disparaging view that the role of government is to maintain order and to fix cases where, regrettably, markets fail to work efficiently.

The collapse in the mid-1970s of the long post-war economic boom had a considerable impact in Australia on attitudes as much as economic conditions. The collapse was manifest in growing unemployment and inflation. For many, it destroyed their faith that governments could solve social and economic problems. It provided the breech in the walls of the Keynesian or welfare state model of government through which the champions of free markets and the supporters of business could enter and transform government in their interests. For these reformers, the appropriate role for governments was to maintain order and ameliorate any damaging consequences of markets by providing a safety net for those who could not sell their labor. To illustrate the change, in the early 1970s, before the collapse, reforming Labor governments nationally and in several states had employed academics or senior public servants in attempts to revivify moribund public services. The goal was to open up governments and make them more directly accountable to the public. After the mid-1970s, the experts hired to advise on all further reforms of government administration and government finances came from business. The goal now was to reduce government and make the remainder more business-like.

The process of transformation was further assisted by a growing specialist financial press and by the emergence of journalists in the national press gallery who mixed economic with political reporting and who championed the new economic reformers within government. The 1980s saw a huge growth in popular business media and in the profile of business leaders. This further helped institutionalize the neo-liberal ideology. Thus while supporters of the Keynesian or democratic socialist model of government lost confidence in its capacity, the reformers were absolutely confident that markets and the organizational form designed to operate in markets—the investor owned firm—could restore the economy. The reformers soon came to dominate: At one stage in the 1980s, all heads of Australia Commonwealth government departments were qualified in economics (Pusey 1991).

The strength of existing arrangements and practices within government and resistance by some interests, such as left factions within the Labor movement, meant that the process of transformation was a long one; indeed, even now political leaders claim that there is still more to be done. One of the first decisive acts of reform (by a Labor government in the early 1980s) was to deregulate financial markets. Gradually reforms were taken up by state governments as well. Many public utilities were privatized (or converted to government owned businesses). Governments focused on reducing government debt and dramatically reduced their investment in any infrastructure that remained in public ownership. When the need for continuing infrastructure investment was realized, they often entered into public–private partnerships.

This transformation in thinking about the role of government had profound implications. According to the most influential account, it involved no less than the institutional transformation of Australia. The "settlement" among government, Labor, and capital that had been laid down at the turn of the twentieth century, a settlement that provided protection for industry in return for high wages for workers, was swept away (Kelly 1992). As part of these reforms, Australia opened its economy more than almost any other country.

The reformers' confidence seems well placed. Since the early 1980s, despite a relatively short recession in the early 1990s, the Australian economy has grown strongly. Although by some measures inequality has also grown, all but the most marginalized groups are considerably better off. The successful transformation of the Australian economy, conducted by Labor and Conservative governments alike, has deeply institutionalized the model. And, given that Labor governments were in office during much of the period of change and enthusiastically championed this transformation, there have been no strong political organizations to argue for a "third way" as emerged in the UK under Blair's "New Labour." An assessment of the first decade of the Howard Liberal-National Party coalition government emphasizes Howard's "effort to entrench the philosophy of economic liberalism" but also his continuity with the preceding Labor government (Kelly 2006). Following the defeat of the Howard government in late 2007, the new Labor government re-affirmed its belief in the efficacy of markets.

The Belief in Business

The second core belief of the reformers was that governments themselves should become more business-like (Alford 1993). As well as converting many of the government agencies that could not be privatized into government-owned business enterprises, this belief also meant that government departments should be managed like a business. This included measuring the performance of individuals and units, emphasizing outputs and outcomes, and insisting on stronger lines of responsibility and accountability, from junior officials to departmental heads. Departments were given the responsibility for employing staff, thus breaking the practice of over a century of vesting such responsibility in public service boards which had been established to remove patronage and the opportunity for corruption from elected officials.

Strengthening this new reaffirmation of hierarchy was the determination of ministers to assert control over their departments. In part, this involved the re-working of the old policy/implementation dichotomy, this time locating responsibility for policy firmly with ministers. Ministerial determination to assert control was justified by a minimalist (or public choice) version of the theory of responsible government. This affirmed that ministers were responsible to the people through parliament and must therefore directly control the activities of the public servants in their employ. Ministers now affirmed the right to dismiss senior managers in their departments, ensuring that those managers paid close attention to the wishes of that minister. In some versions of this hierarchical model of government, there was no place for interest associations, seen as interfering in the policy processes of elected governments.

In addition, agency theory, another outgrowth of the revitalization of neo-classical economics, developed a wide following. Arguing that without the right mix of incentives and oversight, agents would attempt to dupe their principals, it encouraged natural ministerial tendencies toward mistrust of the permanent public service. To strengthen their position, ministers employed in their ministerial offices young party activists to monitor and often to direct senior public servants (Anderson 2006; Tiernan 2007). This in turn generated much conflict between the ministerial office and the public service and consequently a high turnover, loss of organizational memory, and a deeply risk averse culture among remaining and newly appointed public servants.

AUSTRALIA'S NONPROFIT SECTOR

Australia has a large nonprofit sector comprised of approximately 700,000 organizations; around half of these are incorporated, but only around 35,000 of them are employers (Lyons 2001). These figures are only estimates, however, because it is difficult to gain a full or complete statistical or analytical picture of nonprofits in Australia because key agencies such as Australian Bureau of Statistics (ABS) and the Australian Taxation Office (ATO) have yet to be resourced to upgrade their raw data and categorization of the nonprofit sector. This is further complicated by the absence of legislation which categorically defines nonprofit or even charity. Rather each nonprofit organization is seen as belonging to a relatively small group of peculiar organizations (peculiar because they are not government and not business)—for example, private schools, churches, unions, charities, sporting clubs, registered clubs, lobby groups, environment groups, NGOs, and so on. Many of these terms are overlapping. So, at different times laws are made for one group or another without any regard for the whole. This has created a situation where charities are nonprofit organizations, but not all (or even most) nonprofits are charities. Charities are provided with tax exemption, but so are many other nonprofits; some charities are deductible gift recipients (DGRs), but others are not, and many non-charities are DGRs. (This ambiguity and other issues relating to the tax status of nonprofits are discussed later in this chapter.)

The most reliable economic data are from nonprofit organizations that are large enough to employ staff. Based on figures relating to this group, the sector added over $35 billion AUD to the country's gross domestic product (GDP) which is about 3.3 percent of GDP or 4.8 percent when 600 million hours of volunteering are conservatively valued and added in. This was larger than agriculture, forestry, and fishing and around the same economic contribution as the mining industry (Australian Bureau of Statistics 2002). By 2007, the sector's economic value-added was probably in excess of $50 billion AUD.

In terms of its contribution to employment, Australia's nonprofit sector ranked sixth largest in 1996 among the 22 countries included in the Johns Hopkins Comparative Nonprofit Project (Salamon 1999). In 2000, the Australian Bureau of Statistics estimated that these nonprofit organizations employed over 600,000 people, or 6.5 percent of the total employed population. Unlike most countries, where nonprofits from one field (notably health or education) dominate the sector, the nonprofit sector in Australia stands out for its wide distribution of employment. Four different fields each accounts for roughly 20 percent of employment in this sector: 26 percent are employed in social services; 24 percent in education and research (including private primary and secondary schools, parent associations, university unions, and research organizations but including only four universities—the remaining 38 are public universities enabled under state legislation); 21 percent in culture and recreation (including performing arts, sports, and registered licensed clubs); 15 percent in health (including Australia's 102 nonprofit hospitals—the remaining 759 are public hospitals); 2.5 percent in business, professional associations, and unions; and 11.5 percent in other categories (including environment, law, advocacy and politics, religion, development, and housing).[1]

Revenue sources are also diverse. In 1999–2000, about 58 percent of the sector's revenue came from sales of goods and services, 30 percent from government grants and contracts, and 18 percent from fundraising and membership dues (Australian Bureau of Statistics 2002). Charitable trusts and foundations play a relatively unimportant role in supporting the sector. Associational membership is high, as more than 80 percent of adult Australians belong to at least one nonprofit organization. A similar portion supports them with donations, $5.7 billion worth in 2004. In the same year, over 40 percent of the adult population volunteered for at least one nonprofit organization (Lyons & Passey 2005).

Growth of the nonprofit sector in recent years reveals a mixed pattern. Reliable data on rates of change are only available for the last five years of the 1990s. These data show that while employment had grown in some fields, such as education and social services, this was offset by decline in other areas so that, overall, growth in the nonprofit sector was only marginally greater than that of the economy as a whole (Australian Bureau of Statistics 2002). This pattern is likely to have prevailed since.

The two sections that follow review the main forces impacting on the nonprofit sector since the 1980s, starting with those that can be attributed to NPM but then reviewing those that were independent of NPM's approach to governing or of government entirely.

THE IMPACT OF NPM ON THE NONPROFIT SECTOR

Many of the sets of beliefs and related practices that constitute NPM could be expected to impact upon government relations with the nonprofit sector. From the belief in markets would likely come privatization and outsourcing, the encouragement of competitive markets and for-profit enterprise as the organizational form best suited to a market environment, and hostility to public debt. The belief in business would likely produce a determination to measure performance, a focus on risk (and its avoidance), and a desire to protect government decision making from the contending pressures of interest groups. Each of these impacted on parts of Australia's nonprofit sector, generally to its detriment.

Privatization and Outsourcing

Unlike other countries where NPM inspired governments to privatize social and health services, Australia had always had many of these services provided by nonprofits. For this reason, there was little privatization in health and social services and so, little impact on the nonprofit sector. The only field where privatization had a large direct impact was the provision of employment services such as job search and related training and support services for the unemployed. This was a field in which nonprofit providers already operated with government support, but in niche areas and under the dominant presence of the Commonwealth Employment Service (and a growing for-profit influence). The privatization of the Commonwealth Employment Service and the outsourcing of its services, for which private firms and nonprofits were invited to compete, led to growth in the size of many of these nonprofits.

Encouragement of Competitive Markets

The creation of markets and the encouragement of competition was a central tenet of NPM. Anti-competitive practices between businesses had been prohibited since the 1960s, but the NPM reforms were focused on industries where government authorities were sole providers, such as water, power, rail, and telecommunications. The privatization and breaking up of government monopolies and the encouragement of competition was the main strategy. But in many of the social and health services, where nonprofits did most of the work with government financial assistance, the NPM reformers restructured the way this assistance was provided. Whereas previously, nonprofit leaders had worked with government officials to determine where new services were needed and which nonprofits would receive government support to provide them, nonprofits were now required to compete against each other, for both new and continuing government assistance.

These changes began during the 1990s with state governments, especially Victoria, taking the initiative. Beginning in non-institutional health care, state governments began to describe what had been grants to nonprofits to assist them in delivering services as 'payments for services' purchased by the government on behalf of people with certain conditions. The Commonwealth government followed suit for other programs, such as supported accommodation and home care which it shared funding with the states, and for some programs of its own, such as employment support for people with disabilities. With the change in description came competition and more detailed specification of what was to be achieved. What did not change was the amount of money payed for the service, which was rarely enough to cover costs. Relations between nonprofit providers and government officials deteriorated significantly, and cooperation between nonprofits decreased.

Government departments are still finding new business-like ways to construct relations with private providers. Since 2005 two Commonwealth government departments have experimented with franchise models to structure their relationship with private organizations (mostly nonprofits) that they fund to provide services. Organizations that were successful in winning contracts for new government programs were instructed that the offices wherein services were to be provided were to be badged only with the name of the Commonwealth program; all reference to the provider organization, often nonprofits with years of service and high reputations, was to be expunged. They were told that they were franchises of the government program, and as the franchisor, the government determined the badging.

Encouraging For-profit Firms

The belief that for-profit firms are best suited for competitive markets and should be encouraged to compete with nonprofits and other third sector organizations is illustrated in the direct encouragement by governments of the demutualization of most mutual insurers and co-operative building societies during the late 1980s and 1990s. A similar movement, but one that progressed in fits and starts, can be seen in those social and health services that received government funding. These included those where government funding arrangements were being transformed to create quasi-markets, but it should be noted that there were other social and health services where competition from for-profits pre-dated NPM and where changes in government funding arrangements occurred largely independently of NPM.

Prior to the embrace of NPM, there were a few programs in health care or the social services where nonprofits competed with for-profits. Two were nursing home care and child care. In the former, for-profits received some government assistance, but nonprofits were much more generously funded to encourage their growth; in the latter, for-profits received no government assistance. By the late 1980s nursing homes were all funded on an equal basis, and within a decade for-profit child care was also being treated in the same manner as that provided by nonprofits. In both cases, the form of funding was what has been described as quasi-vouchers, with the level of funding dependent on family income or the level of care required by residents. Although these funding arrangements, whereby governments strengthen demand, create a more effective market than the purchase of service arrangements described above, they emerged from efforts to better target government expenditure rather than being a product of NPM (Lyons 1995). Indeed, the first quasi-voucher arrangements, those for school education, pre-dated the emergence of NPM.

In other social and health services, as noted above, governments began by requiring nonprofits to compete with each other for funding. They then encouraged businesses to join the competition by promising them the same treatment as given to nonprofits. Although inadequate levels of government support and a high degree of bureaucratic control have restricted for-profit entry into some programs. For example, in child care the nonprofit contribution has dramatically declined.

Hostility to Public Debt

A further dimension of NPM is hostility to public debt. As well as producing an under investment in public infrastructure, it has also led to a drastic curtailment in capital grants to nonprofit organizations. This meant nonprofits had to use a combination of borrowed funds and donations to expand. While most large nonprofit organizations had the capacity and standing to borrow, it placed some church sponsored and smaller nonprofits at a disadvantage in competing with for-profits (Lyons, North-Samardzic, & Young 2007). However, despite possessing certain advantages for expanding into growing markets, for-profits have only ventured where they can anticipate a reasonable return on their investment; government monopsony pricing and over regulation has kept them out of some specialized social services.

Measuring Performance

One of the key characteristics of the NPM approach to governance has been the growth of performance measurement. Heads of departments have their performance agreements with their ministers; those reporting to them have their agreements and so on. Understandably, government departments that claimed to be purchasing services from private providers wanted to assure themselves that they were getting "value for money." They have sought to specify in greater and greater detail the service to be provided as well as the outcomes to be achieved. This contradictory behavior seems to have been driven by a need to reduce the likelihood of providers choosing to work only with clients who will easily provide the desired outcomes (itself encouraged by governments refusing to pay the full cost of service delivery). Contracts are increasingly voluminous. This illustrates one of the contradictions of NPM, a contradiction between embracing markets while also strengthening bureaucratic forms of control. This contradictory combination of the language of markets and competition along with strengthened bureaucratic controls and reduced accountability of government (via claims of commercial confidentiality) has been called "market bureaucracy" (Considine 1996).

Governments have also required providers to collect and submit ever increasing amounts of information about the persons for whom the services had been 'purchased.' Nonprofit organizations had been required to collect and submit data under earlier funding arrangements, but its growth under NPM regimes has been significant and applied equally to the older models of grants and quasi-vouchers.

Focusing on Risk and its Avoidance

Another feature of NPM has been a focus on the perceived risk to governments which is thought to be inherent in funding private organizations to provide public services. The perceived risk is that with less direct, bureaucratic control there is a higher likelihood of failure with consequent financial and reputational costs. The goal of government is to shift risk, and thus blame, as well as any financial costs of failure onto the provider. This applies whether the service is public transport or social services. This approach has been increasingly obvious in contracts written by government departments with nonprofit and for-profit providers of social and health services. These have made it clear that any detriment suffered by a service recipient is the responsibility of the service provider and not the government funder. One consequence has been to force providers to pay increasing sums from other revenue sources to insure against risks incurred in fulfilling a government contract.

Hostility to Criticism

It has sometimes been argued that another consequence of NPM has been the growing delegitimization of nonprofit advocacy organizations (Maddison & Denniss 2005). The evidence for delegitimization is threefold. One piece of evidence is the Howard government's decision to discontinue annual grants to certain interest groups, representing groups such as women, young people, and the homeless (Sawer 2002). Another is the insertion into many contracts 'purchasing' services from nonprofits of clauses affirming government ownership of intellectual property generated in fulfilling the contract. This has been understood to forbid contractors using information gained in providing contracted services to publicly criticize any aspects of government policy (McGregor-Lowndes & Turnour 2003; Meltz 1997). A third piece of evidence is what is incorrectly described as the attempt to change charity law and regulation to limit advocacy by charities (Staples 2006).

With the exception of the misunderstanding of charity law 'reform,' where the only change was a slightly more energetic enforcement of the existing law by the taxation authorities (described below), these developments are undeniable, but their relationship to NPM is tenuous. Those who argue for a strong link point to those parts of public choice economics which argue that interest groups are a threat to good governance, a proposition publicly endorsed by pro-business think tanks (Maddison & Denniss 2005; Staples 2006). But this view has not been espoused by ministers or officials. The connection between these changes and NPM is less direct. Adoption of the NPM has made governments determined to control the way they are presented in the mass media. An incoming government that wishes to limit criticism is unlikely to continue funding nonprofit organizations that criticized their policies when in opposition. As for attempts to prevent criticism by service providers, NPM thinking would propose that if governments purchase services from private organizations, then those organizations should devote themselves solely to providing those services.

Governments do not understand that for many of these organizations and their staff, advocacy on behalf of those they are assisting has been a long tradition (albeit one restricted to a degree by the operation of the common law restriction on lobbying by charities). Some powerful nonprofits, such as those with connections to the Christian churches, have ignored these restrictions anyway.

OTHER FACTORS IMPACTING THE NONPROFIT SECTOR

During the past 30 years while NPM has exercised its considerable influence over government, parts of the nonprofit sector have grown greatly and other parts declined. But the forces affecting the growth and decline of different parts of the sector are many: population growth and its ageing, rising living standards, changing values and ways of living, and an expansion of services provided by business. Among these forces government policies have been important, but they explain only part of the story. Not all of the ways in which governments acted upon the nonprofit sector were shaped by NPM, and not all of the factors affecting the sector were government initiated at all. A few examples illustrate the point.

Since almost the beginning of European settlement in Australia, nonprofit organizations have been the main providers of social services, including aged care, child care, and services for people with disabilities. These have all expanded greatly since the 1970s in response to growing demand. The growth in nonprofit supply has been greatly facilitated by government financial support which has been increased to help organizations meet that demand. In some cases, as noted above, the way this funding is organized has changed under NPM, but the growth itself was not a product of governments embracing NPM.

Since the mid-1990s there has been a growth of several percent in the number (now over one third) of Australian children attending nonprofit schools, nearly all sponsored by Christian and non-Christian religions. The driver has been growing parental disenchantment with government schools, but the growth in nonprofit schools has been assisted by an easing of the rules restricting the formation of new schools and an easing of access to government subsidies.

As noted above, many parts of the nonprofit sector have declined overall or have seen a growth of large nonprofit organizations at the expense of small ones. Almost all Australian sport is organized by nonprofits . Since the 1980s some sports have prospered financially through the sales of television rights, but even these, along with sports with lower entertainment value, have experienced a decline at the level of the grassroots as fewer people are prepared to commit time to sustaining local clubs. This is a product of increasing time spent working and

travelling to work, the rise of a consumerist mentality, a growing awareness of the risks associated with governing volunteer boards, and the
cost of insuring against other risks associated with physical activity
(Australian Bureau of Statistics 2007). Sports nonprofits have also seen
growing competition from for-profits, both at the local level (from fit-
ness 'clubs') and at the state and national levels (from investor owned
competitions and clubs).

Higher incomes and changing expectations of members probably explain
the growth of some recreation clubs (known as "registered clubs") into large
organizations providing a wide range of services in a flash modern setting
and the related collapse of many small neighborhood level clubs. Many
other member-serving nonprofits have seen declining membership numbers as public values change. Service clubs like the Rotary or Lions, trade
unions, political parties, and the mainstream Christian denominations
have all experienced decline; so too have many advocacy organizations,
such as women's groups, formed during the 1960s. Nonprofit hospitals,
which receive no direct government support, have also declined in numbers
since the 1970s, mostly being sold to for-profit chains. As nonprofits they
were unable to raise the capital needed to reach an optimal size and buy the
technology needed to remain competitive. None of these signs of decline
can be attributed to government, let alone to NPM.

Running parallel with the decline in numbers of nonprofit organizations
and in their membership has been an increase in philanthropic behaviors by
individual Australians and Australian businesses. Between 1997 and 2004,
giving has increased in real terms by over 50 percent and the percentage of
people who volunteer by over 80 percent. Business giving has also increased
considerably (Department of Family and Community Services 2005). The
increased giving is clearly a consequence of 15 years of economic prosper-
ity, although government efforts to legitimate and encourage such behaviors have also been important.

Over the past five years, modest changes have been made to taxation
law to facilitate charitable giving, especially by high income or high wealth
people. People who give through payroll deduction schemes are able to have
their tax adjusted at the time of the donation rather than after they file
a return. Deductions can be made for donations of shares and property,
including works of art, and can be spread over a five year period. A new
form of foundation, the Private Prescribed Fund, has been established and
given certain exemptions to encourage wealthy people to build foundations while they are still living, and companies have been encouraged to
enter into long term supportive relationships with nonprofits in the arts and
social services. These initiatives appear to have emerged from a particular vision of John Howard, Australia's Prime Minister between 1996 and
2007, rather than as part of either NPM or any kind of movement toward
more relational forms of governance.

LEGAL AND REGULATORY ENVIRONMENT

It is in providing a legal framework for nonprofit organizations to operate that governments can impact the largest number of nonprofits. Apart from small changes to encourage giving, the continuing incoherence of the legal and regulatory environment of nonprofit organizations illustrates how Australian governments do not 'see' a nonprofit *sector.*

The invisibility of the third sector is nowhere more obvious than in the many reforms of laws and regulations to assist business. The reform of corporations law has been a central achievement of NPM governments, designed to make it easier for business to operate and raise funds. Some of these changes have inadvertently disadvantaged nonprofits (Boland 2002; Woodward 1999). Task forces and reviews established by governments to reduce the red tape which adds to business costs have consistently ignored the voluminous red tape that increases costs for nonprofit organizations.

By contrast with their multiple efforts to assist business, governments have made no effort to simplify the legal and regulatory environment of nonprofit organizations. The legal and regulatory framework encompassing Australia's third sector is extensive, complex, and incoherent. It has grown in fits and starts, each piece of legislation designed to cover certain classes of nonprofits or certain activities, but at no point has any attempt been made to make it simpler and more coherent. There is still no clear definition of charity in Australia and no requirement that all charities (or other nonprofits) be officially registered, not least because there is no single administrative body overseeing nonprofits with whom to register. However, organizations are required to be endorsed by the Australian Tax Office in order to receive various tax breaks such as income tax exemption, gift deductibility, and fringe benefit tax exemption, but nonprofits are not automatically considered entitled to all or some of these exemptions, and notably many are not endorsed to receive income tax deductible gifts and tax deductible contributions.

A core aspect of this framework is freedom of association which is guaranteed by the common law. There are at least fourteen different acts enabling incorporation of nonprofit organizations for any (legal) purpose, and many more apply to those formed for particular purposes (such as parent associations or trade unions). Australia's federal system (six states and two territories) partly explains this multiplication. Each state has legislation incorporating associations and cooperatives (including nonprofit cooperatives), while the national government incorporates nonprofit companies and aboriginal associations. Each state has two separate laws governing fundraising (depending on whether or not it involves an element of gambling). But many third sector organizations (for example, any with a religious connection) are exempt from these laws. The Income Tax Assessment Act exempts 37 different types of third sector organizations from income tax and some of these from other forms of taxation. It allocates the right to bestow deductibility of gifts on an odd mix of 47 types of nonprofit organizations. Some are charities; many are not. State and Territory governments exempt certain classes of nonprofits from taxes which they levy (McGregor-Lowndes, 1999). And as already noted, nonprofits that receive government assistance to provide services are subject to an extensive array of funding rules that have grown incrementally with little care as to their cost and impact (Lyons 1997).

Over the past five years there has been some modest fiddling with aspects of legal and regulatory arrangements applying to third sector organizations, but rarely to make them clearer or more supportive. Mostly, they were initiatives based on a flawed understanding, even ignorance, of the sector, and they have tended to flounder as a result. Their connection with NPM is tenuous, but neither do they indicate a move to relational governance. Three examples will suffice to illustrate this generalization.

Greater Interest by the Tax Authorities

In 2000, the Commonwealth government introduced a Goods and Services Tax (GST). It was introduced to shift some of the burden of taxation from income tax to a broadly based indirect tax. One consequence was closer scrutiny of some nonprofit organizations by the Australian Taxation Office (ATO). Until then, most nonprofits were entirely free of ATO scrutiny. Any organization considering itself tax exempt was not required to file a tax return and could avoid any contact with the ATO. Those claiming to be able to give a deduction to donors had to obtain ATO agreement, but after that no further scrutiny was applied. Similarly, persons wishing to establish a charitable trust had to have their trust deed and prospective trustees scrutinized by the ATO. Only nonprofits that employed staff had regular interaction with the ATO, being required to deduct income tax from their employees' salaries and transmit that to the ATO. The GST applied to those nonprofits but also to some smaller organizations as well, requiring filing of quarterly returns. It was also extremely complicated with various transactions being free of GST and others exempted. The ATO had no idea about how many nonprofit organizations would be affected by the changes and correctly anticipated a good deal of confusion. As a consequence, it set up a special nonprofits unit. It also decided that it would review those claiming a tax exemption on grounds of being a charity and those that claimed to be able to give a deduction to donors. But they are still not required to file a return, and most nonprofits remain free of any scrutiny.

Confusion over Mutuals

Recently, the ATO sought and obtained a favorable court decision declaring that many nonprofits which were not fully tax exempt but were exempting much of their income under the operation of the common law principle of mutuality could not do so, leaving many, such as large recreation clubs, facing large tax bills. Many of these nonprofits had in their constitutions a clause deemed by the court to make them ineligible to be a mutual (that on winding up, net assets should be distributed not to members but to a similar tax-exempt organization) as a condition of their incorporation or license to provide particular services. In the end, after extensive lobbying, and rather than conducting a comprehensive review, the Commonwealth government legislated to re-establish the status quo.

Charities Inquiry

In 2001 the Commonwealth government established an inquiry into the definition of charity. It did so as part of a deal with a minor party to obtain the agreement of that party to the passage of legislation introducing the GST. Chaired by a retired judge, the Inquiry produced a report that was generally welcomed by those parts of the third sector that were affected by it. After a year of inaction, the government introduced legislation accepting some of the report's recommendations and ignoring others, including the recommendation to establish a Charities Commission. One recommendation, designed to clarify (and narrow) the common law restrictions on political advocacy by charities, was rejected: The government chose instead to reproduce the existing common law interpretation. That brought protests from some advocacy organizations and revealed the profound ignorance of the law and of the sector by ministers, backbenchers, journalists, and most academics who chose to join the debate. After further review, the government walked away from all but a few minor extensions of charity status to self-help groups, nonprofit child care centers, and enclosed religious orders.

HAS THERE BEEN A CHANGE TO RELATIONAL GOVERNANCE?

Inevitably, contradictions have appeared within the NPM approach to governance. Markets and competition created by government fiat often failed to produce the desired outcomes. In the health and social services, when viewed from the perspective of clients or patients, the period of NPM has increased the costs of care while reducing its availability and quality. It has worsened already faltering coordination among services. In response, there have been some attempts to modify the NPM approach with gestures toward relational governance. Some of these gestures are in fields wherein nonprofit organizations are prominent.

For a time in the late 1990s, in response to One Nation, a populist movement with racist overtones viewed as feeding on the alienation of people in shrinking country towns and on the outskirts of the big cities, many government departments, both state and Commonwealth, embraced the importance of building of community "leadership" and "capacity" (Cavaye 2004).

A few modest attempts were made to give government presence in particular areas greater coherence via "place managers." It was in some of these community focused programs that Australian governments came closest to some form of relational governance. A few of these programs have had modest success, but others, such as place management, were abandoned in the face of resistance from functional departments and their ministers. Many programs failed to display any understanding of the economic dimensions of community development. The definition of community was itself confused, sometimes meaning local residents and sometimes (local) nonprofit organizations and sometimes local government. Such confusion ensured policy failure. In the end, many programs degenerated into vote buying.

The term 'community' is a difficult one for policy makers; certainly it does not fit into the NPM framework. Former Prime Minister Howard was fond of invoking a "social coalition"—or a cooperative effort among government, business, and "the community" to address social problems. But just what was meant by community was never clear: Was it groups of people or groups of associations? Nonetheless, under this rubric, the Commonwealth government has had some success in encouraging businesses to 'partner' with nonprofits, mainly social service and environmental organizations. This gradual rapprochement between the nonprofit sector and business has, on balance, benefited the sector, but government statements suggest that a main objective has been to ensure that nonprofits and charities become more business-like, an objective that fits very well within the NPM framework.

In social services, where state and territory governments have important regulatory and funding roles, nonprofit leaders have pushed the relevant government department(s) to negotiate "compacts" after the UK model. Simultaneously, national, state, and territory government social service departments have embraced the language of relational governance (Blacher 2005). They talk of partnerships and nonprofits under contract as "our partners," and they employ "partnership managers."

But generally the behavior of governments belies their language. And, their behavior remains firmly rooted in the NPM model. The case of compacts illustrates this point. The push for compacts came from social service nonprofits, seeking better relations with government funders. These compacts have no relevance for most of the nonprofit sector. Yet, none of the agreements that have emerged, after several years of sporadic negotiations in some cases, addresses the major complaint of social service organizations: the inadequacy of government funding or the risk shifting in contracts. As far as most governments were concerned, compacts have been a gesture, no more.

In one or two cases in one or two jurisdictions, these gestures have produced benefits. Victoria, the state which in the 1990s had most enthusiastically embraced NPM, has modified its position; social service contracts now run for three years rather than one. In an effort to address the fragmentation of services, it requires that organizations tendering for complex contracts specify the other organizations they will call upon to help deliver the wide range of services required. To help them prepare for the tendering process, grants are made to assist in forming the networks needed to bid on such contracts. In 2007 the government has conducted reviews of "community organizations" (small arts and sports nonprofits, as well as those providing social services) and of the legal environment of a wider set of nonprofits. Subsequently it committed itself to modest initiatives, but these will affect mainly social service nonprofits. None of these changes suggests a significant departure from NPM.

Recent Developments

Following its election in November 2007, much of the rhetoric expressed by members of the new Labor federal government appeared to reject the language of NPM. A notable indicator of this linguistic shift was Labor MPs' regular reference to a so-called "social inclusion" agenda. The government went so far as to create a portfolio for this 'agenda' (albeit ex cabinet) with the appointment of Senator Ursula Stephens to the position of the Parliamentary Secretary for Social Inclusion and the Third Sector. There was also a Social Inclusion Board—a group of fourteen government appointed "leading community and business thinkers"—as well as units of Social Inclusion in the Department of Prime Minister and Cabinet and in other key departments. Also, there have been various nonprofit related policy initiatives. The government committed to reforming its contract management with some nonprofit organizations by abolishing "confidentiality clauses" (sometimes referred to as gag clauses) in some funding contracts and reducing red tape. Also, following the lead of the UK, the Rudd government launched a national compact which is a non-binding agreement between the Commonwealth government and nonprofit organizations that promised to provide a framework for allowing both parties to work together productively and for "mutual benefit" (Casey & Dalton 2006). Finally, the government also called on Australia's Productivity Commission to measure the contribution of the sector.

For a variety of reasons, however, these initiatives are likely to fall short of substantive reform. To date, the processes relating to these initiatives have been *ad hoc*, hurried, and noninclusive. Moreover, they are further undermined by a narrow view of the third sector as well as a failure to fully account for the realities of the Australian federalist political structure. In March 2010, the Rudd government launched the National Compact claiming that it will stimulate a significant cultural shift toward stronger mutually collaborative relationships, encouraging the participation of nonprofits in policy development. It should be noted that already all state and territory governments had developed compact-style documents. In the end, these documents were partial agreements covering only the human services area and regulating relations between these organizations and just one or two government agencies. This was primarily due to negotiations failing to involve a more representative sample of the nonprofit sector, that is, one that included those from unions or from fields such as sport, the arts, and the environment. Instead, these compacts were largely driven by 'top-down' forces, with much of the initiative for their establishment coming from government or major peak organizations. Evaluations of these state compacts (and those overseas) have found that they have majority support among participants who are aware and involved in the compact process (Casey et al. 2010). However, there is also widespread lack of knowledge about their existence and significant dissatisfaction in the processes and outcomes, even among signatories in both government and community organizations (see Phillips, Chapter 9, this volume for a discussion of Canada). "Sceptical goodwill" appears to be a common reaction (Craig et al. 2002: 21; see also Casey et al. 2010). Both the content and background of most of the signatories suggest that a focus on nonprofits as deliverers of community services remains. The government also called on Australia's Productivity Commission to measure the contribution of the sector and launched an Inquiry into the Disclosure Regimes for Charities and other Not-for-profit Organizations (although it should be noted that this Inquiry was not a Labor initiative but came in response to a motion by Senators Allison and Murray of the Democrats prior to their departure from the Senate in June 2008). On the one hand, the report recommends useful changes to the regulatory and institutional framework, including recommendations to reduce regulatory and compliance burdens, and proposes consistency across states and territories through the establishment of a Registrar for Community and Charitable Purpose Organizations, an Office for Nonprofit Sector Engagement, and a Center for Community Service Effectiveness. The Report also recommends the creation of a separate chapter in the Corporations Act 2001 dealing with nonprofit companies limited by guarantee (Productivity Commission 2010). On the other hand, it has been criticized by some nonprofits for its overly economic approach and thus its tendency to focus on the role of nonprofits in terms of producers of services and its failure to fully account for their role as advocates or consider those not reliant on government funding and not delivering welfare services (Brotherhood of St Laurance 2009; Fundraising Institute of Australia 2009). As commendable as some of the recommendations are, it remains to be seen whether any are followed up by the government.

Their value aside, the effectiveness of these initiatives is likely to be undermined by Australia's federalist political system. State governments have more direct responsibilities for service delivery and so are more closely engaged with the nonprofit, in particular with the community sector. Therefore, polices directed at funding, contracts, and agreements will have little impact on the majority of nonprofits whose sole government funding relationship is with a state government. For example, gag clauses can only be removed from contracts finalized with the federal government which is limited to a comparatively small group of organizations, principally those supplying employment services. In sum, for the most part, these initiatives do not reflect a vision for a constructive relationship with the sector. While it has promised to abandon clauses in funding contracts that appear to prohibit lobbying, the federal government is not willing to legislate to remove the uncertainty around political activity permitted to charities, as proposed by the 2001 Charities Definition Inquiry. It is questionable whether the national compact will have any more impact than the state government gestures that preceded it. The Rudd government showed no interest in developing a comprehensive understanding of the nonprofit sector to underpin policy development. Indeed, the motivations and processes surrounding these initiatives have been, in many ways, similar to those of the previous Howard government. Much like the Howard government, the Labor government equates the third sector to a collection of nonprofit organizations that deliver social services. Those engaged in promoting sport or recreation, getting together those that share an enthusiasm for a cause, or those that seek to promote arts and culture are rarely top of mind among policy makers when thinking of the third sector. Similarly, advocacy-oriented nonprofits, or what the ABS calls "interest groups," whether they are for the environment or for the rights of workers (such as unions), are often not included in sector-wide consultation or policy development. As a consequence, NPM principles, notably individualization and risk shifting, remain while the opportunity for fundamental reform is missed.

In June 2010 Julia Gillard assumed the Labor leadership. The subsequent election failed to deliver a parliamentary majority to any political party but, after two weeks of negotiations, Gillard secured the support of two independent MPs to form a government (albeit presiding over a hung parliament). To date there have been mixed signals for the nonprofit sector. During the election campaign Labor foreshadowed the establishment of a new Office for the Non-Profit Sector and scoped out the role and design of a one-stop-shop regulator. In the new ministry the Social Inclusion portfolio has been elevated, but the words" Voluntary Sector" dropped from the title. Australia's PM has also indicated that the capacity to deliver on election polices may be constrained in the new parliamentary environment (Coorey & Hartcher 2010).

WHAT OF THE FUTURE: IS AUSTRALIA JUST LAGGING?

The NPM paradigm and the beliefs that underpin it are deeply entrenched in Australian governments. Under it, Australia has enjoyed well over a decade of economic growth. The income and wealth of most people have increased considerably, and unemployment has fallen to its lowest level in thirty years. Few Australians deplore the change to what some have called "market governance" (Donahue 2001) and to being viewed as customers rather than citizens.

While governments have made gestures toward a more distributed or relational form of governance, these have been no more than pilots or experiments: They flourish for a year or two and are then forgotten. Power is increasingly concentrated in fewer and fewer hands. The national government takes power from the states (most recently to restructure industrial relations) and the states from local governments. The current Labor government has promised to work cooperatively with the states to reduce wasteful duplication of administration and cost shifting, but promises even more centralization if the states fail to measure up to the Commonwealth's expectations. This process is not new (it can be dated to the Second World War or earlier), but it is encouraged by NPM with its business model of government. The Prime Minister and premiers accrue more power to their offices, and super ministries combine several previously separate functions under one minister. Security concerns arising from the so-called war on terrorism are used to further justify this process.

In the absence of complete collapse in the world economic system as a result of the recent financial crisis, a major war, or a major sudden environmental and political change, it is difficult to see NPM being replaced in Australia by any other model of governance in the next decade or two. And, any change that was the result of a catastrophe is unlikely to be toward a radical power sharing or relational model. So strong is the grip on Australia of NPM that it raises the question of whether moves to a new model of governance elsewhere are significant rather than symbolic and whether they are likely to be sustained. If those movements are substantial and sustained, then Australia will be increasingly out of step with those parts of the world.

It is unlikely that much will change in relations between governments and the third sector in Australia. Certainly, nothing will change without the third sector clearly establishing that clubs, associations, charities, and unions have something in common and something that is to be valued: in other words, without 'inventing' the nonprofit sector. But even then, such is the hold of NPM that the best that could be expected is less collateral damage from government actions along with a bit more trust and a little less red tape.

NOTES

1. As noted in the Australia Bureau of Statistics' (2002) *Non-Profit Institutions Survey: Satellite Account* report, "In this satellite account nonprofit institutions that are classified to the general government sector (the most notable being universities and public hospitals operated by religious orders) have been excluded, even where they are self-governing and institutionally separate from government."

REFERENCES

Alford, J. (1993). "Towards a New Public Management model: Beyond 'managerialism' and its critics." *Australian Journal of Public Administration*, 52(2): 135–148.

Anderson, G. (2006). "Ministerial staff: New players in the policy game." In H. K. Colebatch (ed.), *Beyond the Policy Cycle: The policy process in Australia*. Crows Nest: Allen and Unwin.

Australian Bureau of Statistics. (2002). *Non-profit Institutions Satellite Account, Australian National Accounts 1999–2000*. Cat No 5256.0. Canberra: Australian Bureau of Statistics.

Australian Bureau of Statistics. (2007). *Motivators and Constraints to Participation in Sports and Physical Recreation*. National Centre for Culture and Recreation Statistics Report prepared for the Standing Committee on Recreation and Sport Research Group Available at <http://www.ausport.gov.au/__data/assets/pdf_file/0011/142220/ABS> (accessed 16 March 2010).

Blacher, Y. (2005). "Changing the way government works." *Public Administration Today*, 5: 38–42.

Boland, P. (2002, May). "Enforcement of the Principles of Mutuality under the Corporations Act: Is it possible without legislative intervention?" *Keeping Good Company*, pp. 209–214.

Brotherhood of St Laurence. (2009). *The contribution of the not-for-profit sector: Submission in response to the draft report of the Productivity Commission December 2009*. Available at <http://www.bsl.org.au/pdfs/BSL_subm_Productivity_Comm_draft_report_NfP_sector_Dec2009.pdf> (accessed 14 March 2010).

Casey, J., and Dalton, B. (2006). "The best of times, the worst of times: Community sector advocacy in the age of compacts." *Australian Journal of Political Science*, 41(1): 23–38.

Casey, J., Dalton, B., Melville, R., and Onxy, J, (2010). "Strengthening government-nonprofit relations: International experiences with compacts." *Voluntary Sector Review*, 1(1): 59–76.

Cavaye, J. (2004). "Governance and community engagement: The Australian experience." In W. R. Lovan, M. Murray, and R. Shaffer (eds.), *Participatory Governance: Planning, conflict mediation and public decision-making in civil society*. Aldershot: Ashgate.

Considine, M. (1996). "Market Bureaucracy: Exploring the Contending Rationalities of Contemporary Bureaucratic Reform." *Labour and Industry*, 7(1): 1–27.

Department of Family and Community Services. (2005). *Giving Australia: Research on philanthropy in Australia, summary of findings*. Canberra: Department of Family and Community Services.

Coorey, P., and Hartcher, P. (2010). "'All bets are off,' says PM." Sydney Morning Herald, 18 September. Available at <http://qqq.amh.com.au/national/all-bets-are-off-says-pm-20100917-15gbl.html> (accessed 19 September 2010).

Department of Parliamentary Services. (2004). *Extension of Charitable Purpose Bill 2004*. Bills Digest, no. 164, 2003–04. Available at < http://www.aph.gov.au/library/pubs/bd/2003–04/04bd164.pdf> (accessed 15 March 2010).

Donahue, J. D. (2001). "Market-based governance and the architecture of accountability." In J. D. Donahue (ed.), *Market-Based Governance: Supply side, demand side, upside and downside*. Washington: Brookings Institution Press.

Flynn, N. (2002). "Explaining the New Public Management: The importance of context." In K. McLaughlin, S. P. Osborne, and E. Ferlie (eds.), *New Public Management: Current trends and future prospects*. London: Routledge.

Fundraising Institute Australia. (2009, October). *Submissions in response to recommendations of productivity commission draft research report–contribution of the not-for-profit sector*. Available at <http://www.pc.gov.au/__data/assets/pdf_file/0006/92697/subdr222.pdf> (accessed 12 March 2010).

Hood, C. (1990). "A public management for all seasons?" *Public Administration*, 69(1): 3–19.

Kelly, P. (2006). "Re-thinking Australian Governance: the Howard Legacy." *Australian Journal of Public Administration*, 65(1): 7–24.

Kelly, P. (1992). *The End of Certainty. The story of the 1980s*. St. Leonards: Allen and Unwin.

Lyons, M. (2001). *Third Sector: The contribution of nonprofit and cooperative enterprise in Australia*. Crows Nest: Allen and Unwin.

Lyons, M. (ed.). (1997). Contracting for Care. *Third Sector Review*, 3, Special Issue.

Lyons, M. (1995). "The development of quasi vouchers in Australia's community services." *Policy and Politics*, 23(2): 127–139.

Lyons, M., North-Samardzic, A., and Young, A. (2007). "Capital access of nonprofit organisations." *Agenda*, 14(2): 99–110.

Lyons, M., and Passey, A. (2005). *Australians Giving and Volunteering 2004*. Canberra: Department of Family and Community Services. Online. Available at <http://www.bus.qut.edu.au/research/cpns/documents/ga_volunteering.pdf>. (accessed 1 July 2008).

Maddison, S., and Denniss, R. (2005). "Democratic constraint and embrace: Implications for progressive non-government advocacy organizations in Australia." *Australian Journal of Political Science*, 40(3): 373–389.

McGregor-Lowndes, M. (1999). "Australia." In Thomas Silk (ed.), *Philanthropy and the Law in Asia*. San Francisco: Jossey-Bass.

McGregor-Lowndes, M., and Turnour, M. (2003). "Recent developments in government community service relations: Are you really my partner?" *Journal of Contemporary Issues in Business and Government*, 9(1): 31–42.

Meltz, D. (1997). "Contracting for care: A legal overview." *Third Sector Review*, 3, Special Issue: 181–203.

Osborne, S. P., and McLaughlin, K. (2002). "The New Public Management in context." In K. McLaughlin, S. P. Osborne, and E. Ferlie (eds.), *New Public Management: Current Trends and Future Prospects*. London: Routledge.

Productivity Commission. (2010). Contribution of the Not-for-Profit Sector 11 February 2010. Available at <http://www.pc.gov.au/projects/study/not-for-profit/report> (accessed 12 March 2010).

Productivity Commission. (2002). *Independent Review of the Job Network*. Report No. 21. Canberra: AusInfo.

Pusey, M. (1991). *Economic Rationalism in Canberra: A nation-building state changes its mind*. Cambridge: Cambridge University Press.

Salamon, L. et al. (1999). *Global Civil Society. Dimensions of the Nonprofit Sector*. Baltimore: The Johns Hopkins Center for Civil Society Studies.

Sawer, M. (2002). "Governing for the mainstream: Implications for community representation." *Australian Journal of Public Administration*, 66(1): 39–49.

Staples, J. (2006). *NGOs out in the cold: The Howard Government policy toward NGOs, Audit Discussion Paper*. Canberra: Democratic Audit of Australia. Available at <http://democratic.audit.anu.edu.au/categories/ngos_partfrm.htm>. (accessed 1 July 2008).

Tiernan, A. (2007). *Power Without Responsibility*. Kensington: UNSW Press.

Woodward, S. (1999). "Not-for-profit companies: Some implications of recent corporate law reforms." *Company and Securities Law Journal*, 17(6): 390–405.

Yeatman, A. (1994). "The Reform of Public Management: An Overview." *Australian Journal of Public Administration*, 53(3): 287–295.

Yeatman, A. (1990). *Bureaucrats, Technocrats, Femocrats: Essays on the contemporary Australian State*. North Sydney: Allen and Unwin.

11 Global Perspectives on the Legal Framework for Civil Society and Relational Governance

Douglas Rutzen

> Moscow, ahead of Washington, has come to comprehend a key fact: the world is becoming a polyarchy—an international system run by numerous and diverse actors with a shifting kaleidoscope of associations and dependencies.
>
> —Sergei Lavrov, Russian Foreign Minister,
> March 2007, quoting the *Boston Globe*

INTRODUCTION

Governments increasingly recognize the inter-connectedness of governance. Their response to civil society engagement, however, is starkly different. Some have embraced the "associational revolution" (Salamon 1994), while others have embarked on an "associational counter-revolution" (Rutzen & Shea 2006). History vividly illustrates these competing approaches: Consider, for example, June 5, 1989. On that day, Solidarity won the elections in Poland, triggering a series of events that led to democratization in Central Europe. Reflecting on trends, Fukuyama (1989) famously argued that we reached the "end point of mankind's ideological evolution and the universalization of Western liberal democracy as the final form of human government" (4).

Many of us, however, were not focused on the Polish elections that day. Rather, we were mesmerized by another image—a man, in a white shirt, on the "Avenue of Eternal Peace" in Beijing. He stood in front of a column of tanks, shifting left and right to block their advance. The tanks, of course, had come from crushing the democracy movement in Tiananmen Square. These are extreme examples, but they illustrate the competing approaches to civil society's engagement in matters of governance.

As Kuti (Chapter 6, this volume) observes, "advocates of relational governance take it for granted that social actors are able and willing to share responsibilities with government." The following sections examine this assumption, analyzing the extent to which legislation enables—or disables— civil society participation in relational governance. (For purposes of this chapter, "relational governance" is an approach that focuses on interactions among the public sector, civil society, the business sector, concerned citizens, and other actors on issues of societal concern.) Specifically, this chapter reflects upon cases presented in previous chapters and expands the analysis to a diversity of other jurisdictions with less enabling environments for civil society to engage in relational governance. Through this analysis, it examines how specific legal provisions affect the ability of civil society to engage in relational governance. The chapter concludes with observations on current challenges and opportunities in the field of governance, providing a general synthesis for the volume as well as a look to the future.

THE ROLE OF LAW

The legal framework for civil society 1) reflects governance theories, and 2) serves as an agent of change. In other words, the legal framework reflects views on the role of the state, the role of civil society, forms of engagement, and other societal norms. At the same time, the legal framework helps determine whether civil society can influence these norms.

Continuing the Chinese narrative, in 1998, President Jiang Jemin and President Bill Clinton participated in an internationally televised debate that addressed issues of democracy and governance. When asked about the status of Tiananmen Square dissidents, Jiang Jemin dismissed the issue, asserting: "Law-breaking activities must be dealt with according to law. I think this is true in any country of rule of law" ("Clinton in China," 1998). More recently, the President of Vietnam was asked if his country should improve its human rights record. He responded: "It's not a question of improving or not. Vietnam has its own legal framework, and those who violate the law will be handled." (Baker 2007). These are but a few examples of how countries have co-opted concepts, converting the "rule of law" into the "rule by law" (Lowenkron 2006).

The international community has become increasingly concerned about the use of law to constrict civil society. In November 2007, representatives from over 125 countries gathered in Bamako, Mali, under the auspices of the "Community of Democracies." They issued the *Bamako Ministerial Consensus*, which recognized the importance of civil society to democratic governance and which resolved to:

> Support and encourage non-governmental organizations by urging countries to adopt legislation aimed at strengthening civil society and to ensure that registration, formation, funding and operation of

non-governmental organizations and their peaceful activities be carried out. (Community of Democracies 2007: para 44)

This concern is well warranted. In recent years, over fifty countries have introduced or enacted legislation limiting civil society and civic space (see ICNL 2006).

THE FORMATION AND OPERATION
OF CIVIL SOCIETY ORGANIZATIONS

Legal frameworks regulate the formation, operation, sustainability and other issues that impact the ability of CSOs to engage in relational governance. This section examines six specific themes:

- organizational forms and the blending of sectors;
- shared (or imposed) values;
- CSO registration and incorporation;
- the definition of charity;
- empowerment and advocacy; and
- transnational challenges.

Organizational Forms and Sectoral Blending

In the late nineteenth and early twentieth centuries, so-called progressive public administration sought to "keep the public sector sharply distinct from the private sector" (Hood 1995: 93–94). Subsequent privatization theories similarly depended on clear delineation between sectors. After all, the point was to transfer certain functions from one sector (the public sector) to another (the private sector). Under New Public Management (NPM), the sectors began to blend (Salamon 2001). This trend continued under relational governance (Skelcher 2004). As Smith (Chapter 8, this volume) observes: "[t]he diversification of policy tools has in turn led to the 'hybridization' of organizational forms, both formal and informal. Many of these new forms embody a more relational and collaborative approach to the government–nonprofit relationship."

Prominent longstanding examples of hybridization include low income housing organizations, land trusts, and workforce development programs (Smith, Chapter 8, this volume). Continuing this trend, in April 2008, Vermont introduced the "low-profit, limited liability company" or "L3C." A hybrid form, the L3C must have a charitable purpose but is permitted to distribute profits to owners and investors. Similarly, in the UK, social enterprises are commonly organized as Community Interest Companies (CICs). Also a hybrid form, a CIC must pass a community interest test, but it may sell shares and distribute profits to members under certain circumstances.

As these examples illustrate, some countries are clearly attempting to adjust their legal frameworks to reflect the blending of sectors. In other countries, however, sectoral distinctions are firmly entrenched in law. For example, Armenia, Ukraine, and Belarus prohibit public associations from directly engaging in economic activities, drawing a sharp distinction between the commercial and non-commercial sectors. Similarly, in neighboring Bulgaria, CSOs (but not commercial companies) have been prohibited from registering as health institutions, including hospitals.

Various policy motivations surround the blending of the nonprofit and public sectors. While this is an attribute of relational governance, interestingly it is also common in countries with authoritarian tendencies. For example, Syria has used "government organized NGOs" and "quasi-NGOs" as a tool to monopolize civic space, attack legitimate CSOs, and defend government policy under the cover of being independent (ICNL & World Movement 2008). Similar challenges have arisen in China, Russia, and Venezuela (National Endowment for Democracy 2006).

Shared (or Imposed) Values

Gaster and Deakin (1998) speak about the importance of "shared values" as an essential component of genuine partnership. Relational governance is consistent with this theme, as it reflects the movement away from the government as the "central source of the 'authoritative allocation of values' for the society" (Peters & Pierre 1998: 224). This notion is also implicit in the compacts of various countries and in the European Economic and Social Committee's (1999) *Opinion on The Role and Contribution of Civil Society Organisations in the Building of Europe*:

> In a pluralist society every member of the community determines his or her contribution, and the community tries to improve the conditions of co-existence. . . . What is remarkable is that this public is not purely factual, but that the parties involved also exchange value judgments (5).

This view, of course, is not universally accepted. Putting aside broader discussions of pluralism, many governments use the law to limit the values advanced by civil society. For example, in Mali, CSOs cannot undermine "good morals:" This provision was used to deny registration to a gay rights association. Morality provisions also appear in the laws of countries such as Algeria, Egypt, and Malaysia. Other countries rely on government officials to determine if a CSO's activities are, in their view, necessary. For example, in Bahrain, the government can deny registration to an organization if it decides that, in its opinion, society does not "need" the organization's services.

In countries trending toward relational governance, the concept of shared values is often reflected in compacts and policy documents, and the voluntary sector is given broad discretion to pursue pluralistic objectives. In other countries, we find that the CSO legal framework contains explicit provisions permitting the government to deny legal existence to organizations that contradict the government's view of morality or values.

CSO Registration and Incorporation

The foregoing discussion links to a broader issue—the extent to which countries facilitate or hinder the formation of civil society organizations. As Morris (Chapter 2, this volume) observes, recent legislation in England and Wales included a number of reforms of an enabling nature. For example, a new form was created, the Charitable Incorporated Organisation, and registration procedures were streamlined. The law also exempted more charities from registration and introduced other reforms to reduce administrative burdens on charities.

In sharp contrast, other countries have used the legal framework to erect barriers to entry. These barriers take myriad forms.[1] Sometimes restrictions impose high burdens on founders of new organizations. For example:

- In Turkmenistan, national-level associations require 500 members.
- In many countries, including Thailand, Malaysia, and Qatar, only citizens or nationals may found an association. This was also the rule in Bosnia-Herzegovina through the mid-1990s, which disenfranchised a number of refugees and stateless persons.
- In Kenya, founders of foreign organizations must prove they are of "outstanding character," supported by "satisfactory" references.

In other contexts, capitalization requirements serve as a key impediment. As one example, under Eritrea's Proclamation No. 145/2005, local NGOs must have access to the equivalent of $1 million US in order to engage in relief or rehabilitation work.

In other cases, the law contains vague criteria, vesting authorities with broad authority to determine whether to register or incorporate a CSO. A few illustrations include:

- The Ministry of Social Affairs and Labor in Oman has the right to prevent an association from registering if it finds that the services to be provided by the association are not needed, or if there are other associations that are meeting the need that would be filled by the new NGO. The Ministry may also reject an application for "any other reasons according to the decision of the Ministry."
- In Croatia a foundation can be denied registration if it is obviously lacking in "seriousness."
- In Uganda CSOs may not engage in any activity that is "prejudicial to the national interests" of the country.

A related issue relates to who interprets these provisions—in countries such as Egypt and Uzbekistan, members of the security service are formally or informally part of the vetting process.

Considering other aspects of an organization's lifecycle, the freedom of association would be largely theoretical and illusory if a government could arbitrarily disband an organization once formed. In many countries, however, governments retain broad discretion to terminate an organization's existence. For example, in Argentina, the government can terminate an organization if it finds that the organization's activities are no longer "necessary" or "in the best interests of the public." Oman has a similar provision.

In summary, in many countries, the law serves a gatekeeper function, keeping individuals from establishing CSOs as legal entities, thereby substantially diminishing the specter of relational governance.

Defining Charity

Significant challenges also arise when countries attempt to define and promote a class of charities (or public benefit organizations) distinct from the general voluntary and nonprofit sector. Ford addresses this point in his chapter on Scotland. He observes that, until recently Scotland sought to promote the voluntary sector *writ large*, reflecting notions of partnership and relational governance (Ford, Chapter 3, this volume). In 2005, however, Scotland adopted a new law that imported from England the more narrow concept of "charity." According to Ford, "[t]his legislative emphasis on a Scottish version of English charities regulation threatens to distort the effect of other measures aimed at developing relational governance for the third sector in Scotland" (Ford, Chapter 3, this volume).

The definition of charity has proved to be an issue in a number of other countries, including Canada. Illustrating this theme, Phillips (Chapter 9, this volume) references a Supreme Court case involving the Vancouver Society of Immigrant and Visible Minority Women. The society was denied registration as a charity because the organization's life skills and job training did not qualify as the advancement of education under the common law. In addition, the class of beneficiaries (immigrants and visible minority women) was insufficiently broad to be considered beneficial to the community under the fourth head of charity. Moreover, it failed to satisfy the "relief of poverty" test because not all the beneficiaries were disadvantaged. The Supreme Court of Canada refused to expand the common law definition of charity; it did, however, invite the Parliament to address this issue legislatively, but neither the Parliament nor the government accepted this invitation.

Religious historians have come to the US to study traditional religious practices because practices, in some instances, have changed less quickly than in the country of origin. To a certain extent we witness a similar phenomenon with charity law. England and Wales passed a new charity law in 2006, but other Commonwealth countries are still burdened by antiquated concepts of charity.

This concept of charity is also an issue outside the Commonwealth. A number of other countries, including most of the countries of Central and Eastern Europe, have undertaken ambitious initiatives to define a class of public benefit organizations entitled to special tax/fiscal benefits. In addition, China has been working on a "charity law" for a number of years. A key issue is how to define charity. There seems to be pronounced interest in promoting organizations engaged in fields like health, education, and culture. But, as one might imagine, there are deep concerns about advocacy groups. The issue of advocacy—which is directly related to relational governance—is addressed more thoroughly in the next section.

Empowering Civil Society

Empowerment is a prerequisite for relational governance. As Phillips (Chapter 9, this volume) argues, in contrast to the view of 'cold charity' that emanated from Victorian England in which the main role of the voluntary sector was to help the less fortunate by providing services and support, the emerging approach emphasizes empowerment by which communities have resources, possess political voice, and are capable of representing and helping themselves. Raymond Atuguba (2007) echoes this theme when speaking about a partner organization in Ghana, noting that the group works:

> to empower their partners to demand from duty-bearers (especially government) their rights and entitlements as full citizens of the Republic. This is a *political* process of building citizenship and has very little semblance to what charities traditionally do.

In democratic countries, a key issue often relates to the ability of tax-benefited organizations (e.g., charities) to engage in advocacy and the public policy debate. Unless greater latitude is provided, advocacy is chilled and relational governance is impeded (Phillips, Chapter 9, this volume). The point is well taken, and it also highlights the impediments to relational governance by countries with even more stark constraints on advocacy and empowerment. For example:

- In Equatorial Guinea, CSOs are prevented from promoting, monitoring, or engaging in any human rights activities.
- In the United Arab Emirates, the Law on Associations requires associations to follow government censorship guidelines and to receive prior government approval before publishing any material.
- In Belarus, the Criminal Code was amended to prohibit the dissemination of "dishonest" information about the political, economic, or social situation in the country, punishable by up to six months in prison.

In a theme addressed later in the chapter, governments often distinguish among CSOs. They tolerate—if not promote—organizations that support governmental policies or engage in service delivery. But if the organization seeks to challenge governmental policies, the law is often the tool of choice to clamp down on dissent.[2]

Enabling Transnational Operations

A cutting edge issue relates to transnational CSO operations. To engage effectively in many of the challenges of today—whether related to climate change, public health, the Millenium Development Goals, or the economic crisis— CSOs must engage across frontiers. This raises interesting legal issues because CSO issues are almost exclusively the province of country-level, domestic legislation. That said, there have been some important developments in this area.

As Dunn (Chapter 7, this volume) observes, there is renewed interest in reviving the Statute for a European Association. Similarly, the European Foundation Centre is actively promoting a European Foundation Statute. In January 2009, the European Court of Justice issued its judgment in the case of *Hein Persche v Finanzamt Ludenscheid*. In this case, the Court held that where donor incentives are available for donations to domestic recipients, they must also be available for donations to foreign recipients based in EU Member States or the European Economic Area, provided that the recipient is equivalent to a domestic public benefit organization. Initiatives are also underway in other jurisdictions to create a more conducive tax and fiscal framework for cross-border giving.

At the same time, there is a cross-current of isolationism, seeking to restrict foreign organizations, international cooperation, and cross-border funding. To illustrate:

- The 1999 Law on Associations in the United Arab Emirates restricts members from participating in events outside the country without governmental permission.
- Eritrea's Proclamation No. 145/2005 prohibits CSOs from receiving funding from the United Nations and creates a presumption that all other donor funding be provided to a Ministry or other government agency.
- Belarus, Bahrain, China, Egypt, Ethiopia, Nicaragua, Peru, Oman, Turkmenistan, Uzbekistan, and Venezuala are among other countries that have considered or enacted foreign funding constraints.

In sum, while transnational activities by CSOs are an essential component of effective relational governance in contemporary society, the legal framework for civil society is deeply entrenched in country-level, domestic legislation. Absent regional integration or bilateral agreements, progress— particularly in terms of frameworks for international philanthropy—will likely be limited. Moreover, a number of countries are erecting barriers to the globalization of civil society, appealing to arguments of sovereignty, security, and aid effectiveness. Accordingly, transnational CSO operations will likely remain a source of friction and a cutting edge issue for future development.

Financial Resources

A related theme pertains to the importance of a sound financial base to support civil society's engagement in relational governance. Indeed, many of the chapters of this book describe initiatives to develop new tools for financing civil society and promoting private philanthropy. For example, Morris notes that in the UK there was a concern over the declining trend in the levels of individual and corporate charitable giving, which led to a package of tax reforms in 2000. Kuti (Chapter 6, this volume) discusses so-called "percentage legislation" and the National Civil Fund in Hungary. Rathgeb Smith (Chapter 8, this volume) describes a variety of financing tools, ranging from tax credits to tax-exempt bonds. A number of chapters also discuss initiatives to regulate charitable fundraising. Donnelly-Cox and McGee (Chapter 4, this volume) address this issue in the context of Ireland, and similar issues arise in the chapters on Scotland, England and Wales, and Canada. Self-regulation also seems to be an emerging tool in the regulation of fundraising (Morris, Chapter 2, this volume).

At the same time, Lyons and Dalton (Chapter 10, this volume) remind us that some tools are inconsistent with relational governance. In Australia, for example, two Commonwealth government departments employed a franchise model to structure their relationship with nonprofit organizations and other entities. Services were badged in the name of the Commonwealth program itself, and references to the nonprofit organization were expunged.

Extending the geographic scope of the analysis, Mexico further illustrates the way in which the legal framework can impede relational governance. To receive tax deductible donations in Mexico, an organization must seek accreditation from the ministry with jurisdiction over the organization's activities. Ministries have few incentives to grant this accreditation (particularly to advocacy groups which might use their benefits to advocate against the ministry), and few organizations in fact attain these tax benefits. Mexican organizations that overcome these barriers can only spend 5 percent of donations received on overhead. Because few organizations can survive on a 5 percent overhead rate, many people suspect that organizations engage in 'creative accounting.' As such, the rule, which is intended to promote public trust in organizations, actually ends up undermining public trust because of concerns over such creativity in accounting.

In some countries the legal framework is even more blunt, providing little or no incentive for private philanthropy. For example, in Nigeria, individuals receive no tax benefits for charitable giving, while in Russia, corporations receive no tax benefits for charitable giving. In Azerbaijan, neither individuals nor corporations receive tax benefits for charitable giving. In other countries, such as Ukraine, there are limitations on fee-for-service activities. As indicated earlier, a number of countries also impose significant restrictions on foreign funding. Continuing with this trend, under a recent proclamation in Ethiopia, an organization that receives more than 10 percent of its funding from abroad is prohibited from promoting the advancement of human and democratic rights, gender equality, the rights of children, disability rights, and other enumerated objectives.

REGULATING CIVIL SOCIETY: ACCOUNTABILITY AND TRANSPARENCY

Many of the initiatives discussed in this volume seem to be based on the need to promote accountability and decrease prospects of abuse. For example, in Ireland, the *Agreed Programme for Government* stated that a "comprehensive reform of the law relating to charities will be enacted to ensure accountability and to protect against abuse of charitable status and fraud" (Donnelly-Cox & McGee, Chapter 4, this volume). Initiatives in Scotland, England, and Wales were similarly cast in terms of protecting beneficiaries, donors, staff, and volunteers (Morris, Chapter 2, this volume).

The key issue, of course, is balance and proportionality. As Morris (Chapter 2, this volume) states, "[i]deally, a modern and effective regulatory framework should provide a suitable balance so as to support a more relational form of governance, but also to meet the demands for enhanced accountability." Similarly, as Ford observes, "regulatory elements of any system implementing an over-arching policy of support must, surely, be justifiable only as underpinning the facilitative dimension" (Ford, Chapter 3, this volume). Balance and proportionality must also be determined in local context. Kuti (Chapter 6, this volume), for example, explains how a country's history affects its view on regulation: "[a]s a reaction to the strong government control they suffered from under state socialism, the Hungarian nonprofit organizations are extremely reluctant to disclose any financial or management information."

Perhaps not surprisingly, in some countries, the balance tilts strongly toward state regulation. As but a few examples:

- In Vietnam, the government has the right to intervene in all stages of an organization's activities; it may also veto new members of an organization and introduce members of its own choosing.
- Under the NGO Regulations of Uganda, an organization may not undertake direct contact with people in any part of the rural area of Uganda unless the organization provides seven days notice in writing of its intention to do so to the Resistance Committee and the District Administrator of the area.

- Until 2009 in Russia a variety of CSOs, regardless of their size or tax status, were required to meet extensive programmatic and financial reporting requirements, which were premised on undefined terms, such as the requirement to report on all "events."

Some countries also apply what might be called the "Al Capone" approach to enforcement.[3] Instead of closing down organizations on substantive grounds, they establish a thick web of nearly impenetrable rules, regulations, and reporting requirements. They then sanction organizations on ancillary grounds, such as the failure to register a logo, to complete a form properly, or to meet some other technical requirement of law.

SYNTHESIZING THEMES

Are relational and authoritarian governance diametrically opposed in how they treat civil society? Table 11.1 presents the prototypical impact of relational governance and autocratic theories on the legal framework for civil society.

Table 11.1   Relational and Autocratic Governance Compared

Issue	Relational Governance	Autocratic Governance
Organizational Forms	Hybridization as a complement to independent civil society	Hybridization to undermine or co-opt independent civil society
Values	Shared values	Imposed values
Registration/Incorporation	Low barriers to entry	High barriers to entry
Concept of Charity	Evolving concept that reflects emerging contexts and enables the engagement of civil society in governance	Focus on traditional notions of "charity" and/or instrumental approaches focused on service delivery
Empowerment/Advocacy	Promoted	Restricted
Transnational Operations	Broadly permitted	Restrictions on cross-border programs and foreign funding
Resources	Broad range of instruments to enable a CSO sector engaged in governance	Broad restrictions on resources and/or more instrumental approaches focused on service delivery
Regulation	Marked by balance and proportionality, enabling the development of civil society	Marked by intrusive oversight and regulation, impeding the development of civil society

This table is merely an illustration. In reality, governance theories and the impact of these theories operate on a continuum rather than in a binary fashion. Moreover, the legal framework for civil society often reflects different objectives and policies. In part, this is because the framework reflects adaptation (new laws in response to changed circumstances) and layering (new laws imposed on top of existing legislation). Regardless of the process, these competing objectives have a significant impact on relational governance.

In addition, neither the government nor civil society is monolithic. Depending on the country, the "government" may include ministries, agencies, departments, offices, bureaus, and other entities. Depending on the structure of the state, there may also be various levels of national and local governments. Perspectives multiply as these levels are staffed by elected officials, political appointees, civil servants and others, with responsibilities ranging from health care to housing to "homeland security." Of course, civil society is also marked by tremendous diversity. As a result of the diversity of governmental entities, the perspectives of individual officials, substantive responsibilities, and the specific CSOs seeking to engage, there are often a panorama of approaches to civil society within a single state.

As Kuti (Chapter 9, this volume) notes, for example, NPM and relational governance had a "parallel presence" as a result of various challenges confronting post-communist Hungary, including the modernization of public services and the challenge of democratization. One can also easily overstate intentionality; as Kuti explains, "Hungary has made, almost instinctively, important steps toward shared governance without widely using this term or knowing its concept in detail."

Moreover, exogenous factors continue to alter the legal landscape for civil society. For example, after September 11, a number of countries enacted counter-terrorism measures. Many of these measures were layered on top of existing CSO laws, imposing significant 'collateral damage' on legitimate CSO activities (Dunn, Chapter 7, this volume; ICNL & World Movement 2008; OMB Watch 2008; Sidel 2008). Indeed, it seems as though when conflict arises some governments ascribe to a *security-based governance* theory that prevails over relational governance and other theories. In turn, a security-based governance approach affects several layers of this framework. For example, a number of countries have enacted legislation affecting CSO financing as a result of domestic pressures and international bodies, such as the Financial Action Task Force. Security-based governance objectives also impact registration and incorporation laws and the ability of organizations to associate with certain types of groups (ICNL & World Movement 2008; OMB Watch 2008; Sidel 2008).

Even more benign objectives, such as "aid effectiveness" and "donor coordination," can prove problematic. For example, in 2007, the Bolivian President issued a Decree on international cooperation that places new restrictions on the ability of civil society organizations to engage in development activities funded by foreign donors. The restrictions were based, in part, on the Paris Declaration on Aid Effectiveness. Similarly, in September 2008, a bill was proposed in the Mexican Senate that would have given a government body the ability to determine which Mexican entities are eligible to cooperate with foreign partners—whether the cooperation involved funding or even the exchange of information. Again, this bill was justified with reference to aid effectiveness.[4] These are only two examples: an increasing number of countries are attempting to convert 'host country' ownership into 'host government' ownership over development assistance with little room for independent civil society.

In summary, as Kuti (Chapter 6, this volume) suggests, the framework depends on "the legal, political, and cultural traditions, the social environment, the administrative ideologies, the generally accepted values, and the interest groups' competition for power and influence." As a result, the legal framework for civil society is not the product of a single, coherent theory.[5] Rather, the legal framework and its implementation are buffeted by competing objectives, leading to a degree of policy incoherence.[6]

FUTURE OPPORTUNITIES

In October 2008, the *Economist* observed:

> Critics claim that the 'Washington consensus' of deregulation and privatisation, preached condescendingly by America and Britain to benighted governments around the world, has actually brought the world economy to the brink of disaster. . . . Arguments for market solutions in, for instance, health and education will be made with less conviction, and dismissed with a reference to Wall Street's fate ("Capitalism at bay" 2008).

A critical question is whether the financial crisis that began in late 2008 will serve as the kind of 'exogenous shock' that fundamentally alters governance models. Lyons and Dalton (Chapter 10, this volume) note, for example, that stagflation in the 1970s destroyed the faith of many Australians that governments could solve social and economic problems. In its place, a belief in markets emerged. They even note that "[o]ne of the first decisive acts of reform (by a Labor government in the early 1980s) was to deregulate financial markets" (Lyons & Dalton, Chapter 10, this volume). Elsewhere, in the words of Salamon (2001), governance models were predicated upon "new-found faith in liberal economic theories."

Impacts continue to unfold, but it is likely that governance will be influenced by the financial crisis. Among other issues, new governance theories and institutions will emerge, particularly relating to the world's financial infrastructure. In addition, the blurring of the state and the market continues, following massive infusions of public money to bail out commercial enterprises. Moreover, deregulation and market-based solutions have become suspect concepts, at least for now. Tools employed in relational governance, like loan guarantees for low income housing, will also inevitably change.

Moving from the policy to the organizational level, CSOs have been seriously affected by these changes (Salamon, Geller, & Spence 2009). Private giving and foundation support have declined significantly (see Charities Aid Foundation & NCVO 2009; Prizeman & McGee 2009). Governmental authorities are also adopting budget tightening, which will impact the sustainability of a number of organizations. At the same time, new fields will develop, particularly as civil society grapples with how best to hold emerging economic and political powers to account.

In addition, there will likely be calls for change as governments have trouble 'delivering the goods' as a result of economic decline. These pressures will build on both democratic and authoritarian governments. Some new democracies are particularly at risk, in part, because of their existing precarious macroeconomic conditions and, in part, because of the fragility of their democracies. In addition, there is a concern that certain autocratic regimes will implement constraints with renewed vigor as they seek to cling to power and quash dissent.

At a minimum, we appear headed to a period of instability and an era when governance concepts will be challenged and changed. At the same time, one could argue that the fundamental principles of relational governance have been validated. Quite simply, the financial crisis has shown that issues are so complex and inter-connected that they are beyond the capacity of government (or even a collection of governments) to address on their own. Rather, it is necessary to engage key actors from various sectors to address contemporary challenges.

That said, some of the more extreme propositions of co-governance seem less tenable in the current environment. For example, in the late 1990s, some commentators argued that "governance without government" is becoming the dominant pattern of management for advanced industrial democracies (Peters & Pierre 1998, citing Rhodes 1997). Others cast governments as "hollow" states (Jessop 1998; Milward, Provan & Else 1993; Peters 1993; Peters & Pierre 1998; Rhodes 1994), and noted that "[s]tate agencies may place some imprimatur on the policy, so the argument goes, but the real action occurs within the private sector" (Peters & Pierre 1998: 225).

If anything, the importance of government, at least for civil society, has been highlighted in recent years. As a parallel trend, the power of the individual citizen has been strengthened as a result of the Internet and other participatory media. Indeed, we regularly hear that civil society organizations are essential because they give voice to the voiceless—that by joining together we are empowered. While this is certainly true, a college student sitting in her dorm room may well have more amplified voice than the CEO of a large nonprofit in a capital city—if the student has a popular blog. Borrowing from Putnam (2000), we are moving from "Bowling Alone" to "Blogging Alone," with significant implications for both governance and civil society.

In conclusion, the governance field seems to be on the cusp of a new era. It is an important time for the field, and new concepts and institutions will likely be born during this era. In the words of the political cartoonist Walt Kelly, "We are confronting a period of insurmountable opportunity."

NOTES

1. The discussion of restrictions draws heavily on ICNL and World Movement for Democracy's Report (2008) entitled, "Defending Civil Society."
2. This chapter focuses on legal provisions. Of course, funding relationships can also reduce civil society's independence and tether organizations to the state. This is not just an issue in 'liberal democracies.' The governments of Uzbekistan and Azerbaijan recently announced new funding schemes for civil society. CSO representatives have expressed concern that these schemes may be used to compromise CSO independence and to co-opt key organizations.
3. Al Capone was a famous gangster in the US. After unsuccessful trials for racketeering, the US finally convicted Capone of tax evasion.
4. This bill is no longer active.
5. Moreover, as various chapters explain, problems arise even when countries attempt to engage in a more holistic review of government–civil society relations through compacts or other related initiatives. In the English context, compacts "seem to be made up mainly of warm words, platitudes and generalities" (Morris, Chapter 2, this volume, quoting Morrison 2000). Indeed, in a 2005 survey on the impact of the Compact, only 15 percent of respondents stated the Compact made any significant difference (Morris, Chapter 2, this volume). Similarly, in the Australian context, Lyons & Dalton (Chapter 10, this volume) concluded, "As far as most governments were concerned, compacts have been a gesture, no more."
6. Implementation is often key. Toward this end, some countries provide for the periodic review of laws and policy, as well as performance benchmarks and dispute resolution mechanisms (see Morris, Chapter 2, this volume).

REFERENCES

Atuguba, R. (2007, April). "Legal analysis of the Draft Trust Bill 2006 and the Draft NGO Policy Guidelines 2007." Paper prepared for the Parliamentary Advocacy Project of the Legal Resources Centre (LRC)-Ghana.

Baker, P. (2007, June 23). "Bush prods Vietnamese President on human rights and openness." *Washington Post.*

Charities Aid Foundation (CAF) and National Council of Voluntary Organisations (NCVO). (2009). *UK Giving 2009: An overview of charitable giving in the UK, 2008/09.* London: CAF and NCVO.

Community of Democracies. (2007). *Bamako Ministerial Consensus, 'Democracy, Development, and Poverty Reduction'.* Online. Available at <http://

www.bamako2007.gov.ml/PRODUCTION%20DE%20LA%204%E8me%20
CONFERENCE%20MINISTERIELLE%20CD/CONSENSUS%20DE%20
BAMAKO/MasterBamakoDocument.pdf>(accessed on 12 November 2009).

The Economist. (2008, October 16). "Capitalism at bay." Available at <http://
www.economist.com/opinion/displaystory.cfm?story_id=12429544>

European Economic and Social Committee. (1999). *Opinion on The Role and Contribution of Civil Society Organisations in the Building of Europe*, Brussels.
Online. Available at <http://eesc.europa.eu/sco/docs/ces851–1999_ac_en.PDF>
(accessed on 15 February 2009)

Fukuyama, F. (1989, Summer). "The end of history?" *The National Interest.*

Gaster, L., and Deakin, N. (1998). "Local government and the voluntary sector:
Who needs whom—why and what for?" *Local Government*, 24(3): 169–194.

Hood, C. (1995). "The 'New Public Management' in the 1980s: Variations on a
theme." *Accounting, Organizations and Society*, 20(2/3): 93–109.

The International Center for Not-for-Profit Law (ICNL). (2006, August). "Recent
laws and legislative proposals to restrict civil society and civil society organizations." *International Journal of Not-for-Profit Law*, 8(4). Online. Available
at <http://www.icnl.org/knowledge/ijnl/vol8iss4/art_1.htm> (accessed 20 April
2009).

ICNL and World Movement for Democracy Secretariat at the National Endowment
for Democracy. (2008). *Defending Civil Society: A Report of the World Movement for Democracy.* Online. Available at <http://www.icnl.org/KNOWL-
EDGE/pubs/ICNL-WMD_Defending_CS.pdf> (accessed 15 April 2009).

Jessop, B. (1998). "The rise of governance and the risks of failure: The case of
economic development." *International Social Science Journal*, 50(155): 29–45.

Lavrov, S. (2007, March 23). "Munich: World politics at the crossroads." *Moskovs-
kiye Novosti.* Online. Available at <http://www.acronym.org.uk/docs/0703/
doc10.htm> (accessed 2 May 2009).

Lowenkron, B. (2006). "Number of countries fear a tougher UN human rights
body." Interview with the Council on Foreign Relations. Online. Available at
<http://www.cfr.org/publication/10103/lowenkron.html?breadcrumb=%2Fbio
s%2F11891%2Frobert_mcmahon%3Fpage%3D10> (accessed 20 April 2009).

Milward, H. B., Provan, K., and Else, B. (1993). "What does the hollow state look
like?" In B. Bozeman (ed.), *Public Management Theory: The state of the art.*
San Francisco: Jossey Bass.

National Endowment for Democracy. (2006, June 8). *The Backlash Against
Democracy Assistance: A Report prepared by the National Endowment for
Democracy for Senator Richard G. Lugar, Chairman.* Committee on Foreign
Relations, United States Senate.

New York Times. (1998, June 28). "Clinton in China; The leaders' remarks: Hopes
for a lasting friendship, even if imperfect."

OMB Watch and Grantmakers without Borders. (2008, July). *Collateral Damage, How the War on Terror Hurts Charities, Foundations and the People they
Serve.* Online. Available at < http://www.ombwatch.org/npadv/PDF/collateral-
damage.pdf> (accessed 20 April 2009).

Peters, G., and Pierre, J. (1998). "Governance without government? Rethinking
public administration." *Journal of Public Administration Research and Theory*,
8(2): 223–243.

Prizeman, G., and McGee, S. (2009). *Charitable Fundraising in an Economic
Downturn: The first annual report on income and fundraising activity in
Irish charities.* Dublin: Centre for Nonprofit Management, Trinity College
Dublin.

Putnam, R. (2000). *Bowling Alone, The collapse and revival of American community.* New York: Simon and Schuster.

Rhodes, R. A. W. (1997). *Understanding Governance: Policy networks, governance, reflexivity and accountability.* Buckingham: Open University Press.

Rhodes, R. A. W. (1994). "The hollowing out of the state: The changing nature of the public service in Britain." *Political Quarterly Review,* 65: 137–151.

Rutzen, D., and Shea, C. (2006, September). "The associational counter-revolution." *Alliance,* 11(3): 27–28.

Salamon, L. (2001). "The New Governance and the tools of public action: An introduction." *Fordham Urban Law Journal,* 28(5): 1611–1674.

Salamon, L. (1994, July/August). "The rise of the nonprofit sector." *Foreign Affairs,* 74(3): 109–115.

Salamon, L., Geller, S. L., and Spence, K. L. (2009). 'Impact of the 2007–09 economic recession on nonprofit organizations.' Communiqué No. 14, Listening Post Project, Center for Civil Society Studies, Johns Hopkins University. Available at <http://www.ccss.jhu.edu/pdfs/LP_Communiques/LP_Communique_14.pdf> (accessed 15 May 2009).

Sidel, M. (2008). "Counter-terrorism and the enabling legal and political environment for civil society: A comparative analysis of 'War on Terror' States." *International Journal for Not-for-Profit Law,* 10(3). Online. Available at <http://www.icnl.org/knowledge/ijnl/vol10iss3/special_2.htm> (accessed 25 April 2009).

Skelcher, C. (2004). "The public-private partnerships and hybridity." In E. Fairlie, L. E. Lynn, Jr., and C. Pollitt (eds.), *The Oxford Handbook of Public Management.* London: Oxford University Press.

Contributors

Ingo Bode is Professor and Director of the Institute for Social Policy and the Organization of Social Services, Department of Social Work and Social Welfare, University of Kassel, Germany.

Bronwen Dalton is Senior Lecturer, School of Management and Director of the Centre for Community Organisations, University of Technology Sydney, Australia.

Gemma Donnelly-Cox is Lecturer in Business Studies and Academic Director of the Centre for Nonprofit Management, Trinity College Dublin, Ireland.

Alison Dunn is Senior Lecturer, Newcastle Law School, Newcastle upon Tyne, UK.

Patrick Ford is Lecturer and member of the Charity Law Research Unit, School of Law, University of Dundee, Scotland.

Éva Kuti is Professor, Budapest School of Management, Budapest, Hungary.

Mark Lyons was a faculty member for many years at the University of Technology Sydney, retiring as Professor of Social Economy in 2004. He then assumed the position of Director of Research at the Centre for Social Impact, a partnership of the Business Schools of the University of New South Wales, the University of Melbourne, Swinburne University of Technology and the University of Western Australia. Throughout his career, Mark devoted himself unstintingly to the development of nonprofit studies in Australia and internationally. Sadly, Mark died in November 2009 and will be fondly remembered.

Siobhan McGee is an independent consultant with extensive experience in the nonprofit sector and Research Associate, School of Business, Trinity College Dublin, Ireland.

Debra Morris is Reader in Charity Law and Policy, University of Liverpool, and Director of the Charity Law & Policy Unit, Liverpool, UK.

Susan D. Phillips is Professor and Director, School of Public Policy and Administration, Carleton University, Ottawa, Canada. In 2010–2011, she is a Visiting Fellow, Lucy Cavendish College, University of Cambridge, and the Centre for Charitable Giving and Philanthropy, Cass Business School, City University London and University of Edinburgh, UK.

Steven Rathgeb Smith is Professor of Public Policy and the Waldemar A. Nielsen Chair in Philanthropy, Georgetown Public Policy Institute, Georgetown University, Washington, DC, USA.

Douglas Rutzen is President and CEO of the International Center for Not-for-Profit Law, Washington, DC, USA.

Index